— Hell in Flanders Fields —

ALSO BY GEORGE H. CASSAR

The French and the Dardanelles
Kitchener: Architect of Victory
Beyond Courage
The Tragedy of Sir John French
Asquith as War Leader, 1914–1916
The Forgotten Front: The British Campaign in Italy, 1917–1918
Kitchener's War, British Strategy from 1914 to 1916
Lloyd George at War, 1916–1918
A Survey of Western Civilization (co-author)
World History (co-author)

HELL IN FLANDERS FIELDS

Canadians at the Second Battle of Ypres

George H. Cassar

DUNDURN PRESS
TORONTO

Editor: Shannon Whibbs
Design: Courtney Horner
Printer: Transcontinental

Library and Archives Canada Cataloguing in Publication

Cassar, George H.
  Hell in Flanders Fields : Canadians at the second battle of Ypres / by George H. Cassar.

Includes bibliographical references and index.
ISBN 978-1-55488-728-6

  1. Ypres, 2nd Battle of, Ieper, Belgium, 1915. 2. Canada. Canadian Army--History--World War, 1914-1918. I. Title.

D542.Y7C39 2010   940.4'24   C2009-907532-6

1   2   3   4   5   14   13   12   11   10

 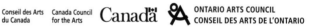

We acknowledge the support of the **Canada Council for the Arts** and the **Ontario Arts Council** for our publishing program. We also acknowledge the financial support of the **Government of Canada** through the **Canada Book Fund** and **The Association for the Export of Canadian Books**, and the **Government of Ontario** through the **Ontario Book Publishers Tax Credit program**, and the **Ontario Media Development Corporation**.

Printed and bound in Canada.
www.dundurn.com

Dundurn Press
3 Church Street, Suite 500
Toronto, Ontario, Canada
M5E 1M2

Gazelle Book Services Limited
White Cross Mills
High Town, Lancaster, England
LA1 4XS

Dundurn Press
2250 Military Road
Tonawanda, NY
U.S.A. 14150

To Bruce and Vicki
And to the memory of Joel

CONTENTS

Maps

Preface

While doing research on an unrelated topic in the Public Record Office (now British National Archives) in 1981, I inadvertently came across a folder of correspondence between Colonel A. Fortescue Duguid, then Canadian director of the Historical Section, and Brigadier-General Sir James Edmonds, the British Official Historian. It began after Duguid read the first draft of Edmonds's official account of the Second Battle of Ypres and transmitted his comments in 1925. The exchange of letters, often heated and less than civil, continued until the publication of the British Official History in 1927 — it would resume again in the mid-thirties while Duguid was writing the Canadian side of the battle. Duguid contended that Edmonds had deliberately played down the role of the Canadians while dwelling on the heroics of the British, and he proceeded to show, on a number of occasions, the points of differences between the two. Edmonds corrected factual errors in his second draft, but not the slant of his narrative. Duguid speculated that the trumpeting of the valiant Canadian stand by both allies and adversaries, often ignoring or only mentioning in passing the presence of the British, had riled Edmonds and that it was his way of trying to set the record straight. Duguid pointed out to Edmonds that it was possible to acknowledge the great gallantry of the British soldiers without giving the Canadians short shrift. However, Edmonds refused to budge, insisting that if the Canadians were unhappy with his account then, like the Austrailians, they should write their own history.

As it happened, Duguid had already been commissioned by the Canadian government to do just that. In the next half-dozen years he accumulated a wealth of relevant material and, in the early 1930s, began the process of writing. His first volume was published in 1938 and focused on the Canadian Army's baptism of fire at Ypres. It was clear, well-written, comprehensive, generally free of mistakes, and went far toward rectifying the imbalance in Edmonds's account and according the Canadians their just due. But Duguid, as with any official historian, had to work under restrictions and there were many incidents that were treated superficially or omitted altogether.

It was with the object of presenting a more rounded picture that I undertook the task of researching and writing about the Canadians at the Second Battle of Ypres. The publication of my book *Beyond Courage* in 1985 was the first account of the struggle since the publication of the Canadian Official History. To a great extent the study was based on sources housed in the Canadian National Archives in Ottawa — official documents, private papers, and interviews of the survivors of the battle conducted by the CBC for its 17-part series on the First World War, which aired in 1964. In describing the events, I brought to light new information, much of which was known to Duguid, but deemed unsuitable in an official history written at a time when most of the leading participants were still alive. Still, *Beyond Courage* integrated few examples of eyewitness testimony — not trendy then — and, as a pioneer work, was hardly free of flaws.

After mulling it over off and on for a few years, I finally decided to revise the study in 2007. This seemed like a propitious time to do so. Since *Beyond Courage* first appeared, there have been several studies of the battle that have used additional personal records, plus the publication of a plethora of biographies, diaries, memoirs, and letters of the participants. On top of this, the Internet, a new discovery, had become an invaluable tool of the scholar. Over the course of my research for this book, I relied not only on Canadian documentary evidence and virtually all available material in print, but also on hitherto untapped sources drawn from British archives. While making amends for earlier sins of omission and commission, I folded in much new material and greatly increased the recollections of individuals who fought face to face with the enemy so as to provide a more evocative and stirring narrative.

The result is a more accurate and much fuller account than the earlier version and one which I trust will bring home the hardship, pain, and exhilaration of those who lived through the battle. Thus, since the new product is quite different from the old one it seemed appropriate to change the title of the book.

Few battles in the First World War are as difficult to follow as Second Ypres. There were many instances where battalions were temporarily detached from their brigades and divisions and added to other formations. Moreover, the nature of the fighting was confusing as troops were constantly moving from place to place. Finally, the overburdened staff officers had little time to attend to their units' war diary so that details of much of the fighting were lost permanently. My hope is that this narrative will help dispel the fog of war, or at least a good part of it, and make the battle more comprehensible to the reader.

Some people might find this work controversial, but I tried hard to be objective and dispassionate, bearing in mind that even a fool can be wise after the event. It is easy to reflect from the comfort of an easy chair with access to dispatches, elaborate and accurate diagrams, and descriptions of the battle from both sides, on decisions taken in the midst of terror and confusion. In the heat of battle, mistakes are inevitable, often excusable. That said, I need also add that commanders should be held accountable for errors resulting from lapses in judgment, professional ignorance, and lack of moral courage.

George H. Cassar
Eastern Michigan University

ACKNOWLEDGEMENTS

Writing may be a solitary activity, but the production of a book is a collective endeavour. My first debt is owed to the scores of soldiers at Second Ypres, who, through their letters, diaries, and interviews, gave me a better feel and understanding of those terrible days. The survivors of Second Ypres have all passed on, but they, together with their comrades who fell in battle, left a legacy of courage, sacrifice, and achievement that should be a source of pride to all Canadians.

It would have been impossible to write this book without the courtesy and help of numerous archivists and librarians. Special mention is due to the following: Sophie Tellier of the National Archives of Canada; R.W.A. Suddaby of the Imperial War Museum; William Spencer of the British National Archives; and Lianne Smith of the Liddle Hart Centre for Military Archives, as well as her former colleague, Caroline Lam. Andrew Powers of Eastern Michigan University never failed to obtain every book that I had requested through the inter-library loan system. Dominick Dendooven of the In Flanders Fields Museum in Ypres gave of his time and resources to research and send me many of the illustrations that appear in this book. To each I wish to express my deep appreciation.

A number of friends and colleagues helped in a variety of ways. I am grateful to Jack Etsweiler for his patience and skill in disentangling my computer-generated gaffes. The department secretary, Claudia Cullen, attended to my many requests with unfailing courtesy. Dr. Steve Ramold provided a sympathetic ear and his probing questions did much to clarify my thoughts and generally to keep me on track. As I had missed the battlefield tour bus on account of my late arrival in Ypres, Steve Douglas, the owner of the company, kindly volunteered to act as my personal guide. Don Lafreniere, an excellent cartographer, drew most of the maps — the others were borrowed from my earlier books.

The research trips I made to Ottawa and London would not have been possible without generous funding from the office of Dr. Robert K. Neely, associate provost and associate vice-president for research, and the Earhart Foundation.

For permission to quote material for which they hold the copyright I would like to thank the following institutions: the National Archives of Canada, the Canadian Broadcasting Corporation, and the Trustees of the Imperial War Museum. Copyright material in the British National Archives is reproduced by kind permission of the Controller of Her Majesty's Stationary Office. In cases where it has not been possible to trace the copyright holder, or where it may have been overlooked, I offer my sincere apologies.

It is traditional for authors to thank their families and I have good reason to conform to that practice. My son Michael undertook many mundane, but no less invaluable, tasks. As usual, my wife Mary tolerated my extended research trips abroad, not to mention the long hours in my office writing.

While I made every effort to accurately credit my sources and ensure that the facts in this book are correct, I alone bear responsibility for any remaining errors.

CHAPTER I

Creating an Army

The moment Great Britain entered the conflict against Germany on 4 August 1914, Canada, as part of the empire, was automatically at war. Like the other dominions, Canada possessed the right to determine the extent and nature of its participation in the war. There was never any doubt, however, that its contribution would be generous and wholehearted. During the years immediately before 1914, leaders of the two major political parties had stated unequivocally on a number of occasions that, in the event of a European war, Canada would stand firmly behind Britain. Indeed on 2 August 1914, two days prior to Britain's declaration of war, the Canadian prime minister, Sir Robert Borden, asked London for suggestions as to how Canada could best render effective aid, observing that a considerable force would be available for service abroad.[1] On 6 August, the British government gratefully accepted the Canadian offer of a contingent and the next day requested that it be made up of a division.[2] In Ottawa, an Order in Council set the strength of the expeditionary force at 25,000 men.

Canada, a nation of less than 8 million people, was ill prepared to fight a major war in August 1914. It had a fledgling navy — an old light cruiser and two submarines — and an air force consisting of two canvas planes still packed in crates. The country's permanent force was small, a little over 3000 all ranks, and only twelve regular officers had completed staff college courses. Its active militia, although numbering nearly 75,000 men on paper, was far from being a model citizen army. Only about three-quarters of the personnel took part in the brief annual course of training, which consisted mainly of two weeks of foot and rifle drill, field skirmishes, physical exercises, and community singing. Many men did not serve out the entire three years of their enlistment and, as the units were always full of raw recruits at each summer camp, training seldom reached beyond the most elementary stages.[3] Moreover, they were poorly equipped and led by officers and NCOs, nearly all of whom lacked combat experience.

The Dominion Arsenal was equipped to turn out small-arms ammunition and artillery shells, but not on the scale to meet the army's wartime needs. Many months would pass before Canada could adapt its industries to mass-produce munitions. Until then it would have to compete with the War Office to have its orders filled by British factories, which had taken on much more work than they could handle.

An even more desperate situation existed with regard to increasing the stocks of heavy guns. Being dependent on British sources of supply, Canada had some 200 artillery pieces when the war broke out, enough to arm two divisions. Shortly after, however, Ottawa generously contributed 98 field guns to Britain so that when the 2nd Canadian Division was raised there were practically no 18-pounders available for its field batteries.[4] Besides the shortages of ammunition and artillery there were deficiencies in many other vital items of equipment, as well as in motor vehicles and horse-drawn transport wagons.

As can be seen, Canada did not have anything resembling the expeditionary force it had promised to put in the field. Nevertheless, it had the potential to create such a contingent and, if necessary, substantially increase its size. That is, it possessed great quantities of raw materials, well-developed industries, a small, but competent professional staff, and a large reservoir of men, many of whom were partially trained.

It was the government's wish that the expeditionary force should be composed only of those who volunteered for overseas service. The only question was how to assemble the detachment. A mobilization plan had been prepared in 1911 by Colonel Willoughby Gwatkin, a British staff officer at Militia Headquarters, with the object of raising for service abroad a volunteer force of one division and one cavalry brigade.[5] It provided for a decentralized system and was sufficiently detailed to reduce chaos and confusion to a minimum. Military districts were responsible for recruiting and, as far as possible, equipping the men and sending them to training camp. Enlistment was to be for the duration of the war and preference was given to those with military experience or militia training. The troops were to concentrate at Petawawa in summer but, in the event that mobilization occurred in winter, they were to be moved directly to the port of embarkation. The scheme, while not perfect, "did supply a considered plan for the provision of troops on a fair ratio throughout the Dominion and for a force of the same composition as that called for in August 1914."[6]

The mobilization plan, carefully prepared against the precise emergency that had now arisen, was consigned to the wastepaper basket by the minister of militia, Colonel Sam Hughes.[7] A man of great resource and energy, but obstinate, impulsive, overwhelmingly vain, and heavy-handed, Hughes made his own rules as he went along, with the result that many of the things he did had to be undone later on. Why he discarded the prepared scheme is difficult to determine. Some historians feel that it was due to political partisanship, reinforced by his insane egotism. Others attribute his motive to an almost obsessive antipathy toward professional soldiers and regular army methods. Whatever the cause, Hughes substituted his own improvised measures, which went into effect on 6 August when he sent 226 night telegrams directly to unit commanders of the militia. With this he short-circuited the whole militia organization, bypassing district commands while he placed himself in the centre of the mobilization picture. Unit commanders were instructed to interview prospective volunteers between the ages of 18 and 45 and forward to Ottawa lists of those who could meet the prescribed physical standards. After Militia Headquarters had examined the lists, each commander would be told how many to enlist until the required number of men had been obtained.[8]

The selection of 25,000 individuals by this cumbersome system produced instant chaos from Halifax to Vancouver. Hughes realized the impracticability of the process and on 10 August the duties of the district commander, as envisaged in the 1911 scheme, were restored. Three days later Hughes modified the instructions again. Orders often contradictory and confusing continued to flow from Ottawa, but, eventually, most of the volunteers joined through existing militia units in virtually the same manner prescribed by the pre-war mobilization scheme.[9]

In January 1916 the minister of militia attempted to justify his actions to Parliament, in terms not only absurd but disingenuous:

> For the first contingent, our recruiting plans were, I think, different from anything that had ever occurred before. There was really a call to arms, like the fiery cross passing through the Highlands of Scotland or the mountains of Ireland in former days. In place of being forwarded to the district officers commanding, the word was wired to every officer commanding a unit in any part of Canada to buckle on his harness and get busy. The consequence was that in a short time we had the boys on the way for the first contingent, whereas it would have taken several weeks to have got the word around through the ordinary channels.[10]

Hughes is scarcely justified when he asserts that adherence to the original plan would have entailed needless delays. On the contrary, had he used the usual military channels of communication, the time required to warn militiamen would have been a matter of hours, not weeks. For example, in 1866, when the Militia Department's organization was much more rudimentary and communications much less developed than in 1914, orders sent through the usual channels twice brought under arms a force of 14,000 Canadian Militia in less than 24 hours. "It is quite certain," the militia report of that year went on to say, "that in place of the … men called for, 30,000 could have been mustered within 48 hours."[11] Indeed, because of the confusion caused by Hughes's irregular call to arms, the militia organization quickly regained its normal place in the mobilization scheme.

The most striking feature, given the sharp conflicts that had characterized external affairs in recent years, was the almost complete unanimity with which Canada entered the war. There would be rifts later, when it became apparent that the conflict would not be over and won in short order, but at the outset scarcely a dissenting voice could be heard. At the special session of Parliament, held on 18 August, Wilfrid Laurier, Opposition leader, speaking on behalf of his party, insisted that it was the duty of Canada to support the mother country and to help "save civilization from the unbridled lust of conquest and power."[12] The *Globe* in Toronto urged its readers that regardless of their political affiliation, "Our duty now is to join together to meet the real emergency."[13] *La Presse* of Montreal stated boldly that "citizens of this country stand united, ready to defend, first our native soil against all invasion, and then to place our surplus strength at the disposal of the United Kingdom ..."[14] Even ardent Quebec nationalist Henri Bourassa, who had opposed Canada's participation in the Boer War as an issue of British imperialism, sided with the government's official policy in a rare moment of accord. In the prestigious *Le Devoir*, which he founded and edited, Bourassa published a statement that it was Canada's duty to contribute according to its resources, asserting that "I have not written and will not write one line, one word, to condemn the sending of Canadian troops to Europe."[15] All Canadians, from the staunchest Tory to the nationalist of Quebec, appealed for a truce to party and racial disputes and for a vigorous prosecution of the war.[16]

No one had any idea of what the war would be like. As in all belligerent nations, Canadians greeted the declaration of war with an almost carnival gaiety. In Montreal, the patriotic tone of the French-language press contributed to the wild excitement of the people parading through St. Catherine Street, singing "La Marseillaise" and "Rule Britania." In other towns and cities across Canada, the story was much the same, with crowds gathered to listen to patriotic speeches or surging through the streets singing, cheering and waving flags. Frank Jamieson, then a member of the 48th Highlanders, recalled one such spectacle:

> I'll always remember the first night war was declared. Never forget it. We was all down the armouries. We was there in the hundreds. The 48th Band come out, played Rule Britannia, and that was the spark that ignited

Courtesy of Library and Archives Canada.

Enlistment centres such as the one above in Ottawa were crowded with eager volunteers during the opening days of the war.

the thing. Away we went in crowds down through the streets. There was a French flag come on the scene, and Union Jacks. I know I got home very tired about 2 or 3 o'clock in the morning afterwards and then we was called on parade the following Friday, the 48th. And we couldn't get through for traffic and they were pulling the poles off the streetcars and the people was mobbing us. You'd have thought we was coming back from the war, let alone going there.[17]

The rush to volunteer for overseas duty in 1914 was unprecedented in the short history of the Canadian nation, far exceeding the 8300 who had enlisted in the British army to fight the Boers in South Africa. From the workshops and offices in the cities, lumber and mining camps, vast wheat fields of the prairies, farms and orchards in the east, the manhood of the country converged upon the recruiting centres.[18] "The call went out and ... there were thousands trying to enlist," recalled E.J. Owens, destined to serve in the 2nd Battalion. "They were coming from all over. We had one fellow in our mob came from down the Yukon Trail and paid his own way to get in."[19]

"It was a great occasion and everybody was afraid they wouldn't have a chance to participate," G.R. Stevens explained. "That feeling was very widespread." [20] Long lines formed outside the recruiting stations. C.E. Longstaff of the 48th Highlanders was on the scene at one such centre: "They had to have a guard on the main door there ... with fixed bayonets to keep the fellows back, pouring in, too many."[21] Within a month the government found that the number of men at its disposal far exceeded the 25,000 it had requested, compelling the Militia Department to issue orders suspending the enrollment of additional recruits.[22]

The Western provinces showed the highest percentage of enlistments, partly because the ratio of single men to married men was higher there than elsewhere in Canada. French Canadians had the lowest volunteer enlistment rates. To be sure, many men of French stock were not attracted to the idea of fighting a war to assist Great Britain or volunteering in an army dominated by English-speaking officers. But it is equally true that Sam Hughes threw cold water on the initial enthusiasm in Quebec by his insensitivity toward French Canadians. An avid Orangeman with an abiding hatred of Catholics, he considered French Canadians untrustworthy and laggards. French Canadian officers with distinguished war records were passed over or given inconsequential commands. Moreover, Hughes would not allow a group of prominent Quebecers to raise a French-speaking battalion until political pressure forced him to relent. When everything is considered, it is difficult to resist the conclusion that Hughes's racist attitude undermined the recruiting drive among French Canadians.[23]

A statistical breakdown of the First Canadian contingent shows that only 33 percent were born in Canada (3.5 percent in Quebec) with the United States and other countries providing another 3 percent. The remainder, about 64 percent, were recent emigrants from Great Britain. In fact in some units there were practically no native-born Canadians.

Canadians flocked to the colours for myriad reasons. A powerful inducement to enlist in the early days was love of the Empire. There were over 1 million British-born citizens in Canada, the majority of whom had settled in Ontario and the prairie provinces. They naturally retained strong loyalties to their homeland and the fit men of military age were among the first to volunteer for service.[24] E. Seaman (3rd Battalion) remarked in hindsight: "I think first and foremost now I'm a good Canadian, although … I will admit that when our boat docked at Plymouth I literally got down on my knees and kissed the soil of England, no fooling. I don't know what prompted me but I did it." A.G. Jacobs (Lord Strathcona's Horse), who arrived in Canada in 1912, felt the same way: "Like ninety percent of the population in Saskatoon at that time we were English immigrants. 1914 came and for two mornings we lined up to get in to enlist and as far as my unit was concerned I was actually the first man in Saskatoon." [25] The pull was equally irresistible for O. Bright, a police officer from Regina who took a leave of absence to enlist: "I had only been in Canada two years, but I felt I had to go back to England. I was an Englishman, and I thought they might need me."[26]

Most militiamen, particularly officers, joined as a matter of course. It was not unusual for whole militia units to volunteer, though always, it seemed, it was the result of a nudge from the commanding offices. C.E. Longstaff recounts the following: "When the war broke out old Colonel Currie … said to us one night, this was on the parade, 'Boys I'd like the whole regiment to volunteer. So will the whole regiment step forward two paces.' So the whole darn regiment stepped forward, see." G.T. Boyd had an identical explanation for his enlistment: "On August 4th, the 90th Winnipeg Rifles was mobilized under Col. J.W. O'Grady. He says, 'Now … war has been declared and I have offered the regiment for service. Who goes?' Naturally everyone says 'We go.' So that's what happened."[27]

For many weaned on stirring tales of Victorian heroes and clinging to the prevailing perception that war was a glorious undertaking, the conflict of 1914 presented a marvellous occasion to fulfill dreams of excitement and adventure. "I wanted to see the world and I thought this would be a good opportunity," remarked H.L. Christopherson (5th Battalion), a 21-year-old bank clerk. "I didn't see how else I was going to ever get out of Yorkton, Saskatchewan, and see the world."[28] S. Ellis of Lethbridge, Alberta, was another young man eager to escape from the humdrum of daily life: "My brother had enlisted and he made it sound like a real nice life. I figured, well, it will be a change — I would get overseas to see the world. I had no intention of ever getting killed."[29] Victor Odlum, a 34 year-old newsman from Vancouver, maintained that all "who were on the younger side had the spirit of adventure in us and I think that a spirit of adventure took most of us there."[30]

Still, there were others who placed duty and patriotism above everything else. A young officer remarked that "if ever there was a war that appealed to the chivalry and patriotism of all, this was the one."[31] A Canadian-born lad in the 16th Battalion told his mother that he enlisted not "for want of a fight or the love of adventure," but "to fight for our country."[32] "It seemed not only the natural thing to do but the inevitable thing to do," exclaimed J.M. MacDonnell (4 Division Artillery).[33]

There were other motives as to why men offered their services — caught up in the excitement of the moment, under pressure from friends or co-workers, the need to prove their manhood, exaggerated courage and bravado after they had guzzled a few beers with the boys, and because of family tradition. Thus there was no single reason that drove Canadians to the recruiting stations.

The early influx of recruits ruled out lowering medical or physical standards or altering the age range for enlistment. Most men who were rejected returned home disconsolate. "Some men that were turned down, I remember them weeping because they weren't accepted," N. Nicholson (16th Battalion) would recall 50 years later.[34] As might be expected, there were always a determined few who succeeded in overturning their initial rejection or found ways to deceive the medical authorities. Harold Peat refused to give up when told that "we have too many men to be taking a midget like you." Accordingly, he resorted to what should have been a transparent subterfuge to win over the medical officer. As he explained in his memoirs he went to the doctor's home to plead his case:

> "Excuse me Doctor," I said when he appeared, "but I'm sure you would pass me if you only knew of my circumstances."

"Well?" snapped the major.

"You see, sir, my two brothers have been killed by the Germans in Belgium, and my mother and sisters are over there. I *must* go over to avenge them." I shivered: I quaked in my shoes. Would the major speak to me in French? I did not then know as much as *Bon Jour*. But luck was with me.

To my great relief Major Farquarhson replied ... "Report to me this afternoon; I will pass you."[35]

Arthur Shelford of British Columbia was turned down because of flat feet. Puzzled, he asked the doctor why flat feet should disqualify him from being a soldier:

"Why," said he, "you can't march."

"I may not be able to march," said I, "but I walked the forty-five miles to Houston over a rough, muddy road in twenty-five hours."

"Yes," said he, "but you couldn't move the next day."

"Maybe," said I, "but I walked thirty miles along the track to Telkwa that day and I will take an eighty pound pack on my back and walk up the Bulkley Valley against any man you like to choose."

"Well," said the Doc, "if that is the way you feel, I guess I had better pass you."[36]

Squib Walker, a scout with the Toronto Maple Leaves, wanted to enlist with his friends from the university, but he had no hope of passing the eye test. Conn Smythe, who would later become the principal owner of the club, tells us how Walker devised an ingenious ruse to cover his physical disability:

When the eye examinations were held in the old mining building on College Street in the basement, Squib, who could not see five feet without his glasses, had us drill a

hole in the door and he backed up there, and when they called out the initials in the lineup, the best visual man we had whispered in his ear from behind the door, and he passed with flying colours.[37]

The range of ages among the recruits varied greatly. Some, barely sixteen, were obviously too young to be wearing khaki as were those in their fifties, well past the cut-off age. Craigie Mackie, although only sixteen, was able to join the Gordon Highlanders because he lied about his age: "When I went to join the first time in the morning the doctor … knew me, so I couldn't fool him about my age. I waited until later in the day and then I tried again. By that time another doctor had had taken his place, so I told him I was eighteen and he enlisted me."[38]

Fred Fish (4th Division Artillery) and his brother received the shock of their lives shortly after they had commenced their training program:

> We were at Valcartier, my brother and I, and we saw a distinguished looking gentleman walking along in civvies, carrying a suitcase and I said to Colin my brother, "That looks like old Dad, the way that fellow walks, doesn't it?"
>
> He said, "Yes." And sure enough it was my father. He had sent his papers in … and was told to report. He was fifty-four.[39]

From local assembly areas the volunteers marched to the rail station where they entrained for Valcartier, sixteen miles northwest of Quebec City. The government had selected the site in 1912 as a central training area for the Quebec militia, but when the war broke out it was still a wilderness of wooded and sandy flatlands. The official reason for building a new camp at Valcartier, rather than using the facilities at Petawawa, was that its proximity to the embarkation port of Quebec City would reduce transportation costs.

Under the supervision of Sam Hughes, ably assisted by William Price, a timber baron, and James McCarty, a civil engineer, the work of building a

The First Contingent at Valcartier.

training facility began on 8 August. Overnight the new campsite swarmed with lumberjacks clearing bush and trees; labourers constructing sewage, roads, rail links to Quebec City, and rifle ranges; and contractors hastily delivering horses, wagons, boats, tents, and other paraphernalia of war. Mounted on a horse and dressed in his colonel's uniform, Hughes seemed to be everywhere, greeting new arrivals, barking orders to workers, dressing down officers in front of their men, interfering with the training of the recruits, and "boasting of his achievements to admiring journalists."[40] Canon Frederick Scott wrote: "The dominating spirit of the camp was General Hughes,[41] who rode about with his aides-de-camp in great splendor like Napoleon. To me it seemed that his personality and his despotic rule hung like a dark shadow over the camp."[42] Still, his methods produced phenomenal results. In less than a month, the place was transformed into a huge military camp with facilities to accommodate the thousands of recruits. Valcartier stands as a monument to Hughes's

unbounded optimism and driving power, but Professor G.F.G. Stanley was probably correct when he observed that it was "wasteful and unnecessary."[43]

The first wave of volunteers arrived on 18 August amid construction and confusion and by 8 September the number of all ranks had reached the maximum of 32,665. Among these was a battalion raised by Hamilton Gault, a veteran of the South African War and a long-time militia officer in the Royal Highlanders of Canada. A wealthy Montreal businessman, the 33-year-old Gault not only contributed $100,000 (about $2 million in today's currency) toward its costs, but volunteered to serve in it. The regiment was commanded by Lieutenant-Colonel Francis Farquhar, a highly talented British soldier loaned to Canada, with Gault as the senior major. With the permission of the Duke of Connaught, the governor general of Canada, it was named after his popular and beautiful second daughter, Princess Patricia. She was described by a member of the unit as "six feet tall, slim and straight, lithe and graceful as a fawn" and "is the most beautiful of her sex that I have ever seen."[44] Moved by the honour, the princess personally designed and made the badge and colours for the regiment to take overseas. Named colonel-in-chief, the princess would play an active role in the regiment until her death in 1974.

Princess Patricia's Canadian Light Infantry was different from the other battalions. Besides being created by one man, it was recruited at top speed and consisted of former British regulars and Canadian veterans of the South African War.[45] Since the "Patricias," or "Princess Pats," as they are commonly called, required less training than the other units, they were the first Canadian troops to land in France. The Patricias did not serve in Flanders as part of the 1st Canadian Division, but nevertheless were involved in the later action at Ypres where they forged a reputation, which they have maintained to this day, as one of Canada's finest fighting forces. Lady Patricia Ramsay (formerly Princess Patricia) issued a statement in 1964 on the fiftieth anniversary of the start of the Great War, paying tribute to and underscoring her pride in the regiment:

> It would be difficult to express in any way … the intense pride and affection I have always felt for my famous and magnificent Regiment.

The gallantry, bravery and devotion to duty which the Regiment has shown unflinchingly ever since it came into being are beyond any powers of mine to praise. I can only render homage, and this I do with all my heart.

Believe me, I am indeed honoured that my name should be borne by such troops as Princess Patricia's Canadian Light Infantry have shown themselves to be.[46]

The authorized strength of the Canadian expeditionary force was 25,000 men, not the more than 32,000 that had been assembled at Valcartier. Thus 6,000 or so of them, after eagerly volunteering for service, faced the bitter prospect of being sent back home. During a visit to Valcartier on 21 September, Prime Minister Borden, having concluded that the 1st Division would require reinforcements and reserves once it reached the front, decided to send the entire force. Hughes, who had agonized over the choice of who should go and who should remain, "broke down and sobbed" in relief.[47]

There was no blueprint on how the battalions should be formed and the process in some cases, as described by Freeman and Nielsen, "was much like the way youngsters choose sides for a sandlot baseball game."[48] According to Major Victor Odlum, (7th Battalion), this was essentially how his unit came into being: "The 7th battalion was formed very largely by what you would call military politics. The groups were there, there was no one in command to organize them. We got together and we just reported that we had formed a battalion. And Sam Hughes took it."[49] F.B. Bagshaw (5th Battalion), gives a similar explanation:

> We didn't know who we were. We didn't know who the officers were. But we were all called out on parade and this dapper officer, boots shining, and as immaculate as could be, he stood on a soap box. He said "This unit will be known in future as the 5th Canadian Battalion …" So that's how we were formed.[50]

On 1 September, after some reshuffling, the infantry was organized into four brigades, each comprising four battalions of 1000 men. The 1st Brigade, made up of the 1st, 2nd, 3rd, and 4th Battalions from Ontario, was commanded by Lieutenant-Colonel Malcolm Mercer. The 2nd Brigade under Lieutenant-Colonel Arthur Currie consisted of the 5th, 6th, 7th, and 8th Battalions, all from the West. Colonel Richard Turner's 3rd Brigade was composed of one battalion from Montreal and the Maritimes, the 14th, and three Highland Battalions from across Canada: the 13th, 15th, and 16th. The 4th Brigade, consisting of the 9th, 10th, and 11th Battalions from the Prairies, and the 12th from the Maritimes, was allocated to Lieutenant-Colonel J.E. Cohoe. Another battalion (the 17th) was formed to handle the surplus infantry as a result of a decision on 21 September to send all medically fit volunteers overseas.[51] To command the Divisional Field Artillery, Hughes chose Lieutenant-Colonel Harry Burstall, a member of Canada's pre-war army and a graduate of the staff college. All those appointed to command brigades, battalions, and artillery units were almost exclusively Canadian-born. Selection was often based on political favouritism, but, as Professor Desmond Morton pointed out, "it is not obvious that better officers were available."[52]

The new battalions, designated as they were by numbers only, failed to perpetuate the time-honoured names of militia units.[53] The more than 32,000 men making up the expeditionary force represented some 200 militia organizations across Canada. Naturally each unit wanted to prove its mettle in action under its own name and its own officers. The new system, in addition to creating hard feelings, particularly among units with a long and distinguished record of service, hindered training and retarded the growth of regimental esprit de corps.

Of special interest to Hughes in the early weeks of training was the selection of a commander for the Canadian Division. There is not much doubt that the minister of militia would have relished the post himself.[54] On 14 August, Borden cabled Sir G.H. Perley, the acting Canadian High Commissioner in London, that Hughes would probably go overseas "if convinced that he would command Canadian division ... and be in fighting line."[55] Although a colonel in the militia, Hughes was by experience and temperament totally unsuited for combat leadership. Lord Kitchener,

British secretary of state for war, settled the issue when he told Perley that it would be a mistake to change the minister of militia "at this juncture."[56] Thereafter Hughes, having accepted the judgment of the War Office, did not even insist on the appointment of a Canadian. Indeed when Kitchener recommended a choice from three Canadian-born officers serving in the British Army, Hughes considered none of these sufficiently senior or suitable for high command. Instead, he had in mind three British officers with whom he was familiar and of these he thought that Major-General Edwin Alderson was "the best qualified by far."[57] On 5 September, Kitchener notified Perley that he was glad to be able to comply with Hughes's wishes.[58] Alderson's appointment was made official on 25 September, and he was promoted to the rank of lieutenant-general effective 14 October, the day the first Canadian units arrived in Great Britain.

Now that a commander had been chosen, the next step was to resolve the delicate matter of the relation of the Canadian contingent to the British Army. In the past, Canadian forces sent to fight overseas had been dispersed among British units. The same procedure might have been followed in 1914, but the Canadian expeditionary force was the outcome of the nation's will and pride and the government was anxious that it should remain a national formation. Kitchener apparently raised no objection.[59] However, there is an account that suggests otherwise.

In late October the minister of militia sailed for England to brief Alderson "respecting officer and other important matters."[60] While in London, Hughes visited the War Office and, according to a Canadian officer who was present, was told that the Canadian contingent would be broken up and integrated into the British Army.[61] Supposedly Hughes told Kitchener to go to the devil and in the end succeeded in having the order rescinded. The story is probably untrue. The statements of the officer in question were made in June 1934, 20 years later, and no evidence can be found either in private or official records to corroborate them. If such an event had occurred, Hughes most assuredly would have proclaimed it loudly to the country since he was not in the habit of concealing his accomplishments, especially as a champion of Canadian rights.

Early on, the Militia Department made arrangements for the Canadian force to complete its training on Salisbury Plain in England.

Valcartier was deemed unsuitable as a winter camp and besides Hughes was anxious to get Canadian troops overseas.[62] All the leading military authorities in Europe, with the exception of Kitchener, had predicted that the conflict would last six months or less. The most frequent fear of Canadian soldiers of all ranks was that the great adventure would be over before they could reach the field. W.C. Sterling (4th battalion), captured the general sentiment among the men at the time:

> Nobody seemed to think that it would amount to much . They'd say, "Ha, ha, you don't mean to tell me you are going over. Why the thing will be over before you get there."
>
> "Well," I said, "we are going to have the boat ride over and see the Old Country anyway."[63]

The weather was pleasant enough and the men experienced little hardship at Valcartier, although there were shortages of practically everything in the beginning. The time for training, already limited, was further shortened by interruptions of one kind or another. The recruits, arriving with no unit organization, had to be medically examined, inoculated, attested, and issued clothing and equipment, which, in many instances, came belatedly from the manufacturers. There were changes, practically on a daily basis, in the composition, location, and command of the units. To make matters worse there was the omnipresence of Sam Hughes, who exercised close and erratic control in matters of administration and training and made appointments in a seigniorial manner without reference to the Militia Council or to his colleagues.

The above disruptions naturally hindered the men's training, which was hardly rigorous to begin with: V.W. Odlum admitted that training "was based upon the use of the rifle." He added: "We were sure that the British Army was the finest and the last word in an army, and all we had to do was to go over there and pick up their ways." Victor Lewis's (4th Battalion) brief comments were even more to the point: "We didn't actually soldier until 1915 when we were on Salisbury Plains."[64]

The instructions guiding the cavalry were equally sketchy. A.G. Jacobs has left his impressions of his stay at Valcartier:

> Never anywhere did thirty thousand ... men get gathered in such a small area, and oh, how untrained we were. We went to the range and started banging away without any preliminary training of any kind.
>
> The type of officer who commanded didn't consider that you needed to be much of a shot as long as you had the guts to get up and go straight at 'em or wait till you see the whites of their eyes.[65]

An artilleryman, J.W. Ross, for his part, recalled an episode that under different circumstances would have been humourous:

> During our stay at Valcartier, Constantine, who later on became General Constantine, came to me one day and said, "We have some shells made in the Dominion Arsenal, and I want you to try them out." So I had my little Sergeant, and he had his gun put out on a hill top, and we fired over the cavalry lines and we fired at a sheet, but I was told to be careful and not hit the sheet if possible, because it was the only one they had.[66]

Training at Valcartier was based on principles contained in a manual entitled *Memorandum for Camps of Instruction, 1914,* issued by the Department of Militia and Defence. This pamphlet outlined the method of training to be followed in militia summer camps. The first few days were devoted to elementary squad and foot drill and rifle instruction. Then came route marches of increasing length, together with daily physical exercises, necessary for the hardening process. But as Fortescue Duguid, then a young junior artillery officer on the scene, and later the army's official historian, remarked, there was a world of difference between training a professional army and a summer militia unit. Further interfering with the training of the troops at Valcartier

Marching at Valcartier. The fact that the soldiers are carrying pieces of wood rather than rifles is clear indication that the country was unprepared for the war

were the repeated changes of the units' composition and command. Many officers and NCOs were provisional and on probation until a few days before departure. Duguid wrote that "one provisional battalion had four lieutenant colonels, another none, and so with the lower ranks; new appointments, promotions replacements, transfers and reductions were of bewildering frequency in the hectic, alternating process of shaking up and shaking down."[67]

Although a significant core of recruits had served in the militia or saw active service in British-led campaigns, the vast majority were untutored in the ways of the military and came from every sector of society. "We had engineers and lawyers and doctors," R.L. Christopherson told CBC during an interview. "We had everything enlisted as privates. One of my best pals was a burglar. He said he wanted to join the army so they let him out of jail … He went right back to his old profession after he returned."[68]

J.I. Chambers (7th battalion) added the following: "The thing I remember mostly about Valcartier was trying to make civilians into soldiers. When we joined up we'd go to the Colonel and say, 'Say, Bub, when do we eat?' something of that kind, you see. We always got into difficulty through not knowing what we were supposed to be doing." C.B. Price (14th Battalion) offered an explanation for the lapses in discipline: "Considering the heterogeneous state of the units in the Division and the fact that so many men had no training, the surprising thing wasn't that there was a lack of discipline, but that there wasn't far more."[69]

It would have been helpful if the men had something to occupy their idle hours in the evening. Sam Hughes was a teetotaler and he was adamant in applying a decades-old army regulation prohibiting alcoholic liquor in camps. R. McLaughlin (14th Battalion) revealed what happened to confiscated alcohol: "They ran a railroad siding into the camp site and there was a long platform, and at the end of it was a pile of stones, and those rocks were there expressly for breaking flasks and bottles on."[70] Worse still, there were no nearby towns and officials, overburdened with their professional responsibilities, had no time to organize concerts or other forms of entertainment for the men. The YMCA did provide recreation rooms and writing materials, but it was not enough to suit most of the men. One day an enterprising individual came to camp, not to serve his country, but for financial motives. He set up a movie operation in a tent and charged an admission of ten cents. The films were of a poor quality and shown over and over again to the fury of the paying customers. Their patience exhausted, the aggrieved men held a council at which they unanimously agreed to drive the shady profiter out of business. Sergeant-Major William R. Jones, a cavalryman, has left a record of what subsequently occurred:

> The time for action was fixed and that evening a large party assembled about the show tent … Certain men were detailed to cut, at a given signal, the guy ropes. No plan was more expeditiously carried out. At a signal a shout went up and down came the tent and down came the tent upon the head of the proprietor. Smoke at once arose and soon the tent and the entire establishment was a sheet of flames with the boys dancing about in the wildest sort of a war dance imaginable. The ending of the show enterprise in this spectacular fashion gave the boys

more real entertainment during the half hour it lasted
than it had given during its entire existence in camp.[71]

After six weeks, the Canadian expeditionary force, still relatively
disorganized and untrained, prepared to leave for England. The
contingent of nearly 33,000 men consisted of 17 infantry battalions,
in addition to the Patricias, three field artillery brigades, and three
cavalry formations — the Royal Canadian Horse Artillery, the Royal
Canadian Dragoons, and Lord Strathcona's Horse. Initially, plans for
the Canadian division had not included any units of the Permanent
Force, an organization that Hughes had never regarded with particular
favour. But, as so often happened with the unpredictable Hughes, orders
changed, and in the end it was decided to send one artillery brigade and
two cavalry regiments. Given the lack of trained officers at the senior staff
level, it would have benefited the volunteer force if Hughes had sent the
Royal Canadian Regiment along, as well. Unfortunately, he allowed the
only regular infantry regiment in Canada to be dispatched to Bermuda
in order to free a British battalion for service in France.[72]

Sam Hughes's parting words to the men did not win him any admirers.
Captain T.S. Morrisey (13th battalion) recalled with some bitterness: "He
gathered us all around him at Valcartier and his last remarks ring in my
ears were: 'Well good bye boys, many of you won't come home, but never
mind there will be others to take your place ....' He got a rousing boo
from the troops for that."[73]

As the troops passed through Quebec on their way to the docks,
they were greeted by thousands of cheering, flag-waving residents
lining the streets and from their homes. William Jones vividly recalled
the spectacle after the war: "I can see it now. Flags were waving people
cheering, laughing and crying, and waving handkerchiefs, flags and caps.
Kisses were wafted to us from windows, flowers showered upon us, and
those who could do so, ran by our side seeking an opportunity to grasp
our hand and bid us a good bye and Godspeed."[74]

The embarkation of the force began on 23 September. William Price,
the man who had performed such prodigious feats of construction
at Valcartier, was appointed to supervise the embarkation. He was

Courtesy of Library and Archives Canada.

Convoy carrying Canadian troops to England.

not provided with a staff to assist him and his own efforts to obtain experienced officers from Valcartier proved unsuccessful. With no plan to follow, Price had to improvise as he went along and it is not surprising, to use the words of a high-ranking official, that "chaos reigned supreme."[75] Many units were split up and separated from their equipment, stores were left behind, and some ships were grossly overloaded while others were half empty.

On the last day of September, the transport ships, one by one, began to move out into the St. Lawrence, on their way to rendezvous with escorting British ships in Gaspé Harbour. Here Sam Hughes, in a rented tugboat, passed through the convoy, distributing printed copies of his stirring farewell speech to the troops.[76] On one of the convoys there were tense moments when the minister's launch was seen approaching. The men were lined up for their ration of beer, which had been provided by a kindly benefactor from Quebec City. A ministerial order, however, had prohibited the consumption of alcoholic beverages on board ship. The captain was spared embarrassment and possible disciplinary action when Hughes's launch veered off at the last moment.[77]

At 3:00 p.m. on 3 October, in clear weather, the flotilla sailed. The 32 ships, strung out over 21 miles, took three hours to stream through the harbour's narrow exit into the Gulf of St. Lawrence.[78] Once out at sea, the ships moved into three lines, two miles apart, each led by a British cruiser, with a fourth cruiser lying well back astern. The Canadian division was the largest armed force ever to cross the Atlantic. No one knew at the time that it was only the vanguard of a much larger host.

Life aboard was easy and, as the sea was calm, the men had a fine leisurely trip across the ocean. But with so many ships carrying thousands of men from different backgrounds, there were bound to be minor disturbances. W.S. Lighthall (Royal Canadian Dragoons) described one such incident:

> One day we suddenly put on all brakes and with propellers in full reverse slowed to a stop and dropped a boat to the water. Presently the boat returned to our ship and was hauled aboard and out of it came a bedraggled individual who turned out to be a Provost Sergeant from one of the ships ahead of us who had raised the ire of his shipmates until they had just tossed him overboard. The lookout spotted him and our ship signaled to pick him up, which we did , and carried him to England — but a more deflated NCO one seldom saw and he certainly gave us no cause to hand him on to the next ship in line.[79]

Christopherson also relates several tumultuous scenes that occurred on the ship he was travelling:

> They set up a canteen on the boat and we used to buy our chocolate bars and apples and cigarettes and one thing and another until we discovered printed on them that they

were donated as gifts to the first overseas contingent by these different chocolate companies. And then the boys, of course, went to town and wrecked the canteen and helped themselves. Oh, there were a lot of little things. There was a mutiny on board because they were serving up rotten fish. Somebody set fire to the boat on the way over. There was quite a cross section of people on the boat.[80]

On the last day of the crossing, reports of German submarines in the English Channel caused the convoy to change its destination from Southampton to Plymouth. The leading transports entered Plymouth Sound on 14 October and, as the other ships arrived, the port became congested, delaying the landing of some units until the 24th.

The townspeople, kept in the dark until the last moment, lined the waterfront and wharves, shouting "bravo Canadians" and greeting the

Courtesy of Library and Archives Canada.

Canadian ships arriving at Plymouth. The soldiers were warmly greeted by the local citizens as they disembarked.

Lieutenant-General Edwin Alderson. Although not a great field commander, he transformed the unconventional raw Canadians into a superb fighting force.

disembarking troops with cheers, handshakes, and gifts. Factory whistles and church bells joined in the welcome. The press was no less effusive in greeting the Canadians, stressing the enormous value their arrival meant to the Imperial cause. The first to do so was the *Western Morning News* of Plymouth: "To Canada belongs the immortal distinction of sending the first contingent of Dominion troops to war. Canada has always been foremost in great imperial movements, and in advance of the empire's honour." The *Morning Post* wrote of the Canadians: "They will soon be of great value in the fighting line ... But they are also of great value to the empire because they are the symbol of its unity and potential strength." The *Times* also expressed its gratitude to Canada for its assistance: "We welcome it for the addition it brings to our numbers in the field, and for the exceptionally fine quality of troops it gives us ... but far more for the incalculable moral support which it brings us in the great struggle for principles that conflict and cannot be reconciled."[81]

The Canadians were awed by the wild reception they received wherever they went.[82] Major Kirkpatrick wrote: "We are the first troops to arrive from the overseas Dominions and the papers say so many kind things of Canada and of us that we will have difficulty in living up to the high standards they are setting us."[83]

Some of the local inhabitants were evidently led to believe that Canada was a primitive land, inhabited mostly by Indians, trappers, and frontiersmen. An old lady walked up to R.F. Haig, a calvaryman, and asked, "Are you a Canadian?"

He replied "Yes."

She then said, "Where are your feathers?"

As the Canadians were parading through Plymouth, H.A. Marlow (Lord Strathcona's Horse) overheard a woman yell out, "Come on and see the Canadians comin'" and a woman appeared and exclaimed, "Oh blimey, they can speak English."[84]

Among the many dignitaries on hand was General Alderson, commander of the Canadian force.[85] Born in 1859, Alderson had seen much active service in Egypt, the Sudan, and South Africa, where Canadian units (Royal Canadian Dragoons and 2nd Canadian Rifles) had formed part of his command — a decisive factor in his present appointment. Short, dark, with a bushy moustache, he was respected for his dedication and kind, gentle character. He was not a great field general, but sound enough as a soldier. All in all, the Canadians could have done worse. With his 36 years of experience in the army, he knew how to train troops and deserves credit for helping to mold the raw and unruly Canadians into a superb fighting force.[86]

From Plymouth, the Canadian division faced a seven-hour train journey, followed by a march of eight or ten miles, before reaching the wilds of Salisbury Plain. The camp, acquired by the War Office in 1900, was approximately 12 miles long and six miles wide and dotted by isolated farms, and small villages and bearing the massive stone slabs of Stonehenge. It had been used as a military training ground for the Regular Army and Territorial Forces. The Canadians were assigned to four main areas extending along a five-mile strip on the western side. There were no permanent barracks available for them, but, while the convoy was crossing the Atlantic, fatigue parties from the Territorial Force, assisted by a group of New Zealanders who had recently enlisted in England, had set up thousands of bell tents, marquees, and kitchen shelters.

The last Canadian units had not yet arrived in camp when the fine autumn weather broke. A heavy downpour brought a quarter of an inch

Slogging through the legendary mud on Salisbury Plain.

of rain on 21 October and a full inch in the next five days. It was the start of what would turn out to be the worst winter in recent memory. From the middle of October 1914 to the middle of February 1915 rain fell on 89 of the 123 days, with intermittent frost and biting winds in between. The 29.3 inches of precipitation for that period almost doubled the average for the preceding 32 years.[87] "I know now why the English people invented the word rotten — no other word would do justice to this weather," Major Kirkpatrick confided to his diary.[88]

Conditions in the camp grew progressively worse. A layer of chalk several inches below ground level prevented drainage.[89] The field, cut by marching men, horses' hooves, and wagon wheels, turned into a quagmire. "No one tries any longer to keep clean and we look like barbarians," observed Lieutenant-Colonel John Creelman (2nd Field Artillery Brigade). "The mud here absolutely beggars description ... and our English visitors remark that an English regiment would mutiny if it were kept here."[90] The unheated tents were not waterproof and the poor quality of the canvas merely broke the heavier drops into fine particles of spray that settled and drenched everything within. "We simply went to sleep with our blankets on top of a rubber sheet and we climbed out of the hole in the morning that our bodies had made," K.C. Hossick (13th battalion) recalled. "I'm sure if we had slept for 48 hours we'd have been in a complete cave-in. It was terrible."[91] The men learned quickly that there was only one way to cope with the resulting discomfort. According to R.D. Haig that "was never take your clothes off, because it was much easier to get up in the morning damp-wet than get up in the morning and try to put on, cold damp clothes."[92] On 11 November, and again a month later, storms reaching gale proportions levelled tents, leaving the occupants shivering and wet, scattering correspondence and articles over the muddy field. Major Kirkpatrick has provided us with a graphic account of his tribulations during one such stormy day:

> Pouring rain again. After parade, I changed my wet clothes in a very wet tent, snatching my dry things out of my tin box, with water dropping all the time. Books, papers and everything uncovered are wet through. At 5 p.m. walked down to 2nd Battalion mess tent to a lecture. Pitch dark, black as a hat and blowing a gale. Fell over a tent guy and took a roll in the mud. Lecture inaudible on account of the roaring of the wind and the rain on the tent. Suddenly at 5:30 with a report like a shot, snap went the guy ropes, crack went the pole and down on our heads came the soaking canvas, chasing us all out into the driving rain, now turned to sleet. So cold and pitiless was the wind one could hardly stand up. Nearly all the large tents went down ... I found myself up to my knees in mud in the wild blackness searching for the road, then struggled back, joyful to find the men's tents standing and mine also. But the rain, driven by that wind, went clean through our rotten tents, soaked everything inside and gave us a very miserable night.[93]

Training was resumed during the first week of November. All instructors were members of the Canadian contingent except for two officers and five NCOs loaned by the War Office. The time for basic infantry training was devoted chiefly to physical conditioning, route marches, foot and arms drill, musketry instruction, and entrenching. Target practice was stressed in the training schedule. Each infantryman shot off his allotted 155 rounds and, for about 10 minutes a day, practiced charger-loading and rapid-fire with dummy cartridges. The object was to attain the speed and precision of British Regular soldiers who could fire 12 to 15 aimed shots a minute.[94] Considering that the material at hand consisted of green recruits, many of whom had never fired a rifle before, the results were quite spectacular. It was only a slight exaggeration when Sam Hughes later boasted that he had formed "the finest shooting army in the world."[95]

Needless to say, the miserable weather played havoc with the training schedule. Cold conditions or mist hampered range practice; heavy storms of wind and rain interrupted tactical exercises. Men had to plough through ankle-deep mud all day, their clothing soaked by rain or caked with slime. Much of the time little or nothing was done. Indeed, one unit historian records that out of a total of 130 days spent in England only 40 were available for training.[96] Duguid wrote: "Few of those who served on the Western front in the next four years were called upon to suffer such prolonged and unavailing misery as was endured on Salisbury Plain in the fall and winter of 1914."[97] The Canadians would have been much better served if they had remained at Valcartier. As a matter of fact, it was because of the experiences of the Canadians on the Plain that the Canberra government ordered the Australian and New Zealander troops to disembark in Egypt instead of proceeding to England.[98]

The year 1914 came to an end with the Christmas season, which for the men was one of the few constant things in their chaotic world. For most, who presumably were lonely and homesick, it was a time unlike anything they had known before. But they made the best of it. Ian Sinclair (13th Battalion) delighted in recalling his experience: "They let half the battalion go on leave at Christmas and half at New Year. The officers waited on the men at Christmas dinner and everybody got mildly tight, and we had a wonderful time." C.B. Price (14th Battalion) reminisced about attending a spiritual event which had left a lasting and fond impression:

> Canon Scott was our Padre then and he had a New Year's Eve service in Ainsbury Parish Church, a beautiful old Norman Church. And it was one of the few perfect nights with a full moon and a white frost, and we walked across the plains to the Church. And it was a wonderful service. They had the choir and everything there and quite one of my happiest memories of the war really.[99]

It is remarkable, in view of the prevailing conditions on Salisbury Plain, that the soldiers, whatever their innermost thoughts, generally remained uncomplaining.[100] The same feeling that had existed at Valcartier, that is, that they might not be ready to play a role in the imminent rout of the German Army, spurred them on, enabling them to withstand all hardships and overcome all difficulties. The Canadian High Command naturally worried lest the prolonged period of inclement weather affected the level of morale. On the last day of November, after a brutal stretch of rain and sleet, General Alderson visited the camp and talked to some of the officers. He asked if the men were complaining about the field conditions. On receiving a negative answer, he remarked, "Wonderful! Simply wonderful!"[101]

The letdown that the military leaders feared never occurred. Early in January 1915, weather conditions improved and there was a noticeable change in the attitude of the men even though training was intensified. The haggard and painful look on their faces disappeared, they joked and engaged in horseplay during idle moments, and even their most blasphemous comments on the weather and mud were salted with good humour. On route marches they sang and, like the British troops, their favourite tune by far was the lilting "Tipperary," a pre-war music-hall hit.

The time in England was spent not only to train, but also to reorganize battalions and exchange defective equipment. At Valcartier there had been eight companies per battalion. In November, the War Office decreed that the battalions, in accordance with British establishment, should reorganize on a four-company basis. In the next two months the War Office changed its mind half a dozen times until finally adopting the four-company system.

A good deal of effort and expense had gone into equipping the Canadian division. The months on Salisbury Plain revealed that some of the items distributed back in Canada were not up to British standards and were ordered replaced. Of immediate concern were the men's boots. Each recruit was supplied with a single pair of boots, which had become standard issue for the Permanent Force since the South African War. The Canadian boots were not designed for heavy marching and continual soaking in mud. In fact, they not only leaked, but literally disintegrated. Major Lester Stevens (8th Battalion) remembered that they "were like sieves, the water just went through them." He went on to say: "I used to empty the water out of my boots every night and I used to wring my socks out and lay them on the bed and lay on them to dry them to put them on in the morning."[102] On Alderson's recommendation each soldier was issued a pair of the sturdier British regulation boots.[103]

The Division had only five battalions that brought web equipment from Canada. The remainder wore the obsolescent Oliver pattern that had pouches for about half of the requisite rounds of ammunition, no pack facilities for carrying entrenchment tools, and were uncomfortable.[104] The War Office drew web equipment from its own stock to outfit seven Canadian battalions.

New outfits had to be found for the Canadian contingent. The tight-fitted khaki tunics with stiff collars, which were apt to split at the seams, were abandoned in favor of the looser, sturdier, and more comfortable British jacket. Unable to resist cold or rain, the cheaply made greatcoats gave way to the British model. The British also provided the Canadians with vehicles, both horse-drawn and motorized. Wagons brought over from Canada were in danger of collapsing when loaded with artillery ammunition. As for Canadian-made cars and trucks, some were worn out, while others had mechanical defects for which no spare parts were available in Britain.

Similarly, the MacAdam shovel, intended for use as a shield and as an entrenching tool, proved unsuitable for service in the field. Hughes had taken a special interest in this device that was patented by and named after his secretary, Ena MacAdam. When stuck into the ground in front of a prone rifleman, it was supposed to serve as a bulletproof shield.[105]Quite apart from the fact that it was heavy, difficult to carry, and practically useless to dig with, tests showed that it could not stop a bullet.[106] The shovels were replaced by British entrenching equipment and eventually sold as scrap metal

Unfortunately, the most important item used by the soldier was not exchanged. The Canadians were armed with the Ross rifle, which was less reliable than the British Lee-Enfield. In 1902, during the South African War, the Canadian government, frustrated that British manufacturers were unable to meet its orders for Lee-Enfields (the British army was given priority), adopted the Ross rifle and entered into a contract with the inventor, Sir Charles Ross. Faults of varying seriousness plagued the Ross rifle from the outset, but Hughes, a shooting enthusiast and extreme nationalist, became its most ardent champion. The failings of the Ross, about which critics had warned, surfaced again at Valcartier, and later on at Salisbury. Experienced soldiers freely admitted that the Ross, under the orderly conditions of the target range, fired with more precise accuracy than the British rifle. On the other hand they were equally convinced that it was unsuited for the harsh exigencies of field service. They observed that it was longer, heavier, and required constant cleaning; that the bayonet, when fixed, had a tendency to fall off; and, more significantly, that it jammed under rapid fire.[107] H.R. Alley (3rd battalion) summed up the attitude of the men towards the Ross rifle: "It was an exceedingly accurate rifle if you could take your time to shoot at one man at about 500 yards. It wasn't worth a hoot if you were dealing with a battalion of Germans at 200 yards. With rapid fire over any lengthy period, say three or four minutes, the darn thing would heat up so you couldn't open the bolt."[108]

Alderson received no satisfaction from Ottawa when he forwarded the many complaints that had poured into his office. Hughes considered himself a rifle expert and dismissed the perceived faults as essentially irrelevant and insisted that with slight modifications the Ross would meet his earlier claim of being the "most perfect military rifle in every sense in the World today."[109] In the final analysis it was the Canadian soldiers who would bear the heavy cost of Hughes's misplaced faith in the Ross rifle.

The general health of the troops was surprisingly good given their continued exposure to the wretched weather. The number of sick did increase, however, after the 2nd, 3rd, and 4th Brigades moved into permanent accommodations. The building of huts on the Plain had begun early in October but at Christmas time 11,000 Canadians were still under canvas — indeed the 1st Brigade remained in tents until departing for France. The huts were intended to accommodate 30 men, but they were invariably overcrowded. The proximity of the men to one another, together with improper sanitary precautions, resulted in outbreaks of various contagious diseases. "A fearful lot of sickness in these huts," recorded a member of the 16th Battalion. "Flu reigns supreme in the shape of sore heads, sore throats and racking coughs. At night it sounds like hell with all those graveyards coughs around."[110] Far more serious was an outbreak of meningitis, a highly contagious and often deadly disease. Of the 39 cases that were treated, 28 proved fatal.[111]

Posing no less a worry to Canadian Headquarters than the rampant sickness in the camp, was the widespread ill discipline among the rank and file. A large portion of the contingent consisted of unseasoned recruits who were independent-minded, hardy with a devil-may-care attitude, and wholly ignorant of standard conduct in the army. They dressed sloppily, did not snap to attention like the British soldier when the national anthem was played, frequently called their superiors by their first name and, if they saluted their officers at all, did so in the most casual and indifferent manner. Few among them seemed to be concerned that a pass was required before leaving camp; and those that obtained formal leave often created disturbances in the neighbouring towns or returned late and drunk. Early in November it was announced that the king, accompanied by Kitchener and other dignitaries, would visit the camp.[112] Before their arrival, a high-ranking officer addressed a battalion and urged the men to behave:

> Lads, the king and Lord Kitchener and all the big-bugs
> are coming down to review us to-day, and for once in

your lives, men, I want to see you act like real soldiers.
When they get here, for the love o' Mike, don't call me
Bill ... and, for God sake, don't chew tobacco in the
ranks.[113]

It was not long before the Canadians wore out their welcome in
nearby towns and acquired a reputation for unruly behaviour that would
dog them until the end of the war. "We must not expect Canadians,"
one newspaper warned the angry local citizens, "to behave as our men
do. Anglo-Saxon though they are, they come to us from a rude frontier
country where class and rank are unimportant."

Besides the existing conditions on Salisbury Plain, there were other
factors, according to artillery captain Harry Crerar, that exacerbated the
troops' tendency for mischief:

1. The Expeditionary Force, barring a few officers, had
    no leave granted since mobilization at Valcartier end of
    August till arrival at Salisbury or Plymouth end of October.
2. No canteen of any kind permitted during that time.
3. Practically 2 months pay on hand on their arrival in this
    country.[114]

Generally the offences were not serious, but inconsequential and
harmless; most could have been stopped with a simple warning. However,
the newly appointed officers and NCOs had not developed the talent
to manage men and they frequently created hard feelings by employing
bullying tactics or imposing punishments that exceeded the nature of the
infractions.

Alderson personally took the matter in hand and, disregarding the
army's long-standing policy, announced at the end of October that he
would establish wet canteens in the camp, at which beer would be sold
at certain hours and under careful supervision. This, he was convinced,
would reduce the men's visit to nearby villages where "they get bad
liquor, become quarrelsome and then create disturbances."[115] Despite
protests from temperance groups in Canada, the new arrangements were

put into effect. "The wet canteens is a Godsend and drinking has been reduced to a minimum," observed an officer. "A man who is free to buy a mug of beer a couple of times a day does not try to keep a bottle of whisky in his tent."[116] Another welcomed measure entitled a deserving soldier to a six-day pass with a free ticket to anywhere in the British Isles. At the same time, those in charge of discipline came to understand that a blend of firmness and subtle cajolery would cause men to conform willingly.[117] All of this produced the desired results. Morale improved while drunkenness dwindled and offences of all sorts decreased.

In mid-November, the most experienced battalion, the Patricias, moved to Winchester to join the 80th Brigade, which formed part of the 27th (British) Division. On 20 December, re-equipped with the Lee-Enfield rifle, they sailed for France.[118] A month later, rumours swirled that the Canadian Division would soon follow. While the men waited impatiently, there occurred a change in the structure of the cavalry. On 1 February 1915, the Canadian Cavalry Brigade was formed, consisting of the Royal Canadian Horse Artillery, the Royal Canadian Dragoons, Lord Strathcona's Horse, with the addition of the 2nd King Edward's Horse, a mounted unit of the British Special Reserve. Kitchener placed the new formation under Colonel J.E.B. Seely, the late secretary of war in the British Cabinet, much to the dismay of Borden, who wanted a Canadian to fill the position.[119] As a reserve unit, it remained in England for the time being and did not join the division in France until May.

On 2 February came the announcement that a royal review would be held in two days. This meant at long last that the Canadian Division would be departing for the front in the next few days. There was a stiff breeze and, as usual, it was pouring rain when the Canadian contingent was paraded to Knighton Down (near Stonehenge) on Salisbury Plain and drawn into two lines for an inspection by King George. Just before the small bearded monarch stepped out of the royal coach and onto the platform, the rain stopped and a pale wintery sun broke through the clouds. Accompanied by Kitchener, the king walked down the entire line, almost two miles long, stopping to shake hands with commanders and wishing them and their regiments "good luck." The king was in good spirits and looked fit. Once he returned to the stand and read from a prepared speech, he waited at the salute while the division marched past in double lines. The troops then lined the railway four deep and, with hats aloft on bayonets, "cheered like mad" as His Majesty stood at the window of the royal coach and waved farewell.[120] The review, one witness commented, "had a dignity that was very inspiring."[121] A message by the king was conveyed to all units after his departure. It read in part:

> By your deeds and achievements on the field of battle I am confident that you will emulate the example of your fellow-countrymen in the South African War, and thus help to secure the triumph of our arms. I shall follow with pride and interest all your movements. I pray that God may bless you and watch over you.[122]

In six months Canada had mobilized, assembled a division out of the civilian sector, equipped it, and partially trained it; then sent it off to England where some of its equipment was replaced and its training and organization completed. For a country that had no military tradition and whose men were forced to complete their training in abysmal weather conditions, it was an incredible accomplishment. Indeed, the actual training time allotted to the Canadian force was less than British military analysts had calculated would be required to put their own Territorial divisions in the field. The Territorials, like the Canadian militia, had some training, but the first division did not arrive in France until 24 February 1915. On the other hand, Kitchener's New Armies (British divisions raised from volunteers at the outbreak of war) began the crossing only during the early days in May.[123]

CHAPTER 2

Off to the Front

The units of the Canadian division began to leave Salisbury on 7 February, boarding trains that proceeded to take them to Avonmouth on the Bristol Channel. The first to make the crossing were fortunate. The later groups, crowded below decks in the cold, dark holds of small cargo boats, experienced a most disagreeable journey. A westerly gale and raging seas pitched and rolled the ships, causing severe sea sickness to all but a few on board. Not even the passage of half a century could dim C.B. Price's recollection of that turbulent journey: "The weather was appalling. We had to have a submarine guard on deck, and everybody down in the hold. They were so sick that you had to search to find enough men to form that submarine guard." E. Seaman (3rd Battalion) recalled that the "stern of the boat was going up and down, and I'm watching the waves to see if I can see a periscope bob up, but all I can see is the roast pork we had had for dinner." To add to the unpleasantness, cold waves broke over the deck and drenched the men huddled in the holds. But, as J.W. Ross, pointed out, the soldiers were not the only ones affected by the deluge of water sweeping across the deck: "The waves were so terrific that they came right over and knocked the horses down on the steel deck and I went round trying to raise them up with the help of some of the men from the 16th battalion. And when they were too exhausted we'd just shoot them and throw them overboard."[1]

The short crossing normally took about 36 hours, but there were so many tedious delays at either end that some men were forced to remain on board for five days. Yet practically all bore their adversity with admirable patience, no doubt relieved "at leaving the misery of Salisbury Plain."[2]

The ships docked at the port of St. Nazaire and, as a strike of stevedores was in progress, the unloading was done by work parties furnished by the units themselves. Generally the men arrived well equipped to deal with the raw, cold French winter but, if not, they were issued such items as they required.[3] Many soldiers supplemented their two days' rations of bully beef and hardtack by buying a loaf of bread (*baguette*), which they carried under the straps of their packs. The Canadians, like the British troops that preceded them to France, were admonished to behave themselves. Pasted in each man's pay book was a printed message from Lord Kitchener:

> Be invariably courteous, considerate and kind. Never do anything likely to injure or destroy property, and always look upon looting as a disgraceful act. You are sure to meet with a welcome and to be trusted; your conduct must justify that welcome and that trust. Your duty cannot be done unless your health is sound. So keep constantly on your guard against any excesses. In this new experience you may find temptations, both in wine and women. You must entirely resist both temptations, and, while treating all women with perfect courtesy, you should avoid any intimacy.[4]

The arrival of a Canadian contingent on French soil was a historic occasion. There were messages of welcome from the mayor and other officials of St. Nazaire. The townspeople lined the streets, becoming doubly excited on hearing their native language spoken by Canadians of French descent. Along the way the Canadians were supplied with refreshments and showered with blessings, good wishes and shouts of "*vive le Canada.*" At the railway station the troops were crammed into dirty little freight cars marked "H*ommes 40, Chevaux* 8" (meaning 40 men to a car or, alternatively, eight horses).[5] What the authorities did not consider was the space required for the men's equipment. J.C. Mackie

(7th Battalion) has described the predicament that he and his mates experienced: "They loaded us into boxcars ... and I remember we were jammed in so tight that if you sat down, you couldn't get up and if you stood up you couldn't sit down."[6] Private Peat's recollection, much the same, is slightly more detailed:

> We could not sit down. If we attempted it we sat on some one, and then there was a howl. We tried all manner of positions, all sorts of schemes. In the daytime we sought the roof of the cars, or leaned far out the open doors. If the country had not been so lovely, and if all our experiences had not been new and out of the ordinary, there would have been more grousing.[7]

As Peat mentioned in passing, the excessive congestion in the boxcars led some men to disregard their own safety and seek other places that were less confining. Captain Paul Villiers (on the staff of Turner's 3rd Brigade) tells us that a handful of these soldiers relaxing in one dangerous spot met fatal accidents: "Some men in the Division were killed through riding on the roofs of carriages and getting their heads knocked off in the tunnels or falling off."[8]

Given the unusually cold weather, the men had been provided with goatskin coats for the journey. They were quickly discarded because, as one soldier wrote, the odor emanating from them "made us believe that they, at least in some former incarnation, had belonged to another little animal family known as the skunk."[9] Another likened them to a "leather jacket without sleeves," adding: "The smell was something wicked. They got damp you know, oh it was vile. Believe me they disappeared, a lot of them never even seen the end of the journey. Some of the boys could't take it."[10]

There were frequent stops along the 500-mile journey to Hazenbrouck (on the Belgian border), which allowed the men to step out and stretch their cramped legs. French Canadian soldiers mingled with the townsfolk and delighted them with the singing of popular Quebec songs such as "Alouette" and "En Roulant Ma Boule."[11] As the trains passed close to the front, the rumble of artillery fire could be heard and spectacular flashes from the fireworks lit the sky at night. The Canadians reached their billeting area on 15 February.[12] Five days later, Sir John French, the British commander-in-chief, inspected units of the Canadian division and pronounced himself quite satisfied with them: "They presented a splendid and most soldier-like appearance on parade," his report to Kitchener read. "The men were of good physique, hard and fit. I judged by what I saw of them that they were well trained and quite able to take their places in the line of battle."[13]

The Canadians were about to enter a conflict that had become deadlocked after the initial exertions of the belligerents. At the start of the conflict in August 1914, both sides relied on long-standing plans to gain a quick offensive victory. The first phase of Germany's Schlieffen Plan worked with almost clockwork precision. The German army swept through Belgium, poured into northern France, and by early September was within 40 miles of Paris. In the meantime French armies drove into Alsace-Lorraine only to be hurled back after some of the fiercest fighting in the war. The French commander-in-chief, General Joseph Joffre, then redeployed his armies northward and westward to meet the invading Germans. Aided by a small British contingent, he launched a counterattack along the Marne River. The Germans, who were exhausted and bewildered, were halted and fell back to prepared positions on the Aisne. The Battle of the Marne dashed Germany's hopes for an early victory over France and forced it into a protracted war on two fronts.

Behind their defences on the Aisne, the Germans beat back all attempts to dislodge them. As a stalemate settled in on the Aisne front, both sides tried to outflank each other in what popularly came to be known as the "race to the sea." As each manoeuvre failed, the line moved farther and farther north until it reached the sea. At the close of 1914, the opposing armies faced each other along a line of twisted trenches that stretched some 450 miles, from Switzerland to the Channel Coast. The line that took shape after the first four months of fighting would not change appreciably until 1918.

Throughout the winter of 1914–1915, the opposing armies began the process of fortifying their trenches, which became increasingly

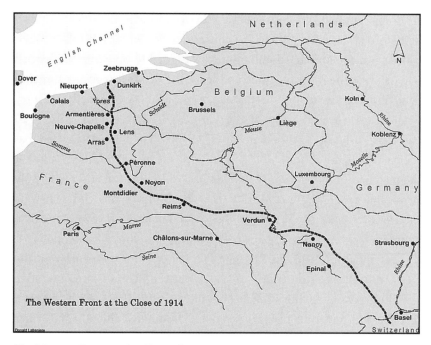

The Western Front at the Close of 1914.

sophisticated as the conflict wore on. The trench system usually consisted of three parallel lines, the front, support and reserve, all protected by thick belts of barbed wire. The lines were not straight, but zigzagged at right angles to minimize the effect of shell blasts and enfilading fire and were entered from winding communication trenches. In between the opposing front-line trenches lay "no man's land," a strip of desolation filled with shell holes, tree stumps, corpses, and the general debris of constant fighting.

Since flanking movements were no longer possible, the enemy had to be assaulted frontally. The generals believed that a coordinated attack would pierce the German line, into which the reserves would pour through, fan out, and rout a disorganized and demoralized enemy. But the greatly increased firepower of modern weapons, particularly machine guns, together with fortified trench networks, gave the defence a clear advantage. Trained during the late nineteenth century, army commanders were confronted with the weapons technology of the twentieth. Rather than re-evaluate the premise upon which the new war was being fought, most generals continued to place their reliance on the offensive and, in so doing, applied old concepts or merely improvised tactics for local battlefield situations. Initially, the conventional plan for a break-through called for a preliminary bombardment designed to break up the barbed wire, silence the machine guns and leave the occupants in the trenches dead or dazed and demoralized. Then, as the artillery ceased, the infantry would climb over the top of the parapets in waves, and, with fixed bayonets, rush toward the enemy lines. All too often it was discovered that the barrage had not done what it was supposed to do with the result that the machine-gunners were able to get back into position and mercilessly strafe the advancing columns. If the assaulting troops did penetrate the front trenches of the enemy, they would soon be thrown back by a counterattack. As a result, gains were minimal and losses tremendous.

For much of 1915 the Germans remained on the defensive in the west, concentrating on trying to knock out the Russians. The initiative therefore passed to the French and the British. The French, because of their preponderant military strength, dominated the alliance. Their strategy was governed by the idea of liberating northern France by means of frontal assaults. Thus, the Anglo-French armies were in the unenviable position of having lost ground during mobile warfare and then committed to retaking it under conditions that gave every advantage to the defenders.

By the end of 1914, British commitment to the Western Front had grown from six to sixteen divisions (eleven infantry and five cavalry). This enabled Sir John French to divide his forces into two armies. The First Army, under General Douglas Haig, occupied an 11-mile line between Bois Grenier and Givenchy. On its left was General Horace Smith-Dorrien's Second Army, which carried the front for 17 miles to Ypres.[14] The Canadian contingent was assigned initially to the First Army.

Before the Canadians were allowed to participate in active operations, they had to be given a brief introduction into the intricacies of trench warfare. After leaving their billeting area, they happened to pass by Smith-Dorrien, who wrote in his diary that they were "really a magnificent body of men and marching real well." He went on to say: "General Alderson told me their discipline had improved very much and he was most hopeful about their doing well."[15]

The Canadians were attached for a week to British units holding the line in front of Armentières. Each soldier, from company commander down to private, spent 48 hours with a corresponding member of the host unit for individual instruction. The Canadians were pleased at the way they were treated. In a letter to his father in Manchester, a sergeant wrote: "My respect for the British Tommy has gone up many hundredfold. First, because of the princely way they have acted towards us in the trenches; probably the finest reception we have had — not consisting of flag-waving, but the things that count."[16] Following the initiation process, each platoon, under the supervision of British officers and NCOs, was assigned a stretch of the front line.[17] Many of the Canadians were scared stiff when they were exposed to enemy fire for the first time and, as a rule, were thankful for the calming influence of their British cousins. Victor Lewis, a member of the 4th Battalion, admitted that he was steadied by their words of encouragement: Often they would tell Canadians, "Come on now, straighten up. Nothing to be afraid of."[18]

Pronounced ready, the 1st Canadian Division received orders to take over 6400 yards of line in the Fleurbaix sector (south of Armentières).[19] Alderson visited many of the units before they entered the line. He cautioned the men to refrain from exposing themselves unnecessarily, to avoid shooting at nonexistent targets, and to "sit low and sit tight" during the bombardment "for there is nothing else to do." He observed that if there was one thing the Germans could not stand, it was a bayonet attack. He encouraged the Canadians to use the bayonet whenever practical, confident that they had the strength to drive it home. He ended, like a cheerleader, on a reassuring note:

> My old regiment, the Royal West Kent, has been here since the beginning of the war and it has never lost a trench. The Army says, "The West Kents never budge." I am proud of the great record of my old Regiment. And I think it is a good omen. I now belong to you and you belong to me: and before long the Army will say: "The Canadians never budge." Lads it can be left there, and there I leave it. The Germans will never turn you out.[20]

Between the 1st and 3rd of March, the Canadians reached their assigned place in the line. In an interview A.S. Rae (16th Battalion) gave his impression of the night march, which was evidently an unpleasant experience for everyone in the battalion:

> It was one of the darkest nights I recall in my life. Although the men were issued white patches so you wouldn't run into the other man in the dark. Even the white patches you couldn't see them it was so tremendously dark. And the guides that was taking us in there got lost. The roads were muddy and several men fell off planks and pretty well were drowned. And finally we got into these trenches. [21]

The first thing that struck the Canadians was the flimsy nature of the trenches, which provided little security. George Hancock, attached to the Patricias, had been in the area earlier and recalled that the "trenches weren't continuous — they were just more or less ditches" All the trenches were shallow because the water table was close to the surface, so it was vital to construct a parapet with a wall of sandbags to at least allow the men to stand upright. The Canadians were often forced to rely on sod or mud because of the scarcity of the requisite material. Some found less conventional ways to acquire sandbags. C. Scriven (10th Battalion) explained: "The sandbags were so scarce that we used to listen at night until we could hear a German work party working and then we used to go out and swipe their sandbags, and the first piece of trench I ever built was built with stolen sandbags from Fritzie."[22]

The Canadian front was divided into three sections, each of which was held by one infantry brigade with an affiliated field artillery brigade. There were now only three infantry brigades — the 1st, 2nd, and 3rd. The 4th disappeared as a formation after Alderson decreed on 18 January that its battalions, along with the 17th Battalion, would supply reinforcements for the other brigades.[23]

Each brigade had two battalions at one time in the front line, the remainder being kept in the rear. Each battalion spent four successive days on duty at the front. At the end the fourth day, the battalion was

Brigadier-General Malcolm Mercer. The most senior of the Brigade commanders, he played only a minor role at Ypres.

replaced by a fresh one and went back to rest in billets. Once relieved, there was little opportunity for a change of scenery. Week-long furloughs to England were granted only once a year to the ordinary soldier.[24] According to H. Campbell (14th Battalion) the transition from boy to man occurred practically overnight. He went on to say: "You learned more in twenty-four hours in the front-line than what you'd learned with all your training that you'd had previously."[25]

The three infantry brigade commanders had each a long and distinguished record of service in the militia. All were promoted to brigadier-general. At 55, Malcolm Mercer, a name that is all but forgotten today, was the oldest of the brigade commanders. A bachelor and a successful lawyer in private life, he devoted much of his spare time to the 2nd Regiment (Queen's Own Rifles of Canada), which he rose to command in 1911. He was an excellent marksman and participated in many rifle-shooting contests at the provincial and national level, and journeyed to England in 1909 for the prestigious Bisley Rifle Competition. He collected antique furniture and works of art that included European and Canadian paintings, porcelain, and sculpture. Although he had never seen active service, his appointment to head the 1st Brigade owed much to the fact that there were few competent senior militia officers available. Besides, he had the advantage of knowing Sam Hughes, with whom he had travelled throughout Europe, observing military manoeuvres prior to the war. Standing six feet tall, his posture as straight as an arrow, and with

Brigadier-General Arthur Currie. The most able of the Canadian commanders and one of the best in the British Army. Had it been politically feasible, Lloyd George may very well have called on him when he was contemplating replacing Haig.

a large mustache that covered his mouth, he radiated an air of confidence and authority. By all accounts he was quiet and reserved, hard-working, personally fearless with a firm grasp of detail, and a real capacity for administration.[26]

Born in 1875 outside the tiny Ontario village of Strathroy, Arthur Currie grew up on his father's farm and studied to become a teacher. He moved to British Columbia, where he taught at public schools for five years before entering private business as a an insurance agent and real-estate broker. At the urging of friends, he joined the 5th Regiment of Canadian Garrison Artillery in 1897. Commissioned in 1900, he rose rapidly through the ranks until he was appointed to command the regiment. Undoubtedly because the 5th Regiment attained a very high standard of efficiency under his watch, he was asked to take charge of the newly formed 50th Regiment, Gordon Highlanders of Canada, in January 1914. Currie was well known to Sam Hughes. Both had served on the executive of the Dominion Rifle Association, not to mention that Currie was a close friend of the minister of militia's son, Garnet. Currie's dismal financial prospects deterred him from volunteering for active service at the outbreak of war, but, upon being approached by Sam Hughes, accepted the offer to command the 2nd Brigade, saying later that he could not turn down "the chance of a lifetime."[27]

Currie had little training by professional standards. Nor did he cut a very soldierly figure. Tall and bulky with a jowled face, sizeable

Brigadier-General Richard Turner. Personally fearless, he was unsuited for command in the field.

Courtesy of Library and Archives Canada.

paunch, and a seat of generous proportions, he resembled one of the first lumbering tanks. Nevertheless, he had a flair for military command. An intelligent, thoughtful person, free of the prevailing military ideas conceived and employed, he brought to his task a fresh eye and an open mind. As later events would show, he rapidly adapted his tactics to the exigencies of trench warfare and gained the reputation, deservedly so, as one of the finest commanders in the British army.[28]

Richard Turner was 43, a short, bespectacled man who looked as if he might feel more at home in the office of his wholesale firm than on the battlefield. Gazetted 2nd lieutenant in the 10th Queen's Own Canadian Hussars in 1892, he served in South Africa, where he won the Victoria Cross at the battle of Leliefontein (7 November 1900) by deflecting a Boer attack on Canadian guns despite being wounded twice. Upon returning to civilian life, Turner remained in the militia and was placed on the Reserve of Officers in 1912. The respect and awe that he commanded as a pre-war hero, in addition to his friendship with Sam Hughes, made his selection to command a brigade inevitable — the 3rd, as it happened. He was the only one among the brigade commanders to have experienced active service and no one could doubt his courage under fire, energy, and zeal. Nevertheless he was out of his element as a commander in the field. In his first major battle, he was bewildered and unable to exercise good judgment in the face of conflicting reports and the normal fog of war, a sorting-out process that is extremely challenging, but vital, for any successful

Lieutenant-Colonel Louis Lipsett. Loaned by the War Office prior to the war, he was the most experienced and talented of the Canadian battalion leaders.

commander.[29] It did not help that his brigade-major, Garnet Hughes, who was incompetent, had undue influence on his tactical decisions.

Of the battalion commanders, two were professional British soldiers. The rest were long-time militiamen and only a few of them had seen active service. As a group they were relatively young, conscientious, unflappable, and too courageous for their own good — three would be killed leading attacks — but, like the brigade commanders, handicapped by lack of leadership experience in battle. It might be helpful here to identify the commanders who would play a central role during the Second Battle of Ypres. Lieutenant-Colonel Frederick Hill (1st Battalion) was 48 years old and a former mayor of Niagara Falls. Gazetted as a lieutenant with the 8th Royal Rifles of Quebec in 1900, Lieutenant-Colonel David Watson (2nd Battalion) at 43 was, in private life, managing director of the *Quebec Chronicle*. Only slightly older than 40, Lieutenant-Colonel Arthur Birchall (4th Battalion) was an experienced British officer with 14 years in the 7th Royal Fusiliers. Lieutenant-Colonel George Tuxford (5th Battalion) was born in Wales in February 1870 and in the 1890s he and his wife immigrated to Canada and settled on a farm near Moose Jaw where, over the next few years, they worked hard to increase their stock of cattle. At the height of the Klondike gold rush, the rugged Welshman led a herd from his farm to Dawson City, Yukon, an epic journey across the

A drawing of Lieutenant-Colonel Frederick Loomis, who played a prominent role in the defence of Ypres.

Rockies that is considered the longest cattle drive in Canadian history. Lieutenant-Colonel William Hart-McHarg (7th Battalion), Irish born, was a 45-year-old lawyer from Vancouver and a superb marksman, having represented Canada in several international shooting competitions. Born in Ireland in 1874 to Welsh parents, Lieutenant-Colonel Louis Lipsett (8th Battalion) was a British soldier who had participated in several campaigns, including operations on the northwest frontier of India. An excellent officer, he had been loaned to the Canadian army in 1911 to help carry out the policy of standardizing military training among Britain and its dominions. Only 34, and yet a veteran of the South African War, Lieutenant-Colonel Russell Boyle (10th Battalion) owned a ranch near Crossfield in Alberta. Over six feet tall, broad-shouldered, and strong as an ox, Boyle was an imposing figure. A harsh disciplinarian, he learned that, on the crossing over to Plymouth, four of his men had been loud in condemning his rules and expressing a desire to punch the hell out of him. At the battalion's first parade on Salisbury Plain, he took off his coat and laid it on the ground, rolled up his sleeves, and challenged any of the malcontents to a fist fight. None stepped forward. A native of Sherbrooke, Quebec, Lieutenant-Colonel Frederick Loomis (13th Battalion) attended Bishop's University and was a private contractor by profession. The last of the group, 45-year-old Lieutenant-Colonel

Edward Leckie (16th Battalion), was a mining engineer from Vancouver. A graduate of the Royal Military College in Kingston, he had served in the South African War and subsequently organized and commanded the 72nd Seaforth Highlanders.[30]

More than two-thirds of the officers in the expeditionary force were Canadian-born and practically all of them had been trained in the militia. The British provided the rest of the officers, especially for senior general staff positions — it must be remembered that up to 1914, few Canadians had passed through the Staff College at Camberley. Duguid writes that the British staff officers selected to serve in the Canadian Division were soldiers of high quality.[31] Captain D.H. Mason (3rd Battalion) went a step farther, conceding that Canadian staff officers would never have reached a level of excellence without the knowledge and guidance of their British counterparts: "The British army loaned some of their own best staff officers, and without whom we would never have been what we were and it was they who set the pattern and trained our own officers with the result that we did eventually have an excellent staff, mostly all Canadians. But without those fellows we never would have been."[32]

In a memo, Alderson reminded his brigade commanders that the role of the Canadians was essentially defensive and stressed that the front line must be held at all costs. If driven back, it was imperative that a counterattack be mounted before the enemy had an opportunity to organize and strengthen its newly acquired trenches. These instructions did not preclude the need, as Alderson pointed out, of maintaining an ascendancy over the Germans: "Bold patrolling, persistent and accurate sniping and prompt enterprises against any sapheads…. Ambushes must be prepared, hostile patrols cut off and in fact everything done to force the conviction on the enemy that the Canadian Division is his superior."[33]

The Canadians were naively self confident, an attitude fostered by their inexperience of warfare. "It was ignorance that caused the enthusiasm," M.C. McGowan (1st Battalion) recalled. "Ignorance of what they were going against, or what you had to face, what we were going against."[34] Encouraged by their officers, they tended to underestimate the fighting capacity of the German soldiers, whom they referred to, usually in the singular, by such derogatory nicknames as "the Boche," "Heinie,"

"Fritiz," "Kraut," and "the Hun." All had heard from the local population stories about German atrocities in Belgium (in some cases untrue or exaggerated) and this had undoubtedly contributed to their hatred of their enemies. In some places, the opposing lines were separated by less than 100 yards and it was not uncommon for Canadians to be harangued by the Germans. Private Peat included a piece on this subject in his memoirs: "When we went into the trenches at first, the enemy would call across the line to us, 'What have you come over here to fight us for? What business is it of yours? Why did you not stay back home in Canada and attend to your own affairs, and not butt into something that does not concern you?'"[35]

Still the Canadians gave much as they took and their retorts were usually peppered with insults and salty language. Interviewed by CBC for the program "Flanders Fields," Private Sidney Metcalf (10th Battalion) gave the following response:

> I remember one instance where there was a German hollered across about him living in Edmonton. He mentioned some of the names of the streets and buildings and so forth, and he said he was going back to Edmonton after the war. And the Canadian soldier is not backward in any way in using a little profanity, especially to the Germans, and I would not wish to repeat on here what actually was said.[36]

The division quickly fell into the routine of trench life. Duties began shortly before first light when every man stood guard for half an hour or so — a procedure known as "stand to"— in case of a possible attack. This was followed by breakfast, usually slices of bacon cooked over an open fire — a practice later abandoned because it drew enemy fire. Movement was kept to a minimum during the daylight hours. Some men snatched what sleep they could, while others shaved (often with water drawn from shell holes), performed minor chores, or simply rested. At dusk there was a repeat of the morning stand to and rations were brought up and distributed to the men. Hot food from field kitchens was available in the rear areas, but in the front line the men usually had to settle for an unpopular diet of corned beef and biscuits — which were so hard that one trooper speculated that its chief ingredient must have been cement and that it could only be broken by using "the handle of your entrenching tool or a stone."[37] At night, the men worked to repair barbed-wire entanglements and trenches if damaged by artillery fire, set out on dangerous patrols or raids, and fetched water, food, building supplies, and ammunition.

It was bad enough that the Canadians had to put up with the harsh winter season, but their front was in a low-lying area and water and mud were everywhere. "This Flemish mud is of a gooey sticky consistency which is hard to beat," grumbled Harry Crerar, an artillery captain. "I never saw anything the way it sticks. After I've been walking ten minutes, I have at least five pounds of it on either foot."[38] In particular, the Highlanders, wearing khaki kilts, suffered horribly as Private Andrew Rae (16th Battalion) testified: "You were so cold you would feel almost the marrow was frozen in your bones. We were wearing a kilt, and at night time you would freeze into the ground and when you rose up you would have to pull part of the earth away with you. You had some trouble getting the earth loose from your kilt."[39]

A solace at the end of the day was a ration of rum, which offered some protection against the marrow-chilling cold. Another measure was a one-pound cardboard container of anti-frostbite grease issued to each man. The substance was nowhere as popular as the rum, but two enterprising soldiers found a profitable way to dispose of it, though their business practices were deplorable by any standard. P. Palin (14th Battalion) jokingly relates a story that his victims would not have found quite so amusing:

> We didn't use the stuff, so we got quite a stock on hand, so Mike Conroy he got an idea. Him and I volunteered to go out and bring in the officers' rations for B Company. Well we did it two nights running and we snaffled all this Hartley's Strawberry Jam in … jars and hid it. So we took all the anti-frostbite grease and we put in two

inches of Harley's Pure English Strawberry Jam, wiped it off, put the cover on top, put it in the sandbags.

So that night we got out two sandbags apiece. We got over the bridge going into Armentières and we got into a café and I said, "*Monsieur vous desirez acheter da confiture anglais?*"

"*Oh oui, oui, oui,* come in the back."

So we go in the back and I had my spoon ready in my puttee. I opened up the sandbag and I take out one of these cartons, take off the cover and take out my spoon and I said, "*Bien, Monsieur, gouttez ça. Première classe.*" Well we made quite a few francs in that load, brother. I think it was around four hundred francs. *Confiture Anglaise*, anti-frostbite grease.[40]

Heavy rainfall was a curse for, when it happened, the water level would rise above the trench floor boards, sometimes up to the knees or even higher. Practically every day men had to pump out water. Long periods in mud and cold water in standard issued boots caused men's feet to swell — known as trench feet, the ailment was similar to frostbite — which was excruciatingly painful. If the men took off their boots, they found they could not put them back again without adding to their agony. In the absence of proper anti-trench feet measures, the men tried to cope as best they could. J.W. Ross indicated that most men followed a simple practice: "Clean socks were brought down by the ration party and, after stand-down in the morning, the men took off their hip boots, dried their feet, anointed them with whale oil and put on the clean socks and their dirty socks were sent back to be washed and dried."[41] But the partial relief from such treatment was only temporary. With men's feet immersed in cold water for much of the time, trench feet would be a continuing problem.

Given the miserable conditions, the last thing on the minds of the soldiers was personal hygiene. Baths in the front line were out of the question and simple washing was possible only on rare occasions. "For some periods, as long as two or three weeks, we wouldn't even have our clothes off except our boots, and they were muddy all the time," J.W. Ross maintained.[42]

"The lice are getting to be a torment," Lieutenant Louis Keene wrote. "You have no idea how bad they are."[43] Within a few days of entering the trenches, the men would be itching and scratching, a sure sign that they had contracted lice. Lice spread easily, lived in the seams of clothing, irritated the skin, and was known to cause typhus. No one, it seemed, escaped the infestation of these troublesome pests. John McCrae, a surgeon attached to the 1st Field Artillery Brigade, worked incessantly to keep his dressing station highly sanitized, determined to avoid his unpleasant experience with the loathsome little creatures while serving in the South African War. According to L.V.M. Cosgrove (1st Division Artillery) the struggle ended suddenly one night after McCrae went over to play a game of bridge with members of the 4th Field Battery.

> We were bunking together at the time and I heard John come in and "Well," he said, "that's the 4th Battery. That's where I got them, that's the 4th Battery."
> I said, "What's the matter, John?"
> "I've got enough lice here to sink a battleship and I've been laying down the law about sanitary conditions."[44]

The Canadians in the front line tried different ways to keep the lice at bay. "I have tried smearing myself with kerosene," Lieutenant Keene maintained, "but that does not seem to trouble them at all."[45] Some Canadians borrowed an unconventional technique from the British. Percy Whitehouse, an English signaller (attached to the 8th Howitzer Bde, RFA 5th Division), revealed in his unpublished memoirs how it was done: "The lice laid their eggs in the seams of our clothing and it was a common sight to see men running along the seams of their tunics with a lighted candle endeavouring to scorch them out."[46]

W.D. Dodds (13th Battalion) described a slightly more scientific process available to the men out of the trenches. "They brought in ovens and you … stripped yourself naked and handed all that clothing in and they put it in the ovens and then dished you out stuff that had been washed … Some of them only did half the job."[47] No matter what device was used, it proved impossible to get rid of them permanently. After taking a bath and putting on clean clothes, J.W. Ross pointed out, he and his buddies would "go back to the trenches again, only to get lousy [term for lice] once more."[48] Few would have disagreed with K.C. Hossick's (13th Battalion) statement that lice was probably "our greatest enemies in the first year of the First World War."[49]

Although the Canadians were in a quiet sector, the threat of danger was constant. Units suffered a dozen or more casualties a week. Night patrols, sent to explore enemy defences or find gaps in the wire, tested men's nerves for at any moment they were apt to be exposed by flares in no man's land and subjected to deadly machine-gun fire. German snipers, with their telescopic sights on their rifles, were especially adept at picking off the unwary. W. Stevens (14th Battalion) described what happened to one of his careless mates: "Pat Rattigan, he was on top of the trench pounding down sandbags and somebody said, 'You crazy something, get down out of there.' And the next thing some of us heard was a 'crack, phut,' and Pat got it in the tummy and that was our first man."[50]

The most dreaded experience among soldiers was the heavy barrage, which accounted for about two-thirds of the casualties that the Canadians sustained in the war. They had nicknames — undoubtedly borrowed from the British — for the various shells lobbed by the enemy. Heavy explosives, with a loud preceding whistle, were known as "Jack Johnsons," after the American heavyweight boxing champion of that name. Lighter shells were dubbed "Whizz Bangs." The Germans had a huge preponderance of heavy guns and, with their infinite supply of shells, their bombardment posed a persistent threat to the men in the trenches. Liable to strike without warning, artillery shells, dropping in rapid succession, created a deafening noise that caused the earth to shake, sent fragments flying in all directions, and could blow victims to pieces, bury them alive, or maim them horribly. Even brave men cringed and prayed. Charles Harrison, one of many Americans in the CEF, gives a vivid description of what it was like to endure a merciless enemy bombardment:

I am terrified. I hug the earth, digging my fingers into every crevice, every hole.

A blinding flash and an explosive howl a few feet in front of the trench.

My bowels liquefy.

Acrid smoke bites the throat, parches the mouth. I am beyond mere fright.

I am frozen with an insane fear that keeps me cowering in the bottom of the trench. I lie flat on my belly waiting ...

Suddenly it stops.[51]

In many places along the Western Front, both sides had adopted the policy of "live and let live." The Canadians were astonished to discover this strange unwritten rule when they were briefly attached to British units. F.C. Arnold (7th Battalion) was among those who received a rude awakening:

It was a bright moonlight night and I could see the Germans working by their wire and I wanted to shoot. I got my rifle and I was going to shoot and this Hampshire fellow he grabbed my arm. "Don't shoot," he said.

I said, "What's wrong?"

"Oh," he says, "if you shoot they'll shoot and we got a working party out too."

Well, I thought, this is a devil of a war. Come six thousand miles to shoot Germans and the first one I had a look at I couldn't shoot them.[52]

As a rule, however, the Canadians eschewed the policy of "live and let live" when they moved into their own sector. According to a recent study, they "maintained a constant level of harassment that the Germans came to fear and hate."[53] Many were hunters or trappers, accustomed to stalking their prey and able to move as stealthily as cats. There were frequent night raids, the object of which was to collect information, demoralize the enemy, or bringing back a few prisoners. R.L Christopherson (5th Battalion) later explained how he and his friends generally approached and carried out their mission:

> Everything had to be done very quietly. And we would sneak up the face of their parapet and club the sentry over the head, jump in the trench and when you came to a dug out you'd pull a pin and throw a bomb [grenade] and generally clean them up. And they panicked of course. They weren't expecting it and they got at last so they never knew when a raid was going to take place.[54]

There were instances when hand-to-hand combat was involved. Charles Harrison (14th Battalion) from Montreal left a gruesome account of his experience in one such foray. Sliding down into a trench, he came upon a solitary German and drove his bayonet between his ribs. But then Harrison was unable to pull the bayonet out. He explained why and what action he took in response:

> He gripped the barrel of my rifle and he was pulling it as if he was trying to help me pull it out of him. I put my foot against his body and I tried kicking him off but he wouldn't come off. He kept screaming. It was too much. I let go of my rifle. He collapsed in the trench. He was still holding the barrel and I ran. Suddenly I hear voices and I hear his cries for help and I suddenly realize I don't have a weapon and I hear the voices coming near so I run back. I grabbed the butt of my rifle and I tried pulling it out of him and he's holding the barrel like a little child saying "no" this is mine you can't take it. I kept pulling and pulling and the blade was working on his insides. Suddenly I realized what I was supposed to do. I pulled back and he was quiet and then I pulled the trigger. "Bang!" and then he collapsed.[55]

The Canadians were no less effective as snipers. Armed with a Ross rifle, in this case an asset rather than a liability, men sometimes worked singly, but standard practice was to operate in pairs, one to observe with a telescope or periscope, the other, an expert marksman, ready to shoot. Germans who exposed any part of their body were likely to be fired on, but the highest priority was to locate and eliminate their snipers. Native Indians were among the best of the Canadian sharpshooters who would prove second to none. Natives tended to be patient, steady, possessed iron nerves and knew how to camouflage themselves so that they could blend with the terrain. A member of the Mississuaga tribe, Johnson Paudash (2nd Battalion), brought down 42 Germans — some accounts put the total at 88 — by March 1918. Philip McDonald, an Iroquois from Ontario, picked off 40 Germans while Henry "Ducky" Norwest, a Cree, tallied 115 hits. Both would perish during the war, the former on 3 January 1916 and the latter on 18 August 1918. But the deadliest marksman in the Canadian army was Francis "Peg" Pegahmegabow (1st Battalion), who accounted for at least 378 Germans.[56] It is unlikely that any other sniper in either camp approached that total, let alone eclipsed it.

The Canadians acquitted themselves admirably during their introduction to trench warfare, and won high praise from both Alderson and Sir John French. During the first week in the Fleurbaix region, their principal duty was to man the line. Their work, for the most part, was dull and mechanical. Their interest rose, however, when told they would undergo their baptism of fire in a few days.

At the beginning of 1915, General Joffre had evolved a plan aimed at severing the huge German bulge between Reims and Arras. He asked the British to attack in the direction of Aubers Ridge while the French Tenth Army, immediately on their right, advanced between Arras and Lens. The joint movement in the north was to synchronize with and support Joffre's own offensive in Champagne. Sir John French agreed to co-operate for he wished, not only to assist his ally, but also to foster an offensive spirit in the British Army after its trying and enervating winter in the trenches.[57]

Sir John also consented to relieve two French formations, the IX and XX Corps, around Ypres, which were required by the Tenth Army. French was counting on the arrival of the 29th and 1st Canadian Divisions to carry out the promised relief. But the 29th, a division made up of British regular battalions from overseas garrisons, was diverted to another theatre of war and its replacement, the 46th (North Midland Territorial) would require additional training before it could be sent to the front. In these circumstances French notified Joffre that he could not deliver his attack and simultaneously extend the British line. Sir John remained adamant in spite of being told that the Tenth Army could not carry out its part in the operation without the troops at Ypres. Joffre broke the impasse when, in a fit of anger, he cancelled the French offensive in the north. Instead of abandoning his own plans, as well, Sir John, for a number of reasons, not the least of which was to show that the British could fight, decided to act alone.[58]

Sir John anticipated a breakthrough, but in retrospect, it is apparent that he had neither the trained men nor the weapons to breach the German line. Prior to 1914, Britain had placed its reliance on the Royal Navy and limited the army's functions to police duties around the Empire and minor landings in remote areas. The British Army had grown since the start of the global conflict, but it would remain comparatively small until the first detachments of the New Armies took the field in the spring of 1915. The British Army was further handicapped by acute shortages of heavy guns and ammunition essential to wage siege warfare. Between 1906 and 1914, insufficient government funding had compelled the army to reduce its purchase of vital equipment. Additionally, by the spring of 1915, the conversion from shrapnel — effective against troops in the open, but useless in demolishing fortifications — to heavy explosives was not yet completed. It was not until 1917 that the British government was able to provide the army with the means to effectively fight a war of position.

The Battle of Neuve Chapelle was the first major attempt by the British to break the German trench system. The operation was entrusted to General Douglas Haig, who commanded the First Army. His objective was to capture the village of Neuve Chapelle, which lay opposite his front, and then push on to Aubers Ridge, three miles farther east. The Canadians were to supply artillery fire along their entire front and be ready to advance in the event of a breakthrough.[59]

At 7.30 a.m. on 10 March, Haig's artillery opened fire, signalling the beginning of the battle. When the barrage lifted 35 minutes later, the infantrymen of the First Army clambered out of their trenches and advanced on a two-mile front into no man's land. The bombardment had proven effective. The enemy's trenches were shattered and the surviving Germans were either surrendering or running away. Within 45 minutes, the British were in possession of their initial objective, Neuve Chapelle. Although setbacks had occurred on both flanks the centre had torn a gap well over a mile wide and nearly a mile deep in the German front. Because of excessive caution and poor communications, the British assault was not resumed for five hours. The delay enabled the Germans to rush reinforcements to the endangered area and hold the British gains to a minimum. By 13 March when the battle ended, the British had lost 13,000 men, about the same number as the enemy.[60]

The battle was seen as partially successful for it showed that it was possible to break into a well-defended trench system. But it would take a long time before the British (as well as the French) High Command grasped the difference between a break-in and a breakthrough. In the case of a simple break-in, enemy reserves would arrive to the threatened area within a few hours, ready to hurl back the attackers with machine guns, artillery, and counterattacks.

The Canadians played only a minor diversionary role in the battle. Their task, so Brigadier-General Burstall's instructions ran, was to "create the belief that we are about to assault" opposing enemy forces.[61] General Currie noted in his diary: "We kept up supporting fire all day. Terrific cannonading and rifle fire."[62] Most Canadians had not witnessed an intense artillery barrage before and the experience could not help but leave a deep impression on them. Half a century later, Captain Morrisey claimed that it was "the biggest noise I've ever heard," but what struck Private Fred Arnold (7th Battalion) the most was that "the ground just rocked."[63] Because of the dearth of artillery ammunition, gunners had been directed to use no more than fifteen rounds per gun, but, as it turned out, they expended twice their allotment. Consequently, in the days that followed, their normal ration of 10 shells per gun was reduced to three.

Courtesy of Library and Archives Canada.

Brigadier-General Harry Burstall. A member of Canada's small pre-war army, he commanded the three brigades of artillery.

The men found different ways to amuse themselves as the remainder of their stay in the Fleurbaix sector passed without serious incident. General Currie wrote in his diary: "Germans put up toy horse on parapet, we knocked it down, they put it up again bandaged round neck and hind legs."[64] An officer from Winnepeg described in a letter home how the men in his unit (8th Battalion) celebrated St. Patrick's Day:

> They started off by sticking the Irish flag, the Union flag, and the tricolour [French flag] on the paraphet. Where they conjured them from the Lord only knows! Then they sang the National Anthem, the Marseillaise, the Maple Leaf and Wearing o' the Green. They riddled the tricolour with bullets, but left the other two alone.[65]

Relieved by the 8th British Division on the 25th and 26th, the

Canadians marched to new billets at Estaires, five miles behind the line. Here they received daily instructions in trench fighting with emphasis on rapid entrenching, getting out of trenches, charging over cultivated ground, crossing wire entanglements, and assaulting hostile lines.[66] All this activity seemed to infer that the Canadians were being groomed to take part in the next attack in the Neuve Chapelle region.

But in war plans often change. Toward the end of March, arrangements between the French and British High Commands meant that the Canadians would be going elsewhere. On 24 March, Joffre wrote to Sir John, suggesting that combined operations be resumed in about six weeks and reiterating his request that the French IX and XX Corps be relieved in the Ypres sector as quickly as possible by British troops. Replying on 1 April, the British chief welcomed the opportunity to participate in the proposed offensive and, noting that he expected reinforcements from home later in the month, also agreed to extend his front as far north as the Ypres-Poelcappelle road.[67] Lieutenant-General Sir Herbert Plumer, whose V Corps was a component of the Second Army, assumed responsibility for the new sector.[68] The addition of five miles to the British line meant that only the northernmost portion of the salient, extending westward from opposite Poelcappelle to the Yser Canal at Steenstraat, would remain in French hands.

Sir John had decided that the Canadian contingent should make up part of the relief force earmarked for the Ypres salient. On the same day that he consented to co-operate with Joffre (1 April), he issued orders transferring the Canadian Division to the Second Army, placing it under the command of the V Corps.[69] Four days later, the Canadians began their march northwards and by the 7th, all units had arrived in the Cassel area — some 17 miles west of Ypres. They were scheduled to spend a week there in preparation for their new assignment.

General Smith-Dorrien inspected the Canadian infantry brigades before they left Cassel. Speaking afterwards, the general welcomed them to his command and observed that, because of his previous association with Canadians in South Africa, he considered the Division to rightfully belong to his army.[70] He complimented the men on the work accomplished at Fleurbaix and intimated that they were about to take over the most vulnerable part of the British front. The Canadians, he said, would have to contend with a foe "more truculent" than had been supposed, but he was sure they would comport themselves "as becomes such an excellent fighting force."[71]

On 14 April and for the next two days, the Canadians marched up from their billets. They passed smashed and broken farmhouses and cottages on their way through the town of Ypres, and, after zigzagging to evade battery pits, torn-up mounds, and cuttings in the marshy ground, reached their assigned place in the Ypres salient. The men were in high spirits and ready for war. Little did they realize that within a week they would be engaged in one of the fiercest and most terrible battles of the Great War.

CHAPTER 3
Unheeded Warning

During the last phase of semi-open warfare, the Germans had attempted to sweep down the Belgian coast and crush the flank of the attacking Allies. They came very close to achieving their objective. The British, assisted by the French, engaged in some of the most severe fighting of the war in the Ypres sector. The end of the First Battle of Ypres in mid-November left the Allied line in front of Ypres in the shape of an arc 17 miles in length, stretching from Steenstraat in the north to St. Eloi in the south.[1] On 15 November, the French took over the Ypres salient and the British consolidated along a continuous front between Wytschaete and Givenchy. Thereafter there was little fighting along this perimeter and both sides settled down to construct trenches and rearward defences.

The salient was about six miles deep, with the town of Ypres at the centre of its base. Ypres, pronounced "Eepryh," but known as "Wipers" to many Canadians and Britons who lived through or grew up in the shadow of the Great War, is situated in the northwest corner of Belgium, practically on the French border. Sitting on flat land, Ypres was the dominant town in the area, and, like the hub of a wheel, roads ran out from all sides and connected it to neighbouring communities.[2] Ypres was an architectural showpiece, a blend of medieval and 17-century buildings highlighted by two magnificent Gothic monuments, Cloth Hall and St. Martin's Cathedral.

The town had been the outlying fortification of the port of Dunkirk and over the centuries, as French, Dutch, and Spanish armies in turn trampled over the region, it had known bombardment, siege, fire, and

Cloth Hall before the war. Built in the 13th century, with its ornate facade 136 yards in breadth and an imposing belfry tower 77 yards in height, it recalled the importance and splendor of Ypres at that time.

pillage.[3] In the medieval ages, it attained great importance as the centre of the cloth industry and its population was said to be over 40,000. But wars, revolts, and migrations drastically undermined its lucrative cloth trade. In the 19th century, Ypres experienced a bit of a revival, thanks mainly to the growth of agriculture in the countryside. Before the Great War broke out, Ypres was a quaint little town with a population of some 17,000. The inhabitants there lived quietly and reasonably well, and for the most part were devoted Catholics.[4]

The intense German bombardment during the First Battle of Ypres had driven away most of the people and significantly wrecked sectors of the town. A large number of buildings were intact or sustained minor damage, but in places the destruction was extensive, with shell holes eight to ten feet deep yawning at intervals and groups of houses reduced to piles of brick and splintered woodwork. The celebrated Cloth Hall had sustained considerable damage: the roof had disappeared, the

Courtesy of In Flanders Fields Museum.

The destruction of Cloth Hall after German artillery fire devastated Ypres. Between 1933 and 1967 it was rebuilt as closely as possible to the original structure.

carved walls and statues were smashed, and the interior woodwork was destroyed by incendiary shells. The cathedral suffered an even harsher fate. A fire, started by incendiary shells, destroyed most of its treasures and left the building in ruins.[5]

As the fierce fighting settled down to the routine of trench warfare, many of the inhabitants returned to the town, electing to live at home rather than face the trouble of removing themselves and their belongings to a safer location. Soon, workmen were busily repairing the damage done by the previous bombardment: debris was cleared, shell holes were filled, and houses were mended. In the fields, farmers tended their crops, some to within two miles of the firing line, and their cattle grazed placidly in the green pastures. The streets of Ypres were again active and military policemen kept the traffic routes clear and the crowds moving. An occasional shell would fall on the town, but for the most part it was business as usual.

A brief description of the topography of the area is necessary in order to understand its relationship to the tactics employed by both sides during the Second Battle of Ypres. On the eastern side of Ypres, at a distance of three to six miles, was a semi-circle of ridges, some rising 150 to 200 feet above sea level. The Germans occupied much of the high ground on the distant ridges, and from there enjoyed a clear view of the wide plain below, including Ypres itself. The Yser Canal, which constricted the movement of Allied troops to the salient, passed behind Ypres and continued northwards through Steenstraat to the sea.[6] Near the southern extremity of the salient lay Hill 60. From there the main ridge, rising no more than 200 feet above sea level, or 150 feet above Ypres, ran in a northerly direction for over four miles, passing through Sanctuary Wood and Broodseinde and on to Passchendaele.

From purely strategic considerations, it made no sense for the Allies to have retained Ypres and the salient. The Germans held enough of the high ground to observe movements around Ypres and their artillery could rain shells on Allied positions from three sides. To make matters worse, only a handful of Allied troops would have been able to escape in case an enemy break-in could not be closed swiftly. There were only several pontoon bridges over the Yser Canal in the rear. It would have been far more sensible to fall back behind Ypres to a more defensible line along the Yser Canal. This also would have shortened the front and required fewer men to hold it. But Ypres was the only remaining town of any size left unconquered in Belgium and, to the Allied authorities, it stood as a symbol of defiance and determination.[7]

The French held the salient through the winter and, for reasons already explained, turned over about two-thirds of it to the British V Corps in mid-April. Defending the French front were two divisions, the 45th Algerian, adjoining the Canadians, and beyond it, the 87th Territorials. These two divisions, together with French units holding the Nieuport sector to the sea, deployed on the left of the Belgian army, constituted the *Détachement d'Armée de Belgique*, headed by 56-year-old veteran General Henri Gabriel Putz. General Ferdinand Foch directed all the French forces in the northern sector, which formed the *Groupe Provisoire du Nord*. Foch's command was broken into three parts, giving him authority over the troops in the

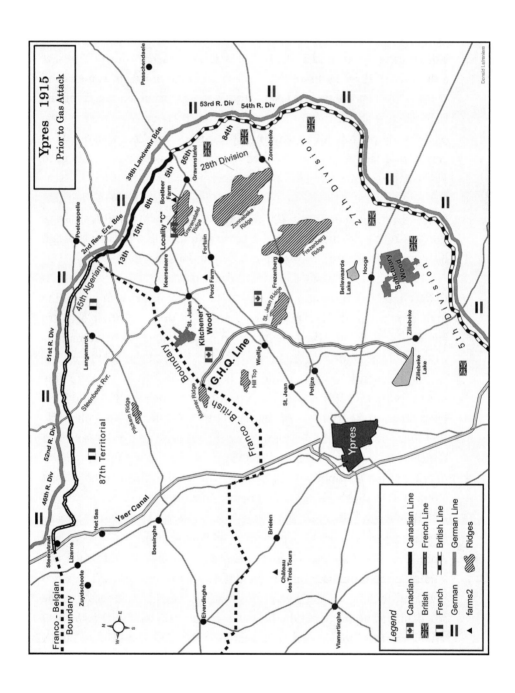

Courtesy of In Flanders Fields Museum.

Alderson's Headquarters at Château des Trois Tours, a luxurious two-storey house on the west side of the Ypres Canal.

northern part of the Ypres salient and between the Belgians and the coast, as well as over the Tenth Army, which lay south of the salient. As Joffre's deputy, Foch had the added responsibility of coordinating the operations of the *Groupe Provisoire* with those of the British and Belgian forces.[8]

At a point opposite Poelcappelle, the French joined up with the Canadians, whose line, running in a southeasterly direction, ended in front of the village of Gravenstafel. On the right of the Canadians were the other two divisions of the V Corps, the 28th and, next to it, the 27th. The Canadian sector was 4500 yards in length and was divided between the 2nd Brigade on the right and the 3rd Brigade on the left. Each brigade had two battalions in the line, one in support and one in divisional reserve.[9] The 1st Brigade was in corps reserve at Vlamertinghe, several miles west of Ypres. Alderson formally assumed command of the Canadian line at 10:00 a.m. on the 17 April and set up his headquarters in the Château des Trois Tours.

The Canadians inherited a front-line defensive system that was in deplorable condition and in stark contrast to British standards. The Canadians had been warned about the state of the French trenches, but what they saw exceeded their worst expectations. The lengths of trenches were shallow and unconnected, with parapets that were only about two feet high and seldom thick enough to stop bullets. There was no parados to give protection against shells bursting in the rear and no traverses to reduce the damage of a direct hit, or guard against enemy troops — who might break into a section of the trench — from firing along its entire length. Wire entanglements and machine-gun posts were good or adequate, but the dugouts were so carelessly constructed that they offered little more than shelter from the weather.[10] F.C. Bagshaw (5th Battalion) complained that "they weren't real trenches at all," being "typically French, careless work … holes in the ground, dirty, lousy."[11] Sgt. Alldritt (8th Battalion) feared that "we shall suffer severely if we get heavily shelled."[12]

To make life even more unpleasant, sanitation had been entirely disregarded. Shell holes and broken-down little side trenches were used as latrines. Many bodies were buried in shallow graves and even in the parapets; scores lay where they had fallen in no man's land. "These [trenches] were extraordinarily filthy, and, well actually they were paved with dead Germans," commented Major Dan Ormond (10th Battalion). "There was one place in the trench where there was a hand dangling through the parapet. The men used to shake hands with it."[13] Large rats, some the size of cats, wandered everywhere and fed off the corpses that littered no man's land. "We were not so hardened and hoped never to be called upon to endure such horrible sights day after day," recalled Sergeant Fred Bagnall (14th Battalion).[14] The line was a breeding ground for disease, not to mention that it required a strong stomach to endure the acrid smell of death permeating the air.[15] The official report on the condition of the trenches, apart from describing their pitiful weakness in detail, advised that "large quantities of disinfectant should be sent into the trenches immediately for liberal use."[16]

A subsidiary line appeared on French tactical maps, but the work had been neglected and it existed merely as a series of unlinked strong points or supporting trenches. The most important of these, known as "Locality C," lay on the western side of Gravenstafel Ridge in the centre of the Canadian sector. The site of furious fighting in the upcoming battle, it has been described as "consisting chiefly of a rather poor trench, 200 yards long, facing north-east, built in the usual French thin parapet style, with no depth, no thickness, and no parados." Along its front lay twisted strands of barbed wire. Some 800 yards farther east, a second strong point covered Boetleer Farm; while still another, southeast of the farm, had been constructed near Gravenstafel. In common with Locality "C," both were in a less than half-finished state.[17]

Better prepared for defence was the so-called GHQ (General Headquarters) Line, which lay between one and three miles behind the Canadian front. It ran from Zillebecke Lake to a point half a mile east of Wieltje where it turned northwest to Mauser Ridge. It consisted of a series of redoubts, 30 yards square, spaced about 450 hundred yards apart, and protected by a thick belt of barbed wire with gaps in a few places to permit the passage of friendly troops. It was well situated in that it generally overlooked flat ground and provided a good field of fire.[18]

French indifference at protecting their forward defensive position was directly related to their method of conducting war. French Army Headquarters (*Grand Quartier Général*) clung jealously to the doctrine of the offensive as the only way to drive the Germans out of France. It did not believe in building strong fortifications, associating trenches with a defensive spirit, and viewing them as a temporary, rather than as a long-term, measure. Thus, it held forward positions with a minimum of troops. If attacked in strength, the men were taught to fall back and rely on the effective fire of their 75 mm field guns to halt the Germans. On the other hand, British policy, reflecting traditional faith in the defensive ability of its infantry, mandated that front-line trenches be resolutely held. In case of an enemy penetration, the commanding officer was expected to counterattack promptly and make every effort to recover the lost ground.[19] It should be pointed out that even if the British had wanted to emulate the French and adopt a defence-in-depth strategy, they would have been unable to do so because their supply of guns and shells was woefully inadequate.

For nearly a week every available Canadian was put to work to upgrade the deficiencies in their line. They laboured mostly at night to avoid the threat posed by snipers. They connected isolated portions of trenches and added traverses and communication trenches. The water table in this area was close to the surface so that trenches could not be dug to a depth of more than several feet. To achieve the desired protection, the only option was to build up the parapets into breastworks. In front of their defensive network the Canadians laid obstacles and an unbroken belt of barbed wire.

The French gave the relieving Canadian troops the impression that they were moving into a quiet sector of the Allied line. To be sure, the level of activity in the Ypres area had been low throughout the winter and early spring, in comparison to the intensity of the fighting in the previous autumn. There was the usual daily shelling and sniping, and, from time to time, each side raided each other's trenches, which resulted in light casualties and occasionally yielded a few prisoners. There was some air activity with planes dropping bombs on the villages or coming over to assist artillery registration. But it cannot be said that the Canadians felt threatened, even though German trenches were only 150 to 300 yards away. "I am really enjoying this trip in the trenches very much," J.E. Lockerby of Vancouver wrote in a letter to his parents. "The weather is beautiful now and the trenches are drying up fine."[20] During the day the men relaxed, joked with one another, did odd chores and found ways to pass away their idle time. One individual, as reported by J.E. Lockerby, played a musical instrument that he had created out of discarded material:

> One of our chaps made a banjo out of a tin biscuit box, and he can play it well. You know I was always fond of music, that is why I volunteered to pack it in and out of the trenches for him. When the shells start coming close we always get the banjo and have a little "Grand Opera" just to show the Germans (who are less than a hundred yards away) that we are quite unconcerned and enjoying life as usual.[21]

Be that as it may, the Canadian position was far from secure, and not only because of the inherent disadvantages of trying to hold on to a salient. The two French divisions squeezed between the British and the Belgians were of inferior quality. Moreover, no arrangement had been devised to bring the three contingents under a single command. Finally, the sites where the armies joined were chosen haphazardly. The junction of the French and British forces was in an awkward place, on the shoulder of the salient; while that of the French and Belgian was on opposite sides of the canal. If the Germans intended to launch an attack in the west, they could scarcely have found a more inviting sector.[22]

As it happened, early in 1915, General von Falkenhayn, the German supreme commander, planned a limited attack in the west as a means to cover the transfer of troops to Galacia.[23] It was principally by default that the Ypres area was selected as the target for the gas attack, not because, as has sometimes been reported, it was there that the winds were most favourable. The High Command was trying to find a way to break the deadlock of trench warfare as conventional methods of attack had proven ineffective. The whole idea behind the battle was to see what the effects of gas might be.

There was nothing novel about the idea of utilizing toxic agents in war. The beginnings of chemical warfare are difficult to trace, but one of the earliest uses was said to have occurred around 600 B.C.E. during the siege of Cirrha, near Delphi, in Greece. According to such ancient writers as Polyaenus and Pausanias, the Cirrhaeans were seized with incessant diarrhea after a drug had been dissolved in their drinking water. During the siege of Plataea in 429 B.C.E., the Spartans, according to Thucydides, produced arsenic smoke (by setting fire to wood saturated with pitch and sulphur) under the walls of the city so as to choke the defenders and render their assault less difficult. In 80 B.C.E., the Roman General Quintus Sertorius used an ash-like sand, driven by wind, to flush the Charakitanes in Spain out of their caves. The drifting fumes caused pulmonary problems and blindness, inducing the Charakitanes to surrender after three days.

These and other variants of toxic chemical warfare were employed during the Middle Ages. The Byzantines employed an incendiary mixture (the exact composition of which is still a mystery), known as "Greek Fire," with considerable success in their campaigns up to the 13th century. Delivered in pots by catapults, the weapon was probably the forerunner of napalm. In 1485 an alchemist, creating a toxic cloud by burning rags dipped in a chemical mixture, saved Belgrade from the attacking Turks.[24]

Noxious gas had been used infrequently in wars through the ages, and, at the close of the 19th century, European statesmen worried that, with the introduction of new and more toxic compounds, there would be greater temptation for nations locked in conflict to use this weapon, either to gain the upper hand or avoid defeat. The issue was addressed at the first Hague Convention in 1899, in which representatives of 26 countries, including Germany, adopted a resolution forbidding "the use of projectiles, the object of which is the diffusion of asphyxiating or deleterious gases." At the second gathering in 1907, the signatories extended the prohibition to "poison or poisoned weapons as well as weapons causing unnecessary suffering."[25] It should be noted that the wording was restricted only to gas released by explosive shells, but the clear intent of the Hague Conventions was to prohibit the kind of gas warfare that Germany initiated in April 1915.

Despite the international agreements, experimental work with chemical agents continued in a number of European countries. In Britain, a shell containing a small portion of lachrymatory substance — disagreeable, but not deleterious — was considered but ultimately rejected as infringing on the spirit, if not the letter, of the Hague Declarations.[26] Germany, too, conducted research into the possibilities of chemical weaponry, but without tangible results.[27] The French were more advanced than either the British or the Germans in the development of a chemical program. It was an investment that they reckoned might pay dividends some day.

Interest in the combat possibilities of toxic chemicals varied considerably during the early months of the First World War. The conflict was barely one month old when Lord Kitchener rejected a proposal to use incapacitating noxious gas because he felt it was ill-suited for land warfare. The Admiralty studied the matter during the winter of 1914–

1915 and, by the end of March, experiments were being conducted with the view to possible employment of non-lethal gas in the Dardanelles campaign. But Winston Churchill, then first lord of the Admiralty, abandoned the plan, partly out of fear that it would invite reprisals and partly out of ethical considerations.[28] The French had a small stock of tear-gas projectiles when the war broke out and appear to have been the first among the belligerents to resort to toxic substances to assist their attacks. These *cartouches suffocantes* were filled with ethyl bromoacetate and fired from a specially adapted rifle. They were employed sporadically in 1914, mainly against fortifications. A hand grenade with the same chemical agent, called *grenades suffocantes*, was devised early in 1915 and used to assault open trenches. The gas released by the two types of chemical weapons did not cause anything more serious than irritation to the defender's eyes and throat.[29]

Germany's efforts to develop chemical weapons began in earnest after the Battle of the Marne in September 1914. In October, von Falkenhayn assigned a group of scientists to develop a chemical shell that would produce irritating reaction so as to drive enemy troops from inaccessible places. By modifying the 105 mm howitzer shell to include dianisidine chlorosulphonate, an agent known to cause violent sneezing, a batch of so-called "Ni-shells" were hurriedly produced, 3000 of which were first used on 27 October 1914, against British and Indian troops in the Neuve Chapelle area. The effects were so slight that the defenders were unaware that anything out of the ordinary was being used against them. Consequently, the Germans abandoned this design. In November, a chemist, Hans Tappen, introduced the idea of filling an artillery shell with a highly lachrymatory liquid made up of xylyl bromide and benzyl bromide, which upon exploding, emitted a vapour similar to tear gas. The OHL (German High Command) gave its approval after the gas projectiles worked well in trials. The first consignment of some 18,000 T-shells (named after its inventor) was shipped to the Eastern Front and fired in large numbers against the Russian position at Bolimow on 30 January 1915, but the outcome was a fiasco. It was not realized at the time, although it should have been foreseen by the experts, that the extreme cold would prevent vaporization of the liquid.[30]

German shed near the front line. Note the gas canister.

To counter the cold weather, bromoacetone was added to the contents of the T-shell. A batch of new shells was sent to the Fourth Army in Flanders and used in the Nieuport sector. They burst upon hitting their targets, but the irritant gas went unnoticed, just as it had at Bolimow. Since it became obvious that the T-shell did not provide a strong enough concentration to incapacitate the intended victims, the OHL looked for a novel solution. It was found by Dr. Fritz Haber, director of the Kaiser Wilhelm Institute in Berlin, who changed the focus of chemical warfare from an irritant to a lethal agent by using chlorine.[31] Toxicologically, chlorine is a powerful irritant to the respiratory organs, causing inflammation, which in turn produces a massive amount of fluid that blocks the windpipe and fills the lungs. Prolonged exposure to a high concentration of the gas causes blindness, death, or, at least, severe injury to the lungs.[32]

Initially, Haber intended to load the lethal chemicals into shells, as was being done with irritant agents.[33] However, when dwindling stocks of shells ruled out this method of delivery, he proposed instead that the chlorine be discharged from cylinders embedded in forward trenches and propelled toward the opposing lines by a suitable wind.

The arguments in favour of employing such a weapon were appealing. The effects were immediate, either killing or disabling the victims. It was cheap, simple to produce, and could easily be transported in cylinders already available because of wide industrial use in Germany. Lastly, it was heavy and would cling to the ground as it rolled forward and yet would not leave any residue that would harm the attacking troops. There were some drawbacks. One of the most obvious was that the chemical weapon depended entirely on optimal wind conditions. Another, and more difficult to overcome, was the moral issue posed by the Hague Conventions.

Haber's proposal was adopted after successful trials had been carried out.[34] The OHL had a difficult time determining where the new weapon should be tried. A number of front-line German generals wanted no part of the lethal weapon, describing it as immoral, unchivalrous, and cruel.Only Duke Albrecht of Württemberg, whose Fourth Army had been repulsed at the First Battle of Ypres, was willing to cross the moral boundary.[35] It was decided that the gas should be tried out against the southern side of the Ypres salient. The Germans did not select the best spot for their gas attack.[36] The prevailing winds around Ypres, except for a brief spell in the spring, blew from west to east. That is, toward the German lines.

Haber understood the tactical value of gas. He advised the OHL to assign large reserves to exploit the breakthrough, which he was certain would occur.[37] But von Falkenhayn's expectations were much more modest and did not extend beyond a local success. The primary objective, as he saw it, was to test the new weapon and see what would happen. He refused to assemble large reserves rearwards in anticipation of a breakthrough.[38]

It was incomprehensible, some would say foolhardy, for the Germans to risk, among other things, worldwide condemnation over a battlefield experiment from which no startling results were expected. The plain truth was that the OHL distrusted the efficacy of toxic weapons. Their judgment was shaped not only by the traditional reluctance of the military mind to accept new methods, but also by the unsatisfactory results of earlier experiments.

The question of which power initially violated the terms of the Hague Conference was a subject of charge and countercharge during and after the First World War. German statements seem to have been based on a desire to appear in the best light. The German Official History claimed that by using tear-gas shells and grenades the French committed "the first breach of international agreement in the sphere of gas warfare."[39] Technically, the statement may have been correct. Other German writers argued that chemical warfare, as practised by the German Army at Ypres, did not contravene the Hague agreements. With extraordinary cynicism, they attempted to make a distinction between gas delivered as drifting clouds from cylinders and gas disseminated from artillery shells. The German leaders themselves appear to have been aware that they were breaking the spirit, if not the letter, of the conventions, for they made no reference to the use of poison gas in their communiqué announcing the attack at Ypres in April 1915.

That issue laid to rest, we continue with our story. Under the supervision of Haber, the work to conceal preparations from the Allies proceeded mostly at night. The first of the gas cylinders were installed late in February along a line near the village of Gheluvelt. By 10 March, all 6000 cylinders had been put in place. Assembled German troops stood in readiness, waiting for the signal to move forward, but each time the attack was cancelled because of adverse wind conditions. His patience exhausted, Albrecht decided to establish a "new front" on the northern part of the salient, between Steenstraat and Poelcapelle, about 10 miles away.[40] By April 5,730 cylinders had been embedded under a layer of dirt in the second front. All that remained was for the wind to blow in the right direction

The German High Command worried about the delay. Quite apart from the impracticability of keeping troops on high alert in the trenches indefinitely, there was a chance that word of its secret weapon might leak out, as it actually did. But, as will be seen below, the Allies attached insufficient importance to the warning signs.

Late in March, German prisoners (belonging to the XV Corps) captured southeast of the salient, disclosed that the trenches in the neighbourhood of Zillebeke held many gas cylinders, ready for use at the first favourable wind. They gave a detailed description of the method of discharge, adding that their troops had been supplied with a medicated cloth pad for protection against the gas. The local French commander placed so little faith in the report that he did not even bother to bring it to the attention of the British when they arrived to take over his front. Curiously enough, particulars of the incident appeared on 30 March in the French Tenth Army bulletin, which was circulated only in the Artois district, over 100 miles away.[41]

A fortnight later, French military authorities came into possession of more concrete evidence. On 13 April, a disgruntled German soldier, private August Jäeger, a 24-year-old automobile driver attached to the 234th Reserve Regiment, 51st Reserve Division, quietly left his post and crawled through the tangle of bodies that littered no man's land and surrendered to elements of the French 11th Division near Langemarck. Taken to Divisional Headquarters, Jäeger stunned his interrogator when he revealed that the Germans planned to use gas and he proceeded to describe the extent of the preparations already made. He explained that the gas would be released through pipes fitted to cylinders buried in the German front trenches. He added that three red rockets fired from an artillery position would be the signal to open the valves and the escaping gas would be carried by a favourable wind toward the French line. The gas was intended to asphyxiate the defenders in the trenches and allow the Germans to occupy them without losses. To guard against inhaling the poison gas, the assaulting troops carried a packet of gauze and cotton, soaked in a chemically neutralizing solution. The German deserter produced one of those crude respirators as proof of his claim.[42]

The divisional commander, General Edmond Ferry, having talked to the interpreter who had interviewed Jäeger, considered the intelligence data to be of paramount importance. He knew absolutely nothing about the new weapon, but it had always been his policy to leave nothing to chance and so he proceeded to take "those precautionary measures which appear to us to be necessary." Accordingly, he alerted his brigade commander in the affected sector and instructed him to 1) thin out his forward line to reduce casualties; 2) shell the German trenches in an attempt to destroy the reported gas cylinders; 3) send an agent to warn the 28th British Division and the Canadians who were due in the sector that night to exercise the greatest vigilance and to improvise some means to prevent gas inhalation.[43]

At the same time, Ferry sent a special messenger to the headquarters of his superior, General Balfourier, commander of the XX Corps, to warn him of the imminent peril. By chance, a liaison officer from *Grand Quartier Général,* or GQG as it was more commonly called, was there when the messenger arrived. They were shown a copy of the interrogation of the German prisoner and a list of the measures taken to meet the contingency of a gas attack. Balfourier, thinking that Ferry was a gullible fool, ignored his recommendations. GQG should have at least investigated the matter for, as Ferry points out, the intelligence service of the War Ministry had been aware for some time that the Germans possessed gas.[44] Instead, it showed itself to be highly skeptical, telling Ferry that "all this gas business cannot be taken seriously." To add insult to injury, it rebuked Ferry, first for bypassing usual channels to warn the British, and second, for tampering with the density of the troops in the front line without regard for official policy.[45] Nor did Ferry profit when his prediction proved correct. He was dismissed from his post by General Foch, who sought to cover up the bad judgment and mistakes that had preceded the battle. Gen. Ferry's resentment over the injustice that cut short his military career "rankled until he could no longer hold his peace." In 1930 he divulged the entire story to an interested France. Ferry indiscreetly named Jäeger as the source of his information. Jäeger, now a civilian in Germany, was arrested after an investigation and brought before the Reich Supreme Court in December 1932. Found guilty of desertion and treason, he was sentenced to ten years in the penitentiary and forfeited his civil rights.[46]

On 16 April, General Putz assumed charge of the northern part of the salient, replacing Balfournier, whose XX Corps was due to participate in Joffre's projected offensive in Arras. Before leaving, Balfournier alerted his successor of the information Jäeger had revealed under questioning. Putz was sufficiently intrigued to order that the German deserter be re-interrogated. On reading the report, Putz concluded that the chauffeur was too forthcoming with details of Germany's plans and security arrangements and that he must have been primed and sent over to mislead the French. Consequently, he did not bother to circulate the news to his divisional commanders, much less instruct them to take precautionary steps.

Jäeger's data, however, was corroborated by other sources. On 15 April, a Belgian spy, whose intelligence in the past had been reliable, reported that the Germans were planning an attack on the Ypres salient on the night of 15–16 April and intended to make "use of tubes with asphyxiating gas." The next day the Belgian General Staff notified GQG that the Germans had purchased 20,000 respirators from a factory in Ghent to counter the effects of asphyxiating gas, which they "intend to discharge towards the enemy lines, notably on the front of the XXVI Reserve Corps."[47]

Equally convincing evidence was provided by the German authorities themselves. German broadcasts and official communiqués alleged that the Allies were firing asphyxiating gas shells in the vicinity of Ypres.[48] It was typical of the Germans to justify their criminal behaviour by blaming their opponents in advance — like when they falsely accused French airplanes of violating German territory on 1 August 1914. The only logical conclusion from the latest unsubstantiated charge was that they intended to use the new weapon themselves. The Germans were evidently aware they were violating the spirit, if not the letter, of international law. The Hague Convention had evidently intended to outlaw the use of poison gas even if the exact wording did not include its diffusion by means of cylinders.

Still, for the French there were clues that tended to cloud the picture. Allied intelligence had not detected the arrival of German reinforcements to the forward area. Then, too, nothing unusual occurred on the night of 15–16 April — as it happened, the attack had been scheduled for that time, but was postponed due to an unfavourable wind. The French overlooked a key point, namely that the wind had to be just right. To further complicate matters, a second German deserter contradicted the testimony of the first.

At 7:00 a.m. on 15 April, a former German NCO, Julius Rapshal, gave himself up to a French party belonging to the 69th Regiment, 11th

Division. A member of the 4th Landwehr Regiment (52 Reserve Division, XXVI Reserve Corps), occupying the trenches between Poelcappelle Road and Passchendaele, Rapshal had been reduced to the ranks for striking an officer, a demotion that had left him bitter and probably accounted for his decision to desert. Although disgruntled, he remained loyal to his country's cause and denied there were any gas cylinders on his unit's front. He explained that the cotton packet in his possession had been issued to him for protection in case the Allies used asphyxiating agents.[49] The French were inclined to believe him, rather than the earlier deserter, partly because he had served on the front and would have known if a gas attack was pending, and partly because they assumed he nursed a grudge against the German Army. They paid no further attention to what they considered to be German misinformation, calculated to spread terror among the troops or to prevent units from being withdrawn from Ypres to assist in Joffre's forthcoming offensive. It did not dawn on them to at least invite the opinion of a reputable chemist, something that could have been done without compromising classified information.

Putz passed on the circumstantial evidence in his possession to a British liaison officer attached to Smith-Dorrien's Second Army and made it clear "that he did not believe it."[50] Smith-Dorrien shared Putz's skepticism. There is the following entry in his diary on 15 April:

> Reports have come in through agents employed by the French and also one or two prisoners captured by the French, that the XXVI Reserve Corps has made all its plans for attacking us tonight on the front which we have taken over, partly by the 28th Division and partly by the Canadians.
>
> The details given by the prisoners are so voluminous and exact that I am sure they are untrue — in fact, possibly the prisoners have been allowed to be captured to spread these stories of German attacks to prevent us attacking them and to keep us on the jump … However, one cannot take chances in a war like this and in case there is any truth in it I have to let all commanders know.[51]

Plumer notified his divisional commanders of the French intelligence "for what it was worth," observing that he, too, did not take seriously the nature of the threat. The British drew up contingency plans of a sort, but these were sketchy. Warnings subsequently went out on 15 April that a German attack was expected to strike the French front that night. Since the Canadians were next to the French, some precautions needed to be taken in case their neighbours experienced a setback. Plumer ordered two reserve battalions to move closer to Ypres and that battalions in the trenches, when relieved, should remain east of the town. Aerial reconnaissance was intensified, but revealed no unusual activity in the enemy's rear that might suggest preparations for an attack. Again on 18 April, Plumer signaled his divisional commanders to expect some kind of enemy offensive action in the next few days. Such an attack, he predicted, would likely "include a heavy artillery bombardment and possibly a mine explosion followed by an attempt to rush one or more of the trenches."[52] In a note to Brigadier-General J.E. Edmonds, the official British historian, after the war, Major-General E.S. Bulfin, commander of the 28th British Division, recalled that he had received an intelligence memo around 16 April, "stating that the Germans to the North in front of the French were believed to be preparing for a gas attack but I do not remember any indication being given as to what we should do to combat such an attack."[53] Edmonds confirmed that Plumer neither suggested nor ordered steps to be taken against a possible gas attack.[54]

It would be perhaps unfair to condemn Smith-Dorrien and Plumer too severely for failing to heed to the early warnings of a gas attack. Both were intelligent and perceptive soldiers with an abundance of moral courage. Their failure to act may be explained by the fact that they had no frame of reference. They had no idea what a gas cloud would look like, what effects it would have, and how to defend against it. Besides, it was inconceivable to these generals that the Germans would flagrantly violate the laws of civilized warfare.[55] Even if the unthinkable were to occur, it was supposed that the noxious gas could be fanned away or, at worst, affect only a small area that could be regained with the delivery of an immediate counterattack.

Beyond divisional commanders, it is not known for sure how far down the British chain of command the warnings were passed. In the Canadian formation, brigade and battalion leaders were informed of the reports of an impending gas attack and urged to adopt measures to guard against such a contingency — even though Alderson admitted later that he did not take the rumours seriously.[56] Currie wrote in his diary on 15 April that an attack was "expected at night to be preceded by the sending of poisonous gases into our lines."[57] Similarly, Victor Odlum, second-in-command of the 7th Battalion, recalled after the war:

> McHarg and I were together one day and we received a message from Brigade which had come down from higher authority saying, "The Germans are expected to attack with gas. Take the necessary precautions," and we looked at each other and we said, "What are the necessary precautions?" We hadn't the faintest idea. We'd never heard of gas before. We called Brigade and we said we'd received this message. "What are the necessary precautions?"
>
> They said, "We don't know any more than you do. If we find out anything we'll let you know. In the meantime do whatever you can." …
>
> We thought it over seriously, and we said, "As we do not know the answer, to send word out that there will be a gas attack will only terrify and confuse everyone. It won't do any good. We can't tell them what to do." So we did not pass that message on to the battalion.[58]

The inaction of other battalion commanders meant that the vast majority of the men in the trenches had not heard of the gas rumours. "We had no warning at all … and it had never been mentioned to us as a matter of fact," grumbled George Kyles (15th Battalion).[59] Still, word had gotten around to a few of the units. Some members of the 14th Battalion had been alerted by a French soldier while he was guiding them to the front. Sergeant Fred Bagnall recorded the following in his memoirs:

"Their intelligence was on the job; he told us the Germans were going to poison us with gas. He said they had compressed containers so arranged that it came out from under the trench and to float with the wind."[60] But those forewarned were uncertain of what they were supposed to do. It was not untypical of Canadians to resort to humour when facing danger or the unknown. In a few places along their trenches they had set up signs in large German letters which when translated read: "You may have a long wait for the right wind to blow."[61]

Beside the intelligence reports sent by V Corps Headquarters, there was, it can now be seen, plenty of other evidence that something was afoot. At night, Canadian troops could hear the constant rumblings of wheels, and gun flashes were observed as being nearer than usual. German airplanes came over with greater frequency, flying low to drop bombs or to register targets. A map found inside one such plane, brought down by French fire, showed new battery positions. While on sentry duty several soldiers (16th Battalion) noticed that pipes were being installed in the enemy's parapet and reported the incident to their superior.[62] An investigation followed, but evidently uncovered nothing suspicious. Had the Canadians possessed more experience they might better have interpreted the series of warnings.

At all levels of command, from Alderson downwards, the degree of apprehension was slight. Nevertheless, at least one officer took the warning seriously and made an effort to determine if there was substance to the alleged threat. Currie ordered his artillery to fire shells every 20 yards along the German breastworks and look out for signs of gas cylinders rupturing. Despite the pinpoint accuracy of the shelling, nothing unusual was detected because the gas cylinders were located farther north. There may have been others who adopted a similar approach, but, if so, no other counter-measures were taken. Why? The idea existed that if noxious gas were discharged it would be localized and on the French front. Then, too, some believed that any reference to the new weapon would inspire terror among the men or violate instructions from the Second Army issued on 15 April, calling for reticence in dealing with secret or confidential matters. But two factors are crucial to understanding Canadian inaction. The first was that the conception of gas did not convey much meaning,

Courtesy of Bruce Liebowitz.

A side view of Hill 60 today.

and the second was the lack of information and direction from Corps and Divisional Headquarters. Odlum aptly describes the state of mind of his fellow Canadian officers at the time:

> We could not visualize an attack with gas, we could
> not guess where the gas would come from or how we
> would recognize it when it did come and we did not
> know what were the necessary precautions. And no
> one else could tell us. So in the end, like all the others,
> we simply did nothing except to lay plans for action in
> case of an ordinary type of attack … [63]

Thus, while there was intelligence suggesting that the Germans intended to use some sort of disabling gas, no special precautions were taken. As nothing unusual happened on the night of 15–16 April, the warning was disregarded and probably forgotten after attention was distracted by two other events, the British attack on Hill 60 and the heavy shelling of Ypres.

Now filled with water, the crater, one of three, was produced by an underground explosion which virtually delivered Hill 60 to the British on 17 April 1915.

Hill 60 on the southern end of the salient was a man-made mound formed years earlier from the cutting of an adjacent railway. It had fallen to the Germans in December 1914 and the French attempt to recapture it in February 1915 had failed. The knoll was of considerable tactical importance since it commanded the flat Flanders plain and allowed the Germans to observe all traffic leading into Ypres from the south and east. When the British took over the sector from the French, the High Command made it a high priority to regain possession of the hill. Since conventional methods had not worked, a more complex scheme was tried. British sappers, working day and night in shifts, tunnelled under the mound and laid five tons of explosive charges. On the evening of 17 April, the mines were exploded, creating three big craters in the hill and killing most of the 150 defenders. Before the smoke cleared away, units of the 13th Brigade (5th Division) sprang up from their trenches and rushed up the hill, hardly encountering any resistance from the dazed survivors. After midnight on the 18th, the Germans counter-attacked and reached the British position before being driven back with the bayonet. For the next three days there was no let-up in the fighting. Early on the 21st, the 1st Canadian Brigade, released from army reserve, was placed at the disposal of the 5th Division and ordered to be prepared to move to Hill 60 at an hour's notice. The routes to the forward area were reconnoitered, and the morning of the 22nd found the 2nd and 4th Battalions standing by. Within 24 hours, the 1st Brigade would find itself in action, but not on Hill 60.[64]

On 20 April, while the fighting for Hill 60 was raging, the Germans opened a violent bombardment of Ypres, sending columns of black and yellow smoke several hundred feet up in the air. It was one thing to block the routes through which the Allies supplied their forces in the salient, but quite another to gratuitously destroy the old medieval city. Huge 42 mm shells rained upon the town, remorselessly grinding away streets and buildings, and killing scores of civilians.[65] After one such shell fell in a field, a Canadian stretcher-bearer claimed, "You could put three ambulances in it."[66] The British interpreted the German action as nothing more than retaliation for the loss of Hill 60.[67] They were wrong. It was the prelude to the rumoured German gas attack.

After the cylinders were in place, the OHL issued orders for the gas attack on 8 April, but they could not be carried out owing to the absence of an accommodating wind. Because the OHL had doubts as to what the gas could accomplish, it limited the objective to the capture of Pilckem Ridge and the adjoining ground to the east, an advance of about one and a half miles. The plan, to be carried out by units of two corps (the XXIII and XXVI), was simple enough. On the German right, the 45th Reserve Division was to march on Steenstraat, while the 46th Reserve Division was to break across the Yser Canal and establish bridgeheads at Het Sas and Boesinghe. Their objectives attained, the two divisions would then march on Lizerne. The main thrust was to be on the left with the 51st Reserve Division directed to take Langemarck, and the 52nd Reserve Pilckem. If all went well, Albrecht anticipated that the Allies would be compelled to evacuate the salient.[68]

With the passage of each day, OHL was becoming increasingly impatient at the delay. Fourth Army Headquarters had no control over the direction of the wind, and on 15 April and again on the 20th, it was forced to counterman the gas alert order. On 22 April, two attempts in the morning to activate the gas had to be postponed because wind conditions were unsuitable and the attack was rescheduled for later that afternoon.[69] No tactical instruction had been given to the infantry, but otherwise everything was ready. The men, in full gear and densely packed in the trenches, kept waiting for the signal to go over the top. Cylinder had been laid over the parapet along a front of 3.75 miles, and German engineers had cut passages in the wire. High German planners were understandably on edge lest all the telltale signs that something was afoot might draw the attention of the French. In such an event, the deadly 75 mm field guns would be turned on the German trenches and there was a likelihood that some of the cylinders would be ruptured by the shelling. Since only the leading German troops were given respirators, as there were not enough to go around, the consequences would be catastrophic.

There was a great sense of relief in the afternoon when the winds shifted and began to blow from the northeast. German artillery unleashed a furious bombardment on French entrenchments and, at 4:40 p.m., Fourth Army Headquarters issued orders to start the attack at 5:00 p.m. The troops were scheduled to move forward ten minutes after the gas had been released. Thus, the cylinders were opened between Steenstraat on the Yser Canal, to a point east of Langemarck, releasing 180,000 kilograms of chlorine that drifted slowly toward the French trenches. For undetermined reasons, the cylinders west of Steenstraat and south of Poelcappelle remained sealed.[70] At 5:20 p.m., when scouts had reported that the air was safe to breathe, wave after wave of German troops clambered out of the trenches and, with fixed bayonets, advanced cautiously across no man's land.

CHAPTER 4
A Higher Form of Killing

Thursday, 22 April, was a pleasant, sunny day with an occasional light wind and the temperature in the seventies. Throughout the morning the Germans had directed the fire of their 17-inch and 8-inch howitzers on Ypres and the nearby towns, but by early afternoon all was quiet. Air reconnaissance revealed considerable activity behind the German lines, including a long column of troops on the march, but V Corps Headquarters was not overly concerned. It was assumed that the Germans still had their sights on recapturing Hill 60.

The daily routine of the troops of the 1st Canadian Division continued uninterrupted. The 1st Brigade at Vlamertinghe, although alerted for possible action at Hill 60, carried on with training. Two battalions of the 3rd Brigade, the 13th and 15th, had worked hard all night, filling sandbags, building breastworks, digging and repairing barbed-wire entanglements. These battalions occupied the left of the Canadian line, next to the Zouave and Turco (Algerian) troops of the French 45th Division. The 14th Battalion was in support near the village of St. Jean, a short distance away, and the 16th Battalion was in reserve outside Ypres. On the right, the 8th and 5th Battalions of the 2nd Brigade carried the Canadian line until it joined with the 28th British Division. These 2nd Brigade units, like the 13th and 15th Battalions, were busy shoring up defensive works. The 7th Battalion was in support nearby (at the village of Fortuin) and the 10th Battalion was in reserve near Ypres.

As work on the front line during the daylight hours attracted enemy shells, the men typically looked for things to do to pass their idle time. Some basked in the sun, others simply chatted or wrote letters. For Lieutenant Herbert Maxwell-Scott (15th Battalion), his account shows that he and several of his friends had gathered outside a dugout and were enjoying tea and biscuits, "all of us being very cheerful." After their break was over, "we retired to our respective parts of the trench."[1] As for the men in reserve in the rear, they had even more free time on their hands. In a field near a barn half a dozen men were kicking a soccer ball while nearby a quartette played a game of quoit — similar to horseshoes.[2] One officer put in a request for some playing cards and mouth organs.[3] Another made arrangements to conduct a cockfight, a popular local diversion novel to most Canadians.

Soon after 4:00 p.m., the Germans unleashed a furious bombardment directed initially on the French positions along the north of the salient and gradually extending to the Canadian trenches, then to the nearby roads, villages, and Ypres itself. French field guns replied and kept firing even after German artillery had ceased.[4] Around 5:00 p.m., French troops heard a loud hissing noise coming from the German lines. As it continued, they saw an "uncanny vision" in the form of an approaching greenish-yellow cloud.[5] The sight prompted French frontline commanders to alert their men to expect an attack, as they were under the impression that the Germans were using smoke to cover their advance.

The Canadians (left companies of the 13th Battalion adjoining the French colonial troops) witnessing the peculiar-coloured wall of fumes advancing toward the French were puzzled. "At first we thought it was just the intense musketry creating the yellow haze," recalled Lieutenant Ian Sinclair.[6] As the acrid cloud enveloped the Africans, they disappeared from the view of the Canadians. Those on points of vantage saw two greenish-yellow clouds drifting slowly across no man's land, on either side of Langemarck. The clouds spread laterally until they united into one long, low bank of fog, and, under the impulsion of a light breeze, rolled down on the trenches of the Algerian Division.[7]

The African troops in this sector may not have been of the highest quality, but even the most experienced and hardened soldiers would not

Ground over which the Germans released gas on 22 April 1915.

have reacted differently. Within seconds of inhaling the fumes, the men choked, their eyes and lungs burned, and they were gripped by violent nausea and stabbing pain in the chest. Clutching their throats and gasping in agony, some, struggling to suck air into their bursting lungs, turned blue and coughed up mouthful after mouthful of yellow fluid. Others writhed at the bottom of the trenches, where the gas was thickest and suffocated to death in a matter of minutes. Their morale broken by this unknown terror, the rest, half-asphyxiated, with eyes streaming and noses and throats burning, sought to escape. Most fled to the rear, but some drifted over to the trenches manned by the 13th Battalion. Initially, the horrified Canadians were unsure of what was happening. Ian Sinclair told the CBC that the Algerians "started pouring into our trench, coughing and bleeding and dying all over the place, and then we realized what it was."[8]

A French position captured on 22 April 1915.

The gas and panic spread to the French 87th Territorials and they, too, bolted and joined their fleeing comrades. Singly or in groups, the French infantrymen stumbled across fields, through hedges, over ditches, and down the roads in the direction of the canal bridges. Many did not halt their flight until they reached Ypres or crossed over to Vlamertinghe and put the canal between themselves and their diabolical enemies.[9] Most of the fleeing soldiers could not outdistance the gas, which travelled five or six miles an hour.[10] But, in an effort to do so they took deeper breaths, resulting in more acute poisoning. "A lot of the fellows … had sort of started to scoot away from the gas," James Pratt (4th Battalion) observed from near Hill 60, "in fact doing the very thing they shouldn't have because the gas was drifting with them and the result was that you found them dead and lying all over the place."[11]

As if by magic, almost two French Divisions had disappeared in a matter of minutes. Only slightly affected by the gas, the right of the 1/1st Tirailleurs Algeriens, next to the 13th Battalion, remained in position, as did the 1/2nd bis Zouaves who were in support. Between Steenstraat and what remained of the 45th Division there was a four and a half mile breach in the Allied line.

Canadian rear units, in the path of the retreat, were amazed at the surreal sight of the panic-stricken rabble of Turcos and Zouaves with their reeking, yellowed clothing and ashen purple faces twisted and distorted by pain, pointing at their throats and vainly trying to gain relief by vomiting. It left an indelible mark on Canadian observers. Major Andrew McNaughton, then a gunner, recalled many years later that they were running "as if the devil was after them, their eyeballs showing white, and coughing their lungs out — they were literally coughing their lungs out; glue was coming out of their mouths. It was a very disturbing, very distressing sight."[12] Captain Paul Villiers saw the Algerians from 3rd Brigade Headquarters at Mouse Trap Farm, and described them as "suffering the agony of the damned, grey-green in the face and dying from suffocation."[13]

The fugitives were incoherent and other than the word "asphyxia" — which at the time had little meaning to observers — it was impossible to understand what they said, but from their appearance it was evident that they were terrified and in severe distress. Behind them came stragglers from the 87th Territorial Division, sobbing hysterically "*La guerre est finie! La guerre est finie.*"[14]French officers tried to halt their flight in vain. Recognizing the danger to their comrades at the front, French-speaking Canadian officers tried their hand, but with no better luck. "Some of our own French-speaking officers stopped the few running men they could make hear," Private Peat wrote, "and begged of them to reform their lines and go back to the attack. But they were maddened ... by fear, and paid no heed."[15] Then the onlookers sniffed something in the air, something which brought tears to their eyes and caught at the back of their throats, filling their mouths with a metallic taste.

Lieutenant-Colonel G.G. Nasmith, an analytical chemist, was one of the first, if not the first, to determine the nature of the gas. A native of Toronto, the four-foot-six-inch Nasmith had been ruled ineligible for combat service on account of his diminutive stature. But he was enthusiastic and eager to help in some capacity. His persistence paid off and he eventually received authority from the minister of militia to organize a laboratory in order to test and clear the drinking water of the Canadian troops overseas.[16]

Grizzly work of the poison gas on 22 April 1915. The soldier on the left is French, the one on the right is a Canadian Highlander.

On 22 April, Nasmith, on his way into the salient, stopped at an Advanced Dressing Station at Wieltje where he ran into his old friend Captain F.A.C. Scrimger, a surgeon from Montreal who was the medical officer of the 14th Battalion. Leaving the car at the edge of the village, the two men were walking towards St. Julien when they saw a long cloud of dense, yellowish-green smoke rising and drifting in their direction. "That must be the poison gas we have heard vague rumours about," Nasmith remarked. As the gas continued to ascend and expand Nasmith noticed that here and there that the clouds were streaked with brown. "It looks like chlorine," he said and Scrimger agreed that it probably was.[17] Half an hour later the gas reached them, making them cough and causing tears to stream down from their eyes. Nasmith inclined to believe that the gas was essentially chlorine, but he was uncertain whether the irritation to their eyes had been caused by the presence of another agent.

Upon reaching his laboratory, Nasmith conducted a series of tests and determined that the gas was "largely chlorine but with probably some bromine present." The next day he wrote directly to Divisional

Headquarters, bypassing normal channels in order to save time. He revealed his findings and suggested, as the best means to protect the men, the use of a pad soaked in hyposulphite of soda. On 28 April, a team of prominent chemists, brought over from Britain in haste, confirmed Nasmith's analysis and identified the same antidote that he had recommended five days before.[18] Shortly afterwards the pad was distributed to the men in the front line.

Although most of the Canadians had escaped the worst of the chlorine gas, those closest to the French zone were in danger of being overcome, or at least severely incapacitated, by its ill effects. "We weren't equipped with a gas mask," J. Sprostin explained. "Men were coughing, spitting and choking, and we didn't know what to do until the M.O. of the 14th battalion, Colonel [should be Captain] Scrimger, was running up and down telling everyone to urinate on your pocket handkerchief, tie it over your mouth, and he saved thousands of lives."[19] Unpleasant though it may have been, the ammonia in the urine partially neutralized the chlorine gas.

Chaos reigned behind the front. Shells fell incessantly and with mathematical precision on Ypres, turning the town into a flaming inferno and creating, what one writer described, "a spectacle that would have driven a Nero to ecstasy of delight."[20] Forced out of their homes, frightened men, women, and children surged through the streets in a desperate attempt to exit the city. There were dead bodies everywhere, often mangled beyond recognition, and cries of agony came from those hurt by bomb blasts or collapsing buildings. For N. Nicholson (16th Battalion), on leave in the city, not even the passing of half a century could dim the recollection of that shocking scene: "People were screaming and running hither and thither. As a matter of fact, I saw one woman carrying a baby and the baby's head was gone, and it was quite devastating."[21]

Outside the city, the human procession, moving westward, merged with the leading traffic from the salient. Civilians who had been reluctant to leave their farms and cottages, despite the proximity of the battlefield, were now struggling to get away. Some drove their animals before them, others helped the elderly or carried children, and still others pushed carts laden with their most cherished belongings. They had mingled along the road with streams of soldiers on foot or on horseback, motor vehicles, and wagons drawn by teams of horses. Former editor of the *Ottawa Citizen*, Lieutenant-Colonel Edward "Dinky" Morrison, on his way along with his artillery unit to take positions in the salient late in the afternoon, has left a record of what he saw:

> The French troops were absolutely in rout and were coming across country in a very demoralized condition. Ambulances loaded with unwounded men, ammunition wagons, transport vehicles crowded with infantry, were galloping across country through hedges, ditches, and barbed-wire. In many cases artillery horses had been unhooked from guns and limber, and were being used for quick transportation, sometimes with two or three men on their backs. After this rabble came men on foot, without arms, singly and in groups, alternately running and walking, and only intent on getting away.[22]

The panic spread well beyond Ypres. A British officer, Lieutenant F. Hawkins (Queen Victoria's Rifles, 13th Brigade, 5th Division) was in the vicinity of Elverdinghe, on the west side of the canal, along with several of his friends, when he witnessed what he considered was "an unnerving spectacle." He wrote the following in his diary:

> As far as the eye could see ... came a flying mass of men, horses, limbers, and waggons; men without rifles and teams without guns. Those nearest to us forced their way frantically through the hedge and when they came close we saw that they were French native troops, Tirailleurs Morrocain [sic] from Morocco. Their faces were gastly, they gasped for breath and staggered about like drunken men. Among them was a Zouave whom I stopped and asked what was wrong. *"Des Gazes Asphixiantes — la retraite — la retraite"* he croaked and stumbled on after his comrades ... Asphixiating gases — no one had

ever heard of them. The traffic on the road paused and shouted for information. A British motor ambulance came hurtling from the direction of Ypres, the driver shouting at the top of his voice — "Run for your lives boys. The Uhlans are in Ypres."[23]

It was impossible for the French High Command to ascertain what had actually happened. Colonel Jacques Mordacq, who commanded the 90th Brigade (45th Algerian Division), learned of the gas attack almost immediately, although it would take many hours before he could assess the scope of the disaster. The colonel reported that at 5:20 p.m. he received a call from Major Villevaleix of the 1st Tirailleurs, announcing in a gasping voice, barely audible and broken by coughing, that he had been violently attacked, that columns of yellow fumes emanating from German trenches had spread across his entire front, and that his men were being asphyxiated. Mordacq admitted that, given the contents and manner in which the information was conveyed, he questioned for a moment whether Villevaleix had taken leave of his senses or suffered from a blow to the head. But a second phone call from a different officer belonging to the 1st Tirailleurs confirmed Villevaleix's account. Minutes later Mordacq again heard from Villevaleix who managed to utter the words, "Everyone is falling around me, I am quitting my command post." Then there were a few inaudible words before the line went dead. [24]

Distraught, Mordacq rushed out of his headquarters, mounted his horse, and, accompanied by a small party, rode toward the front. As they approached the town of Boesinghe, Mordacq recalled that they "were seized by a violent tingling in the nose and throat, the ears began to buzz, breathing became difficult, and an intolerable odor of chlorine surrounded us." When the horses stubbornly refused to move on, they dismounted and entered the town, where they saw a terrifying spectacle. Everywhere, all types of fugitives were without weapons and greatcoats, running around like madmen, crying loudly for water, spitting blood, and a few were even rolling on the ground, making desperate efforts to breathe. No real attempt was made to halt their flight. They were no longer fleeing soldiers but, as Mordacq described, "poor souls who had suddenly become insane." All along the canal this scene was repeated. Mordacq was able to rally units that had not been in the front line to defend key positions. But with all the guns lost and most of the 87th and 45th Divisions fleeing, killed, or incapacitated, an immediate counterattack was out of the question.[25] This meant that the inexperienced Canadian Division, the formation closest to the breech in the line, was left with the unenviable task of trying to block the German advance.

The sounds of the German bombardment and the initial reply by the French 75s and rifle fire, followed by reports of the penetrating stench of the chlorine, alerted Canadian Divisional Headquarters that something serious was going on. For several hours it was impossible to ascertain precisely what had occurred because of the completeness of the French collapse and the disruption of the telephone lines by artillery fire. In the meantime, unit commanders were issuing quick, independent orders in an effort to combat the strange menace that was developing to the north.

The Canadians on the front line, witnessing the gruesome effect of poison gas on the Algerians, were naturally distressed, but for the most part remained astonishingly calm. Fifty years later McNaughton explained: "Somehow we felt it was the normal course of war. It was unpleasant, it's true, but nobody got very excited about it. Now later on, when we'd learned a little about war, we wouldn't have been there at all; we'd have been off within the next couple of hours."[26] Other survivors spoke in similar terms:

> Victor Odlum: Fortunately we were neither alarmed nor excited. Had this event occurred later in the war, when we knew more, we might have been both. [27]

> Elliot Green (4th Division Artillery): If they were better troops they would have withdrawn immediately and if they'd been worse troops, they wouldn't be there at all — they'd have panicked.[28]

> George Patrick (2nd Battalion): No one had any idea of getting out. We didn't know enough about it to know

that we were licked. We went in there and we were going
to stay there, and that was that.[29]

Advancing into the gap created by the discharge of chlorine, the
Germans quickly gained their objectives except in three places — on
either wing and in between at Langemarck — where resistance was
obstinate. As already noted, the gas, through some unknown glitch, was
not released at the western end of the German line, allowing Steenstraat
to hold out against the 45th Reserve Division until late in the evening.
Farther east, the discharge of gas had barely touched the garrison at
Langemarck, which greeted the 51st Reserve Division with a torrent
of firepower. A hectic struggle ensued, but by 6:00 p.m. the Germans
were in possession of the village, or what was left of it, and subsequently
crossed the Steenbeek with the object of capturing St. Julien.[30] On the
eastern fringes of the gap, the Germans had failed to turn on the valves
of the cylinders so that most of the Canadian units were not affected by
the gas. Here, the left of the 51st Division ran unexpectedly into elements
of the 13th Battalion.

Three platoons of No. 1 Company, under Major D. Rykert Mc
Cuaig, occupied the trenches at the left end of the 13th Battalion. Major
Edward Norsworthy, second in command of the battalion, with two
platoons of No. 3 Company, was in support some 800 yards yards to
the rear. The rest of No. 3 Company was in St. Julien with the battalion
commander, Lieutenant-Colonel Frederick Loomis. The distance
between Norsworthy's outpost and St. Julien, a stretch of more than a
mile, was unguarded except for the 10th Field Battery below Keerselaere.
A heavy battery of British guns in Kitchener's Wood (the name was not
associated with Lord Kitchener, but was a literal translation of the French
bois de cuisiniers), about half a mile west of St. Julien, constituted the only
manned position between the village and 3rd Brigade Headquarters at
Mouse Trap Farm.[31] This lightly defended stretch presented the greatest
danger, not because it was longer than the one north of the village, but
because it was nearer the centre of the attack.

Around 5:00 p.m., McCuaig, worried by reports that the French
were under heavy attack and curious about the sun's peculiar greenish

tint, went over to investigate, taking a platoon with him. As he made his way into the continuous trench he came upon a party of 1st Tirailleurs, who, having flung their line at right angle from their original front, were exchanging a brisk fire with Germans occupying a parallel hedge 150 yards away. Insufficient cover prevented McCuaig from extending the French line farther to the rear, so he took a position in echelon in the ditch along the east side of the Poelcappelle road. There he was soon joined by a second platoon and then part of a third. McCuaig did not appear to have realized the extent of the French debacle and the seriousness of his own position until around 6:00 p.m. when a salvo from a battery scored four direct hits on his trenches, causing a dozen or more casualties. Shells continued to rain, frequently blowing up the flimsy trenches and causing heavy losses.[32] "Our line of trenches promptly disappeared so we had nothing except a foot or eighteen inches of cover and so we fought from that," Ian Sinclair later maintained.[33] All indications were that the Germans, presumably using a captured gun, were firing from the left rear. McCuaig concluded, correctly as it turned out, that the Germans had swung in toward the Canadian flank and were heading in the general direction of St. Julien. Eventually the Germans were able to dislodge the Tirailleurs from their isolated breastwork, but McCuaig was able to rally about 200 of them and use them to reinforce his line. He also ordered two machine guns to be brought up. Sinclair later recalled: "There was some pretty stout fighting on the part of the Battalion, there's no question of that. Our machine-gun section did a magnificent job."[34]

McCuaig was faced with myriad problems that would have tested the resourcefulness of a much more experienced officer. He was heavily outnumbered, his communications had been cut, he was without artillery support, and his men were suffering severely from heavy enfilading fire. By all the rules of war he was a beaten man, and, as such, should have retired while the going was good. The longer he remained in his position, the less likelihood there was that he would be able to make it out safely. "The Germans had us completely cut off," Ian Sinclair subsequently told his mother, "and could have got us to a man, so much so, in fact, that we thought we were gone anyway and might as well make it as dear as possible."[35] By sticking it out, McCuaig apparently deceived the Germans into thinking that behind him lay a much larger force which, of course, was not the case.

Half a mile to the south, Norsworthy and his two platoons, supplemented by a handful of Algerians originally driven back by the gas, lined the ditch on the west side of the Poelcappelle road. Inspired by the gallant leadership of Norsworthy, the Canadians and Algerians put up a fierce struggle, thwarting several attempts by the enemy to work around McCuaig's rear. With their numbers dwindling, they refused to surrender, until overwhelmed by sheer weight of numbers. One of the few who survived described how Norsworthy was killed:

> Major Norsworthy was hit in the neck by a bullet but it did not stop him from walking up and down our line, encouraging our men to hold fast. It was not until he received a second bullet that he had to gave in and lie down. We bound him as well as we could, but the second wound was serious and he died about forty-five minutes later.[36]

Norswothy and his men, however, had not died in vain. In his report, McCuaig not only paid tribute to Norsworthy's courage, but was convinced that his "devoted defence was of immense assistance in delaying the German advance and in gaining time for bringing up reinforcements."[37] Also among the dead was 26-year-old Captain Guy Drummond, a staunch Conservative and son of a former president of the Bank of Montreal, who was being groomed for a career in politics before enlisting in the army. Friends and acquaintances would not have been surprised if someday the bright, handsome, and fluently bilingual young millionaire had ascended to the post of prime minister.[38] Lieutenant-Colonel J.A. Currie, who knew him well, wrote: "When he fell Canada lost a valuable and useful citizen. His training, education and charm of manner, coupled with his intense patriotism, marked him for a great career."[39] Interestingly enough, his remains were not discovered until 1919, when soldiers, in the process of clearing the Ypres battlefield, found a makeshift grave. Once identified, he was buried again in a cemetery near St. Julien.[40]

As the Germans surged toward St. Julien they were unaware that Major William King's 10th Field Battery, deployed in an orchard near the village of Keerselaere, stood in their way. The artillerymen, with their four 18-pounders, were firing in support of the 13th Battalion when they saw swarms of Algerians running past them. At 7:00 p.m., a French sergeant, who had stayed with the battery, suddenly gripped King's arm, and, pointing to a hedge to the west side of the road, cried *"Allemand."* King turned, and, to his amazement, saw a large column of grey-clad infantrymen above the intervening hedge marching south, less than 300 yards away. King ordered two of his guns to swing 90 degrees to the left and commenced firing over open sights. The Germans provided the sort of target that gunners dream of and within a few minutes their dead lay in heaps on the ground. The survivors turned and ran, taking cover some distance away. After digging themselves in, they directed a steady rifle fire at the Canadian gunners, bringing down showers of leaves from the willow trees above them.[41] The Germans eventually withdrew, but King realized that they would return after dark, and, as his position was exposed, requested help from the garrison in St. Julien.

Loomis detailed a party of 60 men, which included a machine-gun crew headed by 19-year-old Fred Fisher, to assist King. Fisher needed help with the machine gun. Private F. Palin (14th Battalion), whose company formed part of the St. Julien garrison, remarked in hindsight: "We were out in the sun doing a bit of cleaning up, and the first thing we knew we got a 'Stand-to' and I remember one Lance-Corporal Fred Fisher of the 13th Battalion, he came down looking for eight volunteers to carry up a machine gun, so eight of us stepped out."[42] Just barely out of a public school in Toronto, but showing the skill of a veteran, Fisher led his crew forward under heavy fire and set up his Colt gun in an isolated building, which enjoyed a commanding view of the enemy. In the fading light, the Germans attacked again and again, only to be driven back each time. Members of his crew went down, but Fisher kept working the gun, ripping and spraying the enemy's ranks. He contributed in no small measure to checking the German advance and providing cover for King to withdraw his guns. Attached to teams of horses, King instructed his drivers to forge ahead "any way you can get out." The guns made it back to St. Julien.[43] For his skill and daring, Fisher was awarded the Victoria Cross, the first Canadian soldier in the Great War to receive that honour. He was given the medal posthumously for, regrettably, he was killed in action the next day.

The way was open for the Germans to march on to St. Julien, but it was getting dark and they were reluctant to press ahead. They had taken heavy losses as a result of King's artillery and Fisher's machine gun and they may have been under the impression that they would run into similar defences elsewhere. The failure of the Germans to exploit their opportunity would allow the Canadians time in the evening and during the night to shore up their flank between St. Julien and the front-line battalions.

Back at Divisional Headquarters, such information as trickled in from the front was often unclear, inaccurate, or contradictory. Alderson happened to be near St. Julien with Brigadier-General Henry Burstall (RCA) to inspect artillery emplacements just before the attack began. Suddenly, his attention was drawn by the sound of heavy rifle fire to the north in the French zone. "I believe the Germans are trying a surprise attack on the French without any previous bombardment," he said to Burstall. When the rifle fire died down he concluded that "the Germans are over the French trenches."[44] A few minutes later he reported that "two clouds of gas appeared."[45] As he was on foot, Alderson hurriedly made his way back to his horse. He then rode though crowds of fugitives to his headquarters in the Château des Trois Tours, arriving shortly before 6:00 p.m. The first reports were already in. One from the 2nd Brigade indicated that its front had not been attacked.[46] Another from the 3rd Brigade advised that an attack had been launched against the French to the north.[47] No further news of importance came to hand until receipt of a series of telegrams, brought by a messenger from Brigadier-General Richard Turner's 3rd Brigade Headquarters, conveyed an entirely wrong impression of the condition of the Canadian flank.

Turner realized, after witnessing the Algerians fleeing in panic, that the French had suffered a defeat, but he was unaware of its dimensions. He immediately ordered his nearest reserves, three companies of the 14th Battalion (the other company as already noted was in St. Julien)

Mouse Trap Farm today. The farm shown in the illustration was built after the old one was completely destroyed during the battle.

billeted near St. Jean, to occupy the GHQ Line near Mouse Trap Farm. There was a certain amount of consternation at 3rd Brigade Headquarters for practically all the staff had no experience of war. Turner was a mediocre field general at best, but his personal courage was above reproach. Turner, according to Captain Paul Villiers, "gave us a very fine example bucking on his revolver, saying that he was quite prepared to die, but surrender he would not."[48] Beginning at 6:25 p.m., Turner sent a series of alarming messages to Divisional Headquarters: "Left of our sub-section is retiring." In a second note at 6:32 p.m. he repeated what was said in the first: "The left of our left section is retiring having been driven in," adding, "Will you be able to support us." At 6:45 p.m. and again at 7:10 p.m. he gave an even more disturbing picture: "Our left driven back and apparently whole line forced back toward St. Julien." And then: "We are forced back on GHQ Line."[49] By 7:10 p.m., there had been some fighting on the periphery of the gap by elements of the 13th Battalion, but the 3rd Brigade's flank remained intact and certainly not on the verge of collapsing.

Andrew Iarocci, in a recent study entitled *Shoestring Soldiers: The First Canadian Division at War, 1914–1915*, has challenged my interpretation of Turner's messages. He argues that Turner was essentially correct, that he was referring to the Allied line, and not, as I contended, to his own.[50] Iarocci's case is based on Turner's telegram to Alderson at 6:32 p.m., in which he states: "The left of our left section is retiring having been driven in" — implying that Turner was referring to the French on his left. In fact, in the telegrams sent throughout the battle, Turner always differentiated between the French line and his own. If he had been alluding to the French, he would have said so. His focus is on the left end of his own front. Besides, Turner himself admitted that he was wrong later in the morning when he sent a note to Alderson that "Our left subsection reported holding on."[51] Finally, there was never any doubt at 1st Division Headquarters, as outgoing messages at the time show, that Turner had drawn attention to the left of his own line.[52]

Alderson, having relayed Turner's faulty intelligence to the V Corps, impressed upon the 2nd and 3rd Brigades the need to stand their ground. He directed one of his divisional reserve battalions, the 16th, to report to Turner. The other, the 10th, was given similar orders, but, as it was held up by the stream of fugitives, turned into the GHQ Line east and southeast of Wieltje.[53] In response to Turner's plea for help, Currie, whose headquarters were at Pond Farm, southeast of St. Julien, placed the 7th Battalion on alert. An hour and a half later, as a precautionary move, Currie ordered the 7th to Locality C where it occupied a supporting position behind the junction of the 2nd and 3rd Brigades.

By evening, a stand-to order had passed down to all Canadian units. Those in reserve positions were directed to plug the spot nearest to where they were. "The bugle came along for fall-in … and we got orders to march off right away," George Bernier (14th Battalion) later related. "When I left I just had my rifle and the light equipment. I didn't take my haversack nor water bottle. We didn't know where we were going."[54] The Canadians seemed to be under the impression that they had nothing to fear; that they were facing inferior adversaries. "We were not frightened," Private Peat claimed. "No; none of us showed fear. Warfare such as this does not scare men with red blood in their veins. The Germans judge others by themselves. A German can be scared, a German can be bluffed. They thought that we were of the same mettle, or lesser."[55] R. McLaughlin (14th Battalion) recalled the words of his platoon commander: "Remember, boys, that man for man you're much better than any of these fellows ever will be. You can lick them and we're going to do it."[56]

Orders to unit leaders were at times so vague they had no clear idea of where they were supposed to go. Odlum recalled the experience:

> We were told to find out where the gap was and go and fill it. And I had to find out in darkness of night with all that turmoil going, what had happened where it had happened, where we were to go and how we were to get in. And I remember going over and seeing Colonel Loomis of the 13th Battalion who was just on the edge of the break — casualties all around him, his Headquarters just filled with moaning, groaning, bleeding men. All Loomis knew was that it happened out that way. So I went back to Colonel McHarg and told him the situation as I had found it and then we started to move into that black darkness and be ready to block it when day-light came. We had a pretty bad time. The Germans were there with the aftermath of the gas and they were all around us. The great bulk of our men got down into trenches or ditches or anything low because you avoided bullets by doing that, but you didn't avoid the gas, you took it … Fortunately for us it was thinning out by the time it had reached us … and we were able to make a plug at a point where the break had occurred, and somewhere on the other side of that hole the Germans were. They couldn't do anything more until the morning came, too.[57]

The first report of a gas attack did not reach Second Army Headquarters until 6:45 p.m., although General Smith-Dorrien, who was returning on foot to Ypres after visiting Hill 60, had himself observed the cloud moving toward the French lines. At 7:45 p.m., two messages arrived, indicating that a disaster had occurred. The first told of the French retirement and the second erroneously reported that the left of the 3rd Canadian Brigade had been forced back to Wieltje. Subsequently General Putz confirmed that the enemy had used asphyxiating gas, adding incorrectly that his right was at Pilckem. Even at that, it meant that a gap of over 3000 yards had been forced open between the French and the Canadians. Smith-Dorrien was in despair. Currie recorded his feelings when he spoke to him early in May 1915:

> He told me that when he first heard of the gas attack and retirement of the French Colonial troops he threw up his hands and foresaw the greatest disaster that ever overtook the British Army. He said that if every man in the salient had tried to get out that night he would not have blamed them, and when he pictured all the men, guns and transport crossing the few bridges over the canal, with a victorious army thundering at their heels, he shuddered. Then, he said he got a message that the Canadians were holding on. At first he refused to believe it and sent his own staff officer to verify the report.[58]

As a first step toward re-establishing the line, Smith-Dorrien released the 1st Canadian Infantry Brigade from army reserve and placed it at the disposal of the V Corps. Plumer, whose headquarters were at Poperinghe, in turn, handed back half the brigade, the 2nd and 3rd Battalions, to Alderson. At the same time, Plumer turned over to Alderson the 2nd East Yorkshires, then in hutments a mile northwest of Ypres.[59] This unit, which formed part of the 28th Division's reserve, was the first of 33 British battalions to come under Alderson's command during the battle.

By 8:45 p.m., V Corps Headquarters had received sufficient information to conclude that both of Putz's divisions had been driven from their first and second lines of defence, with the loss of all their guns, and that there were no formed bodies of French troops east of the canal, except at Steenstraat. A glance at the map showed that the gap was not

3000 yards, but nearly 8000, providing the enemy with a clear path to menace Ypres and take in the rear the three British divisions still holding the salient. It was clear to Plumer that other reserves had to be found before such a threat developed into an overwhelming disaster.

Alderson's counterparts on the right, Major-General Edward S. Bulfin and Major-General Thomas D'Oyly Snow, who commanded, respectively, the 28th and 27th divisions, had grasped the fact that, except for a few Canadian dispositions scattered here and there, the Second Army's left flank lay open. On their own initiative, these two divisional commanders dispatched some of their own reserves to the threatened flank. The 27th Division moved the 4th Battalion and the 2nd KSLI (King's Shropshire Light Infantry) to the St. Jean-Potijze area. The 28th Division contributed four battalions. The 2nd East Kents, more familiarly known as the Buffs, and the 3rd Middlesex, in billets and bivouacs near St. Jean, marched to the ridge north of the village and deployed westward as far as the Yser Canal. The 1st York and Lancaster Regiment, in reserve west of Ypres, was called forward to reinforce St. Jean. The 5th King's Own Royal Regiment was held in reserve. These four battalions were placed under the command of Colonel A.D. Geddes of the Buffs, and for the next five days fought at the disposal of the Canadian Division.[60] It should be pointed out that the composition of Geddes's force varied almost from day to day and, for that reason, was simply known as "Geddes's Detachment."

As the various British units marched toward their allocated places, Alderson received a hand-delivered note from 3rd Brigade Headquarters. In it, Turner reported that the rumours his brigade had been forced back were erroneous and that the original line was still in place.[61] This was good news, but the situation remained highly dangerous. The left flank of the Second British Army ended abruptly just west of Mouse Trap Farm and in the whole of this distance only three points were held: McCuaig, with several hundred Highlanders and Tirailleurs, occupied a ditch at the northern end; two and a half companies under Loomis covered St. Julien; and the 14th Battalion was in the vicinity of Mouse Trap Farm. These dispositions left unguarded three great gaps of 2000 yards, 1000 yards, and 3000 yards. Even after the arrival of reinforcements, it was hard

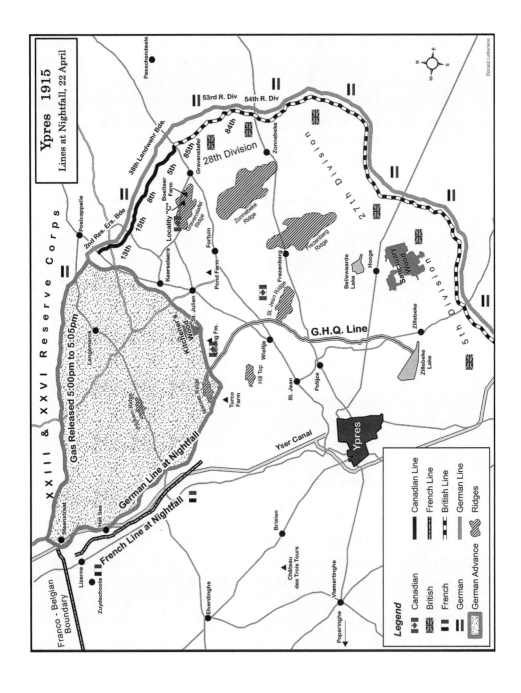

Ypres 1915
Lines at Nightfall, 22 April

Donald Laffenière

Passchendaele

53rd R. Div   54th R. Div

38th Landwehr Bde.

84th

85th

Gravenstafel

28th Division

Zonnebeke

27th Division

Bootleer Farm

Locality "C"

5th

8th

15th

13th

Gravenstafel Ridge

Zonnebeke Ridge

Frezenberg Ridge

Bellewaarde Lake

Hooge

Sanctuary Wood

2nd Res. Ers Bde.

Poelcappelle

Keerselaere

Fortuin

Pond Farm

Frezenberg

St. Jean Ridge

Zillebeke

X X I I I   &   X X V I   R e s e r v e   C o r p s

Gas Released 5:00pm to 5:05pm

St. Julien

Kitchener's Wood

Vanheule Fm.

Wieltje

Hill Top

G.H.Q. Line

Zillebeke Lake

Langemarck

Mauser Ridge

Pilckem Ridge

Turco Farm

St. Jean

Potijze

German Line at Nightfall

French Line at Nightfall

Steenstraat

Het Sas

Yser Canal

Ypres

5th Division

Lizerne

Zuydschoote

Franco - Belgian Boundary

Brielen

Château des Trois Tours

Vlamertinghe

Elverdinghe

Poperinghe

N
E
W
S

Legend

Canadian Line
French Line
British Line
German Line
Ridges

Canadian
British
French
German
German Advance

to see how the new flank, unprotected by wire and with only makeshift trenches, could possibly maintain a prolonged resistance.

Suddenly, with victory practically in their grasp, the Germans halted their drive. Von Falkenhayn, underestimating the effects of the new weapon, had not provided the means to convert the break-in into a breakthrough. Only one division was available in army reserve and when released the next day, was given to the XXIII Reserve Corps, not the XXVI, which had made the deepest penetration. There had been no arrangements to carry out special tactical training for the troops following up the gas cloud. The attacking infantrymen advanced two miles when they stumbled into their own poisoned fumes and cautiously held back. They had only been issued crude respirators, which many had not bothered to wear owing to the difficulty in breathing. Passing through the French trenches, they were struck by the unprecedented scene of horror and apparently became concerned about their own safety. The fear of gas, together with the high-spirited stand of the Canadians, made the Germans only too willing to stop and dig in as soon as they had reached their assigned objectives. Canadian survivors, interviewed for CBC, make it clear that the Germans were unwilling to press forward upon meeting the slightest resistance. Typical was the experience of Sergeant-Major C.B. Price (14th Battalion) who, along with a certain Stewart Le Mesurier, had been sent out to investigate whether the large bodies of troops ahead were French or German. Price explained:

> Just then he [Le Mesurier] saw two men coming fairly close down this hill to us and he challenged them, and one of them put up his rifle and shot him, shot him through the hand. So then just instinctively I put up my rifle and I shot both of them. And I rather think that the fact that their scouts were shot made them feel that there was a force there and instead of being able to go right through as they could have, they stopped and dug in themselves.[62]

By holding back, the Germans failed to discover the extent of their success and the weakness of the Canadian line hastily thrown in the path of their flank. And on the days that followed they showed the same lack of ardour, merely moving forward to occupy the patches of ground that their artillery and gas had practically swept free of defenders. If the Germans had pressed their advantage on the 22nd, there is good reason to suppose that the Ypres salient, with its garrison numbering upwards of 50,000 men and 150 guns, would have fallen.

Chapter 5
The Deadly Counterattacks

As darkness fell on 22 April, and enemy pressure slackened, large numbers of wounded were evacuated from the trenches, where some had been languishing near death, groaning for hours in their own blood and feces, waiting to be carried to medical facilities. With too few stretcher-bearers — only four to a company — there were those who did not need or want to wait for help. The slightly injured could walk rearward for treatment. There were others, bleeding badly or with broken limbs, who should not have been standing, let alone moving, often stumbling and crawling in an attempt to make it back on their own.

The work of stretchers-bearers was not only exhausting, but dangerous. Racing across the muddy, pitted battlefield under the rain of shells, they brought in their pain-wracked burdens to the Regimental Aid Post (RAP). The RAPs were set up immediately behind the lines, normally at every battalion's support trenches, and as far as possible equidistant from each of the companies at the front. At each RAP, a medical officer, aided by an NCO and several orderlies, assessed the condition of the patients walking in or carried in. The RAP was not a place where delicate surgery was performed, but rather it was a sort of casualty ward where the patient was given stabilizing care.

After the patients received first aid, they were taken by field ambulances to a rearward Advanced Dressing Station (ADS), located within the fire zone at some place along the road — such as at Wieltje or Mouse Trap Farm. Here, their wounds were checked, their dressings changed, their broken limbs set if possible, and morphine administered to dullen the pain. Ambulances conveyed the disabled to the next relay point, the Main Dressing Station, where they were sorted out and classified according to the nature of their injury. Given that the doctors were badly overworked, they tended to bypass men deemed lost causes and administer care to those with a greater chance of surviving. Private David Shand and his British regiment (1st Gordon Highlanders) stopped in a trench next to an ADS on their way to the front.[1] He described a scene of severely gassed soldiers who were dying or already dead:

> There were about two hundred to three hundred men lying in that ditch. Some were clawing at their throats. Their brass buttons were green. Their bodies were swelled. Some of them were still alive. They were not wearing their belts or equipment and we thought they were Germans. One inquisitive fellow turned a dead man over. He saw a brass clip bearing the name CANADA on the corpse's shoulder and exclaimed, "These are Canadians!" Some of us said, 'For the love of Mike! We never knew that!" Some of the Canadians were still writhing on the ground, their tongues hanging out.[2]

Minor cases were operated on and kept at the MDS (Main Dressing Station) until they were fit to be transferred to the Casualty Clearing Station. Patients with superficial wounds were given rest and treatment for a few days and sent either back to their units or to a convalescent camp in the neighbourhood. Those requiring specialized surgery were transferred to other hospitals.

The Casualty Clearing Station was well behind the firing line so that it could not be shelled by enemy artillery and was always situated in the vicinity of a railhead. Its primary function was to provide immediate post-operative care. The patients were then placed aboard an ambulance train and carried to the base, the final stage in their journey.

For everyone concerned, the early days of the Second Battle of Ypres were a nightmare. As the wounded continued to pour into the aid stations, additional accommodations were sought in adjoining houses and in billets of nearby army units. The clearing of the wounded was no less urgent and everything imaginable was used for transport — horse-drawn vehicles, motor lorries, omnibuses, village carts, and gun limbers. Doctors and the medical staff laboured by the dim light of lamps and candles, and, in spite of their unremitting work, the long rows of stretcher cases in the courtyards never seemed to diminish. Frequently, aid stations were forced to move on account of enemy shelling.

It is not known exactly how many wounded passed through the hands of the Canadian Army Medical Corps throughout the Second Battle of Ypres. No. 3 Field Ambulance alone treated some 5200 cases.[3] A member of the staff wrote that within a 24-hour period, they attended to 1800 cases:

> The wounded came at such a great pace, it was a great job to attend them all. Some awful wounds were attended to, gashes large enough to put your fist in, many came with bullet wounds, many poor boys will have to have there [sic] arms or legs taken off. Other poor fellows will never live to tell the tale. As fast as possible we take the wounded a distance of 6 miles to Poperinghe, ready for a departure to the base, England or elsewhere.[4]

Since the start of the war probably no other unit of the British Army attended to as many wounded during a comparable period as did the Canadian Army Medical Corps. Yet, in an age before the use of antibiotics, the quality of medical care was remarkably effective. Despite severe abdominal and head injuries and the septic conditions at the front that encouraged infections and gas gangrene, 93 percent of wounded soldiers seeking medical treatment during the war survived. Strangely enough, it was a rate higher than even in the Second World War.[5]

At 8:00 p.m. on 22 April, before it was known that the Germans had halted, a French liaison officer arrived at Alderson's Headquarters with a request from General Putz for Canadian assistance in a counterattack that the 45th Division was preparing to launch toward Pilckem. It is incomprehensible why such an appeal was made.[6] The Algerian Division was in no position to attack as it had lost all its artillery and its surviving

Courtesy of In Flanders Fields Museum.

Panoramic view of Kitchener's Wood today.

infantry was in terrible disarray. This was unknown to Alderson, who felt that concerted pressure on both sides of the breach might compel the enemy to fall back. Thus Alderson ordered Turner to clear Kitchener's Wood and then, in co-operation with the French, direct his advance slightly east of Pilckem. Turner was told to begin his counterattack as soon as his reinforcements had arrived.[7]

The assault to retake Kitchener's Wood was the only counterattack mounted during the Second Battle of Ypres that was operationally sound in its conception. The Canadians were not expected to attack, and under the cover of night would retain the element of surprise practically until the moment of impact. The Germans had neither the strength of numbers nor the time to prepare fixed defences. Then, too, the objective was well chosen. The capture of Kitchener's Wood would deny the Germans of an obvious jumping-off place for an attack against nearby St.Julien; and cause them to interrupt their advance or risk a British buildup inside their left flank.

Aerial view of Kitchener's Wood taken by a German pilot in April 1916.

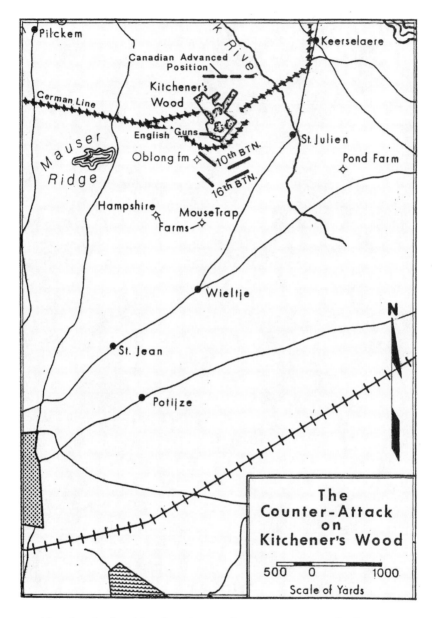

The Counter-Attack on Kitchener's Wood

Scale of Yards

Alas the deplorable planning and execution ruined what was an eminently feasible operation. There was no prearranged set of objectives beyond clearing the Germans out of the woods or plan to consolidate gains. Artillery support, vital in any ground operation, was practically non-existent. "The only artillery preparation I was aware of was that about three shells were fired at the wood," Lieutenant-Colonel Leckie, commanding the 16th Battalion, later told Duguid. "I understand there was no ammunition."[8] The enemy's exact location was unknown, as there had been no time for reconnaissance. Consequently the two Canadian battalions would be advancing blindly toward a dark blur. On top of this, the standard formation of men advancing shoulder-to-shoulder in straight lines may have been suitable for early 19th-century warfare, but certainly not after the invention of the magazine rifle and machine gun.

Although the instructions for the assault were issued at 9:40 p.m., it was not until almost midnight that the troops for the purpose, the 10th and 16th Battalions, were ready to move out. The 16th was late in reporting. "We had a lot of difficulty getting up that road," H.H. Oldaker explained. "You see there was only the one road going up there and there was artillery traffic and supplies and civilians and ambulances coming back."[9] For a time 3rd Brigade Headquarters feared that the 10th Battalion would have to go in alone.

The two battalions, with the 10th in the lead and the 16th in close support, formed up about 1000 yards from the enemy. The 10th was divided into four lines, each separated by 30 yards, with the ranks shoulder-to-shoulder along a two company front (about 300 yards). The 16th, 30 yards in the rear, was in the same formation, except the distance between each line was 20 yards. A hundred bombers drawn from the 2nd and 3rd brigades accompanied the 1500-man force.[10]

While the troops stood in silence, officers synchronized their watches at 11:30 p.m. for the attack scheduled to start 15 minutes later. Words of encouragement were given to all ranks. "We have been aching for a fight," Lieutenant-Colonel Boyle (10th Battalion) told his men, "and now we are going to get it."[11] The much-beloved Canon Frederick Scott of Montreal, who had accompanied the 16th, passed through the ranks, shaking hands and proclaiming "A Great Day for Canada, boys! A Great Day for Canada, boys!"[12] The mood among the men was upbeat, for they were anxious to prove themselves in their first big fight. "Belive me there was some excitement in the ranks," Sergeant J.C. Matheson wrote in a letter to his father. "We didn't seem to realize what we were up against."[13]

The troops took off their packs and greatcoats and fixed their 17-inch bayonets. There was no moon, so the night was dark and only a dim outline of the wood could be seen. As a guide, the men were told to follow the North Star, which appeared to be directly above the wood.[14] At 11:45 p.m., the signal was given and the Canadians moved forward, only the steady tramp of over 3000 feet and the slap of empty scabbards against the thighs could be heard. The men had covered half the distance to the wood when the leading wave of the 10th Battalion ran into an unexpected obstacle — one of the unfortunate consequences of failing to reconnoitre the lay of the land. It was a hedge, four to six feet high, with a thick strand of wire threading through it, presumably at one time to act as support. There was a momentary pause as the men in the lead, using entrenching tools and wire cutters, wriggled through and resumed their advance. With so many men stumbling and running into each other in the dark, noise was inevitable. Boyle's adjutant, Major Dan Ormond (10th Battalion) had this to say: "There was no talking, not a word, but with your entrenching tool and bayonet scabbards and the rifle butts, that created a great deal of noise."[15] Predictably, the noise alerted the enemy. Suddenly, a shower of flares lit up the countryside and the Germans opened rapid fire with rifle and machine gun. The Canadians immediately hit the ground.[16] A.M. McLennan (16th Battalion) remarked that "to green troops ... it was an appalling experience to start with, a stunning experience."[17] Suddenly Major James Lightfoot, a company commander (10th Battalion,) rose, and cried out "Come on boys, remember that you're Canadians," and charged towards the enemy's trench, some 40 yards in front of the woods, inspiring the others to follow his lead.[18] Over an open field, the Canadians advanced by a series of rushes. "We went down flat, then up, then down again," wrote a platoon commander, "but the only distinct impression is that of a bare flat piece of ground, the German flares going up, and the ceaseless, angry, zip, zip of the bullets and machine gun fire. Then came the cries of those who were hit."[19] Private Percy Allen (10th Battalion) saw his company commander, Captain F. Pott, fall "right in front of his men — his revolver empty and only a cane for defence."[20] Bunched as they were, the Canadians presented an ideal target. Enemy machine guns ripped out and rifles crackled, tearing large gaps in the advancing line that others behind filled, until they fell in turn.[21] A soldier on the scene recalled that "the whole front line seemed to melt away, only to be instantly closed up again."[22]

An especially troublesome spot to the west was Oblong Farm, from where enemy machine guns added to the deadly toll. Boyle had turned down the suggestion made by some of his officers that he should send a platoon to take the farm.[23] Boyle speculated that the element of surprise would enable his men to dash across the open field before the enemy had time to react. It was a serious miscalculation.

Some the survivors of the attack have left their impressions of the gruesome scene. "The wood seemed to be literally lined with machine guns, and they played these guns on us with terrible effect," Sergeant Matheson wrote. "Our men were dropping thick and fast."[24] Private Gerald Hartman (16th Battalion), said that the fire was so intense that it seemed no one could live through it unscathed. "We went down in hundreds," he noted.[25] Another soldier of the 10th Battalion recalled that "the rank in front of me seemed to melt away." An NCO (10th Battalion) painted a more graphic picture: "Men fell all around me. It was a ghastly sight … Our dead and wounded were lying in heaps."[26]

Given the murderous wall of fire coming from the front and left flank, the ranks wavered and swayed for an instant, but encouraged by their officers — in particular Captain John Geddes of the 16th, a former football player, who, although mortally wounded, struggled valiantly on hands and knees, shouting "Come on!"— they recovered their balance and, with cries and cheers, jumped over the bodies of their fallen comrades and surged forward until they reached the enemy's trench.[27] "We bayoneted the Germans who remained in the trench and chased the balance who had made for the wood in the rear of the trench," Captain H.A. Duncan (16th Battalion) noted.[28]

Here it was so dark that the men could not see more than a few feet in front of them. Marching over unknown ground, the units lost direction and cohesion after encountering large bodies of Germans. The ensuing strife, much of it hand-to-hand, was fierce. One participant described what happened:

Pressing on into the wood the struggle became a dreadful hand-to-hand conflict; we fought in clumps and batches, and the living struggled over the bodies of the dead and dying. At the height of the conflict, while we were steadily driving the Germans before us, the moon burst out ... The clashing bayonets flashed like quicksilver, and faces were lit up as by limelight.

Sweeping on, we came upon lines of trenches that had been hastily thrown up and could not be stubbornly defended. Here all who resisted were bayoneted: those who yielded were sent to the rear. The trench fighting presented a spectacle which is not pleasant to recall.[29]

A diarist, lucky to have avoided the fate of many of his comrades, related his own experience:

I vaguely saw some Germans and rushed at the nearest one. My bayonet must have hit his equipment and glanced off, but luckily for me, another chap running beside me bayoneted him before he got me. By this time I was wildly excited and shouting and rushing into the wood up a path towards a big gun which was pointed away from us. Going through the wood we ran into several Germans, but I had now lost confidence in my bayonet and always fired.[30]

A good deal of the fighting centred around German strong points, which were scattered throughout the woods. Private Sid Cox (10th Battalion) described what happened to him when he entered one of these little forts:

It was all so mixed up you just didn't know for anything. That's where I got the biggest scare of my life. I went into a bit of a hut there. I went to go in and a great big German stepped out and he may've been going to surrender, I couldn't tell you, but I got out of there in a hurry. I pulled the trigger and ran. Boy that man startled me. I didn't expect anything.[31]

The Germans were driven back farther and farther into the woods by the almost uncontrollable fury of the Canadians. "Many Germans were encountered in the woods, some of whom surrendered, but the majority were bayoneted or shot," Leckie's account recounted. "Many, however, escaped by dodging through the underbrush".[32] Private Percy Allen and his friend Billy Neal were in the lead with a group Canadians, "jabbing here — stabbing there — killing wounded men, because if we didn't they'd shoot us in the back as we went past." At one point while Allen was engaged with an opponent, Neal came face to face with a Prussian estimated to be six-foot-six. He "parried, lunged and then lunged again quickly," taking "all the lower part of the Prussian's face away." Later they tried to "stick the part to the whole," only to discover that the Prussian was dead.[33] In the woods, the Canadians stumbled upon four guns that Leckie judged to have been abandoned by the French. In fact, they belonged to the 2nd London Battery, which had been captured during the Germans' first rush the previous evening (22 April).

The two Canadian battalions halted when they reached the northern fringes of the wood and proceeded to dig in. Around 1:00 a.m. Leckie dispatched a message to 3rd Brigade Headquarters. He reported that the wood had been carried and that four guns had been recaptured. He requested reinforcements to secure his flank and a team of horses to remove the guns.[34]

At this moment, trouble developed in the rear. The sound of musketry fire was punctuated by a shout in good English, "We have you surrounded: surrender."[35] The demand was ignored, but an investigation showed that this came from a German redoubt at the southwestern extremity of the wood, about 15 yards from the captured trench. A mixed party of 34 men, led by Major Ormond, was detailed to deal with the stronghold. But as the men tried to outflank the German position, they were cut down by machine-gun fire or blown to bits by bombs and grenades. After half of his force was killed or wounded, Ormond withdrew, whereupon it was decided to dig a cross trench to cover the Canadian flank.[36] Subsequently, it was discovered that the redoubt was part of a strongly held trench system extending westward. East of the wood, on the opposite flank, the Germans were in force and touch could not be established with the garrison in St. Julien. There was, moreover, continued rifle fire from the northwest, indicating that the enemy still occupied that corner of the wood.[37]

The position now held by the Canadians in the woods was 1000 yards behind the enemy's line. Whether they could maintain control over all the ground regained was another matter. The anticipated French attack on the left had not taken place. The absence of a post-battle plan, the intermingling of units and the losses, especially among the officers, hampered consolidation. Further difficulties were created by the enemy's tremendous concentration of artillery fire, which swept "the wood as a tropical storm sweeps the leaves from the trees of a forest."[38]

The senior officials of the two battalions met to discuss the next course of action. Surrounded as they were on three sides, the consensus was that it was too dangerous to defend the woods. Ormond told the CBC that "we knew we were over half a mile in behind the Boche, right in the middle of them, the only thing I could see was to go back because the forces we knew were assembled by the Boche, they'd get in behind us and scupper the works."[39] Thus, they withdrew most of their forces to the former German trench while leaving a handful of men to hold on to the advanced line in the hope that reinforcements would be forthcoming.

The assault on Kitchener's Wood was still in progress when the 2nd and 3rd Battalions (1st Brigade) reported to Mouse Trap Farm shortly after 1:00 a.m. Divisional Headquarters had sent these units earlier with instructions to Turner that he was to use them primarily to extend his left so as "to fill the gap between you and the French."[40] But instead Turner kept the two battalions nearby, in anticipation that they might be required to assist in the assault on Kitchener's Wood. When he received word that the attack had been successful, he directed Lieutenant-Colonel David Watson to move his 2nd Battalion forward to reinforce the 10th and 16th Battalions. Watson made his way in darkness, arriving at Juliet Farm, Leckie's Headquarters, shortly after 3:00 a.m. A conference with Leckie followed, during which both men agreed that it was vital to strengthen the flanks. The major threat to Leckie's position was the troublesome redoubt at the southwest corner of Kitchener's Wood. Watson dispatched No. 1 Company, under Major George Bennett, to attack the strong point; No. 3 Company (Captain Geoffrey Chrysler) to swing farther left and take Oblong Farm; and No. 2 Company (Captain Claude Culling) to extend the right of the 16th Battalion in the direction of St. Julien.[41]

As the companies set out toward their objectives, they were hampered by the darkness, unfamiliarity with the ground, and broken fields. On top of this, Bennett was unable to make a night attack because he had spent too much time reconnoitering the German position. As dawn approached, his men crept silently forward, but at 200 yards the mist suddenly lifted and they were spotted by German machine-gunners, who opened fire. Over open ground with little protection to hide behind, the company was cut to ribbons, and, of the dozen or so who managed to drag themselves back, nearly all were wounded. "My God! What an awful night we have had," a depressed Watson wrote in his diary. "Lost almost 200 men and 6 officers of No. 1 Coy."[42] The attack, though unproductive and costly, had created a diversion sufficient to allow the other companies to achieve their objectives. No. 3 Company captured Oblong Farm while No. 2 Company cleared a German outpost on the right of the 16th Battalion and established a line 200 yards toward St. Julien.

The failure of Bennett's attack raised fears that the Canadians on the north end of the wood might be cut off. Therefore, after another consultation between the officers on the spot, orders went out to evacuate the forward position. As the horses had not yet arrived, the guns could not be removed, but their ammunition was destroyed.

The coming of light revealed the enemy's grisly work of the night before. Hundreds of dead and wounded lay upon the open field, piled on one another or at intervals so close that it would have been almost impossible to walk through the area without stepping on a body. Pitiful groans could be heard and some of the bodies moved or twitched, but, in the face of German fire, rescue attempts had to be abandoned. For the survivors of the 10th and 16th Battalions, the nightmare was not over. Inside the trench, G. Dunlop (16th Battalion) recalled that "we were

What remained of Kitchener's Wood in 1919.

crawling over dead bodies and guts and everything sprawled all over the place."[43] Although the captured trench was in reasonable shape from a defensive standpoint, it was far from providing iron-clad protection against the enemy's almost constant artillery and machine-gun fire. The men were cold, hungry, and thirsty as they had discarded their greatcoats and packs before the attack. Additionally, enemy activity in the distance seemed to suggest that an attack was impending — as it turned out nothing materialized. The men, one diarist recorded, "looked frightfully tired and discouraged."[44] Despite the adverse conditions, however, they remained steadfast until relieved on the 24th.

The Canadians had suffered staggering casualties. The 10th was able to muster only five officers and 188 other ranks out of more than 800 men. Lieutenant-Colonel Boyle died from multiple bullet wounds and his second in command, Major Joseph MacLaren, also hit, was killed by a shell while on his way to the hospital. The command passed to Major Ormond. The 16th had lost its adjutant and three company commanders.

Memorial to the 10th and 16th Battalions at Kitchener's Wood.

Only five officers and 263 other ranks were able to answer the roll.[45] Later, when the troops acquired experience, they would learn to attack in open formation, preserve momentum by reinforcing the points of ongoing progress, consolidate in stages, maintain a reserve against the unforeseen, and bring stores with them in the third or fourth wave. But all of this was unknown to them at the time, and, as a result, they paid a high price for their ignorance. The number of German casualties is unknown. But according to Leckie, who observed large clusters of German bodies in and outside the woods, their losses "must have been very severe."[46]

The two raw battalions had done everything that was humanly possible in their first major action, displaying courage, discipline, and an esprit de corps. Their efforts had earned them the grudging respect of the enemy. A German officer captured by the 10th Battalion remarked, "You fellows fight like hell."[47] After the fighting was over, Private Allen spotted a German who "raised himself to a sitting position and saluted us saying 'Brave men, brave men,' and then he fell back dead."[48] Nor did the mettle of the Canadians escape the attention of Allied leaders. Foch considered the Canadian counterattack as "the finest act of the war,"[49] and made a similar statement during an interview in 1919.[50] Smith-Dorrien was equally complimentary when he visited the 16th Battalion on 5 May and spoke to the surviving officers. According to a diarist, the general said that the German gas attack had placed the Allied position in critical danger and produced great anxiety in the minds of Allied leaders. He went on to say, "The counter-attack by the 10th and 16th Battalions was launched at such a moment and did everything to restore the situation and confuse the enemy. The General … asked Col. Leckie to thank all ranks for maintaining the high tradition of the British Army."[51]

For the weary Canadian survivors, who only a few hours earlier had been itching to fight the Germans, the action at Kitchener's Wood and its grizzly consequences, shattered their naive assumption about the nature of modern warfare. In fact, their experience had a numbing effect. Many wept openly after the names of comrades, with whom they had established a close rapport, were called out and met only with a silence. Percy Allen explained how he felt:

> I have wanted to see a fight and now that I have done so I don't want any more. I think … of all the dead and dying lying about in contorted shapes. One poor chap lay with his chin in his hands — eyes wide open … but a little blue hole in his forehead. That sight, combined with the cries of the wounded during the night, I shall never forget.[52]

To fill the 500-yard gap between the right of the 2nd Battalion and the St. Julien garrison, Turner sent up two companies of the 3rd Battalion under Major Kirkpatrick. Their objective was a German trench some 400 yards in length about a mile and a half away. Leaving at 6:00 a.m., Kirkpatrick and his men had gone about a mile when they ran into heavy enemy fire. "Our lads were falling pretty fast; our officers even faster," Private Peat wrote. "The machine-gun fire was hellish. The infantry fire was blinding … It seemed that no one could live in such a hail of lead." In the lead, Captain Joseph Straight, whom the men idolized, was wounded in the leg, but continued to crawl ahead, crying out "Come on, lads — come on." The Canadians continued to surge forward with one soldier remarking afterwards, "Fellows, I'd have followed him to Hell, and then some!" Coming to grips with the Germans, they took possession of the trench after fierce hand-to-hand combat. Out of 750 men, only 250 were left standing at the conclusion of the engagement.[53]

At 2:00 a.m., prior to giving Kirkpatrick his orders, Turner telephoned 2nd Brigade Headquarters and urgently requested help on the grounds that the enemy was in strength at Keerselaere and north of it.[54] Currie, whose front was relatively quiet, at once ordered, the 7th Battalion (less one company) under Lieutenant-Colonel William Hart-McHarg to march westward from Locality C and fill the gap between St. Julien and the end of Gravenstafel Ridge. No resistance was encountered in the darkness and by 3:20 a.m., Hart-McHarg reported that his left was in touch with the St. Julien garrison and his right with support troops of the 15th Battalion. His request from 2nd Brigade Headquarters that he be allowed to attack nearby Germans was turned down and he was ordered to fortify his position.[55]

But, north of Keerselaere, for a distance of over half a mile, the Allied flank still lay open. The next defended area was the new apex of the salient where the 13th and a small group of Zouaves lined the ditch along the Poelcappelle road. For McCuaig and his dwindling band, the situation remained desperate. The Germans, apart from enjoying an overwhelming superiority in guns and numbers, had plenty of flares, and, being able to command light at their pleasure, kept up the pressure all night. They rained shells on the trenches below and twice followed up with grenades and bayonet charges. Bleeding and exhausted though they were, McCuaig's men drove back both attacks after inflicting severe losses. The defenders kept up a steady fire all night. McCuaig's purpose in doing so, notwithstanding the expenditure of his limited stock of ammunition, was to disguise from the Germans the weakness of his force.

Reinforcements arrived shortly before dawn — to the delight of McCuaig's weary troops. These consisted of No. 2 Company of the 2nd East Kent (Buffs) — loaned by Geddes — under Captain F.W. Tomlinson and two platoons of No. 3 Company of the 13th Battalion which, until a few hours ago, had formed part of the St. Julien garrison. The mixed force was led by Major Victor Buchanan, who, as a result of Norsworthy's death, was now second in command of the regiment. Buchanan assumed control of the operations upon arrival.

Not long afterwards, a cluster of figures, apparently wearing French uniforms, but indistinct in the early morning light, appeared in the rear of the Algerian trenches, crying out "We are the French." McCuaig, Tomlinson of the Buffs, and a French officer were standing at a point where the trenches crossed the road. They suspected a ruse, and, after failing to receive satisfactory responses to their queries, ordered their troops to open fire. Scrambling for cover, the imposters replied in kind.[56] No attack materialized, although German shelling was nonstop, and, directed by airplanes, extremely accurate. As the trenches were shallow with no parados, they did not offer good protection. "I lost during the day a considerable number, but I think, all from the rear or from 'whiz bang' bursts," Tomlinson wrote. The British officer put his finger on another problem they faced during daylight hours: "We could not ... engage the German trenches in front, because in doing so we expose ourselves to fire from the rear, so we kept our eye on the trenches with periscopes, and dealt with the enemy in rear."[57] Although the Canadian garrison continued to take casualties, it remained unwavering in its determination to hang on.

A dangerous gap of some 3000 yards remained west of the 2nd Battalion's flank at Oblong Farm. Had the Germans driven down the road from Pilckem to Ypres, they would have been able to encircle the whole Allied forces in the salient. Thus at 1:05 a.m., Alderson ordered Colonel Geddes to push forward from St. Jean and fill the gap between the left of the Canadians at Kitchener's Wood and the right of Putz's battalions, "driving back any enemy that may have penetrated."[58] Duguid acknowledged that Geddes was a fine soldier, to use his words, "a regular officer, a graduate of Staff College and tried in the 1914 campaign." Nevertheless, since his force had been put together only a few hours earlier, he had to improvise a staff, and there was bound to be a lack of coordination because his units were scattered. It is interesting to speculate why the task was not assigned to Mercer, an obvious choice. His men were ready to move out, and he was closer to the scene, enjoyed a complete headquarters staff and was senior to Geddes. Duguid hints that Mercer was bypassed because Alderson did not have confidence in his leadership.[59]

Told that haste was essential, Geddes got his detachment underway before daybreak. His plan called for the Buffs to move forward and link up with the left flank of Turner's 3rd Brigade, the 3rd Middlesex to try to gain touch with the French right, and for the King's Own Rifles to advance in the centre. From Wieltje, the Buffs pushed northward over open, practically level ground, and, passing west of Mouse Trap Farm, came under furious machine-gun fire. After losing two officers and 80 men they sought cover in some old trenches beyond the farm where they eventually established contact with men of the 14th Canadian Battalion. The 3rd Middlesex, in the course of driving forward between Hill Top and Pilckem, was surprised when its two left companies came into contact with the 1st and 4th Canadian Battalions. Geddes's operation was in progress when he was informed of the movement of these two Canadian battalions.[60] What had caused them to take the field?

During the night, 1st Divisional Headquarters hurriedly improvised a second counterattack, to be carried out by such forces as were available. Foch had urged Putz to organize a counterattack with the ultimate object of regaining the lost ground. The idea was for Mordacq (90th Brigade) to advance on Pilckem with two battalions, while his flank was covered by the 87th Territorial Division, which was expected to force a crossing of the Yser. These French units were too shattered to execute the plan, yet Putz requested that the British co-operate by attacking northwards from their exposed flank. Shortly after midnight, Plumer and Alderson conferred to discuss the proposed operation. They might have had second thoughts if they had known that the French had failed earlier to support the 10th and 16th Battalions in Kitchener's Wood.

Alderson had no clear idea of the location of the French right, so, as a preliminary move, he ordered the two remaining battalions of the First Brigade, the 1st and 4th, to take up a position east of the canal. It was not until 3:45 a.m. that Alderson received his instructions, whereupon he immediately contacted Mercer: "At 5 o'clock two French battalions are to make a counter-attack against Pilckem with their right resting on Pilckem-Ypres Road. You will co-operate with this attack at the same time with your left on this road."[61] To say that Mercer did not have much time to organize his attack would be an understatement. He received Alderson's telegram at 4:15, 45 minutes before the projected French attack was timed to begin. The Canadian push northward was to take place on the left of Geddes's flank.

At 4:30 the two Canadian battalions, the 1st under Lieutenant-Colonel Fred Hill, and the 4th commanded by Lieutenant-Colonel Arthur Birchall, assembled slightly behind the crest of Hill Top Ridge. The 4th Battalion, deployed in four lines along a 200-yard front, was in the lead. No. 2 and No. 4 companies of the 1st Battalion were to follow in two lines with the remaining two companies held in reserve. A short time earlier, as already noted, the Canadian right had come into contact with two companies of the 3rd Middlesex, part of Geddes's Detachment. At the request of Mercer, the two British units agreed to join in the counterattack.

The first objective was to seize Mauser Ridge, a low hill some 1500 yards to the north. The field between the Canadians and the ridge was dotted with piles of manure and bisected by willow trees. Beyond Hill Top Ridge, the ground sloped slightly for several hundred yards when it began to rise gently to the top of Mauser Ridge, approximately 30 feet above the surrounding plain. The defenders had a clear view of the field, particularly the last half. "There was about two thousand yards of open country up to the Pilckem [Mauser] Ridge," recalled G.W. Twigg (4th Battalion).[62] Another participant claimed that most of the field over which they had to cross was "as level as a billiard table."[63]

As the sun rose, the Canadians could clearly see swarms of Germans digging assiduously and laying barbed-wire entanglements. Also visible a few yards from the summit of Mauser Ridge, were a farmhouse and a barn, which came to be known as Turco Farm. Everything was ready at the appointed hour, but the French had not yet appeared.

At 5:25 a.m., Birchall, mistakenly assuming that the French movement on his left was hidden by intervening trees and hedges, gave the order to advance. As it happened, the French attack never occurred in any meaningful manner, leaving the Canadians to charge up Mauser Ridge alone. Only eight light field guns and eight 4.5-inch howitzers were available to support the attack. These guns were incapable of bringing down anything like the kind of firepower needed to neutralize the defenders.

Duguid described the leading companies of the 4th Battalion as moving forward "by sections extended to ten yards and leap-frogging, followed by the other five coys."[64] What he meant was that the initial

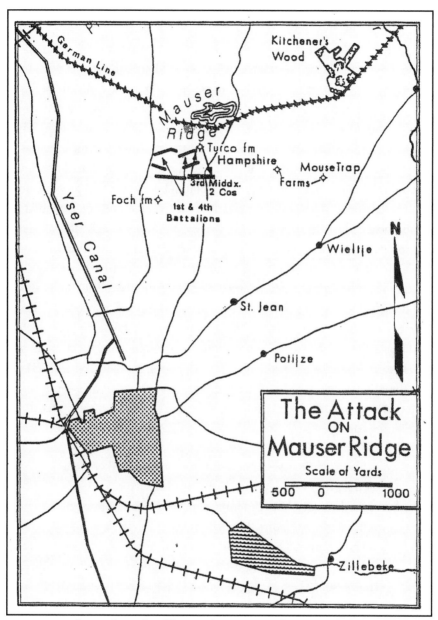

The Attack
ON
Mauser Ridge
Scale of Yards
500 0 1000

waves conformed to the "fire and movement" principles outlined in *Rapid Training of a Company for War*, a training manual Birchall had authored.[65] The idea was for small groups like a company or platoon to advance in short rushes, covered by their neighbours who would themselves rush forward under similar cover.

Along the way, the infantry lines passed Foch's Farm, where the supper from the previous evening lay untouched on the kitchen table. Looking through his binoculars, Mercer could see "the whole advance being carried out in most perfect order as if on parade," until the last line disappeared from view.[66] Mercer was kept informed of the progress of the battalions. The 4th Battalion reached the halfway point with only light casualties, prompting Birchall's counterpart, Fred Hill, to report that "all goes well so far."[67] But the good fortune of the Canadians was about to change. The Germans were holding back their fire, presumably until their field of fire was completely unobstructed and the Canadians approached closer. As the Canadians swept past the line of trees and were within about 600 yards, the Germans opened up, supplementing rifle and machine-gun fire with an intense and well-directed artillery barrage. "It did not seem possible that any human being could live in the rain of shot and shell that began to play upon us as we advanced," Corporal Edgar Wackett (1st Battalion) wrote. "For a time every other man seemed to fall."[68] As the bombs struck home, men crumbled in a hail of shrapnel or were tossed into the air by the blast of high-explosive shells. Major Kelley of the 4th was wounded and went down, but he was never seen again. Private George Bell (1st Battalion), a fortunate survivor, described the sickening carnage:

> Ahead of me I see men running. Suddenly their legs double up and they sink to the ground. Here's a body with the head shot off. I jump over it. Here's a poor devil with both legs gone, but still alive. A body of a man means nothing except something to avoid stumbling over. Its just another obstacle. There goes little Elliot, one of the boys from the print shop where I worked in Detroit, only ten yards from me. Poor devil. There's nothing I can do for him. What's one man, more or less, in this slaughter?[69]

As the field beyond the trees was open, the men looked for anything that might afford them some cover. As N.M. Young (4th Battalion) observed, the choice of many of his mates proved counter-productive: "We ran into a lot of difficulty because one of the fields we had to cross was dotted with manure piles and our men looked upon that as shelter and of course the manure piles were not only no shelter, but they were simply target attractors and we suffered a lot of casualties."[70] With men and officers falling at every step, the advance reached a row of pollard willows, which marked the shallow depression between Hill Top Ridge and Mauser Ridge, before coming to a halt. Now Major Albert Kimmins, commanding No. 2 Company of the 1st Battalion, tried on several occasions to contact the French to urge them to distract the enemy. Two of his runners were killed trying to run across the bullet-swept ground. Finally, Kimmins set out himself, only to suffer the same fate.[71]

On the right, the Middlesex companies, living up to the regiment's nickname of the "Diehards," advanced over the valley and up the slope to within 400 yards of the objective. Around 7:30 a.m., Birchall requested reinforcements from Hill. Accordingly, reserve companies of the 1st Battalion were sent into action and, together with the Middlesex, pushed forward another 100 yards and drove the Germans out of Turco Farm. Captain G.H. Wilkinson, in charge of No. 3 Company of the 1st Battalion, has left us the following record:

> We advanced ... as far as a little old farm — I don't remember its name — on the top of Pilkem Ridge [actually, it was in front of the ridge], which we took at the point of the bayonet, surprising Fritz somewhat, because I don't imagine he thought we were able to do it. The centre of that old farm and the stink-pot in the middle of the courtyard was a regular shambles. I saw more wounded and dead men in a radius of about fifty yards than I think I ever saw before or hope to see again.[72]

The capture of Turco Farm would prove to be the high watermark of the advance. Unfortunately, the Anglo-Canadian troops were forced to abandon it. From the start of the attack, the 2nd Canadian Field Artillery had been shelling Turco Farm. The Anglo-Canadian troops were unable to remain in the farm because they had no way to signal their own gunners to stop firing. Frustrated, they fell back to a less exposed position at the bottom of the slope.

Mercer's fury at the French for not showing up mounted as he watched his men cut down in bunches without coming close to the enemy's line. Earlier, he had received assurances from Mordacq that he had assembled five and a half battalions to act in conjunction with the Canadian advance.[73] At 8:30 a.m., Mercer, seeing no evidence of a French attack, ordered his two battalions to dig in.

The 1st and 4th Battalions were pinned at the bottom of the valley, unable to retreat across the long, open field. If the weary and isolated Canadian survivors dared to look around from their shallow pits or improvised cover, they would have been able to see hundreds of khaki-clad figures sprawled on the ground, some lying still, while others moaned or made convulsive movements. To some, like George Twigg, it was certainly a relief, but strange, given their desperate plight, that the Germans made no effort to finish them off:

> I looked back and there wasn't a sign of anybody and my section sergeant said to me, "My God, if they had any sense at all, or any guts at all, they'd come over here and they wouldn't have to fire a shot. They could just take us all prisoners." There wasn't a sign of anybody for two thousand yards back of us, and they were up on a ridge there, and they were thicker than thieves.[74]

In the absence of the French, Mercer worried about his exposed left flank. A request was accordingly sent to French headquarters to fill the gap between its forces and the 1st Brigade. To that end, a battalion of Zouaves moved up and established contact with the Mercer's left shortly after midday.[75]

At this point the 13th and 15th Battalions held the original front. There was a gap of about 1000 yards between the flank of the 13th, under McCuaig and Buchanan, and Keerselaere. From there a line, more or less continuous, but flimsy, stretched down, and, curving westward at the edge of Kitchener's Wood, ended at a point occupied by the right of the French. The tenacious resistance of scattered parties of Canadians along the periphery of the gap, together with the counterattacks delivered during the night and early morning, had deterred the Germans from pressing home their advantage. Still, the position of the defenders remained critical. The seventeen and a half Canadian and British battalions in the first and second lines, rushed up at utmost speed during the night or early morning, were weary, hungry, forced to fight from unprepared positions frequently located on lower ground, in many cases sadly reduced in numbers, and supported only by the artillery of a division. These faced 42 German battalions, which enjoyed an overall advantage of at least five to one in guns, as well as a huge preponderance in heavy artillery.[76]

CHAPTER 6
Securing the New Flank

Throughout the day on 23 April, the Germans contented themselves with a few isolated attacks against the improvised flank and slightly improving their position wherever necessary. The advance on the previous day had exceeded their expectations and the short pause that followed allowed them to bring up supplies and make preparations for the next step. To facilitate their further movement forward, their guns, frequently using tear-gas shells, subjected the Canadians to a violent artillery barrage that ranged in the individual sectors from 15 minutes to many hours.

As if the men of the 1st and 4th Battalions had not already suffered enough, they had to contend with heavy enemy shelling throughout the morning. "Lord but I'm hungry and thirsty," wrote George Bell (1st Battalion). "What wouldn't I give for a drink of cold water? Even bully beef and hard tack would taste good. If only the artillery would stop long enough so a man could rest. Its enough to drive one nuts." Then someone smelled gas. A lieutenant who was a druggist in civilian life yelled out, "Piss on your handkerchief and tie them over your face." Those that ignored his advice began rolling on the ground, clutching their throats, and gasping for air. But, judging from what the Germans were using elsewhere, it was probably tear gas and its unpleasant effects (violent coughing and temporary blindness cause by the tearing up of the eyes) would have passed after the shelling ceased. At any rate, the wind shifted and carried the gas back toward the Germans.[1]

In other parts of the line, there was no let-up either. "We were bombarded and shelled all day losing men by 3 and 4 at a time," Ormond's

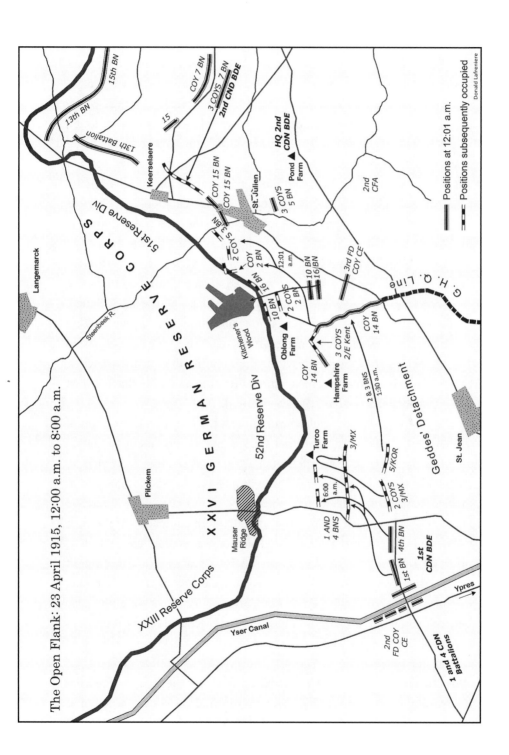

The Open Flank: 23 April 1915, 12:00 a.m. to 8:00 a.m.

Donald Lafreniere

Positions at 12:01 a.m.

Positions subsequently occupied

report ran.[2] "It was an awful day," Captain H.A. Duncan of the 16th Battalion commented in a letter home. "Men blown out of a trench was a common occurrence, leaving nothing but possibly a boot or Glengary."[3] At the apex of the Canadian front, losses from the shelling were so heavy that at 9:00 a.m., McCuaig and Buchanan decided to abandon the redoubt, which protruded several hundred yards into German-held territory and retire to the main trench line.[4] "We finally gave them the slip and got our line joined up again," recalled Ian Sinclair, "thinking ourselves pretty smart in fooling them."[5] On the right of the 13th Battalion, the 15th was showered with tear-gas bombs, but wet handkerchiefs neutralized some of the ill effects. "General Alderson congratulates on the way we have stuck out the shell fire," a proud Captain George McLaren wrote.[6] Even the 5th Battalion, which was not in a very exposed area, recorded a number of casualties from the sustained shelling. The War Diary for the day included: "Enemy artillery very busy shelling of our position and ... heavy shelling of our fire trenches and Headquarters from 4.30 to 6.30 p. m. .... Casualties 11."[7] As nerve-wracking as it was for the men huddled in the trenches, they had no choice but to remain where they were and pray that the next exploding shell did not have their name on it.

For the Canadian brigade commanders, the heavy concentration of artillery fire could only mean that the Germans were about to launch an attack somewhere along their line. Turner was the first to be alerted. David Watson, who commanded the 2nd Battalion, sent a message to Turner at 8:05 a. m. that enemy reinforcements, numbering between 500 and 1000, had been brought up opposite his right company.[8] An hour or so later, a body of Germans estimated at 2500 was spotted concentrating north of Kitchener's Wood with the obvious purpose of attacking St. Julien. There was more distressing news. Columns of trucks carrying infantry were seen moving southward from Langemarck to fill the gaps between some of the German units, and batteries had been brought up presumably to support their assault.

Turner faced other concerns. The arrival of reinforcements had allowed the Germans to cross the St. Julien-Poelcappelle road and fire from the rear at the Canadian units holding the original line. One consequence, as explained above, was that McCuaig was forced to evacuate the redoubt on the road. Turner contacted Division Headquarters at 9:15 a.m. and warned that, as the enemy had dug in behind his left, he would be unable to hold his trenches unless a counterattack could be arranged to regain the original French line.[9] At 10:30 a.m., Loomis, having been kept abreast of what was happening in his sector, informed Turner that the enemy was attacking his left flank and that something needed to be done quickly. He had lost contact with the defenders in that part of the line and could not regain touch with them with the force under his command. He requested reinforcements or a strong counterattack, otherwise he would be compelled to wiredraw his beleaguered men to St. Julien.[10] Loomis sent Captain William Clark-Kennedy, who had just returned from the 13th Battalion's front, to 3rd Brigade Headquarters to plead his case.

Clark-Kennedy made his way to Mouse Trap Farm, whereupon he was ushered into Turner's office. Turner needed no convincing. He discussed the matter with 1st Division Headquarters by telephone. He received a sympathetic hearing, but little else at the time. It was apparent that the Germans were rapidly consolidating their position and could not be driven back without a major effort, and this, for the moment, seemed to be out of the question. Alderson had already dispersed the division reserve and neither the 2nd nor 3rd Brigades had any troops to spare. All that remained of the V Corps reserve were a few battalions borrowed from the 27th and 28th divisions. The Second Army had no reserves left, except the 13th Brigade, currently resting south of Vlamertinghe after its ordeal at Hill 60. All outside reserve units would eventually be turned over to Alderson.

At 11:03 a.m., Division Headquarters replied, suggesting that the 13th and 15th Battalions fall back to support trenches so as to blunt the angle of the apex of the front, which was under heavy pressure. The promise of two companies of the 9th Royal Scots (27th Division) did not turn out to be permanent.[11] No sooner had these arrived than they were ordered to join Geddes's Detachment. Loomis was left to defend his front as best he could.

Until the new line was prepared, the 13th and 15th were to remain in place, but the severity of enemy shelling meant that supplies and ammunition could not be delivered to them, nor could their wounded be evacuated. Short of food and drinking water, the men eventually were reduced to using their iron rations.[12]

Between the 15th Battalion's support units and St. Julien, the 7th (less one company left as a garrison for Locality C) occupied a hill at the foot of the village of Keerselaere. As we have already noted, the 7th Battalion had moved up under cover of darkness and early in the morning received an order to dig and fortify a new trench line. The question confronting the commander, Lieutenant-Colonel Hart-McHarg, was whether the new line should be dug in the open ground, where the battalion then lay, or down at the foot of the hill. Major Odlum, second-in-command, observed that he had already reconnoitered the area, and, in his judgment "our existing position on the high ground was the right one and that if we went down to a forward position at the foot of the slope our communications would be very much exposed and endangered."[13] Hart-McHarg was inclined to agree, but he wanted to go out and see for himself.[14]

Accordingly, Hart-McHarg, accompanied by Odlum and Lieutenant D.M. Matheson of the Engineers, proceeded cautiously down a hill to the wrecked houses and shattered walls of the village. As they looked through a window in the rear of one of the ruins, they were amazed to see masses of Germans lined up behind hedges scarcely a hundred yards away. "Apparently we had been under observation the whole time," Odlum wrote in the battalion's war diary.[15] All three turned and ran, Matheson veering off to the left to take shelter in a ditch while the other two headed straight up the hill. The instant they cleared the ruins they were followed by a burst of rapid fire. Both threw themselves to the ground. Odlum, by luck, jumped into a small shell hole directly in front, and a moment later, Hart-McHarg rolled on top of him, exclaiming "I don't want to get hit again."

"Get what again?" Odlum asked.

"I'm shot," he replied.

"Where?"

"Through the stomach, oh my God."[16] He had been struck from behind, through the left thigh, the bullet penetrating his stomach.[17]

Odlum slid out from under his stricken comrade and did what he could to comfort him. The colonel was in great pain and would not let

Odlum tend to his wound, begging him to get the doctor. "Frankly, I did not want to," Odlum said afterwards. "I felt much safer where I was and I had it in my mind to remain in the shell hole until. … darkness when we could get out safely. But his suffering was too much for me"[18] Awaiting his opportunity, Odlum made a zigzag dash up the remainder of the hill, the Germans firing at him as he went. He found Captain George Gibson, the battalion medical officer, and explained to him what had happened.[19] Gibson volunteered to go out at once, and, with Sergeant J. Dryden, made his way down to the shell hole where Hart-McHarg lay. Between them they moved the colonel to a nearby ditch where Matheson had taken cover and dressed his wound there. They remained with him until after dark when the stretcher-bearers arrived and carried him to a little ruined farmhouse, which served as battalion headquarters.[20]

A robust man might have survived the wound, but the 46-year-old Hart-McHarg was barely 140 pounds and in frail health. He suffered from chronic indigestion that had confined him to a special diet, often mere milk and biscuits.[21] He knew he was dying and during the night he found comfort in gently clasping the hand of Odlum, who, when duty permitted, sat by his side. There were many things he wanted to say, but he had great difficulty in speaking. Toward midnight, an ambulance arrived and transported the sinking colonel to Poperinghe where he died the next day.[22] A born leader with enormous natural ability and a dominating personality, he would undoubtedly have risen to high command in the Canadian Army had he lived. Odlum made the following entry in the battalion's war diary: "Throughout the night of 22nd and 23rd he displayed splendid qualities of leadership. He was cool, collected and daring. His loss at such a time was a heavy blow to the regiment."[23] On a personal level, Odlum was deeply saddened by the death of the man he respected and considered a close friend. "It almost broke my heart to lose him," Odlum subsequently told Hart-McHarg's mother. "We have got along so well together, and he was such a splendid type, that I had learned to love him."[24] To perpetuate Hart-McHarg's memory a tablet in bronze, erected by his comrades, was unveiled in Christ Church, Vancouver, on 13 November 1921. Odlum, wealthy owner of the Vancouver *Daily Star*, succeeded to the command of the 7th Battalion.

The situation in the Ypres salient was under careful scrutiny at British General Headquarters where the piecemeal reports had trickled in during the night of 22–23 April. Since August 1914, the 63-year-old Sir John French had faced more than his share of military crises, which all too frequently he had mishandled. His pre-1914 reputation was based almost exclusively on his leadership of the cavalry in the South African War, especially in the operation around Colesberg and in the relief of the siege of Kimberley. A short, thickly built man with a bushy moustache, he was personally fearless of danger and could inspire his men as few commanders could. His assets, however, could not begin to compensate for his liabilities. He had an unstable personality, veering sharply from optimism to gloom, from confidence to indecision. He was unimaginative, inexperienced in handling large bodies of men, and ignorant of the tactical and strategic principles of modern warfare. French was the classic example of a man who had risen above the level of his competence.[25]

It did not require exceptional perspicacity to determine that the German action on 22 April had gravely imperiled the British front. It seemed to French, given his limited resources, that the only sensible thing to do was to fall back with all haste in order to straighten the line. Before doing so, he needed to confer with General Foch, who was charged with coordinating the efforts of the French, British, and Belgians in the northern theatre. While the fighting and movements were occurring on the Ypres battlefield, Sir John motored to Foch's headquarters at Cassel on the morning of the 23rd.

If we are to understand Foch's behaviour at this time, an examination of his character and military background would be useful. First as instructor and then as commandant of the Ecole Supèrieure de la guerre, Foch had played a key role in shaping the military philosophy of the French Army prior to the First World War. In a series of lectures subsequently published as *Principes de la guerre* (1903) and *Conduite de la guerre* (1904), Foch fascinated his audiences by expounding a doctrine that stressed the transcendence of the moral factors over the material. He contended that the basic formula for victory was Napoleonic audacity, seeking out battle immediately and attacking without thought of cost or possibility of tactical manoeuvre. His teachings permeated the upper levels of the French Army, which incorporated into the new Field Regulations in 1913 the idea of *l'offensive à outrance* — attack to the absolute limit. Included in the Field Regulations was the following paragraph: "Battles are above all else struggles of morale. Defeat is inevitable as soon as the hope of victory ceases. Success comes not to him who has suffered least, but to him who has the strongest will and the highest morale."

Nowhere in the manual is there any emphasis on supplies, firepower, or defensive action. Even after the opening months of the war, in which their armies had suffered shattering defeats, the French military leaders refused to acknowledge they had been wrong to assume that attacking infantry required essentially unflinching determination in order to win.

Now 64, Foch was still remarkably fit and alert, in both body and mind. He was an engaging little man, and, being typically French, was fond of gesticulating to emphasize a point. His unshakeable character and faith in his beliefs made it difficult for anyone in his company to hold firm to contrary opinions. His tactical limitations were at least partially offset by the fact that he looked like a general and possessed many of the qualities of a true leader. He spoke as if he had divine guidance, kept his equanimity even under the most perilous circumstances, and never shied from accepting responsibility.[26]

When Foch learned of the German break-in, he directed Putz (around midnight on 23 April) to ensure that the Belgian army and the remnants of the two French divisions, that is the 87th Territorial and the 45th Algerian, retain their position on the eastern side of the canal; and requested that he organize and deliver a counterattack to reestablish the old line. For the latter purpose he ordered that the 153rd Division (XX Corps, Tenth Army) stationed at Arras be sent up and he warned the commander of the Tenth Army that he might need to borrow more units.[27]

Of all the French generals, Foch alone enjoyed a harmonious working relationship with the choleric Sir John. He understood Sir John's state of mind and in conversation with him was reassuring, tactful, and deferential. However strange and unreasonable Sir John's proposition might be, Foch never countered with a refusal or criticism. He would begin by outlining the merits of the proposal and then gently bring Sir John around, step by step, often leading him to accept his own views. In difficult times, Foch behaved with such firmness and conviction that Sir John, troubled and anxious at the start, would leave the interview comforted and confident.

The meeting on 23 April ended like most of the previous ones with Foch getting his way. There is no record of the exchanges, but the results, included in the report that Sir John sent to Kitchener, show that he committed himself to a course of action exactly opposite to that which he had proposed. Optimistic as ever, Foch assured Sir John that in the next few days he intended to make good the ground lost by the 45th and 87th Divisions. To that end, he had ordered up large reinforcements and already two battalions and three batteries had reported to General Putz — these came from the Nieuport garrison which was under Putz's own command. Foch deliberately deceived Sir John for his promise of large reinforcements amounted to a little more than a division, nowhere near the numbers needed to hurl back the Germans. Intimidated by Foch's theatrics, Sir John agreed to co-operate in the counterattack, even though an hour earlier he had been intent on giving up the salient.[28]

The contracted salient was a potential death trap. The improvised British flank was very fragile, with practically no supports, and at any moment it was apt to be overwhelmed by vastly superior enemy forces. Compounding Sir John's fears was the possibility that a renewed thrust by the German XXIII Reserve Corps, across the canal near Steenstraat, might rupture the line between the Belgians and the French.[29] The field marshal's concerns were well founded.

Euphoric at the progress of his army during the first day's fighting, Duke Albrecht concluded that victory was a virtual certainty. His objectives for the next day, April 23, were considerably broader. His plan called for XXIII Reserve Corps to press across the Yser Canal and capture Poperinghe, six miles farther to the west, in order to drive a wedge between the Belgians and the French, while the XXVI Reserve Corps pressed southward to strike at the rear of the Canadian and 28th British divisions.[30] Albrecht informed the commander of the XXVI Reserve Corps that he regarded the advance of the XXIII Reserve Corps against Poperinghe to be the main operation and that his own was only of secondary importance. Albrecht understood that once the French were driven beyond the canal, the British position would be untenable. The fatal flaw in his thinking was that his resources did not permit him to successfully pursue the two objectives simultaneously. A far more attainable goal would have been to exploit the 1000-yard gap between the left of the 13th Battalion and the right of the 7th, thereby cutting off the salient. That avenue was open on Friday, 23 April, but closed on the following day.

Albrecht's elation faded as the day wore on. The assault of the XXIII Reserve Corps against the French and Belgians encountered extraordinary difficulties and failed to realize any of its objectives. On the other hand, the vigorous Canadian counterattacks in the early morning left the XXVI Reserve Corps in no condition to execute the movement ordered. Later in the day, the German High Command intervened and informed Albrecht "that Poperinghe did not primarily enter the question at all as an objective and that for the present it was strictly a matter of cutting off the Ypres salient."[31]

Back at his advanced headquarters, located at Hazebrouck, French instructed Smith-Dorrien to assist General Putz's advance, making available the infantry of the 50th Division and subsequently the entire Cavalry Corps. The 13th Infantry Brigade (5th Division) was released from Army reserve and placed at the disposal of General Alderson. Furthermore, two brigades of the 4th Division and the Lahore Division (Indian Corps), billeted near Bailleul and Merville repectively, were warned to be ready to move northward at short notice.[32] The British were doing all they could to uphold their end of the bargain.

The same thing could not be said about the French. General Putz was unwilling to fritter away his remaining reserves in hasty counterattacks. He preferred to wait for the arrival of fresh French reinforcements before engaging the enemy. Although a Frenchman, his command included Belgian as well as French divisions and he was responsible only to King Albert of Belgium.

The action of Foch and his generals indicates that they had a poor understanding of the conditions on the battlefield. That is apparent from the instructions that General Fernand Quiquandon, commanding the

45th Algerian, issued to Mordacq (90th Brigade) at 1:20 p.m. Mordacq was directed to strike northward between Boesinghe and the Ypres-Pilckem road and to begin his operation at 3:00 p.m. Mordacq was further informed that the Germans appeared, for the moment, to have exhausted their ammunition and that he would be acting in liaison with British forces advancing toward Langemarck.[33] Quite apart from the fact that this information was inaccurate, as will be shown below, the absence of new reserves to assist Mordacq's shattered battalion meant that the effort would be feeble at best.

Alderson did not receive the French operation order in time to change his own, sent out at 1:30 p.m. It called for the 13th Brigade, led by Brigadier-General Robert Wanless O'Gowan, to cross the Brielen bridge, form up, and advance toward Pilckem with its right on the Ypres-Pilckem road. The uncommitted battalions of Geddes's Detachment were to move forward on the left or east side of the road. The 1st and 4th Canadian Battalions, along with the 3rd Middlesex, were to provide what assistance they could as the operation developed. Following the capture of Pilckem, the attack was to continue until the old French line was restored. The attack was timed to commence at 3:30 p.m., half an later than that of the French.[34] There was no mention of an attack on Langemarck in the orders.

When the commanders concerned received copies of the order, they must have been perplexed. Mercer, recognizing at once the similar objectives of the 13th Brigade and Mordacq's men, contacted Division Headquarters to inquire whether it might be advisable to cancel the smaller French operation. Back came the reply: "No let the French commence their attack and if possible you might cooperate as far as possible and then let 13th Bde. Go through you."[35] Mercer was bewildered. The initial instructions had made no mention of troops going through his men entrenched below Mauser Ridge. Besides the 13th Brigade was west of the road, while the 1st and 4th Battalions were to the east of it.[36]

At the same time that his instructions went out, Alderson sent a message to Mercer and Turner, stating: "French report that Germans are apparently running short of ammunition. They have been ordered to advance. Divisional Commander wishes you to seize the opportunity to push forward." It was a baffling note. In the plan, none of Turner's units had been allocated a role and Mercer's decimated 1st and 4th Battalions were expected to participate only if opportunity occurred. Besides Alderson, his headquarters located far in the rear at Château des Trois Tours, had no idea that German artillery had been plastering Canadian positions along the entire flank. Turner, whose men and own headquarters (Mouse Trap Farm) had been under steady bombardment for hours, shook his head in disbelief, scribbling on the telegram, "An example of the value of information received from the rear."[37] It was another disturbing sign that Alderson did not have a reasonable grasp of what was happening at the front.

As zero hour approached and still no sight of the promised French formations, Smith-Dorrien grew anxious lest a delay enable the Germans to further fortify their position. Following consultations with General Plumer, Smith-Dorrien became convinced that, if an attack was to take place at all, it must be made immediately. At 2:30 p.m., he issued orders to the V Corps for a general attack between Kitchener's Wood and Yser Canal.[38]

The start of the operation was delayed, first to 3:15 and then to 3:45 to permit the British troops to move into position. On the east side of the Ypres-Pilkem road, Geddes's Detachment was lined up and waited for the signal to move forward. Geddes was under the impression that he enjoyed an independent command. He was wrong, but it did not affect his control over the eastern frontage. For reasons that are unclear, the higher command did not notify him that he had been placed under the orders of Wanless O'Gowan until well after the battle was underway.

Geddes had placed in the front line the 2nd East Yorkshire Regiment and the 1st York and Lancaster Regiment with the 5th King's Own Royal Regiment in reserve. In close support on the right were two newly arrived units from the 27th Division, the 2nd Duke of Cornwall Light Infantry, and two companies of the 9th Royal Scots under Lieutenant-Colonel H.D. Tuson. Geddes had ordered the 1st York and Lancaster to keep in touch with the left flank of the 13th Brigade, situated on the other side of the Ypres-Pilkem road. In the same vein, the 2nd East Yorks were told to conform to the movements of Tuson's Duke of Cornwall Light Infantry.

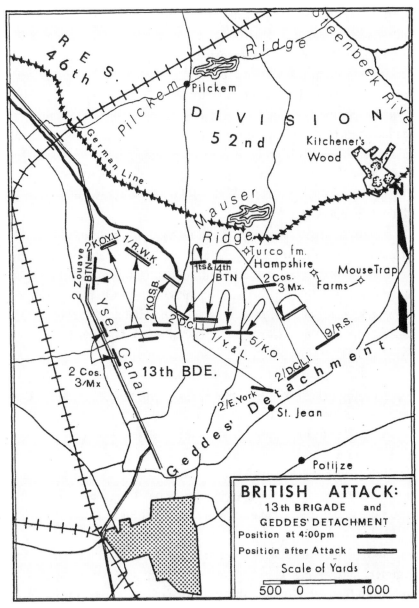

BRITISH ATTACK:
13th BRIGADE   and
GEDDES' DETACHMENT
Position at 4:00pm
Position after Attack
Scale of Yards
500   0   1000

Realizing that he would not be ready even at the new appointed
hour, Wanless O'Gowan asked for a further postponement to 4:15.
As it happened, the 13th Brigade, marching from Vlamertingde, had
swung too far north and entered the French zone, compelling it to
take a circuitous route to avoid confusion and congestion on the road.

Additionally, Wanless O'Gowan insisted that his men, on foot since 9:00 a.m., be fed before the attack. The delay allowed Wanless O'Gowan to ride ahead and personally reconnoitre the ground on which his forces were to assemble. He observed that a gap existed between the canal and the left of the Canadians. Accordingly, he deployed four battalions in readiness for the assault, with the 1st Royal West Kent and 2nd King's Own Scottish Borders in the lead and the 2nd King's Yorkshire Light Infantry and Queen Victoria's Rifles in close support.

The 13th Brigade had been reduced to 3000 men after losing 62 officers and 1300 men in the fight over Hill 60. The men were in good spirits, but physically tired. The attack got underway at 4:25 p.m., and, like the one in the early morning, was directed against Mauser Ridge. It was doomed to fail before it started. The infantry had to advance between 500 and 800 yards in broad daylight over ground that was very open, broken only by a few clusters of hedges and scattered piles of manure. Since the operation was organized in haste, there was a lack of preparation and no reconnaissance even to determine the enemy's exact location. To make matters worse, the infantry assault was launched without the customary artillery support. The gunners, spread out as they were and coming under different commands, were not informed of the change in the time of the attack and opened fire at 2:45 p.m. When the assault actually got underway, a shortage of ammunition prevented another preliminary bombardment.

Spread across a front of about 500 yards, each lead battalion formed up in five or six lines at wide intervals for the advance. Alerted by the earlier artillery barrage that an attack was forthcoming, the Germans opened fire as soon as the leading waves came into view. In the clear light, with every man distinctly visible, German machine-gunners reaped a bountiful harvest. The 13th Brigade maintained its advance despite a fire that became hellish after they passed the Canadian trenches, some 300 to 400 yards from the hidden enemy. Wanless O'Gowan wrote in his report that, owing to the amount of smoke and dust, it was impossible to see anything and the casualties among officers were so heavy that hardly any information came back.[39] It became increasing difficult to direct the battle. To add to the confusion, a battalion of Zouaves, moving too far to the east, suddenly cut across the front of the Royal West Kents, halting their progress and forcing them to veer to the right, into the flank of the King's Own Scottish Borders, and disrupted the firing line. The War Diary of the Royal West Kents describes the problem the movement of the Zouaves created: "In consequence of this the supporting lines were held back under the cover of the canal bank and low ground and only one platoon at a time pushed to support the firing line."[40] Recoiling from the maelstrom of enemy rifle and machine-gun fire, the Zouaves quickly broke off action and withdrew to their trenches. This lame effort, more of a liability than anything else, was the only part played by the French 45th Division during the battle.

The two battalions of the 13th resumed their advance despite terrible enemy fire and calamitous casualties. Wave after wave was decimated, but small groups and individuals continued to work their way forward. Along the canal where the ground was a little more enclosed, some groups pushed up the slope and got as far as the enemy outpost line before being brought to a standstill.

Led by Geddes himself, the detachment did not fare much better. Crossing over the same ground as the 1st and 4th Canadian Battalions earlier that morning, the men came under annihilating fire and the first two lines of the 2nd East Yorks and the 1st York and Lancaster were practically cut down to a man. Watching the slaughter in horror, James Fraser (4th Canadian Battalion) recalled that "they were simply bowled over like ninepins."[41] The dust and smoke offered partial protection to those that followed and they slowly crept forward, regardless of their losses. Now Geddes's reserve battalion, the 5th King's Own, was thrown into the fray to close the growing gap between the East Yorkshires and the Duke of Cornwall L. I. Despite the heroic effort of Geddes's men, at no point were they able to come to grips with the main body of Germans. The CO of the 2nd East Yorkshires reported: "Casualties were so numerous that wave after wave was needed to keep any semblance of a firing line."[42] Some parties advanced a little farther than others, but ultimately all were forced to dig in or fall back to find cover. A small unit of East Yorkshires got closest to the Germans, fighting its way to within 30 yards of their front trenches.

On the far right, the Duke of Cornwall Light Infantry (DCLI) moved off from west of Wieltje and, once past Hill Top Ridge, lost touch with the Royal Scots, who, in the face of murderous rifle and machine-gun fire, were compelled to fall back. The DCLI pushed on alone and, with incredible resolve, managed to reach Turco Farm, where they engaged the enemy in vicious hand-to-hand combat. Filled with hated for the loss of confederates, the Dukes showed no mercy to the few Germans who tried to surrender. But, owing to their depleted ranks, the Dukes were unable to retain control of the farm and were ordered to withdraw. It was the second time in less than 12 hours that Alderson's men had abandoned the hard-fought strategic objective.

Moved by the plight of their comrades, the beleaguered able-bodied survivors of the Middlesex and the 1st and 4th Canadian Battalions jumped to their feet and joined the attack. German machine guns and shrapnel tore large gaps in their already depleted ranks. The 4th Battalion came under particularly devastating fire and wavered for a moment. Its commander, Lieutenant-Colonel Birchall, with a revolver in one hand and a light cane in the other, coolly rallied it as he walked up and down the ranks, urging his men to make further advances. Private Peat recounts:

> Men went down like ninepins at a fair. But always ahead
> was the colonel, always there was the short flash of his
> cane as it swished through the air. Then he was hit, a
> bullet in the upper right arm. He did not stop; he did not
> drop his cane. "On boys, on!" And his men stumbled up
> and forward.[43]

With reckless disregard for his own safety, Birchall, who had personally taken over C Company after its commander was wounded, would pay the ultimate price. Leading a charge toward a German trench, he fell, riddled by bullets. Frank Betts, who was nearby, wrote in a letter home: "Our Colonel Birchall got killed. He sure was a brave man. He went up the field just as if there was no war, and the bullets, shrapnel, Johnsons and war shells were as thick as hail and I'm not exaggerating." Minutes later, Betts was himself struck by a bullet, but fortunately he was not seriously hurt. He described his ordeal while he struggled in the open field:

> How anybody got through it without getting hit is a miracle. After I was hit they tried to get me again. I got my trenching tool out and with my left hand dug a little hole to lie in and the bullets hitting the ground all around me; three shrapnels burst so close I was nearly buried and a piece of shell hit the handle of my trenching tool, just missing my head by about two inches. I lay in the open with the beggars sniping at me and wondering where the next shell would burst. Then I made my mind to beat it for cover. How I got away without getting hit again I don't know. The bullets threw up the ground all around me … It was awful. I don't want to see another day like that one.[44]

The survivors assert that their objective was reached, but they must have been referring to a German outpost that they captured when the defenders fled. Official sources make it clear that the attackers fell short of their territorial objective and eventually withdrew to a point about 200 yards from the enemy. In the end, the initiative by the Canadians and Middlesex had served no purpose other than to add to the already staggering casualty toll.

With the approach of darkness, all movements came to an end. The casualty figures for the day had been appalling, running between 200 and 400 in most of the British battalions. The morning and afternoon attacks of the two Canadian battalions had been especially costly, with the 1st losing 404 all ranks and the 4th a total of 454, including its CO, Lieutenant-Colonel Birchell, and second in command, Lieutenant-Colonel William Buell, both of whom were killed. In facing a gauntlet of fire from an entrenched enemy on high ground and with little chance of success, these men of the 1st Brigade, who were hardly seasoned soldiers, had acquitted themselves magnificently. Looking back across the years, G.W. Twigg declared:

> It was a glorious day for the Canadians because these men had had practically no training. But was I ever proud of them. If they'd have been trained for ten years they couldn't have acted better. To think of those kids that had been pulled from all over the country and the way they behaved! In a murderous fire like that! I never felt so proud of a bunch of boys in my life.[45]

The Canadian commanders, for their part, had supervised the movement of their men in their part of the battlefield and carried out their orders as well as could be expected. They had used up-to-date tactics, kept their men from falling into disarray or withdrawing in disorder, and maintained communications with one another and with brigade headquarters throughout the day.

There are some, however, who cannot escape censure for their conduct. Much blame should be laid at the doorsteps of the French, who were late in showing up and only made a pretense of attacking. Alderson deserves to be criticized, as well. The attack was too hurriedly organized, before he had received the French operational orders and assured himself that their formations were ready to move forward — by then he must have known about their failure to attack in Kitchener's Wood. Moreover, he and his staff had misjudged the time that it would take for the 13th Brigade to arrive in its assigned place. They ought to have known that Wanless O'Gowan's men, on their feet since early morning, would be required to eat before going into battle. Finally, they made no attempt to alert the gunners that the attack had been delayed so that when the time came, the British troops had no artillery support.

Whether the attack at Mauser Ridge was justifiable in view of the terrible cost remains a subject of controversy. From the outset, the chances of success, that is, in dislodging the Germans from Mauser Ridge, had to be seen by Alderson and his staff as practically non-existent. But for them, the attack was necessary in order to deny the enemy the avenue to Ypres and beyond the canal. As they saw it, that strategic goal had been achieved. Colonel Cecil Romer, GSO1 of the 1st Canadian Division, told Duguid a decade later: "From General Alderson's point of view, it was vital to stopping further German advance on the left and to gain time until further reinforcements had come up and the French were able to assume the offensive." Romer makes another interesting point: "Experience of former fighting in 1914 had convinced me that the Germans when counter-attacked, and even when the counter-attack was unsuccessful, always paused and waited to see what was going to happen. Unless this point is clearly brought out the reader must have a wrong impression."[46] J. Sutherland-Brown, who was on Alderson's staff, made similar arguments to Duguid, saying that the counterattacks by the Canadian Division "had a most deterring effect on the Germans in preventing them advancing as far as Elverdinghe and Brielen resulting in the complete abandonment of the Ypres salient."[47] Duguid does not take a formal position on the subject, but tips his hand in a letter to Edmonds a decade later: "There can be little doubt but this deterred the Germans from advancing to the Canal East of Brielen on the morning of the 23rd."[48]

In contrast, the verdict of the British Official History, accepted by most writers, is harsh, observing that "no ground was gained that could not have been secured, probably without casualties, by a simple advance after night to which the openness of the country lent itself."[49] That statement is undoubtedly true. But it is easy to be wise after the event. By the time Edmonds wrote his piece on the battle, he knew that the German High Command's objectives on the 23rd were limited and that it had no plans to assault Ypres. Romer had read Edmonds's second draft of the British Official History of the campaign, and was very critical of it. A copy of his letter to Duguid was forwarded to Edmonds. The British official historian evidently did not think that Romer's defence of the counterattack merited a response. Nor did he take into consideration decisions made in the heat of battle and the virtual absence of the promised French help.

The evening of 23 April was cloudy, without a moon, and, around 9:30 p.m., the British leaders ordered their men to fall back to a new line in rear of the high-water mark of the attack, some 600 yards south of the enemy. Situated in a low point in the countryside, it was not an ideal spot. The Germans could observe most of what was happening below and the ground was completely waterlogged so that it was impossible to dig deep trenches.[50] Organization of this position proceeded only with great difficulty. The units were mixed up and there was such confusion that daylight found some survivors digging in facing the wrong way. The men spent a miserable night, though they were undisturbed by the Germans. Some rations of bread and bacon were brought up, but the distribution was so haphazard that many men remained 24 hours without food.

French assistance on the east side of the canal, which Foch had pledged, did not amount to much. As noted earlier, the Zouaves made a brief appearance on the battlefield before scurrying back to the safety of their own line. During the day, Foch went to see Putz on two occasions to urge him to greater efforts. He received no special assurances. As we have already seen Putz saw no point in sending out thoroughly demoralized troops across bullet-swept ground and, possessing a stronger backbone than Sir John, was less susceptible to pressure.

It would have been better if Foch and his commanders had arrived at a common policy before making commitments that they could not hope to meet. As it was, they forced the Canadians and the British into hurriedly improvised operations and left them in the lurch, ensuring defeat and many more casualties than would otherwise have been the case. Lieutenant-Colonel Gordon Hall, GS02 of the Canadian Division, remarked bitterly about French inaction:

> If we had only ourselves to consider we *might* have organized one proper counter-attack with adequate numbers as soon as they were available. Fewer troops would have been required; we could not have suffered more heavily; we would not have had our troops mixed up and disorganized and at least we might have been able to form a decent flank and avoid the disastrous break at the apex on the 24th. All due to Foch and his Divisional Commanders, whose idea seemed to be that the British must sacrifice themselves in holding on, till they themselves were quite ready to take on the job in a big way with adequate troops and make a spectacular exhibition of it.[51]

The Canadians continued to show the same dogged determination in resisting the enemy as in their counterattacks. All day, shells rained on St. Julien and the covering trenches, ceasing only when an attack was imminent. The Germans came out of their trenches on four occasions and each time they were driven back by rifle and machine-gun fire.[52] But, at the apex of the front, opposite Poelcappelle, the position of the 13th Battalion and its allies was progressively deteriorating. Loomis alerted Turner, who concurred that it would be best to retrench and smooth out the apex as Alderson had suggested. Clark-Kennedy was sent to the front to deliver a message to Buchanan, instructing him to withdraw and occupy a new line at right angles to the 15th Battalion. Before executing the manoeuvre, Buchanan passed the word to bury all the dead that could be reached and to commence the removal of the wounded.

Besides clever planning, it required a good deal of luck to successfully withdraw from an exposed position in the dark while under the nose of the enemy. The retirement had barely begun when the Germans, sensing the move, attacked from the rear. Tomlinson remarked that at one point the advancing Germans were so near "that I was slightly wounded by the splinter of a bomb."[53] Buchanan's forces were in danger of being overwhelmed, as they had exhausted their supply of grenades and were weighed down with large numbers of wounded. This was prevented by the gallant rear guard action of a small detachment, backed by two machine guns, under the command of Lieutenant Charles Pitblado. The German attacks were beaten off and the withdrawal continued, though for a while it was feared that Pitblado and his men might be cut off. Arriving at the place designated by General Turner, the Buffs and the men of the 13th laid down the wounded and began to dig in.[54] The dangerous gap between the 15th Battalion and the 7th Battalion had been closed.

At 9:25 Turner notified Loomis that two companies of the 14th Battalion under the unit's second-in-command, Lieutenant-Colonel W.W. Burland, had been placed at his disposal and would soon be arriving at St. Julien. When they appeared half an hour later, Loomis sent one to reinforce the left of the 13th and the other to take a position west of St. Julien. The Germans made no attempt to interfere with any of these movements, allowing the exhausted Canadians, particularly the 13th, to rest and slake their thirst.[55]

It had been typical of the Germans at Ypres to allow the artillery and the gas to clear the way for them, refraining from making sacrifices in a battle they presumed had been all but won. Whether it was poor leadership, the generals' overconfidence and lack of urgency that spread to the rank and file, the tenacious resistance of the Canadian and British soldiers, or a combination of all these factors, a serious and vigorous effort to crush the salient had thus far not occurred. The War Diary of the XXIII Reserve Corps places the blame, perhaps unfairly, squarely on the shoulders of the foot soldiers:

> Unfortunately the infantry had become enfeebled by trench warfare and had lost its daring and its indifference to heavy losses and the disintegrating influence of increased enemy fire effect. The leaders and the brave-hearted fell, and the bulk of the men, mostly inexperienced reinforcements, became helpless and only too inclined to leave the work to the artillery and trench mortars.[56]

By the end of 23 April, the position of the Canadian flank was slightly better off than on the previous day. However, the improvement had been achieved at the expense of heavy casualties and of having to throw every battalion in divisional and corps reserve, plus two brigades from the Second Army reserve into the fray. Although little ground had been regained, a continuous manned position had been established, running southward from the 15th Battalion, which now held the apex of the Canadian front, to around St. Julien and extending westward to a spot next to the canal where a battalion of the 13th Brigade reinforced the junction with the French right flank.

Anxiety among Canadians remained high, and, even when permitted, few were able to sleep: "We kept a very careful watch all night," wrote Major Harold Mathews, a company commander (8th Battalion), "two officers being always on duty, and no man allowed to be in the dugouts

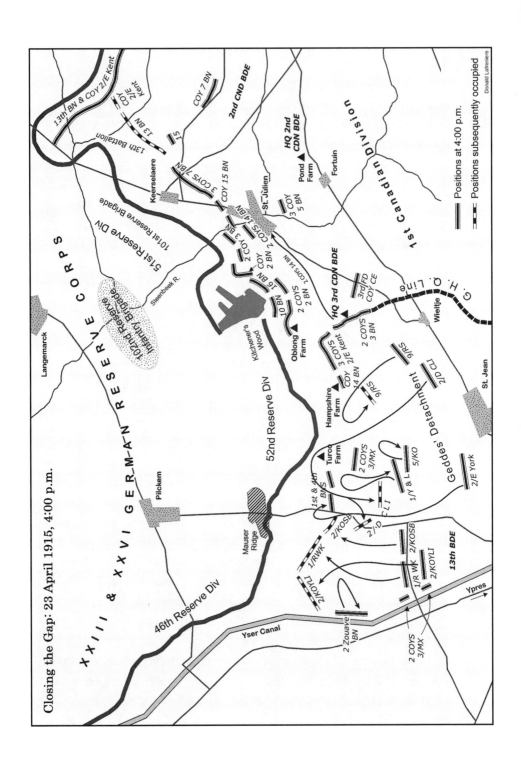

Closing the Gap: 23 April 1915, 4:00 p.m.

Positions at 4:00 p.m.

Positions subsequently occupied

Donald Lafreniere

XXIII & XXVI GERMAN RESERVE CORPS

1st Canadian Division

Langemarck

Pilckem

Keerselaere

51st Reserve Div

101st Reserve Brigade

102nd Reserve Infantry Brigade

Steenbeek R.

52nd Reserve Div

46th Reserve Div

Mauser Ridge

Kitchener's Wood

Oblong Farm

Turco Farm

Hampshire Farm

St-Julien

Fortuin

Pond Farm

Wieltje

St. Jean

Ypres

Yser Canal

G.H.Q. Line

2nd CND BDE

HQ 2nd CDN BDE

HQ 3rd CDN BDE

13th BDE

Geddes' Detachment

13th BN & COY 2/E Kent

COY 2/E Kent

13 BN

13th Battalion

15

COY 7 BN

3 COYS 7 BN

COY 15 BN

15 BN

3 COYS 14 BN

2 COY 13 BN

2 COY 13 BN

COY 16 BN

16 BN

2 COYS 14 BN

10 BN

2 COYS 2 BN

3 COY 5 BN

3rd/FD COY CE

3 COYS 2/E Kent

2 COYS 3 BN

14 BN

9/RS

9/RS

2/D CLI

5/KO

2 COYS 3/MX

1/Y & L

CLI

1st & 4th BNS

2/E York

2/KOSB

2/D

1/RWK

1/R WK

2/KOSB

2/KOYLI

2/KOYLI

1/R WK

2 Zouave BN

2 COYS 3/MX

on any pretext whatever."[57] Another company commander, Major G.H. McLaren (15th Battalion) reported: "German flares appear to be going up in almost a complete circle around us, also two fires to be seen behind us."[58] "The German flares crossed each other in the heavens behind us," Lieutenant-Colonel John Currie, commander of the 15th Battalion, noted in his memoirs. "I could see the angry red flashes of the thousands of guns they were directing against our devoted defenders."[59] The sentries in the 16th Battalion were so jittery that they frequently raised false alarms. "All night it was a case of 'stand to' every half hour, the cry being 'there're coming,'" wrote a member of the unit.[60]

Throughout the night, parties of men at the front were busy "adjusting dispositions, strengthening parapets, filling sandbags, building traverses and digging cover."[61] Odlum reported that his men "worked hard in strengthening and wiring its position."[62] Lieutenant-Colonel John Currie observed: "The 13th were withdrawn from their trenches and were digging in along the slope of our left bank." At the same time, unit leaders took steps to ensure that there were enough rations, water, and ammunition to meet the challenge of the next enemy assault. All seemed to go well. Lieutenant-Colonel George Tuxford's (CO of 5th Battalion) was succinct in assuring Division Headquarters at midnight that he was "[p]erfectly prepared."[63] A few adopted an additional safety measure that would pay huge dividends the following morning. One such commander, Major Mathews, penned the following: "In expectation that we might be gassed, dixies of water had been placed at intervals along the trench, handkerchiefs and empty bandoliers had been wetted hoping that by keeping something damp over our mouths and noses the effect of the poisonous gas would be nullified to some extent."[64]

Reports late on the 23rd and in the early hours of the 24th from the west side of the canal were mixed, giving rise first to hope and then to apprehension. The Belgians not only maintained their front intact north of Steenstraat, but the arrival of fresh units permitted them to extend their right to the outskirts of Lizerne, thus closing a 700-yard gap with the French. In the French sector, however, there was reason for concern. The Germans, aided by a new discharge of gas, had captured Het Sas and Lizerne, gravely endangering the French position on the west bank.[65]

To General Headquarters it appeared that the Germans were delaying their advance against the new British flank in order to concentrate elsewhere. The thinking was that the Germans would exploit their bridgeheads to force a crossing of the canal, thus driving a wedge between the French and the Belgians and then sweeping the former away. If successful, the Germans would be able to overwhelm the left flank of Plumers' Corps and force the surrender of Ypres. On the morning of 24 April, Sir John directed Smith-Dorrien not to place much reliance on the French and to secure his left as soon as his dispositions would permit it. He added that vigorous action east of the canal was the best means of checking the enemy's advance westward through General Putz's troops.[66] One cannot help but question the field marshall's decision given the circumstances — the previous day's losses, the confused and demoralized condition of many of the units, the extreme tactical vulnerability of the British position, and the absence of any effective protection against the gas. However, as so often happened in the war, the Germans struck first.

Chapter 7
24 April: The Onset of the Battle of St. Julien
(4:00 a.m. to 1:00 p.m.)

Aerial reconnaissance made at dawn on 24 April detected the presence of 30 trains at Menin and seven at Ledeghem (four miles north of Menin), but no unusual German movements. The trains consisted of covered coaches and might have brought up reinforcements, but they might also have been empty and intended for the evacuation of the wounded. As a precautionary move, Smith-Dorrien warned the II Corps, which was south of the V Corps and opposite Menin-Ledeghem, to be alert for any signs of an attack.[1]

With the Germans free to select any of a number of options, there was no sure way of knowing where the next blow might fall. As noted at the end of the previous chapter, Sir John, fearing that the enemy would attempt a thrust across the canal to split the Belgians and the French at Steenstraat and Lizerne, proposed to initiate countermeasures. He blamed Joffre for placing inferior troops on his left flank, and, in effect, causing the break-in, and he resented that the responsibility for setting things right had been thrust on his shoulders. He calculated that the best means to check an enemy advance against Putz's forces was to attack east of the canal. In issuing orders to Smith-Dorrien to carry out such an operation, Sir John warned him to take steps necessary to safeguard his left and to not rely on the French. The telegram was sent at 9:30 a.m. on the 24th, five hours after the Germans had opened an attack of their own.

After a promising start, Duke Albrecht had been frustrated by the progress of his men on the 23rd. The attempt to breach the defences between the Belgians and the French and push on to Poperinge had miscarried because of fierce resistance and a shortage of reserves. The suicidal counterattacks by the Canadians and British, although beaten back, had stopped his advance to turn the flank of the defenders in the salient. As a consequence of the day's fighting, the OHL directed Albrecht to simply concentrate on cutting off the salient. By then, Albrecht realized that the salient would not fall into his hands as easily as he had initially imagined and that he would require a vigorous and well-planned effort to roll up the Canadian line.

On the 24th, Albrecht's planned a two-staged operation, one on each side of the salient. The first and most important would be a converging attack on the Canadian-held apex mounted by the XXVI Reserve Corps and supported by the XXVII Reserve Corps. Its object was to crush the stubborn Canadians, capture St. Julien, and, by penetrating into the heart of the salient, force the abandonment of Ypres. To Albrecht's delight, the direction of the wind was favourable, permitting the use of poison gas prior to the attack. The discharge, set for 4:00 a.m., was to be accompanied by a bombardment of T-STOFF shells to thicken the cloud and to increase its psychological effects. The second stage called for the XXIII Reserve Corps to continue the action on the west bank of the canal, circling southward toward Vlamertinghe to cut off the British army's line of retreat from the salient.[2]

The Germans had driven the French out of Lizerne at 1:30 a. m., allowing them to establish a bridgehead on the west side of the canal. The capture of Lizerne put them in a strong position to turn the defensive flank of the Belgians and so, as previously noted, drive a wedge between them and the French. The Germans opened their attack at 3:00 a.m. with a heavy bombardment that included gas shells. The Belgians not only stood their ground, but, by extending their left around Zuydschoote (some 700 yards southwest of Lizerne), outflanked their attackers. In the meantime, the French mounted two counterattacks to regain Lizerne. Although their forces failed to break into the village, they nevertheless succeeded in enclosing it on three sides. This prevented the Germans from making any real progress in the area.

Along the Canadian front the men had made preparations to meet a renewal of the enemy's attack, which was expected at daylight.

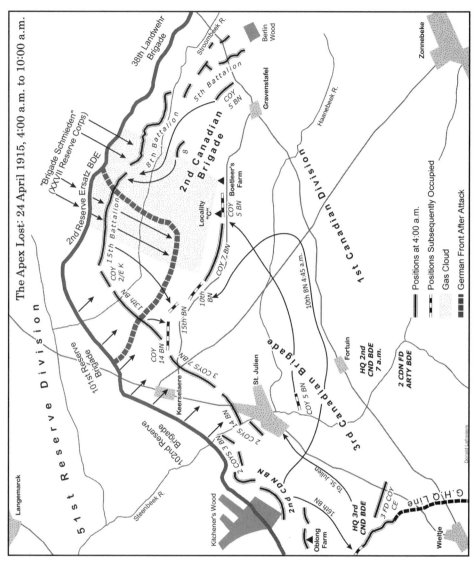

"Knowing as we did something of the tactical situation on our left as it had developed the previous two days, we fully expected a determined attack on our positions," Major Mathews wrote in his account of the battle.[3] Against Albrecht's 24 divisions, the Canadian line, from the apex to St. Julien, and continuing southwest to Kitchener's Wood was manned by the equivalent of eight battalions with only a few companies in reserve

At 3:00 a.m., the roar of the bombardment to the northwest and the flashes of the German guns reflecting in the sky had alerted the Canadians and the order stand to was given. After about an hour, Mathews began to think that because it was so light "nothing would happen after all." [4] Suddenly, at 4:00 a.m., sentries along the northern face of the apex spotted three flares floating down from a German balloon. A few minutes later, German artillery saturated the Canadian line with shells of all calibre, scattering sandbags, collapsing trenches, and exacting a deadly toll. Odlum did not need to underscore the accuracy of enemy fire when he simply wrote in his report: "Our casualties were numerous." [5] H.G. Brewer (14th Battalion), recalled: "People were being blown up all around us, bodies flying up in the air." [6] What stayed lodged in Sergeant Harold Baldwin's (5th Battalion) mind was "the shrieking blast of destruction," with "the hiss and scream of their medium-sized shells and the hated whiz bang, bursting over every section of the trench," and that the only thing "we could do was wait." [7]

At the apex, the men of the 15th and 8th Battalions noticed that something unusual was happening. A number of Germans hopped out of their trenches, and in the dim light they appeared to be wearing helmets that resembled a diver's headgear. A hissing sound was heard, and a greenish-yellow vapour began to flow. The gas cloud, covering a 1200-yard span of the front, was aimed directly at the junction of the 15th and 8th Battalions. Driven by a dawn breeze, the poisonous fog of smoke, estimated to be 10 to 15 feet high and appearing to be thicker in some places than in others, came on rapidly across no man's land. Canadian sentries sounded the alarm and hurried calls for artillery support brought prompt aid to the 8th Battalion. For the 15th Battalion on the left, however, no such help was forthcoming because the 3rd Field Artillery, assigned to the 3rd Brigade, had been moved to cover a rupture in the line from earlier fighting and was out of range. [8]

The two battalions had not been heavily engaged in the earlier action, so, except for a few officers, its members had no sure way of identifying the gas cloud before it reached them. Lester Stevens (8th Battalion) "thought it was smoke and they were going to come up behind it" and therefore "we started firing at them so as to prevent them following up this smoke." It

An idea of what the Canadians faced at Ypres on 24 April may be gleaned from the gas cloud at the battle of the Somme in 1916. Regrettably, not a single photo of the gas attack at Ypres exists, undoubtedly because it was unexpected.

did not take long for Stevens and his mates to feel the effects of the deadly fumes. "It came up and went over the trenches and two fellows, one on my right and one on my left, they dropped and they both died." By his own admission, Stevens was "a bit of an athlete in those days," and able to hold his breathe underwater for two minutes. When he realized what he was facing, he held his breath long enough to wrap a wet bandolier "over my nose and that saved my life."[9] Reacting to the gas cloud, Corporal William Thornton (No. 3 Company, 15th Battalion) wrote: "Well when I saw it coming, I was not curious to find out what it was, but just grabbed a towel, which was a big, thick one, soaked it in water and covered my face, so I came off lucky."[10] Major G.H. McLaren (No. 3 Company, 15th Battalion) suspected that the approaching greenish cloud was the poison gas he had heard much about: "We immediately opened rapid fire but the gas soon rose to about 10 feet and we could not see through it and it struck our trenches in a very short time."[11] On the other hand, Lieutenant-Colonel Louis Lipsett, the CO of the 8th Battalion, had seen the gas first-hand on the 22nd: "At 4 a.m. I could see from my Headquarters the same sort of bluish haze, blowing from the German trenches … as I had seen on the 22nd blowing over the French trenches."[12]

There was no panic among the Canadians, partly because they had not been caught by surprise. Then, too, enough time had passed since the first release of gas on 22 April for the suggestions on how to cope with it percolated down to the men in the field — though it was left up to the various units to improvise those means. Brigade command directives recommended that the men cover their mouth with handkerchiefs or towels wetted with urine or water to reduce the effects of the gas. Thanks to officers like Major Mathews, the 8th Battalion was provided with cotton bandoliers and buckets of water were stationed within easy reach. Still, this measure was not of much value if the gas was in concentrated form.[13] Lieutenant Herbert Maxwell-Scott (No. 3 Company, 15th Battalion), a descendant of the novelist Sir Walter Scott, wrote: "Captain McLaren gave an order to get handkerchiefs, soak them, and tie around our mouths and noses … Even with these precautions it was hopeless to try to stand up against the stuff."[14] What the Canadians hoped for was that they would be able to hold on long enough for the blindness and searing pain to pass. They realized, or at least many of them did, that they were not likely to survive and that their only remaining option was to take as many Germans with them as possible. Major Mathews duly acknowledged their courage and discipline: "I can truthfully say there were no officers or men who did not do their duty by trying to fight down to the best of their ability the effects of the awful chocking gas in their determination to stick to their posts."[15]

The deadly fumes enveloped the whole of the 15th Battalion's right company (No. 1) and much of the centre company (No. 3), as well as most of the 8th Battalion's left company (No. 1) and a small part of the centre company (No. 2).[16] Lipsett reported that the gas "had a most paralyzing effect on one, leaving one almost helpless and gasping for breath."[17] Mathews added the following:

> It is impossible for me to give a real idea of the terror
> and horror spread among us all by this filthy loathsome

pestilence. It was not, I think, the fear of death or anything supernatural but the great dread that we could not stand the fearful suffocating sensation sufficiently to be each in our proper places and able to resist to the uttermost the attack which we felt sure must follow …[18]

Coughing, choking, and with eyes tearing, men held dampened cotton bandoliers or moistened handkerchiefs over their faces. Many were blinded and overcome, then tumbled to the bottom of the trenches where, gasping for air, they died in frightful agony. "The trench presented a weird spectacle, men were coughing, spitting, cursing and groveling on the ground and trying to vomit," Mathews recalled.[19] Those still able to fight, reacting to the order that the line must be held at all costs, dragged themselves up onto the parapet and awaited the enemy.

The 5th Battalion suffered less from the gas than the two battalions on its left. Lieutenant-Colonel George Tuxford was awakened by his adjutant, Captain Edward Hilliam, after the alarm went up. On coming out of his dugout, he saw a huge wall of greenish mist, swallowing up the landscape as it rolled toward his front from the north. He described what happened next:

> "What do you make of that? What do you think it is?" Hilliam questioned.
>
> "I wonder whether it has anything to do with the gas we have heard about," I replied. I went to the telephone and called up Lipsett for his H. Qrs. was now enveloped by the vapour.
>
> He replied himself at once, his voice choking, and gasping for breath. "[sic] its gas — very bad — can't talk" was all that I could make out.[20]

About ten minutes after the gas had been released, the Germans scrambled out of their trenches, wearing their rudimentary respirators. They were so confident that the chlorine had done their work that they advanced, not in open skirmishing order, but in heavy waves.[21] The 5th

Battalion was never in peril that day, although Tuxford had no way of knowing how it would turn out. He had no artillery support. On top of this, his men had to contend with the repeated jamming of their Ross rifles. Tuxford recalled with asperity: "We had spent many months of training to attain proficiency in rapid fire, even telling the men that their safety depended on that efficiency, and now that that efficiency was demanded, the rifle failed … men cursed the rifle and threw it away. I have seen strong men weep in anguish at the failure."[22]

Fortunately, the Germans did not press their assault with great resolution. Private R.L. Christopherson (5th Battalion), a bank clerk from Yorkton, Saskatchewan, was praying that he would not have to rely on the bayonet or debris — bricks, building material, bats — in his trench to fight off the German. As he later put it: "The Germans never came close enough for bayonets, thank God. But they would attack and they'd come so far and then they'd go back and attack again. That went on practically all day. By nightfall there were fellows had died from the gas that we all re-equipped ourselves with Lee-Enfield rifles, and then we could shoot."[23]

On the front of the 8th Battalion, appropriately nicknamed the "Little Black Devils," the right company (No. 4), having escaped the worst of the gas, raked the steadily advancing grey figures with rifle and machine-gun fire, mowing down wave after wave. In the centre and left companies (Nos. 1 and 2), a considerable number of men had been overcome by the gas, but the majority, with tears flowing down their cheeks and gasping for breath, manned the battered parapet as determinately as their physical condition would permit. In one sector of the trench, Corporal John Simpson, having dragged himself up coughing and spitting amid the swirling fumes, waited for the enemy to attack. As the fumes dissipated, he saw the Germans climbing over the parapet, so he called out to all who could stand to open rapid fire. "We killed all who got over and, and, no more attempted ," he wrote to his mother in Dublin. [24] An unsteady Private J. Carey mustered all of his strength and willpower to pull himself to the top of the trench. Then the enemy appeared: "Of the hundreds of Germans in front of me, I see one big fat fellow aiming. I get him and he limps like a big pack rabbit performing in a pantomime. I laugh as I see him come down on his shoulder with his heels sticking up and wiggling funnily. But, nevertheless, I fire again and the wiggling stops."[25]

Backed by an accurate shrapnel barrage that landed at the rate of a ton every two minutes, Canadians poured a deadly fire into the fast-approaching hordes. Under the stress of rapid fire, their Ross rifle, as experts had warned, jammed. In such circumstances, the men had been instructed to pry back the stubborn bolt by striking it sharply with their entrenchment tool handle or using their boot heels. These measures did not always work, and, as the fire slackened, the Canadians threw back the Germans with machine-gun bursts and bayonet thrusts. Many of the wounded, who were sitting or lying at the bottom of the trenches, loaded empty rifles and passed them up to their comrades on the firing step. Stricken by fire they had not expected, the attacking lines wavered, broke up, then stopped. Mathews wrote that the enemy's last-gasp effort on his left was met by machine-gun fire that was so effective that when it was over he estimated that 50 or 60 Germans had been killed. The attack had been repelled with such ease, Mathews went on to say, that "the men wanted to kill and go on killing, and it was hard to prevent them climbing out of the trench and making an attack on the enemy."[26] General Currie later complimented the "Little Black Devils" as the only regiment in the British service to date that, after being gassed, held their trenches."[27]

On the other hand, the fortunes of the 15th Battalion, on the left of the 8th, could not have been much worse. Here, the gas was more concentrated, not the least because its trenches were about 100 yards closer to the enemy's gas cylinders than those of the 8th.[28] Being outside the gassed area, the left company (No. 4) was powerless to provide aid, for it was unable to see the front of the attack. Consequently, the centre (No.3) and right (No.1) Companies, which had received a full dose of the chlorine, were left to their own devices, without either artillery support (which, as noted, was too far away from their front) or enfilading fire. For ten minutes, these soldiers endured chlorine gas and incessant shelling, unaware that there was no help at hand to impede the advance of the Germans. The task of simultaneously trying to keep the choking poison out of their lungs and checking the swarms of Germans following behind the wall of gas proved impossible. The fumes penetrated the wet handkerchiefs and again men and officers dropped to the ground, clutching their throats, writhing and vomiting in a slow and frightful agony of death. Captain Archie McGregor and practically all of the men in No. 1 Company were killed, while in the centre, Major Joseph McLaren's company practically disintegrated. McLaren, himself sick and disoriented, collected what men he could and led them to a trench to the left and rear, which was held by one of his platoons under Lieutenant Smith. A party of Germans pursued them briefly, but were held back by two Colt machine guns. As it happened, that part of the line where McLaren and his men sought refuge had not been affected by the gas. Most of McLaren's men were too far gone to fight, but those able to pick up their rifles joined Smith's platoon in firing into the flank of the Germans as they crossed over the trenches formerly occupied by the two Canadian companies.[29]

Other survivors from No. 3 Company swayed and staggered in disarray toward the reserve trenches. It was probably this group that a captivated Tom Drummond (8th Battalion) sighted from a distance. He wrote that he saw "a line of men on our left leaving the line, casting away equipment, rifles and clothing as they ran," some "writhing to the ground, clutching at their throats, tearing open their shirts in a last struggle for air, and after a while ceasing to struggle and lying still while a greenish foam formed over their mouth and lips."[30] Those who made it back to the rearward defences, according to McLaren, lay practically motionless at the bottom of the trench, while others died slowly from asphyxiation. There were some who lost their way and stumbled back aimlessly, never reaching a safety zone. What exactly happened to these men is not entirely clear. We do know that they ran into a few stragglers from the other company (No. 1) who had miraculously survived, and together they trudged to a wooded area by the Stroombeek, a stream about 700 hundred yards behind the front. Here, with the Germans on their heels, they dug in, as much as their physical condition would permit, and fought to a finish.

Around 4:50 a.m., Lipsett received a telephone message that the Germans were advancing unchecked on the trenches of the 15th Battalion. He immediately sent two platoons of No. 3 Company — which had been held back in the rear in support — under Captain Arthur Morley to cover his left. Morley made his way through the shelling and drifting gas, and, when he reached his destination, reported that the Canadians were all gone and that their trench "was full of Germans who had put up their flag on the parapet"[31] To secure the battalion's open flank, Morley deployed his men at right angles to the front.

The rupture in the 15th Battalion's front, through which poured masses of German infantry, imperiled the rear of Canadian units on either side. Canadian reinforcements for the critical point flowed from different quarters. Turner was the first to respond, but it was for the wrong reason. He had received an erroneous report that the front of the 2nd Brigade had been "driven in."[32] As he had no reserves, he immediately called upon what remained of the 10th Battalion from Kitchener's Wood, where it had been under fire for almost two days with little sleep or food. The unit was ordered to leave the trenches it had won so dearly and move to Locality C on the crest of Gravenstafel Ridge. Although belonging to the 2nd Brigade, the 10th had temporarily passed under Turner's command two days earlier. Now Turner informed Currie that he was returning the battalion.[33] To take over from the 10th, the equally depleted 16th was directed to extend its line farther to the left — a little while later- the 16th would be relieved by the 2nd. Even with the 16th providing cover, it was not a simple matter for the men of the 10th to work back to the rear in broad daylight over an open field. Lieutenant Walter Critchley (10th Battalion) remarked in hindsight: "In full view of the Hun we had to individually get out and race across this ploughed field and reassemble and go up to the Gravenstafel."[34] Sid Cox added: "And they got quite a lot of us coming out, you see because we had to run about fifty feet, jump into cabbage patch or wheat field ... and you would see three or four run and they would get one — and then you'd think, well I'll crawl and they would get one. No, I'm going to run. You had to make up your mind which way you wanted to be hit."[35]

Cox's memory betrayed him a bit, for there were not nearly as many casualties as he implied. "We did very well," was Major Ormond's verdict. Still, 450 men had fallen since the midnight charge, leaving only three officers and 171 other ranks — out of a battalion that had numbered close to 850 before 22 April. As the new CO, Ormond led his men to 2nd Brigade Headquarters at Fortuin. If Currie was shocked by the remnants of the once powerful 10th, as he surely must have been, he gave no indication. Ormond remarked that when Currie came out "he gave the men a cheery word"[36] Ormond was directed to reinforce the defenders on Locality C, a pivotal point in the Divison's defences, and henceforth take his orders from Lieutenant-Colonel Lipsett. After reconnoitering the area, Ormond communicated with Lipsett by telephone (at 5:30 a.m.) and was urged to hold on to Locality C at all costs. Lipsett considered his position to be in grave danger. He had assured Currie at 4:50 a.m. that he had the situation in hand, but whether it was a case of overconfidence or that he had an incomplete picture of what was happening — there was a time lag between the events occurring and receipt of the news — cannot be determined. In any case, he had a change of heart, as the nature of the fighting came into sharper focus. He wrote in his report that he was aware the Germans were working around his left flank, where a 1300-yard gap existed between his trenches and Locality C. He added that he held no hope of stopping a determined attack with the forces at his disposal.[37]

Ormond and his men arrived at Locality C ten minutes later and headed toward a line of shallow trenches to the front and left of No. 1 Company, 7th Battalion — one of two reserve companies Currie had transferred to Lipsett when he had determined the direction of the attack — commanded by Captain John Warden. Ormond went ahead to scout the area when he fell into a pond. As he dragged himself out, he was spotted by the enemy and came under rifle and shrapnel fire. He was hit in the right shoulder and knocked down, but only bruised. He no sooner joined his men in the trench than they were almost overcome by gas. Ormond claimed that he was saved only because Lieutenant Critchley gave him a piece of his wet handkerchief.

As the men regained their senses, they detected swarms of Germans passing over the dead ground (an area inaccessible to artillery fire) between the left of the 8th Battalion and Locality C. After rupturing the front of the 15th Battalion, the Germans were in a position to take in reverse the Canadians holding the northwestern face of the salient. They chose not to do so for the time being. Instead, they mounted further attacks southward, and, as we have previously mentioned, overran the little band in the woods by the Stroombeek before reaching the outskirts of Locality C. "We looked over there and all we could see was masses of the Germans coming up in mass formation," Critchley recalled. "Their officers were still on horseback then." Their first attack having been beaten back, the Germans did not fare any better with the next two that followed. Ormond recalled the feeling of euphoria that swept over him and the other defenders in the aftermath of their triumph:

> We stood up on our parapet and gave them three ruddy cheers and shook our fists at them. We gave them everything we had and they figured it wasn't worth while and they just turned around and went back. They did that again and we did it again. We were quite happy about it. So they did it a third time. When they went back the third time we thought we'd won the war.[38]

During the last attack, the Germans resorted to a subterfuge carried out mostly in front of Warden's section of the line. As the Germans approached, Warden saw a row of men wearing British uniforms with "the enemy behind pretending to drive them along with their bayonets towards us." A major, who had sought refuge in Warden's trench, along with other Highland stragglers, was fooled by the ruse. However, Warden was not similarly deceived, as he later explained:

> As there was a Highland Major in command of my trench, I waited for his orders to fire. Not receiving any, and as the enemy were getting within 50 yards and outnumbering us, I should say 10 to 1, I ordered the men myself to fire. This Major (I do not know his name or Battalion) ordered the men to cease firing, as he said we would shoot our own men in front of the Germans. I shouted "They are not British Soldiers — they are Germans dressed in British Uniforms," and again gave the order to fire. Again he stopped those

near him firing. I ordered my own men to open rapid fire, which they did and succeeded in driving back the enemy. Those in "British Uniforms," who were right up to our entanglement and could have come into our trench had they wished, turned and ran back even faster than the rest, which was sufficient proof that they were not British soldiers.[39]

What made the Canadian stand even more remarkable was the continued unreliability of their Ross rifle. Ormond pointed out that, instead of the twelve or fifteen aimed shots a minute during rapid fire, they could get off only a few rounds before their rifles jammed, thus compelling them "to lay down and take their heel to force the bolt open."[40] Even after half a century, Sergeant Chris Scriven, a member of Ormond's unit and a seasoned militiaman, nursed bitter feelings about the Ross rifle:

> It wasn't even safe to send a fourteen-year [-old] kid out rabbit-hunting in the fields with, never mind going into battle with. I laid in a shell hole with four other men for a day and a half, and out of five Ross rifles in that hole, it took four of us to keep one of them working, banging the bolts out. As soon as you fired a round, you had to sit down and take the entrenching-tool handle to bash the bolt out, to get the [empty cartridge] out, before you could load it again.[41]

The retention of Locality C did not lessen the pressure on the left front of the 8th Battalion. Morley, engaged in a running battle with the enemy, had sustained serious casualties. Lipsett continued to worry about the condition of his left, recognizing that if it gave way before the arrival of reinforcements, a large section of the Canadian line would be lost. Thus, he sent half of his remaining reserve company to assist Morley. The two platoons drew machine-gun fire as they crossed a high bank to occupy a trench. Their leader was shot and a number of the men were hit.

Sergeant-Major Frederick Hall, a 30-year-old Irishman from Winnipeg, brought two of the wounded back into the trench, but groans of suffering indicated that there was another helpless victim on the ridge. Hall and two volunteers, Lance-Corporal Payne and Private Rogerson, went over the parados toward the injured man. Payne and Rogerson were wounded almost instantly, and, with Hall's assistance, scrambled back to the shelter of the trench. Hall rested a few minutes before attempting the rescue again. While he crawled slowly along the ground, bullets ricocheted off the top of the parados and cut the ground around him. He moved up the slope of the bank where, guided by the weakening groans of suffering, he located the wounded man. He lay flat and squirmed beneath his helpless comrade, getting him on his back. As he glanced up to survey the ground over which he had to return to shelter, he was shot in the head and instantly killed. For his act of heroism, Hall was awarded the Victoria Cross posthumously.[42]

Unable to break behind Locality C, the Germans concentrated on trying to smash through the northwestern face of the salient. The Canadian line, from the severed end of the original front to St. Julien and round to Kitchener's Wood, was held by units belonging to the 13th, 14th, 7th, 3rd, and 2nd Battalions as well as the Buffs. The discharge of gas, which preceded the German assaults, was not always effective, drifting in some places almost parallel to the trenches. "The enemy liberated gas fumes on our front," Odlum wrote in his report, "but owing to the direction of the prevailing wind we escaped the full effects of them."[43] However, gas fumes blew over a few sectors, one of which was held by two companies of the 3rd Battalion dug in west of St. Julien. Here, the Germans made a determined effort to break in between the two companies and St. Julien. A 23- year-old Private Frank Asburn remarked in hindsight:

> During the gas attack at St. Julien we lost the first line
> of trenches and had to move back to the supports. At
> the back of those trenches we lay down flat and covered
> our mouths with wet clothes, waiting for the Germans
> to come up. They came slowly, thinking we were all
> dead from their gas, but not so. It drifted slowly over

us and showed the Germans about seventy-five yards away. We were suddenly ordered to rapid fire and I don't think that more than a dozen Germans got away alive. We advanced again and regained our front trench with minimal losses.[44]

Behind the two companies of 3rd Battalion, the St. Julien defenders kept the advancing German hordes at bay in spite of heavy shelling and the jamming of their Ross rifles from the rapid fire. Loomis's garrison consisted of No. 2 Company of the 15th Battalion under Captain George Alexander, whose trenches on either side of the Poelcappelle road, north of the village, slanted southward to the Steenbeek. Slightly to the rear of his position lay two platoons of the 14th Battalion, led by Captain Wilfred Brotherhood, which carried the line on the western side of St. Julien. Captain R.Y. Cory, Alexander's second in command, collected about 200 Turcos, in addition to stragglers from other units, and extended the line toward Mouse Trap Farm. After 6:00 a.m., the Germans tried on three occasions to break into the town from the left, only to be turned back each time.

It was the same story in other parts of the line during the early morning, with the Germans on the receiving end of withering fire. They made excellent targets as they came in close formation over practically open ground. The defenders cut down wave after wave, leaving the dead and wounded lying in long rows on the field. Reeling, the German infantry drew back to allow the artillery to subdue the defenders. German gunners, aided by airplanes soaring overhead to identify the correct range, laid down a dense and deadly bombardment along the front between the apex and St. Julien. Whole stretches of trench were obliterated and casualties mounted rapidly.

The shelling was especially severe at the apex where the 13th Battalion and a handful of Buffs, reinforced by two companies of the 14th, were vulnerable in their shallow trenches. "People were being blown up all around us," H.G. Brewer (14th Battalion) recalled, "bodies flying up in the air."[45] Around 8:00 a.m., after a lull in the bombardment, the Germans redoubled their efforts to reduce the apex. By now, the position of the defenders was hopeless. They were without machine guns, all put out of action by the shelling, and under heavy attack from the front and threatened from the rear by the breach in the 15th Battalion's front. At 8:30 a.m, Major Buchanan, who commanded the left part of the 13th Battalion's line, judged that he must fall back or else he would soon be surrounded. Thus, he passed the order to retire to a reserve line west of Locality C. There was no assurance that the withdrawal could be carried out safely. The men had to scramble back over a long slope that was relatively open and covered by machine gun and artillery that one eyewitness described as "absolutely hellish in its accuracy."[46]

The movement should have begun with the units at the tip of the apex, but presumably the pressure of events dictated otherwise. Three out of the four companies led by Buchanan, along with units of the 14th, fell back in reasonably good order. The right company, under the redoubtable McCuaig, now reduced to two other officers and 40 other ranks, plus the remnants of Tomlinson's company of Buffs at the far end of the line, were not nearly as fortunate. By the time the order reached McCuaig's men, their only chance of escaping was to dash back toward the nearest cover, 50 yards in rear over open ground. Just as McCuaig was about to give the signal to withdraw, a shell exploded in the trench, killing a soldier and burying 28-year-old Colin Alexander. One of the men called out, "Major McCuaig, there is Alexander gone." From beneath the mound of earth, a voice was heard: "No Alexander is not gone but he is pretty well badly hurt." Alexander's comrades pulled him out, but his leg was seriously injured and he was unable to run.[47]

Alexander was the first of McCuaig's men to be taken prisoner. He may have considered himself lucky. As it was, only a few of the men managed to scramble to safety. The Germans, who had been expecting such a move, swept the open ground with intense rifle and machine-gun fire, cutting down most of the Highlanders before they had covered half the distance. It was then that Lieutenant Charles Pitblado showed exceptional courage in carrying back Captain Whitehead, second-in-command, who had been mortally wounded and was delirious. Whitehead lapsed into unconsciousness and Pitblado was compelled to abandon him after being hit in the knee. As he struggled on, he came face-to-face with McCuaig and the two men saw to the retirement of the remnant of the company. McCuaig's report, written after the war, described what followed:

> We were going back together when I was wounded in the knee but was able to proceed. I was shortly after shot through both legs and rendered helpless. Pitblado in spite of my protests refused to leave me and bandaged up the wounds in my leg under a very heavy fire. He was then wounded a second time in the leg, which finished his chances of getting away. I was subsequently wounded four more times while lying on the ground. We both remained there until picked up by the Germans an hour or two later. Their firing line passed us about ten minutes after we were wounded.[48]

For both McCuaig and Pitblado the war was over. The courage and devotion shown by the two men throughout the engagement were later acknowledged when they respectively received the Distinguished Service Order and the Military Cross, the first Canadians to be awarded that distinction in the Great War.

At the top of the apex, Tomlinson's Buffs, adjoining the 15th Battalion, had remained in place for they had not received the order to retire. They continued to fight on until they ran out of ammunition. Then they moved over and connected with the left company (No. 4) of the 15th Battalion. Cut off, bombarded ceaselessly, and pressed on all sides by the enemy's infantry, the Buffs and Highlanders continued to hold out, but, with their ammunition exhausted and most of the survivors wounded, the end was clearly in sight. The Highland commander, Major Ewart Osborne, a 39-year-old stockbroker, suddenly discovered that his headquarters was isolated from the main line. Dashing across an open field under heavy artillery and machine-gun fire, he was hit, but managed to reach a cottage where he was eventually captured by a small German party. From a distance he could see that the Germans had surrounded the Highlanders and Buffs, and, additionally, their guns had started to find the range. He prayed that the defenders would recognize the futility of further resistance and hoist the white flag. To his relief, he did not have long to wait. Left in charge of the Highlanders, Lieutenant MacDonald consulted his subordinates and the second-in-command of the Buffs, Lieutenant Ryder (Tomlinson was apparently wounded), and, to use Osborne's words, "justifiably surrendered about 9:10 a.m. in order to save an absolutely needless slaughter of men."[49]

The penetration into the 15th Battalion's front, followed by the retirement of the 13th, had placed the 7th Battalion, transferred earlier to the 3rd Brigade, in a precarious position. The new commander, Major Odlum, had seen elements of the 13th, 14th, and 15th Battalions stream past his rear in disorder. All telephonic communications with 3rd Brigade Headquarters had been cut, so he was unable to ascertain immediately what was happening to the north. Patrols sent out to investigate reported that there was utter confusion everywhere, but a gap existed between the right of the 7th and Locality C. Odlum sent a runner to inform 3rd Brigade Headquarters that he was in danger of being cut off and asked "for instructions, for reinforcements and for information concerning intentions." His appeal went unanswered. Turning to Currie, he described his plight and added that unless reinforced, there was a danger his line would give way, in which case his battalion would be cut off.[50] But since Odlum was now under Turner's orders, Currie felt he could not intervene.

At 8:30 a.m., rifle fire was heard in the rear on a crest to the east. Thinking that his reserve company might be firing on Canadian troops retreating from the trenches of the 15th Battalion, Odlum sent word that it was to refrain unless the enemy could be identified and were very close. As it happened, the fire came from Germans, who were less than 300 yards from Odlum's rear. The two companies (Nos. 2 and 4) facing west, commanded by Captain Thomas Scudamore and Major Percy Byng-Hall, sent verbal reports that the Germans were advancing in very large numbers against their front, but that they were being mowed down in masses by rifle and machine-gun fire. After each attack was hurled back, the Germans paused briefly before returning to the charge.[51] "The wounded and the dead were lying everywhere," Private Perley Smith recalled, "and there was everything in the German army coming at us over the fields for miles."[52] Smith could still visualize the scene half a century later: "They came over in masses. You couldn't miss if you could fire a gun. That's what made me so sore. If our guns had been working, or just if we had good rifles — some fellows picked up Lee-Enfields and threw the Ross away. There were some fellows crying in the trenches because they couldn't fire their damned rifles."[53] Scudamore, realizing that many Canadian soldiers had perished because of a defective rifle, could not conceal his bitterness: "Those who were in the line with that rifle will never forget, while those who were not will never be able to understand what it was like to be charged by the flower of the German army, confident of victory, and be unable to shoot in return."[54] Sergeant Hugh Peerless did much to contain the men's anger and frustration with their rifles by his courage and inspirational leadership that included cries of "Give the sons of bitches hell, boys."[55] In the early stages, the three machine guns in the Canadian line were instrumental in keeping the Germans at bay. In fact, the two COs were confident, so they told Odlum, that they could maintain their position against any frontal attack.

It was a different story for Captain H.V. Harvey and two platoons of No. 3 Company, occupying a stretch of trench on the northeast side (extreme right) of Odlum's line. A gap in the line had allowed the Germans to break though and close in on their trench. The men of No. 3 Company made the enemy pay dearly, but not without cost to themselves. A stretcher-bearer, R.C. Hunt from Cobourg, Ontario, gives us a glimpse of the suffering the men endured:

> I found them in an awful mess. Poor little Captain Harvey had been wounded twice and I dressed him and asked him if I could carry him down to the dressing station and he said no look after the other men. Then Lieutenant Bromely got one which I dressed. I tried to persuade him to sit down but he said he must look after his men.[56]

A small detachment, which included Private Nathan Rice, a 26-year-old railwayman, was sent to reinforce Harvey. It ran into heavy enemy fire and most of the men were killed or wounded. A friend of Rice staggered and fell after a bullet hit his ammunition pouch, causing a small explosion. Rice ran to his side and saw "that all his insides were hanging out between his fingers like rolls of sausage."[57] The survivors never reached Harvey's trench. Nor did another party that volunteered for the dangerous task of bringing up ammunition. Odlum watch with horror as a shell landed in the midst of the group, killing his brother Joseph, among others. Sick at heart, he had no time to dwell on his personal loss. At 9:30 a.m., with the enemy closing in on his headquarters, he moved to a dugout and shifted the two platoons of his reserve company to protect his rear and to support any troops of the 3rd Brigade in the area. At 10:30 a.m., Odlum received a report that Harvey and his men had been wiped out and that the enemy was in possession of their trench.[58]

As the morning wore on and his position deteriorated even further, Odlum made another appeal to 3rd Brigade Headquarters: "My position becoming desperate. Unless reinforcements hurried up, my batt. will be cut off. Can only get out with difficulty by way of St Julien. Instructions please."[59] Again, he received no answer. Turner was aware that the 7th Battalion had passed under his orders, but he failed to exercise jurisdiction over it. Turner's inaction has never been explained. The only thing for sure was that early on he and his brigade major, Lieutenant-Colonel Garnet Hughes, failed to grasp what was happening on the west side of the apex.

As we have noted, Turner informed Alderson at 4:55 a.m. that the left of the 2nd Brigade had collapsed, when in fact it was the right of his own brigade that had given way. Currie's appreciation to Divisional Headquarters — sent by hand at 5:15, but not received until an hour later — painted a more accurate picture. He maintained that his position was intact, but that the Germans had penetrated a section of the 15th Battalion's trenches.[60] A second message from 2nd Brigade command, delivered at 6:30 a.m., indicated that the 3rd Brigade's line was crumbling and that the situation was critical.[61] Yet twenty minutes later, Turner still had not discovered that the point of danger lay within his brigade, not the 2nd, assuring Alderson, "We do not feel uneasy."[62] At 7:00 a.m., Loomis, who commander the St. Julien garrison, sent a note to 3rd

Brigade Headquarters that finally opened Turner's eyes to the disaster that had occurred on his right — nearly three hours after the front of the 15th Battalion had been breached. Loomis observed that many stragglers were coming back, an indication that the line was broken. Additionally, he had received a message from Lieutenant-Colonel W.W. Burland, acting commander of the 14th Battalion,[63] telling him of the break-in.[64]

Turner responded by sending a flurry of messages, some of which, even accounting for the chaos and confusion prevalent in battle, bordered on the absurd. He directed Loomis to attack with two companies and underscoring "that St. Julien must be held." [65] Loomis could not understand the order to attack with two companies that were already engaged. He collected 15 signallers, orderlies, and runners at his headquarters and set out for Gravenstafel Ridge. Scrambling to the top of the ridge, he could see the remnants of his own 13th Battalion, supported by parts of other units on either flank, fighting off a frontal attack from the northwest. Of greater concern to him were the masses of Germans who had followed behind the gas and were preparing to attack the Canadian rear. As he could do little with 15 men, he decided to hurry over to Mouse Trap Farm, three and a half miles away, to personally explain the situation to Turner and to request artillery support. He gave no thought to leaving his post, which could have cost him his command. Dodging bullets and artillery shells, he reached 3rd Brigade Headquarters, and, in an interview with Turner, persuaded him to withdraw the order to counterattack.

No less illogical was the message sent to Lieutenant-Colonel John Currie, commander of the 15th Battalion, at 7:15 a.m: "Reported that impression exists in your regiment that they are to retire on GHQ line. This must be corrected at once. You are to hold your front line. If driven out, collect your men, organize counter-attack, and regain it. You are *on no account* to retire on GHQ line."[66]

One can only imagine what passed through Currie's mind upon reading Turner's note. A counterattack was out of the question since, by then, the 15th Battalion had been practically annihilated. The casualties for the day were later placed at 671, of whom 223 were killed. During the entire war, no other Canadian battalion suffered as heavily in so

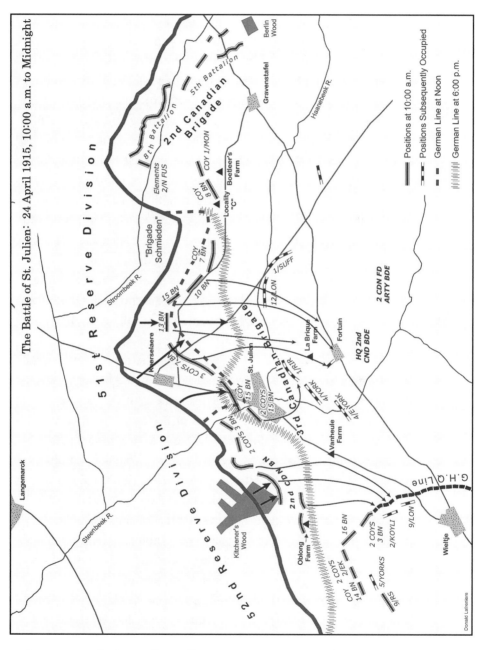

The Battle of St. Julien: 24 April 1915, 10:00 a.m. to Midnight

Positions at 10:00 a.m.

Positions Subsequently Occupied

German Line at Noon

German Line at 6:00 p.m.

51st Reserve Division

52nd Reserve Division

2nd Canadian Brigade

3rd Canadian Brigade

Berlin Wood

Gravenstafel

Haanebeek R.

2 CDN FD ARTY BDE

8th Battalion

5th Battalion

Elements 2/N FUS

COY 1/MON

COY 8 BN

Locality "C"

Boetleer's Farm

"Brigade Schmieden"

Stroombeek R.

COY 7 BN

15 BN

10 BN

13 BN

Keerselaere

3 COYS 7 BN

COY 15 BN

2 COYS 15 BN

St. Julien

1/SUFF

12/LON

1/R/R

4/YORK

4/EYORK

La Brique Farm

Fortuin

HQ 2nd CND BDE

Langemarck

Steenbeek R.

2 COYS 3 BN

2nd CDN BN

Kitchener's Wood

Oblong Farm

Vanheule Farm

COY 2 COYS 2/EK

14 BN

5/YORKS

9/RS

16 BN

2 COYS 3 BN

2/KOYLI

5/YORKS

G.H.Q. Line

6/LON

Wieltje

Donald Lafrenière

short a period of time.[67] Finally at 7:20 a.m., Turner informed Alderson that his right was retiring, a message he subsequently confirmed while requesting help.[68]

Even before receiving Turner's first telegram, Alderson suspected that a minor break-in had occurred, but he had been reassured by confident messages. Upon learning of the predicament of the 3rd Brigade, he acted at once. Among his British and Canadian reserve units were four battalions of the 150th Brigade (York and Durham), 50th Division, which had come under his command earlier that morning and was currently near Brielen Bridge on the west side of the Yser Canal. At 7:30 a.m., he directed Brigadier-General J.E. Bush, in charge of the 150th Brigade, to occupy the GHQ line with two battalions and act as reserve to the 2nd and 3rd Brigades.[69] Alderson then notified both Turner and Currie of the availability, if needed, of the two Yank and Durham battalions and directed them to contact Bush.[70] Less than an hour later, as the enemy continued pressing its attack on St. Julien, Alderson instructed the other two battalions of the 150th to move forward to the GHQ line.[71] Alderson hoped to relieve the 3rd Brigade in the evening with the 150th. Accordingly, at 10:45 a.m., he urged Turner not to call on a battalion of the 150th unless absolutely necessary.[72]

V Corps Headquarters did not hear of the German break-in until 7:40 a.m. and even then had to wait nearly four hours before receiving further news. At 11:33 a.m., a message from the 27th Division reported the new Canadian position after the loss of the apex. Alarmed by the latest developments, Plumer directed Alderson "to take instant action to reconstitute the line." It was an unnecessary order. What did he think the Canadians had been doing since the break-in had been reported? But, in his defence, being a long way from the scene and without precise information, he was acting instinctively, in the only manner that he could think of. What the Canadians needed above all was help. Several hours earlier, Plumer had placed the 151th Brigade (50th Division) under the 2nd Cavalry Corps Division, which was in reserve on the left flank west of the canal. He had also promised Alderson the 10th (4th Division) and 149th (50th Division) Brigades, the only other troops available, but they had not yet arrived in the area.[73] For the time being he could do nothing else.

It is apparent from reading the various reports, telegrams, and exchanges of messages, that the command structure was breaking down — not unusual during major battles in the First World War. Given that

British and Canadian headquarters were well behind the lines, often beyond the sound of guns, the reports they received were frequently erroneous or out of date. The crux of the problem was that they did not have a viable communications system to properly control their widely scattered forces. Thus, as the fog of war spread over the battlefield, the burden of conducting the fighting fell mainly on the battalion commanders. These met periodically in groups of two or three to discuss common problems and share their resources. None had any idea of the general situation. The result was that their action reflected concern over local rather than general conditions.

After the loss of the apex, the Canadian line, from Locality C to north-east of St Julien, was shaped like a rough semicircle. It was manned from east to west by the 10th Battalion, resting near Locality C, followed by remnants of the 15th, 13th, 14th, and the 7th Battalions (less one company). Given no reinforcements, as none were available, they were left to defend a frail line that was in view of the enemy and enfiladed by machine-gun fire from both flanks.

Near Keerselaere, the nightmare continued for the right two platoons of the 7th Battalion, their numbers diminishing steadily by the uninterrupted shelling from guns of all calibers. Odlum had two options: he could retire or remain in place and face extermination. Out of touch with 3rd Brigade Headquarters, Odlum went to nearby colleagues for advice. At 11:00 a.m., he met Lieutenant-Colonel Burland of the the 14th Battalion and Lieutenant-Colonel Currie, CO of the 15th — his No. 2 Company continued to hold a trench on Odlum's left — at a crossroad between Locality C and St. Julien. According to Odlum, he met the two officers separately, not together, as has been reported in the accounts of the battle. His interview with Burland went splendidly, but his encounter with Currie was marred by heated exchanges. Odlum did not paint a flattering portrait of Currie on that occasion:

> He said some things which I took in bad part, and our language towards each other was explosive. He did not realize that the 7th and the 15th were in a position almost back to back and he did not accept my explanation. As a

matter of fact, he seemed to have a very meager idea of what was happening at that part of the field. He believed that his own battalion was still in position, whereas I knew that a large part of it had retired, because in retiring it had passed through my rear and around my flank. I told him this and he became very excited.[74]

It is difficult to believe that Currie was still in the dark five hours after the Germans had smashed through the 15th Battalion's front. But it should be pointed out that Currie may have been in a state of denial as his behaviour, then and subsequently, suggests that he suffered something approaching a breakdown — which would soon led to his recall.[75] At any rate, the decision was taken to withdraw 300 yards to the rear and establish a new line between St. Julien and Locality C. Taking advantage of the dead ground, the 14th and 10th Battalions on the right of Odlum carried out the movement without serious losses. No. 2 Company, 15th Battalion, in attempting to fight its way back to the new line, was pressed so closely by the enemy that only a few individuals escaped and of these most were wounded. The fortunes of the 7th were no better. By the time Odlum returned to his headquarters to organize the retreat, his defences were beginning to crumble. "We got trapped," L.C. Scott explained. "We were out behind the German lines. We stayed too long."[76]

Odlum passed the order that his men were to fight their way back and rendezvous in the new line. With the enemy close and coming from all directions, the left company under Scudamore remained behind to cover the withdrawal. The weight of Germans broke through its defences almost immediately, and the survivors scrambled back, sometimes in small groups, but few managed to escape. Scudamore, who had received a head wound earlier, did not run far when he lost consciousness. When he woke up, he saw a German soldier standing over him and pointing a rifle. Byng-Hall and the men in the right company made a run for it, partially shielded by the thick fog of dust and tear gas created by the shells exploding nearby. They reached the trench in front of St. Julien, which was manned by Captain Alexander's company. Unfortunately, their reprieve was only temporary.

Those who made good their escape owe much to the valour of Lieutenant Edward D. Bellew, machine-gun officer of the 7th Battalion and Sergeant Hugh Peerless. A 37-year-old civil engineer from Vancover, Bellew was a graduate from Sandhurst and served in the Royal Irish Regiment before immigrating to Canada. Bellew had two guns situated on the high ground overlooking Keerselaere, slightly to the left of the right company. He operated one himself after his trained gunners were put out of action and Peerless handled the other. When the front of the right company was penetrated, the two soldiers remained where they were and emptied belt upon belt of ammunition into the advancing enemy. Disgusted that their progress was being held up by the fire of two machine guns, the Germans gradually worked behind them. Peerless was killed. Bellew was struck down by a bullet; nevertheless he picked himself up and kept on firing until he ran through his last belt. Then, smashing his gun, he met the enemy with bayonet and rifle butt. He was overpowered and taken prisoner.[77] When released in December 1918, he learned that he had been awarded the Victoria Cross. Bellew was the first officer of the Canadian Expeditionary Force to have been acclaimed for exceptional valour.

At the specified location, Odlum collected about 100 of his own men, plus a few stragglers belonging to other battalions. From a captured trench north of St. Julien, German fire, directed by balloon and airplane observers, swept the flat ground below Gravenstafel Ridge, rendering Odlum's position untenable. As a consequence, he arranged for another conference with Currie and Burland, this time to be held behind Locality C.[78] Major Ormond, whose men were retiring to the next line below, encountered the three battalion commanders a little after 12:30 p.m. and joined the discussion. Few options were available. Ormond wanted to amalgamate the remnants of the various units and counterattack with the object of sweeping the enemy off the toe (west side) of the ridge.[79] The others considered the plan unfeasible. The proposal to retire to the GHQ line was also vetoed on the grounds that it was too far in the rear and would take them out of the battle. In the end it was decided to withdraw 1000 yards farther south to an unmarked line southeast of St. Julien. It was none too soon, for the Canadians were being heavily pressed by the Germans.

Amid shells bursting everywhere, the retirement was carried out in successive rushes with each party falling back a short distance, flopping to the ground, and covering the withdrawal of the next by its fire. Far from wilting under the strain, the Canadians kept up a punishing fire that caused the troops of the 51st German Reserve Division to break off their attack to await further reinforcements. The discipline shown by his resolute comrades left a lasting impression on Private Fred Arnold (7th Battalion):

> I could see the fellows from where I was going back along a hedge and I never saw anything more wonderful for what you'd call semi-untrained troops. They went out on the brow of a hill and they run at about six pace intervals and most of the time you couldn't see them for bursting shells. The Germans were really throwing the big stuff into them. And these fellows took their position up and then they started to fire. I tell you I was proud to be a Canadian.[80]

The Canadian withdrawal at midday had exposed the right of the St. Julien garrison. The Germans had pulled back after their abortive attempts earlier in the morning and waited for the arrival of reinforcements. In the meantime, they kept up the shelling, which continued unabated throughout the morning. Directed by two airplanes hovering above the battlefield, the artillery fire was so accurate that it forced the defenders to move around from time to time. According to Captain Wilfred Brotherhood (14th Battalion), the bursting shells blew up machine guns and killed its crews, buried men, and leveled trenches.[81] It was becoming a one-sided fight. Turner's headquarters ordered a small party of about 100 men of the 3rd Battalion, commanded by Captain Len Morrison, to reinforce the garrison. Moving up from the GHQ line, it was intercepted by Captain Robert Cory (15th Battalion) on the outskirts of the town at 10:00 a.m. Evidently outnumbered, and with the artillery continuing to inflict casualties, Cory judged that only one outcome was possible. As he saw no reason to add to the toll, he informed Morrison, "You had better go back, there's nothing to be done here." [82] Cory walked back to St. Julien, and, like the others, awaited the enemy's final rush.

The defenders at St. Julien were unaware of the terrible odds they were about to face as the size of the German force was partially hidden by folds in the ground. But 3rd Brigade Headquarters had received information from different sources about the enemy build-up. Around 11:00 a.m., the 8th Battalion had sniped at long range into masses of the enemy passing by their left flank. While Locality C was still in Canadian hands, a dozen or so German battalions were seen moving forward along the Stroombeek toward St. Julien. There were reports that dense columns of German infantry, followed by artillery, were swarming down the main road from Poelcappelle (which led directly to St. Julien).[83]

From three sides, the Germans descended like a gigantic tidal wave upon the village. Captain Brotherhood sent the last message from the doomed village at 11:30 a.m., reading: "Enemy have shelled us out and are advancing from our left and front. Will hold every traverse if we have to retire along right to our line. Captain Williamson killed." [84] An hour later, Brotherhood would suffer the same fate. "They came over and were all over us in a few minutes," recalled Private Nathan Rice (7th Battalion).[85] On the left, part of No. 4 Company, 14th Battalion, managed to withdraw, shielded by the shattered houses, but the rest fought it out to the bitter end. "Our rifles were jammed and the only machine gun that remained had been clogged with mud," explained Private. W.C. Thurwood (8th Battalion).[86] Rice's rifle also jammed in the heat of battle, and, compounding his frustration, the results were the same with the other two he picked up. He did not have an opportunity to grab a fourth rifle. As the Germans had worked their way behind their trench, Byng-Hall (who along with his men had occupied the trench held by Captain Alexander's company) gave the order to cease fire at 12:45 p.m.[87] The Germans, who had seen hundreds of their comrades mowed down, were in an ugly mood. Thurwood was among the lucky who surrendered:

> Though we held our hands aloft and were now unarmed,
> the cold-bloodied crew started to wipe us out. Three of
> our men were bayoneted before an officer arrived and

saved the rest of us. Even then our rough captors struck us with their rifle butts and kicked some of our men who were unfortunate enough to be laid out with wounds.[88]

There were some who, believing the reports of German atrocities, refused to be taken captive. Sergeant Raymond MacIlree (7th Battalion) convinced himself that an order to cease fire should not necessarily be equated with an order to surrender. Preferring a quick death by a bullet rather than being tortured and brutalized as a captive, he shouted to those around him that it was every man for himself, surmising that they had at least a chance to elude the grasp of the swarming Germans. MacIlree felt bullets whizzing by him or hitting his equipment as he, together with five other men, dashed through a hedge and across a field. Cut off by the Germans, MacIlree dropped to the ground and played possum. When the Germans move on, he picked himself up and made his way back to the Canadian lines.[89]

As the remnants of the Canadians were forced back into the village, small groups here and there fought from behind houses and in the streets against enormous odds. Loomis gave the order to retreat to the GHQ line, but only a handful of survivors of the 14th Battalion made it back. It is not known when the last spark was extinguished in St. Julien, but the worst of the fighting was over by 1:00 p.m. Canadian prospects in other parts of the line were no less dismal. We now turn our attention to that story.

CHAPTER 8
24 April: The Crisis Deepens
(1:40 p.m. to 7:00 p.m.)

During the late morning of 24 April, troops belonging to the 2nd and 3rd Battalions south of Kitchener's Wood saw line upon line of German infantrymen emerging from the dead ground for the assault on St. Julien. Both battalions had been placed under the jurisdiction of Turner during the first night of the battle. The 2nd Battalion — which had replaced the survivors of the 10th and 16th Battalions — was holding the trenches on the left and two companies of the 3rd were manning those on the right, in front of St. Julien. The 2nd Battalion from eastern Ontario was commanded by Lieutenant-Colonel David Watson. The 3rd Battalion was raised chiefly from three well known Toronto militia regiments — the Governor General's Body Guards, the 10th Royal Grenadiers, and the Queen's Own Rifles — and was under Lieutenant-Colonel Robert Rennie, with its two front-line companies directed by Major Kirkpatrick.

The sight of many battalions of German infantry advancing in close formation made inviting targets. The 2nd Battalion opened up with rifles and machine guns and the volume of fire rose when the companies of the 3rd Battalion joined the action. Once more, the entire sector was the scene of furious fighting. The Germans assailed Doxsee's House on the 2nd Battalion's front, but a well regulated stream of lead drove them back.[1] Turner was worried about the exposed position of the 2nd Battalion, and at 1:00 p.m. ordered Watson by telephone to withdraw. Watson was loath to do so and sent his adjutant, Captain Willis O'Connor, to plead with Turner to defer his decision until nightfall when disengagement would be easier. Turner agreed to cancel the order.

The Germans had no more success against the 3rd Battalion companies. Then came the German penetration of St. Julien, which spelled trouble, especially for the right company led by Captain John Streight. He notified Major Kirkpatrick that the Germans were in his rear, and, to avoid being cut off, advocated a withdrawal. He received a blunt reply that he was to hang on "*at all costs.*"[2] Kirkpatrick had his own orders: "Do not lose touch with St. Julien. Hang on. A counterattack is being made on your right."[3] The counterattack never took place.

As mentioned earlier, Alderson had sent the 150th Brigade forward to the GHQ Line in response to Turner's call for help. Alderson sent Turner new instructions at 10:30 a.m., telling him that he could use, if absolutely necessary, only one York and Durham battalion as he intended to use the Brigade to relieve his own that evening. With everything around him collapsing, Turner must have wondered what was going through Alderson's mind. Unless the Yorks and Durhams were thrown immediately into the fray, there would be few of his men left to relieve. In light of messages from different quarters of worsening conditions, Alderson changed his mind again and became convinced that the lost ground must be regained. At 11:35 a.m., he assigned two of the York and Durham Battalions to Turner with instructions to counterattack with energy above St. Julien and drive the Germans back — so as to maintain contact with the 5th and 8th Battalions on the north east side of the apex.[4] Bush arrived at Mouse Trap Farm around noon, and, after conferring with Turner, left to prepare the counterattack. However, once alerted to the impending enemy assault on St. Julien, Alderson felt it necessary to countermand his last directive. Colonel Cecil Romer, Alderson's chief staff officer, spoke with Turner by telephone at 1:00 p.m. and a written note followed, directing him not "to counter attack but utilize Bns. of York and Durham to strengthen your line and hold on."[5] The term "your line" was a reference to Turner's present position — from Hampshire Farm to Locality C. There was no hint of anything else. We are told that Turner interpreted the message to mean the GHQ Line, half a mile to the rear. Did he not realize that by falling back he would uncover the flank of the 2nd Brigade? How this misunderstanding could have occurred after Turner had a second conversation with Romer at 1:35 p.m. remains a mystery. Why was he overly eager to quit the battle line? It is a question that remains unresolved to this day. It certainly was not because he lacked courage. The most likely explanation was that he disobeyed orders out of concern for his men. They were being pummelled and he was getting no support from Canadian batteries, most of which were out of range.

At any rate, it was one thing to order the battalions to withdraw, but quite another to extricate them directly from the face of the enemy. On some parts of the front, the fighting was practically hand-to-hand and the ground immediately behind was open and swept by rifle and machine-gun fire. It seemed better to stand fast and kill Germans than to be shot in the back while running away. There were other instances in which isolated groups, their officers put out of action, suspected a ruse — that the order to withdraw had originated with the enemy— and refused to budge; or they were unsure of what they were supposed to do and by the time they reacted sometimes it was too late.

Because of the damaged communications, a well-coordinated withdrawal was out of the question. Once the runner delivered the written message from battalion headquarters to the CO of the unit, the word was passed verbally from platoon to platoon. Thus, the order reached units at different times and not at all in some cases where groups were secluded. George Patrick (2nd Battalion) and a few of his buddies were cut off from the main body, without even an NCO. His recollections are worth noting:

> Our company had left, and the little group that I was in didn't get word to go. I said, "Well, let's get out of here."
>
> My chum said, "Nothing doing. We dug this hole and we are going to stay here."
>
> Well another group came in from the other Brigades, and this officer who had brought them in asked me if I knew the orders … "No, I haven't any idea. But," I said, "the Adjutant and the Commanding Officer are back in that farm."
>
> And he said, "Will you go over and find out for me?"
>
> And finally I said, "All right, I'll go … Excuse me,

Mr. Turner [Asst. Adjutant], are we running away from this gang?"

He said, "Oh no, we are simply retiring to a prepared position."

I said, "That's all right, that's fine." So I went back and I said to my chum, "Let's get out of here."[6]

Watson understood that the withdrawal would be difficult and dangerous so he was dismayed by Turner's decision. The enemy had attacked six times towards Doxsee's House in the course of the morning

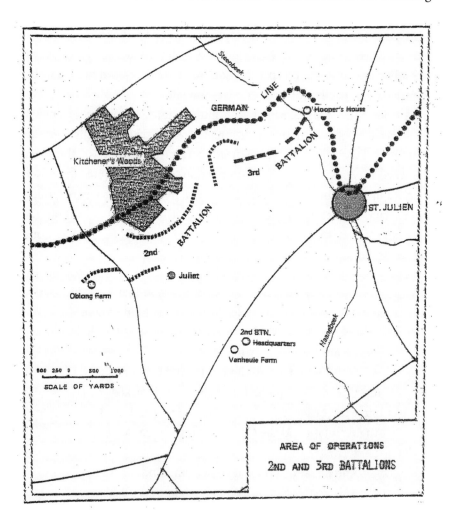

and early afternoon, and each time had been decimated by independent small-arms fire.[7] Watson saw no military reason to retire. In fact, as he would write in his report: "It was during this retirement that we sustained our heaviest losses."[8] In a letter to Turner, he went about as far as he could without explicitly calling his superior's judgment in question. The retirement was "*not compulsory*," he highlighted for the record, "the enemy having been repulsed with heavy losses, on their repeated attempts to advance."[9] Be that as it may, he issued the order to retire at 1:55 p.m.

The 2nd Battalion held stretches of trenches extending over three-quarters of a mile with No. 3 Company on the left, No. 4 Company in the centre, and No 2. Company on the right. The withdrawal was to begin on the left with No. 3 Company, followed by No. 2 Company on the right. In the centre, No. 4 Company would hold and retire when the flanks were clear. There was nothing wrong with the plan. The main problem was that the line was not continuous. It would be difficult to transmit the order to all parts of the line and even greater to those manning the three advanced posts — Oblong Farm on the left, Hooper's House east of Kitchener's Wood, and Doxsee's House on the far right.[10]

As can be gleaned from the reports and diaries of the men involved, the 2nd Battalion was under constant attack along the entire line when the order to retire was received. "Our whole position was shelled and machine guns played on the house [Doxsee's House], until the shots penetrated all three walls," wrote Captain George Richardson in his report of No. 2 Company. "At times men lay on beds and boxes while the machine gun swept the floors. Again they hugged the floor while the bullets passed over their heads."[11] Private Ferdinand Hardyman, 17-year-old from Sault Ste. Marie, had a sinking feeling when he saw the Germans closing in from several directions. He wrote: "The German artillery was more active than ever. We could not get any reinforcements up, and in the afternoon … the Germans came across and we had Germans back and front of us."[12]

On the left flank, Captain Geoffrey Chrysler, commanding No. 3 Company, sent a subordinate to convey the order to retire to his men in the main line and those at Oblong Farm. The men crawled along their shallow trench to the right, and, once beyond Juliet Farm, dashed across the open ground, seeking shelter in some of the barns in the rear. The Germans had anticipated the move and raked the field with intense rifle and machine-gun fire. There were casualties, but most made it back unscathed. The defenders at Oblong Farm were not as fortunate. By the time the order to withdraw reached the farm, they were surrounded and fighting at close quarters. Private Alan Beddoe and some of his comrades tried to reach a trench beyond the house, which would have given them a chance to escape. The Germans, however, had a machine gun sweeping the area. Beddoe explained what happened next:

> It was a most terrifying experience to see your chums going out, one after the other, out the end of this little trench that we had, out into the open where machine gun fire was just squirting in like through a hose, and one after the other they would go over like jack rabbits, and they were piling up there.[13]

Beddoe's elation at getting through was short-lived, for he was knocked unconscious by a shell blast. When he awoke several hours later, the firing had stopped. The other Canadian defenders had seen what happened to those attempting to withdraw. They chose to remain at their posts until the bitter end and were either killed or taken prisoner. Beddoe, too, was captured, for when he struggled to his feet there was a German soldier pointing a rifle at him.

On the right, Captain Claude Culling, in charge of No. 2 Company, passed the word to his men in the line and instructed Captain Richardson to bring in the garrison from Doxsee's House. Because messengers had been killed or wounded en route, the order to retire did not reach Doxsee's House until around 3:30 p.m. A short time earlier, its defenders had broken up the sixth and final assault by the Germans. Richardson estimated that 300 Germans had been cut down. Fifty years later, Wallace Bennett, whose machine gun had been set up on the upper level, described the action:

> I watched till they broke through the hedge, and they had over a hundred yards to cross over to get to our

farmhouse … And, as near as I can remember, I held my fire, because we were short of ammunition, you know. We couldn't have stopped another attack — we didn't have the ammunition, we'd run out. So I had to wait until they got through the hedge … before I opened up on them. I just cut 'em down. For once the gun didn't jam. We beat them back — some of them we killed, some of them were lying there kicking, you know, you could hear them [screaming]…. Those that could get back, crawled back, and carried some of their wounded back.[14]

Richardson hurriedly organized the withdrawal from Doxsee's House. The machine guns were dismantled, with each member of the crew carrying parts. The loopholes were left manned until everyone was clear. Sentries were then withdrawn and the forward trench and house were vacated. All went well in the early stages, but it was every man for himself when they had to cross open ground — against which a torrent of fire was being directed — to reach a trench dug in rear of the house. "The line of men just seemed to dwindle away," Richardson wrote in his report.[15] Bennett gave more details in relating his own harrowing experience:

Out through the back door we ran … The Germans saw us leave and we ran right into their fire which seemed to be coming from all angles. Bullets were flying and hitting the ground around us as we ran. They turned a machine gun on us … I tripped and fell … Two of our men dropped — killed outright. There were two ahead of me crawling along the ground, while over to the left I could see two or three crawling and running, trying to get through … I looked back over the field and it was hard to realize how I had got through to the trench — about 75 yards in the open — under fire all the way across! It was now too late. The others would never make it … The Germans had now captured the place and what had been the fate of our men who had been unable to get out?[16]

Bennett and a few men, including Richardson, were the only ones in the group who got away. The other members of No. 2 Company fared no better. Culling and his men may have felt good about their odds but, as they crossed open ground behind their trenches, machine-gun bullets and shrapnel bursts ripped into their ranks. The field was littered with scores of dead and wounded. Only a few made good their escape and of these nearly all were wounded. A defiant Culling was last seen with a revolver in his hand in an abandoned trench.[17]

There is a postscript to the calamity that had befallen No. 2 Company. When Richardson reached safety, he halted, collected what was left of his garrison, and added a group of stragglers on the road toward Wieltje. On the way, Richardson and his men, about 15 in all, came across two English regiments, the 12th London and 1st Suffolks, moving toward Locality C for a counterattack. Richardson thought that if the ground just lost were retaken, it might be possible to rescue some of their comrades who were lying wounded or helpless. Turning to his men he said, "We're going forward."[18] All were thoroughly exhausted, half-starved, and thirsty, some were wounded, and nearby was the GHQ Line where they could attend to their needs. Yet not a word of protest was uttered. They attached themselves to the British regiments "expecting to be carried back in the direction in which we had come," but the orders were changed and they ended at Fortuin. That night Richardson and the remnant of his little group threaded their way back to 1st Brigade Headquarters near St. Jean.[19]

Before the withdrawal, Major Herbert Bolster, commanding No. 4 Company in the centre, issued orders to remove the bolts from rifles that had to be left behind. It was a sad commentary that it proved unnecessary in many instances where the bolt rings had been broken off by men who, in desperation, had tried to pry them open by using their heels or entrenching tools. Major Bolster acted as a one-man rear guard for his men who withdrew under heavy fire. He was never seen again.

The outcome for the garrison in Hooper's House was equally tragic. Captain Hooper and his men had managed to reach a trench near the edge of Kitchener's Wood. Here, exhausted and loaded with wounded, including Hooper who was nearly helpless, they set up their machine gun and awaited the enemy. Attacked from all sides, they put up a fierce fight, but fell one by one until no one was left. Nearby units heard the battle raging, but firing became fainter and fainter, and then stopped.

For the survivors of the three companies, the withdrawal had been a terrifying and unforgettable experience. Private Hardyman, living up to his surname, wrote that in making his break he had been hit four times — in the chest, left leg, and twice in the right arm. He went on to say: "I had to run, after receiving my wounds, about eight hundred yards to the reinforcement trench to escape from the Germans, and from there I crawled to the dressing station [over a mile]."[20]

Lieutenant-Colonel Watson had seen to the removal of the wounded before leaving his headquarters to personally supervise the retirement of his companies. Watson remained with his second-in-command, Lieutenant-Colonel Rogers, until the last company was on its way. Shaking hands, the two officers separated, surmising that it would increase the chances of one of them getting through the perilous journey to the rear. Running as fast as he could for about 300 yards, Watson paused for a moment by a tree to catch his breath. He happened to glance back when he spotted one of his officers, Lieutenant A.H. Hugill, lying on the ground some 60 yards to the left. Watson hurried over, assuming he was wounded. But it turned out that Hugill was merely exhausted and taking a few moments to recover his breath.

Hugill was barely back on his feet when Private Wilson (2nd Battalion), passing nearby, was shot through the leg. Watson asked Hugill if he was up to helping carry the wounded man over the remaining 700 or 800 yards of fire-swept ground. Hugill said he was, whereupon Watson knelt down and Wilson got on his back. As Watson staggered along with his load, the air was alive with bullets and flying shrapnel. After carrying the wounded private for what seemed an eternity, but in reality was probably less than half a mile, Watson reached his battalion headquarters. By then the place was deserted. After resting for a few minutes, they started off once more and the two officers with a combined effort, managed to get Wilson back to safety. It was one of many such acts of heroism that went practically unnoticed that day.

It must have broken Watson's heart when he took stock and discovered that, for all intents and purposes, his battalion had been destroyed. The casualties for the recent action totalled 528 all ranks. Of the 22 company officers, only seven had emerged among the survivors. Watson would have been inhuman if he had not felt some bitterness toward Turner.

On the right, the two companies (under Major Kirkpatrick) belonging to the 3rd Battalion found themselves in dire circumstances after the fall of St. Julien. Subjected to intense fire from front and flanks, they were unable to break off on receiving the order to retire. "All you could see in the woods was a succession of spiked helmets," recalled Eric Seaman, a member of the machine-gun crew. "And there were hordes of them came at us there."[21] The ground to the rear was open and swept by machine guns, and all those who tried to dash across to safety were killed. Kirkpatrick's only hope, as he would write in his report, "was to hold on until night and break through."[22] In the meantime, there was no place to go. Thus, the men stayed in place and fought, their fate resting essentially on two machine guns mounted in farm buildings. One enemy assault after another was hurled back. Recognizing the source of their trouble, the Germans concentrated their fire on trying to silence the machine guns. An incredible thing happened to John Hewitt, a former mounted policeman and one of the machine-gun crews. A bullet struck him in back of the head and came out between his eyes. His head covered in blood, he fell next to Seaman. The 24-year old Seaman assumed that his buddy was dead. He got the surprise of his life when that proved otherwise:

> I thought he was gone but he began to stir after a while and stood upon his rubbery legs. And I said, "How do you feel John?"
>
> "Oh," he said, "I feel as though I had been on a drunk for a week ... That's all."[23]

By 3:30 p.m. only one machine gun was in operation, ammunition was running low, and the Germans were closing from both sides on the isolated trench. Of the 425 men who had moved into the line, less than

100 could walk. The survivors had been fighting ceaselessly for 36 hours, they had gotten no sleep, and they were drugged with fatigue. When the Germans sprang out of their trenches for one final rush, the men of the 3rd Battalion knew that their day was done. Major Kirkpatrick wrote: "For one moment, like gladiators we stood at gaze, then surrounded and outnumbered, our ammunition all but gone, we bowed to the inevitable and to save useless waste of life, gave in."[24] Among the prisoners was Danish-born Major Peter Anderson, who had been knocked out by an exploding bomb before the surrender. He woke up to find himself a prisoner of the Germans. "What an awful feeling; what a humiliating position to be in," he wrote in his memoirs. "What will people at home think about me. A prisoner of war and not wounded." Anderson may have gotten a measure of satisfaction when a German officer, after gazing at the pile of dead and wounded lying before the Canadian trench, approached him and exclaimed in disbelief, "You do not mean to tell me that you did all this damage with these few men?"[25] Anderson spent only five months in the prison camp at Bischofswerda, near Dresden. Driven by the need to atone for being captured, he escaped on 28 September 1915, and headed for Demark, 600 miles away, and, upon reaching there after an incredible journey, made his way to England (via Sweden and Norway). He was the only Canadian officer to have escaped from captivity in Germany during the Great War, a distinction that earned him an audience with King George and a promotion to lieutenant-colonel.

The Germans who rounded up the Canadians were Saxons, and, unlike the Prussians, who all too often mistreated their prisoners. Corporal Jack Finnegan, who was shot in the leg and unable to walk, expected the worst when he saw a German pointing a bayonet at his chest. He was pleasantly surprised when the German, handing his rifle to a comrade, put him in a wheelbarrow and pushed him to a rear dressing station. Finnegan was convinced that without their act of kindness, "I would have died at the side of the road in a mudhole."[26]

For the two companies of the 3rd Battalion, it had been a disastrous day. Unable to comply with the order to withdraw, they had been cut to pieces. Only 43 men from the two companies dragged themselves back, and, of these, most were wounded, and two were blind.[27]

Alderson had no idea that Turner had ordered his brigade to fall back. At 2:30 p.m., he urged Turner to hold his line as reinforcements were on the way.[28] Not surprisingly, no record of a reply exists. Much of the correspondence exchanged between Turner and Alderson on 24 April cannot be found. In mid 1915, J. Sutherland-Brown approached Henry Lamb (a colleague on the General Staff of the Canadian Division) and asked to see the report of the battle and the correspondence with the 3rd Brigade. Only part of his request was met: "The report of the battle was available but I was informed by Colonel Lamb that the correspondence had been destroyed."[29] This is a likely explanation, but it does not square with the statements given by Alderson and Lamb to the Canadian Official Historian. While both officers denied that it had been deliberately destroyed, neither could account for the missing correspondence. The War Diary of the 3rd Brigade might have been helpful if compiled properly, but, like the Divisional report, it was written after the battle and does nothing to fill the major gaps.

It was not until after 4:00 p.m. that Alderson discovered what Turner had done. He was naturally upset, but it could not have come as a complete surprise. All along, he and his staff had urged Turner to follow a bolder strategy and to use the troops being sent forward to strengthen his line. At 4:35 p.m., he sent a message to Turner in which he listed all the troops that could be utilized in the vicinity of Wieltje, about half a mile behind the GHQ Line: York and Durham Brigade, 2nd King's Own Yorkshire Light Infantry, and 9th London Regiment (Queen Victoria's Rifles) of the 13th Brigade, and part of the 4th Canadian Battalion — unknown to Alderson the two Yorkshire battalions (York and Durham) referred to were then engaged southwest of St. Julien and were unavailable. He urged that, "With these troops you must push … up into your front line and prevent at all costs the Germans breaking through between you and the 2nd Canadian Bde." As further evidence that he was out of touch with events on the front, he ended by saying; "I have no exact knowledge of your situation at the present moment but hope that you are still blocking St. Julien and in close touch with the 2nd Canadian Bde."[30] Of course, neither condition existed at the time.

Alderson's order was in accordance with the Division's scheme of defence issued to the brigade commanders when the Canadians moved into the salient.[31] In keeping with his admonition, it was necessary to establish an unbroken line connecting the 3rd Brigade with the left of the 2nd Brigade. Any fall-back position was to be only temporary. If that occurred, Turner was to hold on to his support line until such time as a counterattack could be delivered to regain the lost ground. Alderson never intended that the GHQ Line should be converted into Turner's new front line. He assumed that Turner was of the same mind. In this he was mistaken.

The movement of the 3rd Brigade to the GHQ Line coincided with the advance of British formations south of Fortuin. Because Plumer was far from the battlefield, he thought it would be advisable to have someone else in control of the reserves in case there was a breakdown in communications. Accordingly, at 9:00 a.m., he gave Major-General Snow (CO, 27th Division), whose sector was on the right of the 28th Division, command of the troops in corps reserve in the area with power to use his discretion in employing them. Neither Alderson, nor the Canadian brigade commanders in the field, were informed of Snow's new appointment.

Snow was a former subordinate of Alderson, and, according to the British Official Historian, both continued to work well together.[32] That may have been true in the past, but now that Snow had an independent command, it appears that their relationship had changed. No two men were more dissimilar in character. Alderson was even-tempered, considerate, helpful, and a gentleman in the best British tradition. Snow, on the other hand, was impatient, ill-temperate, abrasive, and shared with other British officers a low regard for Empire troops. The kind of rapport they enjoyed may be inferred from the tone of an early-morning wire Snow addressed to Alderson even though, it should be noted, he was inferior in rank: "If my guns assist you today as I hope they will, please arrange more definite targets than yesterday. Yesterday we were asked to fire at our extreme range on certain areas. After sighting I found out target was about 2500 yards behind enemy's position. Possibly that was what you wanted but I doubt it."[33]

Although Snow's headquarters were located at Potijze, near the endangered area, he did not appear to be well-informed about up-to-date military developments. He assumed, though the source of his intelligence is unknown, that the Germans had broken through at Berlin Wood — between the 2nd Canadian Brigade and the 85th British Brigade — and were in possession of Fortuin, a scattered group of farms and cottages about half a mile southeast of St. Julien. Unknown to him, the line was still intact and Fortuin was being held by 200 Canadians, mostly remnants of the 7th and 10th Battalions. Operating in ignorance, Snow directed the 1st Royal Irish Regiment, or rather the remains of it (now reduced to only 356 men), from his own divisional reserve to march to Fortuin and drive back the Germans. Since additional troops could not be obtained from either the 27th Division or the V Corps, Snow commandeered the 1st Suffolk and 12th London (Rangers) from the 28th Division's reserve without asking Bulfin's permission and sent them to join the Royal Irish.[34] Incredible as it may seem, he initiated these movements without reference to either Alderson or Turner. Snow did, however, direct Turner at 2:15 p.m. to contact and take command of the three British battalions and to use every man at his disposal to stop the enemy's advance from Fortuin.[35]

The message arrived two hours later at Mouse Trap Farm and must have caused Turner to shake his head in bewilderment. He did not personally know Snow and had no idea that his powers of command had been extended. Here was a British general three miles away instructing him to launch an attack against an enemy in a sector under the control of his Canadian counterpart, Arthur Currie. Although Turner ignored the order, he set out for Fortuin to establish contact with the battalions Snow had allotted to him.

The 12th London (Rangers) and the 1st Suffolk were the first of the battalions ordered by Snow to move into the gap created by the withdrawal of the 3rd Brigade. Currie was alerted when they passed behind his brigade and he sent his brigade-major, Lieutenant-Colonel Herbert Kemmis-Betty, to show them where they were to deploy. The Canadian officer met the two battalion commanders and informed them that Fortuin was already in Canadian hands. Instead, he led

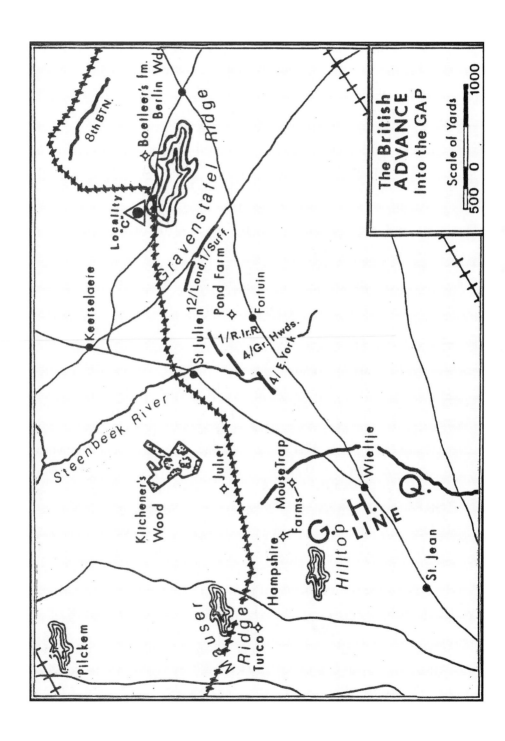

The British ADVANCE Into the GAP

Scale of Yards

500   0   1000

them northeast toward Gravenstafel Ridge to cover the open flank of the 2nd Brigade. In so doing, he was unaware that by 4:00 p.m. the Germans were in possession of Gravenstafel Ridge and St. Julien. From these vantage points, the Germans unleashed their artillery against the advancing British battalions. Adding to their suffering was the shelling from their own artillery. No one had informed the British batteries that the two battalions had advanced northward into an area presumed to be occupied by the Germans. Heavy fire forced the two battalions to stop and they entrenched near the junction of the Zonnebeke and Keerselare roads. In the action the Suffolks, who were in the lead, sustained 154 casualties, while the losses of the Rangers amounted to 59, and included among the wounded, was their CO, Lieutenant-Colonel A.D. Bayliffe. Lieutenant-Colonel W.B. Wallace of the Suffolks assumed command of both battalions.

Farther west, the 1st Royal Irish Regiment was on the move, having left Potijze earlier that afternoon with orders to capture Fortuin. Finding that the village was held by the Canadians, the Irishmen swung north toward St. Julien, unaware that it was occupied by the Germans. As they approached the village, they came under heavy fire, which halted their advance and compelled them to dig in. They were surprised to see the 4th Yorkshire (Green Howards) coming up on their left, for they had no knowledge that any other British unit was in the area. As it happened, the Green Howards, along with the 4th East Yorkshire, of the 150th Brigade (York and Durham), had left the GHQ Line and were moving northeast toward Fortuin. When they approached the Haanebeek they were subjected to machine-gun fire and wheeled left, advancing between Kitchener's Wood and St. Julien. A captain from one of the rear companies spotted a section of the 6th Canadian Field Battery and sent a runner to inquire about the location of the enemy. It was only then that Lieutenant-Colonel M.H.L. Bell — taking charge of the two battalions after Lieutenant-Colonel G.H. Shaw (commander of the East Yorks) was killed — learned that St. Julien had fallen. What he did not realize immediately was that the Germans, having noticed the presence of the British battalions, were advancing out of St. Julien to attack them. However, he was alerted when troops belonging to the 3rd Canadian

Battalion in the GHQ Line saw large bodies of Germans moving southeast and poured rifle and machine-gun fire into them. Bell's green troops met the charging Germans head-on and a furious battle followed.

Several hundred yards behind the Yorkshire battalions lay elements of the 2nd Canadian Field Artillery Brigade under Lieutenant-Colonel John Creelman. An observation officer, turning his binoculars in the direction of the rattle of musketry, saw rank upon rank of Germans crossing an open field from Kitchener's Wood, silhouetted against the red glow of the setting sun. Creelman could also see them from his dugout south of Fortuin. At 5:15 p.m., he ordered two sections of his guns, which were in a position facing northeast toward the Stroombeck, to swing around. The Germans were so close that the gunners fired over open sights. Creelman summed up the ensuing action: "It was the most ideal target any of us had ever seen. Every man at every gun saw his objective. The order to fire was given and in a very few minutes two lines of Germans ceased to exist. Up to dark no third line had attempted to leave the woods."[36]

Although the gunners were blasting away at targets they could hardly miss, they experienced some anxious moments at one point. Firing at the rate of twenty rounds a minute, they feared that they soon would be running short of shells. Just when their supply was about exhausted, they breathed a sigh of relief when, above the din, they heard the cry of "Four wagons of ammunition, sir."[37] It was a young subaltern reporting as his sweating team pulled into the farmyard after braving artillery bursts along the six-mile journey from Vlamertinghe.

Subjected to a shower of shrapnel, as well as accurate rifle and machine-gun fire from the British battalions, the Germans broke and ran, first in small groups, and eventually in the hundreds. The Germans assumed that they were facing a major counteroffensive. They waited until dusk to evacuate St. Julien, moving to higher and more defensible ground immediately to the north.

In the semi-darkness, the German flight was mistaken for a Canadian advance into St. Julien. But no Canadians would occupy the ruined village that night, other than the dead littering its streets. Nor did the British battalions attempt to advance. In fact some of them, owing to Turner's action, were getting ready to withdraw.

Destroyed Buildings in St. Julien.

We last left Turner when he set out on foot toward Fortuin to find the units Snow had allotted to him. It was an act of personal courage, but a risk he should not have taken. Since his route lay across the path of the German advance, he was lucky not to have been killed or captured. After making his way unscathed, he located the 1st Royal Irish stretched out in a field south of St. Julien. He directed the CO of the battalion to withdraw at dusk to the GHQ Line and then returned to his headquarters at Mouse Trap Farm. He did not go in search of the 4th York and 4th East York Regiments, presumably because he had no idea of their location, even though they were nearby. As the Irishmen withdrew, they passed the word to the Yorkshires, who promptly followed suit. Turner was unaware of the presence in the area of the 1st Suffolks and 12th London Regiments, otherwise they, too, would have been pulled back to the GHQ Line. They remained there despite Bulfin's insistence that they be returned to him as soon as possible.[38] Still, the withdrawal of the three British battalions had reopened the gap between the 3rd Brigade and Currie's left.

By early evening, Turner had filled the GHQ Line with a medley of troops belonging to no less than eight battalions — some 3500 in all.[39] For the most part they were tired, disorganized, and unfit for employment in attack. Turner could have, if he had so chosen, dispersed some units along the gap, but he would have been hard pressed to mount any kind of sustained attack. At any rate, he attempted neither. Instead, as the late Daniel Dancocks pointed out, Turner "was obsessed with defending the GHQ line, apparently convinced that it was the salvation, not only of his brigade, but of the entire Canadian Division."[40] He did not seem to understand that most of the line faced east, the wrong way to effectively defend against the tidal wave of grey coats coming from the north. In hindsight Lieutenant-Colonel Gordon-Hall was highly critical of Turner's generalship on the 24th:

> Turner began to sit on his reserves instead of using them to reinforce his forward position as directed by Div. HQ. This policy he pursued to the end and nothing Div. HQ or other commanders could order, or suggest, or implore made him alter his policy, with of course disastrous consequences to all concerned and to none more than to his own troops. I don't think enough is made of the overcrowding in GHQ Line and to the resultant heavy casualties from hostile artillery fire. It had a magnetic attraction for Turner in spite of the fact that it faced the wrong way and could be enfiladed.[41]

Duguid chose his words carefully in the Canadian Official History, written when Turner was still alive. He wrote that the general "understood his instructions to be that he should hold St. Julien as long as possible and then occupy the GHQ Line." [42] But in private he shared Gordon-Hall's assessment of Turner: "The fact is that, in my story, the truth and nothing but the truth has been told but out of consideration for General Turner not the whole truth: his actions and their results are made clear without comment and without stressing what Gordon-Hall describes as their 'disastrous consequences.'"[43]

It is difficult to find an explanation for Turner's behaviour. His priority to save his battered brigade, above all else, had compromised the security of the 2nd Brigade and jeopardized the defense of the salient. And to make matters worse, he did so without notifying Currie, the person most adversely affected by his move. Turner's decision to withdraw out of concern for his men might have been understandable if no other alternative had existed. But there were three battalions in the vicinity with others on the way. He could have reinforced the threatened sectors of his front, and, while he may not have saved St. Julien, he could have averted the slaughter of the 2nd and 3rd Battalions and maintained contact with the left of the 2nd Brigade. Turner's overall conduct was inexcusable and he was very fortunate to have escaped dismissal.

The one positive element in an afternoon fraught with confusion and ferocious fighting was the advance and steadfastness of the British battalions. Although they arrived an hour too late to save the remaining detachments of the 2nd and 3rd Battalions, they may well have averted an even greater disaster. The tenacious resistance of the Canadians, followed by the appearance of fresh British battalions, apparently prevented the execution of an order from the German XXVI Reserve Corps to retake St. Julien that night. This was most fortunate, because, in ordering three of the British battalions back, Turner had reopened the gap between his brigade and the left of the 2nd Brigade at Locality C. The question was whether the British had bought enough time. That thought must have haunted Currie, whose men were already being mauled by a massive enemy assault.

CHAPTER 9
24 April: The 2nd Brigade Stands Fast

For Currie, who was under enormous stress on 24 April, it must have seemed to him that the day would never end. From early morning until practically dusk, the 2nd Brigade was in constant danger of being outflanked. After the first onslaught, the 5th and 8th Battalions continued to cling tenaciously to their trenches, but an ominous opening existed on the left flank, caused by a breach in the 15th Battalion's front. Currie tried to cover the ground between his left and Locality C by sending No. 4 Company of the 8th Battalion and another company from the adjacent 5th to occupy French trenches in front of Boetleer Farm and cover the intervening space with fire. His makeshift arrangement was evidently inadequate to stop a determined German assault from penetrating through his line. Currie had already sent all of his reserves and such troops as he could commandeer to shore up his front. His salvation rested on obtaining reinforcements.

As if Currie did not have enough on his mind, a shell landed on his advanced command post at Pond Farm a little after 7:00 a.m., setting it on fire and destroying his kit, among other things. While the building was ablaze, Currie hastily wrote a note to the British CO of the neighbouring 85th Brigade, asking if he had any men to spare.[1] Then, racing out with his staff, he fled to the headquarters of the 2nd Field Artillery Brigade near Fortuin, about 700 yards to the south. There, in cramped quarters, he set up his new command post and used Creelman's communication network for his own messages.

Before 9:00 a.m., a runner brought the reply from the 85th Brigade's CO, who sent his regrets.[2] But good news had already arrived from

Château des Trois Tours. At 8:10 a.m, Currie learned from Division Headquarters that two battalions of the 150th (York and Durham) Brigade were on their way to the GHQ Line and could be called up if needed. An hour and a half later, there was still no sign of the promised reinforcements. As time was of critical importance, Currie sent out his orderly officer, Lieutenant Murray Greene, to meet them and to lead at least one of the battalions into the gap east of Locality C.

As the morning wore on, conditions on the left of the 2nd Brigade grew steadily worse. Lipsett (8th Battalion) turned to Tuxford and asked if he could help. "He said he was hard pressed," consequently "I gave him two platoons of the Support Company," Tuxford noted. Later in the morning, Lipsett telephoned 5th Battalion headquarters again, saying his situation was desperate and requested additional assistance. Tuxford continued: "I explained that I now had only two platoons left in support of the two companies holding the 1100 yards of front line. However, if Lipsett's front had to give it meant we were doomed, so I sent over the remaining two platoons and we now had nothing behind the front line, and still the line held."[3]

These reinforcements helped in the early going, but fell considerably short of Lipsett's requirements. At 10:50 a.m., he telephoned Currie that the Germans had begun to move around the end of his battalion and were threatening to surround it.[4] But minutes later, he assured Currie that he had spoken with his company commanders and all had "stated that they will stick to the last in their trenches."[5] That message was encouraging, but more than brave words were needed to halt the Germans. About this time, Currie telephoned 3rd Brigade Headquarters, and, according to Hughes, requested reinforcements "or the whole front is lost."[6]

Lieutenant Greene returned at 11:00 a.m., having seen no sign of the British battalions. Currie sent him back to Wieltje with orders to await their arrival. At 11:15 a.m., Lipsett sent another message to the effect that he needed a company to fill the gap between his front and Locality C. "I could send no help [as] our reserves were all used up," Currie wrote in his report.[7] By now the atmosphere at 2nd Brigade Headquarters had become exceedingly tense. It seemed that Currie was running into a dead end at each turn.

In light of two critical developments that occurred between 11:15 a.m. and 11:40 a.m., Currie was reluctantly driven to the conclusion that he must take drastic action, the nature of which he had desperately wanted to avoid. The first was receipt of information from an unknown source that the two battalions of the York and Durham were no longer available. How the 2nd Brigade came to believe that they had been withdrawn, which turned out to be erroneous, is unclear. The second was a reply from Turner indicating that his troops were being blown out of their trenches and that he had no "substantial reinforcements at my disposal to reinforce your left."[8] On the strength of these messages, Currie instructed Lipsett and the neighbouring 5th Battalion and 85th Brigade on his right to retire to Gravenstafel Ridge.[9] As it happened, the withdrawal was not carried out.

Around noon, the outlook brightened somewhat. Lipsett reported that conditions had improved on his front: "Just heard German advance against our left seems to have slackened and come to a halt. I am not uneasy about being able to hold my line if the Germans are prevented walking round my rear."[10] About the same time, a signal message addressed to 2nd Brigade Headquarters reported that the leading battalion of the York and Durham (5th Durham Light Infantry) had arrived at Wieltje. What Currie did not realize until later was that the British battalion refused to move forward. The officer in charge of the 5th Durham Light Infantry told Greene that his orders stipulated that he was to reinforce both the 2nd and 3rd Brigades, but that he would take no action until he found out what proportion should go to each.[11]

Currie knew that the respite Lipsett was enjoying was temporary and that it was unlikely he could hold out once German pressure was resumed. He saw that by bearing down on Lipsett's flank and Locality C, the Germans would be able to envelop Gravenstafel Ridge from the northwest. Their objective, Currie felt, could best be frustrated by a counterattack mounted from the 3rd Brigade area. Such an attack, first suggested to him by Lipsett, seemed feasible now that reinforcements were at hand. Currie contacted 3rd Brigade Headquarters at 12:20 p.m., unaware that Alderson had already sanctioned the move. He asked Turner to consider a local counterattack in the direction of St. Julien, "which will do much towards restoring the situation."[12] Ten minutes later, he received a copy of the message Alderson had sent Turner.

By then Greene had returned to 2nd Brigade Headquarters with the bad news. Currie was frustrated and in despair. While his brigade was threatened with destruction, he could not help but feel that there was a lack of urgency on the part of higher commands. There were British troops in the GHQ Line, but these were unavailable for reasons that seemed specious. If only they could be brought into the line quickly to assist in the counterattack, there was a good chance that the gap between the 2nd and 3rd Brigades could be filled. The more Currie thought about it, the more he became convinced that he should take the extreme course of leaving his command post and going back to the GHQ Line to try to obtain the desperately needed reinforcements before it was too late. In so doing, he put his military career at risk. His duty was to remain in place and direct the battle, not leave in its midst. Currie justified his action on the grounds that, with the survival of his brigade at stake, he needed help desperately and that the York and Durham battalions "might move for me when unlikely to move for officers of lesser rank." When consulted, both Lipsett and Tuxford agreed with his decision, the former "urging me to go and hurry."[13] But the concurrence of subordinates does not justify a commanding officer's questionable action. Currie's initiative, however well intentioned, was ill advised and probably due to his inexperience.

Currie left Lipsett, in whom he had the utmost confidence, in charge of the battle zone during his absence. Tuxford was senior in rank, but he willingly deferred to Lipsett on the grounds that he was a professional soldier and better able to handle the brigade.[14] Before departing, Currie wrote out a retirement order to both Lipsett and Tuxford, a decision that would haunt him a decade later, when his enemies accused him of cowardice and of abandoning his men. In 1926, Currie maintained that he had directed Lipsett not to carry out the retirement unless forced by circumstances. "As he was the man on the spot I left it to his judgment," Currie wrote, "and Lipsett and myself had a clear understanding about it."[15] Lipsett was killed later in the war, but in his report of the battle, dated 30 April 1915, he wrote "Soon after noon I got the order to fall back."[16] Tuxford was still alive when the controversy was raging. His

A drawing of the ruins of a chateau neat Wieltje.

comments to Duguid, also contradict Currie's claim of a conditional retirement: "We had been ordered to retire [on 24 April]. We had disobeyed the orders to retire."[17] On another occasion, Tuxford wrote that during the afternoon on the 24th, "[a] definite order to retire was received by Lipsett from the [2nd] Brigade."[18] Actually, an astute reader can follow the trail through Currie's series of messages reproduced in Duguid's text and in the appendices, plus the reluctance expressed by the battalion commanders to retire, and the protest registered by the commander of the neighbouring 85th Brigade, whose left flank would be left unprotected.[19]

Currie's journey to Wieltje took him across open ground that was under heavy artillery bombardment and crawling with German stragglers, not to mention littered with fallen trees. From the main 2nd Brigade Headquarters at Wieltje, Captain Charles Napier, a 37-year old miner, did a double take when he saw his commanding officer approach alone:

> The roads were being heavily shelled and the open was
> searched by rifle, machine gun and shrapnel. As he
> drew near, a salvo of heavies intended for the road burst
> immediately in his line of approach, but he reached
> the comparative shelter (from rifle fire at least) of the

ruined cottage where I was — making, as he did so, a jocular remark as to the comparative salubrity of Salisbury Plains.[20]

It was about 1:00 p.m. when Currie located the the 5th Durham Light Infantry, the only York and Durham battalion to have arrived in Wieltje thus far. What disturbed him even more was the unwillingness of the commanding officer to act without orders from his own brigadier. While there, Brigadier-General J.E. Bush, commander of the York and Durhams, walked in. He had just come from 3rd Brigade headquarters, where he had discussed the counterattack with Turner. But before carrying it out, he desired to wait for another of his battalions (4th East Yorkshires), which was on its way to the GHQ Line via Potijze. He then left to meet the battalion to hurry it along. Unfortunately, he took a different route and missed it.

Around 2:00 p.m., the 4th East Yorkshire battalion arrived at the GHQ Line and Currie urged its commander, Lieutenant-Colonel M.H.L. Bell, to advance toward St. Julien. But Bell, no more than his counterpart with the 5th Durham Light Infantry, refused to budge without instructions from Bush. Currie's only hope was to find Bush. Just as he was about to leave, he encountered Lieutenant H.F. McDonald, a member of Turner's staff, who passed on the news that the counterattack had been cancelled and that units of the 3rd Brigade in the field had been ordered to retire to the GHQ Line.[21] Currie was stunned. He could not understand why such action had been taken. As noted in the previous chapter, Alderson, having received reports suggesting that the enemy was massing for an all-out assault on St. Julien, had cancelled the 3rd Brigade's counterattack and instead ordered it to strengthen its line with the York and Durham battalions and to hold on. Turner, presumably convinced that the Germans could not be stopped, ignored the directive and pulled his men a mile back to the GHQ Line. The withdrawal left a 4000-yard opening between the 2nd Brigade's rear and the GHQ line except for the remnants of the 7th Battalion, which had reformed south of St. Julien.[22]

Currie caught up with Bush at a farm southeast of Wieltje, and pleaded with him to move his two battalions to fill the gap. As much as he wanted to help, Bush was powerless to do so. He had received orders that his battalions were not to be used as formerly intended, "but to increase the large bodies of troops protecting Potijze."[23] While at the farm, Currie learned that there was a British Division Headquarters several hundred yards away. He assumed that from there he would be able to inform Alderson of the grave situation on his front. Arriving around 3:00 p.m., Currie found out that it was the command post of Major-General Snow, who directed the 27th Division. Currie had never met Snow and he was unaware that he had been given control of all Corps reserve troops in the area.

As Currie entered the dugout of the 27th Division's Headquarters, his attention was drawn to a general sitting at a table immediately to the left of the door. It was General Snow. His elbows rested on some papers spread over the table and his face was between his hands. As Currie walked over to talk to Snow, he was hardly the picture of a spit-and-polish general. He had not shaved in several days, his boots and uniform were caked with mud, he was sweating profusely, and he was haggard-looking, for he had not slept in two days and was utterly exhausted. Snow had just finished an interview with Captain Paul Villiers, a Canadian officer on the staff of the 3rd Brigade. Having failed to elicit satisfactory replies to his rather disjointed questions, Snow had become abusive, shouting and cursing at Villiers for his supposed stupidity. Waving him away, he ended his tirade by saying: "Get out of here. Get back to your Brigade and, when you have some definite information to pass on, send someone with intelligence, if you have such a one, capable of explaining the situation."[24] Lieutenant Edison Lynn of the 2nd Field Company, Canadian Engineers, who was present and recorded the exchanges, was dumbfounded by Snow's boorish behaviour: "I was … surprised that an officer of Genl. Snow should have lost control of himself to an extent as to curse and abuse a subordinate without restraint."[25]

Snow was still upset and angry when he looked up and saw the corpulent frame of a Canadian brigadier standing in front of him. "Well what now?" he bellowed in a loud, raucous voice. Currie identified himself and added, "I am being hard pressed at certain points." With the aid of a map, he proceeded to describe the tactical situation on his front.[26] Currie had no sooner mentioned that there was a gap between the 3rd Brigade and the left of his 8th Battalion when Snow began to shout, asking how dare he allow such a thing to occur. Currie would recall 11 years later: "To hear him you would think that I personally and solely was responsible for that gap, though every man of the 2nd Brigade was fighting in the line at the moment."[27]

Pausing briefly for the interruption, Currie went on to say that it was essential for the safety of the whole line that the area under extreme pressure be reinforced without delay. "Your men are being directed to points in the line which are already well held and in safe keeping. I would suggest that they should be diverted to these points." He simultaneously indicated them on the map. Currie further declared: "Your men are fresh and their assistance at the points mentioned would be of great value."

On hearing Currie's remarks, Snow flew into a rage: "Have you come to teach me my profession and dictate to me how I shall handle my Division?" His following remarks, smothered as they were by his frenzied outburst, were so incoherent and unintelligible that it was impossible to form an estimate of what he intended to convey.[28] Currie suffered through Snow's temper tantrum in silence. When Snow's choleric explosion eventually subsided, more as a result of exhaustion than anything else, the dialogue continued:

> Currie: There was no intention on my part to attempt to teach you your job or to advise you how to handle your Division; but I have been in this sector for some time now and know it pretty well. My Brigade has been in the line for ten days. They were in it when the attack was launched, and have resisted every attack without relinquishing a foot of trench. They have counter-attacked and at many points have been fearfully cut up. They are tired and hungry and require support at many points before nightfall.

> Snow: Do you expect me to wet-nurse your Brigade? You have got yourself and your men into a mess and you will have to get them out of it as best you can.

Currie: I am not in a mess nor are my men. My men and I have held out against fierce onslaughts and will continue to hold out so long as any of us are left. As I have already stated my men have not lost any ground despite the fact that they are played out, hungry and decimated. The support of some fresh troops is essential for the safety of the line.[29]

Snow interrupted before Currie finished: "Enough of this, I have heard enough of your harangue. Get out of here! Take care of your own line, you will get no help from me." [30] Once more Snow started to shout and pour out invectives. Currie stiffened and his icy glare betrayed his contempt for Snow. As he walked away from the table Snow shouted, "Give them hell. Give them hell." Currie wrote in retrospect: "When I considered the position of all the troops of the 2nd Brigade and my inability to move two battalions whom I thought had been sent to our assistance, I confess that at that moment I thought I had never heard a more stupid remark."[31]

Snow's version of the interview is sanitized and is repeated here for the first time:

The brigadier of a Canadian Brigade came in and told me that he had ordered a retirement of his men on to the GHQ Line. I explained to him in rather a forcible manner that if he had done so he had better counterman that order. He told me that he had orders to retire from his Divisional General, but on investigation I found that the order was "if forced to retire, retire onto the GHQ line." I explained to the brigadier that if he considered that it was an order he was at once to consider it cancelled by me and that he was to get his men back into their original trenches, or as near as possible, and stick to his ground at all costs and I impressed on him that there was no question of retiring.[32]

Edmonds, who had served on Snow's staff (GSO1) in 1914, was fully aware of the confrontation between his former commanding officer and Currie. Under pressure from his own superiors he had omitted all mention of the incident in his Official History published in 1927. By then Currie was principal of McGill University, a revered figure in Canada and a strong supporter of the Imperial connection. After reading the preliminary draft of Duguid's official history of the battle in the mid-1930s, Edmonds rushed to Snow's defence, again initiating an acrimonious war of words between him and his Canadian counterpart. In short, Edmonds accused Duguid of besmirching the reputation of Snow in order to cover up Currie's mistakes:

> The account in your galleys now is unfair to General Snow. He did use strong language to General Currie, in fact told him if he had been a Regular [British] Officer he would have put him in arrest. If you record the language, you must not, in fairness, omit the cause. Currie, without saying who he was, stumbled into the 27th Division headquarters, and asked leave to use the divisional signals "to report" to Canadian Divisional Head. On being asked why, he said he had ordered his brigade "out of the line." Snow pricked up his ears and asked on what authority he had done it. Currie produced a conditional order to the effect that if compelled to fall back he was to retire to a certain line. Snow tore the order up ... And then Snow roundly cursed him and told him to get back.[33]

Edmonds maintained that there was plenty of evidence to corroborate Snow's assertion that Currie had ordered the 2nd Brigade to withdraw besides the short-hand notes taken by staff officers (belonging to the 27th Division) during the meeting. He produced Currie's message to Divisional Headquarters on the afternoon of the 24th which read: "I ... ordered 8th Battalion, Section II to fall back to Locality C, the 5th Battalion to conform to their movements and hold the Gravenstafel

Ridge, notifying 85th Brigade of what I was doing."[34] No less compelling was a conversation Edmonds had with Currie himself:

> General Currie during his visit to me asked after the health of General Snow. With this opening, I took the opportunity to say, "You found that he had a pretty rough tongue," and he said, "he had that reputation." Then I asked, "did he tear up your orders?" and he nodded.

Edmonds went so far as to track down and interrogate Lieutenant Lynn, "who told me plainly that if he spoke the truth about the interview he would get into trouble in Canada."[35] Edmonds urged Duguid to adopt one of two options he put forward: that the less said about the interview the better; or, if he chose to dwell on it, he needed to explain the cause of Snow's intemperate outburst. He preferred the former alternative as "Currie's action certainly requires 'covering up' in view of the reputation he subsequently earned."[36] Edmonds's arguments evidently carried the day. When the Canadian Official History appeared in 1938, there was only one cryptic line about the meeting.[37]

It is interesting to note that in the course of their heated exchange Snow did not even tell Currie that he had been placed in charge of the Corps reserves in the area and that he had sent troops to Fortuin. It may have been an oversight, but it was more likely deliberate, a reflection of Snow's contempt for Currie. Snow's only concession to Currie was to allow him to send a situation report to 1st Division Headquarters.

A British officer followed Currie on his way out and half apologetically told him to ignore his commander's tirade. He added that Snow "had the reputation of being the rudest officer in the British army."[38] The officer's kind gesture did not alter the fact that Currie's mission to obtain reinforcements had been unsuccessful. Dejected and bone-tired, Currie paused to gather his thoughts. Out of the corner of his eye, he recognized Lieutenant Lynn, the Canadian junior officer who had witnessed Snow's temper tantrum, standing by the entrance of the dugout. "Well, Lynn," he remarked, "what are you doing here?"[39] Lynn explained the nature of his business with Snow and proceeded to take him to a group of Canadian stragglers who had lost contact with their units and drifted to the rear. Currie called out the men of the 2nd Brigade, which numbered about 100, formed them up, and personally led them forward. As he approached the battlefront, he turned them over to a regimental sergeant-major, who was a member of the party, and ordered him to join the 8th Battalion. Then he made his way to Lane Farm, where he learned that the 2nd Artillery Brigade Headquarters — where his own command post was located — was moving back there on account of enemy shelling. After resting for a few minutes, Currie hurried over to his rear headquarters at Wieltje, expecting to meet his command post staff, who he assumed had already pulled back. When he discovered that they had not yet arrived, he proceeded to 2nd Artillery Brigade Headquarters, which was in chaotic state as personnel, guns, and equipment were moving out. There, Currie found that his staff had just left, but the good news was that the 8th Battalion was still in position. During his journey, important developments had occurred on the fighting front.

Currie had left his adjutant, Major Kirkcaldy, and Lipsett to contact the various units and to organize the withdrawal. Kirkcaldy had an uneasy feeling while writing out the retirement orders. He told Lipsett that if the battalion had to retire "up the face of the hill" it "would be cleaned out." Since the telephone communications with the front were still intact, he suggested to Lipsett that his company commanders and Tuxford be consulted.[40] Lipsett was in the midst of contacting the unit commanders when he received word that the 3rd Brigade was preparing a counterattack. He tried to reach 2nd Brigade Headquarters, but Currie had been delayed in returning from his mission and the brigade major, Kemmis-Betty, feared the worst. "General Currie is missing and we believe he may have been killed," Kemmis-Betty replied. "You will take command of the Brigade."[41] Lipsett next tried to get through to Division Headquarters, but the wires were down. Lipsett remained cool, took stock and ultimately decided that, given the new circumstances, he would be following the wishes of both Brigade and Division Headquarters if he clung to his position.[42] He sent a note to Turner asking when the attack would start, stressing that his answer could determine whether or not the 8th Battalion remained in place. Turner replied that the counterattack had been cancelled.[43] Lipsett's spirits were low when he phoned Tuxford, explaining his order from Currie, and asking him what he thought of it. "I replied that I did not understand why we should have to retire," Tuxford wrote. "In spite of our casualties my men were in good spirits and full of fight ... It was mutually agreed there and then and we stuck." Tuxford recorded the reaction among his men when he informed them that the order to retire had been cancelled:

> Upon telephoning the order to Major Tenaille in the right front line, I can still hear the ringing in my ears the cheer that sounded in the telephone from those unbeaten men. Likewise, telephoning to the left, Major Edgar's bluff voice immediately responded: "We'll stay here till the cows come home.[44]

It was about this time that Lipsett found out that two British regiments (12th London and 1st Suffolks) were moving up on his left. He sent several of his officers to guide them forward. But the British battalions were advancing west of Locality C, so that the gap between the strong point and his left remained open. That the Germans were unaware of the gap was at least partially due to Major Andrew McNaughton's 7th Field Artillery, which fired 1800 rounds over the course of the day. With an observation post in Locality C, McNaughton was instrumental in breaking up the hordes of advancing Germans. A talented artilleryman with a degree in electrical engineering from McGill, McNaughton made ever shell count. He waited for the Germans to line up for an attack before unleashing a barrage. The ground in front of the 8th Battalion was carpeted with grey-clad corpses. An enemy shell fell nearby and a splinter cut through McNaughton's shoulder, but he refused to leave his post. During an interview with CBC in 1963, he related the incident: "A German shell burst into my face. It blew me about ten or twelve feet back and part of it went through my shoulder; it took me a long time to get over it but I was with the battery all day until we had been ordered out... And I was in close touch with Lipsett all that time."[45]

Still there were occasions when enemy groups unwittingly infiltrated through the gap on the left of the 8th Battalion. Canadian stragglers waiting to rejoin their units often took it upon themselves to hunt them down. Tuxford witnessed one such action from his command post on a ridge. A body of Germans advanced 800 or 900 hundred yards and fortified a farm to the rear of the 8th Battalion. Tuxford tried to locate a field gun to reduce the place, but none was available. To add to his despair, he noticed a party of Canadians advancing toward the farm, unaware that it was occupied by the Germans. He had no way of contacting the men and he feared that they would be annihilated if they approached any closer. An officer walked ahead by himself, presumably to investigate if the farm was defended by the enemy, when he was shot down. The rest of the Canadians flopped to the ground and a firefight ensued.[46]

Throughout the day, reinforcements from various quarters, among them the 151st Brigade and the 10th Brigade, were hurrying into the Canadian sector. At Château des Trois Tours, Alderson had originally intended to relieve Geddes's Detachment and Turner's men that evening with the 10th Brigade and the uncommitted York and Durham Battalions (150th Brigade). Once that had been completed, the 10th was to counterattack, together with such troops as were available. But the British High Command's intervention caused Alderson's scheme to be set aside.

British plans were shaped, not only by what the enemy might do, but by the wishes of the French. On the 24th, French gains had been negligible, but at least they had not lost more ground. On the west side of the canal, they had established firm touch with the Belgians, whose timely advance frustrated a renewed German effort to take Zuydschoote. General Codet's men broke into Lizerne around 2:00 p.m., but were driven out. General Roy's bid to recapture Het Sas was equally unsuccessful. On the other hand, the Germans had been unable to enlarge their bridgehead on the west side of the canal.

On the left of the Canadians, four battalions of Zouaves advanced from the canal at 1:30 p.m., with the object of pushing the line forward toward Pilckem. The force was not remotely strong enough for the task it had been assigned. The Zouaves fought valiantly, but they were mowed down by a torrent of fire that the few nearby Canadian batteries could not suppress. Four or five hours after the abortive attack, a patrol found that Turco Farm was no longer occupied by the Germans. From that time on, it became the point of junction between the French and British armies.

Foch was always able to brush aside distasteful truths with fiery rhetoric and smooth assurances. Although he had promised Sir John a strong counterattack to regain the lost ground, there was as yet no sign of the French infantry reinforcements or of the heavy guns so necessary for any hope of success. The British V Corps, which was supposed to play a subordinate role, had shouldered the entire burden, suffering losses out of all proportion to its gains. Plumer realized that it was his duty to fight on as long as possible to allow the French time to recover their balance. If, on the other hand, the French were unable to make any progress, it would be best to evacuate what was left of the salient and direct British efforts to expelling the Germans from the west side of the canal, where they had but a tenuous hold. It was Sir John French who settled the future course of operations. At 4:15 p.m., he sent a staff officer to Second Army Headquarters with the following message: "Every effort must be made at once to restore and hold line about St. Julien, or situation of 28th Division will be jeopardized."[47] "The Germans must be a bit tired by now," French maintained in a subsequent letter to Smith-Dorrien, "and they are numerically inferior to us as far as we can judge. In fact there seems no doubt about it."[48] Considering the Germans at the time outnumbered the Canadians and the British at least three to one, it is difficult to know whether it was a case of hubris or faulty intelligence.

French was living up to an agreement he had concluded with Foch on the afternoon of 24 April to participate in still another French proposed counterattack. It did not seem to have made any difference to Sir John that Foch had made similar promises in the past, only to leave the British in the lurch. Foch assured Sir John that French forces planned a vigorous offense set for Sunday "against the front Steenstraat, Pilckem, Langemarck and east of these places"[49] As a sign of his resolve, he asserted that he was bringing in two fresh divisions, the 153rd, which was currently detraining at Cassel and a second one due to arrive in time to participate in the joint operation. Left unsaid was the fact that the 153rd had been created only ten days earlier, its units were untried, and that the two old ones at the scene were

A French soldier resting behind the lines. To his right is a French tomb.

depleted and exhausted. Under the circumstances, it bordered on the absurd to think that Foch could achieve his goal. In all he had four divisions, three of which were of inferior or at least of questionable quality, and only a handful of batteries to support them. Yet he expected to drive an equal number of German divisions, with momentum on their side and covered by massive artillery fire, not only out of an entrenched position, but back three miles to the original line. Sir John had a tendency to run down Foch and the French in front of senior British officers, loudly proclaiming that it was their responsibility to take the necessary steps to regain the ground they had lost. But in the presence of the fast-talking Foch, he invariably wilted like a flower deprived of sustenance. And so lacking a backbone, Sir John succumbed to the illogical thinking of the little Frenchmen, and, in so doing, sacrificed thousands of British and Canadian lives in a series of fruitless attacks.

French's order was passed down the chain of command and reached Alderson's headquarters at 6:30 p.m. It instructed Alderson to launch the strongest possible counterattack in order to retake St. Julien and re-establish the line. It was to be carried out by the 10th and 150th Brigades, plus six battalions or such of them as could be assembled. The hour of the attack was left up to Alderson, as was the selection of a commander.[50] Upon receipt of Sir John's directive, Alderson cancelled the arrangements he had made to relieve the 3rd Canadian Brigade and Geddes's Detachment with the l0th and 150th Brigades.

Alderson appointed Brigadier-General Charles P.A. Hull of the l0th Brigade to command the counterattack, and, to nullify the effects of the enemy's artillery, set zero hour for 3:30 a.m. on Sunday 25 April. Currie, in reference to Hull, wrote that he had never been "associated with a better soldier or better comrade."[51] For all his energy, courage, and ability, Hull was not a good choice for this difficult task. He did not know the ground, there was no time during the remaining daylight (that is, after 8:00 p.m., when the operation order was issued) for reconnaissance and he lacked an adequate staff to control the battalions under his charge. He was forced to base his plan on what he could glean from a map, assisted by several members on Alderson's staff. Although they were familiar with the area, they were uncertain about some of the latest developments on the battlefield, in particular whether St. Julien had fallen or was only partially held.

The night was dark, it was raining hard, and there was no guarantee that all 15 battalions detailed for the attack could be contacted and assembled in time. Hull sent word to his battalion commanders to meet at his temporary headquarters northwest of Ypres at 9:00 p.m. that night. Only one showed up. The rest were too far away to make it on short notice. Some of them headed units that were taken from their formations and attached to others so that they received the order belatedly or not at all; or, owing to vague directions, could not find Hull's headquarters. The upshot was that Hull delayed the attack by an hour and left for Wieltje to try to bring his force together.[52]

Hull was not the only one trying to round up men. Acting on his own initiative, like any good commander, Lipsett looked to neighbouring British units for help to bolster his battered line. Tuxford, who accompanied Lipsett on his excursions, wrote:

Three times that night Lipsett and I walked over to the Battalion H. Qrs of the Royal Fusiliers from where touch could be obtained with their rear. Our men had been fighting desperately for some days and had been badly gassed. It had not been possible for rations to come up since the Thursday night, and the men were existing on their emergency rations, and what could be gathered from the field. The need of water was imperative, and ammunition was running short, in fact, Lipsett would have been in grave difficulties had I not been able to send over ammunition with the last two platoons that I had sent him. Could their Division make some attempt to relieve our more than weary men. We were ... unable to obtain any prospects of a relief.[53]

After one of these fruitless quests, the two officers returned to Lipsett's Headquarters at Boetleer Farm, where Tuxford observed that every foot of space was occupied by a wounded man. They were surprised and somewhat puzzled when information came in that two British divisions had gathered near Zonnebeke and were only waiting for guides to lead them forward. "It did not seem probable," Tuxford stated, "but in the disordered state of things, there was a possibility, and it seemed like a ray of hope. Major Pragnell (5th Battalion), who had been sent up with his company to support Lipsett during the day, volunteered to go back through the German-infested countryside and act as a guide. But Pragnell had been wounded in three places by shrapnel and he was in no condition to undertake the mission. Since there was no one else available, Tuxford, knowing the area well, obtained Lipsett's permission to go back himself. Tuxford had a keen sense of direction — born perhaps of his prairie experience — which enabled him to make his way in pitch darkness, dodging enemy shelling and outposts on his left rear. He came within a quarter of a mile of Zonnebeke, and, seeing no sign of any troops, returned dejectedly to Tuxford's headquarters.[54]

Lipsett's persistence paid off, for on his last trip he collected an assortment of about a 1000 men, among them the 2nd Northumberland

Fusiliers, a company from each of the 2nd Cheshire Regiment and the 1st Monmouthshire Regiment, and two companies from the 1st Suffolks, who were entrenching behind Locality C. All, except a platoon of Cheshires, which was turned over to Tuxford, were scattered to the west of Boetleer Farm and extended about 800 yards into the gap. Tuxford assisted Lipsett in directing the British units to their new positions. "Posting some of these men in one piece of trench," Tuxford related, "and receiving no reply to my call from the occupants, I jumped down to find that every man was stone dead, lying or sitting in the most natural attitudes. The work of poison gas." Gazing at the sight of the enemy's handiwork, it sickened him to think "there were men in England who wrote to the daily papers and discussed the use of gas, saying that if the Hun descended to such depths, at least let us forbear from the use of it."[55] Tuxford could at least take comfort in the knowledge that it was not up to those self-righteous cretins, sitting comfortably at home and probably without sons in harm's way, to determine policy.

While Lipsett was straining every nerve to secure and extend his left, Turner was experiencing difficulties of his own. At 8:45 p.m., Turner informed Alderson of his position and added, "Some of our troops still are in St. Julien surrounded, this number originally 700 now possibly 200."[56] Turner's information was incorrect. As previously noted, there were no living Canadian or, for that matter, enemy troops in St. Julien at this hour. Turner was silent on the issue of re-establishing contact with the left of the 2nd Brigade. Although his orders had been specific, he decided that it was up to Snow to maintain the link. Sometime during the afternoon movement of the British units in the gap, Turner learned that Snow was in charge of the reserves. Without taking time to check, Turner assumed that Snow was directing the proper countermeasures to stop the German advance southward.

Turner's messages to 27th Division Headquarters in the evening alerted Snow that a grave misunderstanding had occurred.[57] Snow notified the V Corps, which in turn dispatched a wire to Alderson shortly before midnight. Plumer blasted Alderson for allowing the 3rd Brigade and its attached units to withdraw to the GHQ Line. He went on to say that this meant giving up all the ground "for which such a struggle has been made today" and leaving the 2nd Brigade's flank in the air. He ordered instant action to re-establish the line as far forward as possible in the direction of St. Julien and in touch with troops on both flanks. If necessary, Alderson was to appoint an officer to take command.[58]

Alderson was shaken and at a loss to understand the apparent inconsistency between his own instructions to Turner and Plumer's revelations of a serious breach in the line west of St. Julien. He sent a senior staff officer, Lieutenant-Colonel Gordon-Hall (GSO2), forward with plenary powers to take what action was necessary to straighten out the tactical situation. On the way to confer with the brigade commanders, Gordon–Hall passed Turner, who was on motorcycle pillion. Baffled by the attitude and directives from Snow, Turner had set out for the Château des Trois Tours to ascertain exactly from whom he was supposed to take his orders.

Gordon-Hall arrived at Wieltje shortly after midnight and proceeded to summon a meeting of the officers concerned at the headquarters of the 2nd Brigade. In attendance besides Currie and his brigade-major, Kemmis-Betty, were General Mercer, Lieutenant-Colonel Hughes, and General Bush of the York and Durham Brigade. Upon learning of the dispositions of these units, Gordon-Hall issued orders to stabilize the defensive line. Currie was to use the remnants of the 7th and 10th Battalions to extend his left to the Haanebeek. Mercer, with the 1st and 4th Battalions, would carry the line westward to the Zonnebeke-Langemarck road. From there, Bush was to occupy the stretch of ground to the southern branch of the Haanebeek. Turner was to move units northward from the GHQ Line to link up with the York and Durham, thus sealing the breach.[59] But since some of the units identified were committed elsewhere or diverted to help other formations, it was uncertain how many would be available to carry out Gordon-Hall's instructions.

The one notable absentee at the gathering was Turner, who was currently trying to straighten out matters with Alderson. There is no known record of the interview between the two men. Apparently there were sharp exchanges and the meeting ended on a discordant note. After that day, Alderson would never again trust Turner, concluding that he was unfit for command in the field.[60] In view of his attitude, the obvious question was why did he not send Turner home, especially after he had received the green light from Plumer? Given his compassionate nature, was it out of desire to avoid humiliating a national hero? Or was it because he was uncertain of how Ottawa would react? The last thing he wanted was to become embroiled in a controversial issue that might dampen the strong pro-British feeling in Canada. Whatever his motive, he must be faulted for having tolerated insubordination, occurring as it did during a moment of crisis on the battlefield. "Had we been a British Division and under the War Office," Sutherland-Brown wrote a decade later, "I am quite certain that either General Alderson or General Turner, or both of them, would have lost their commands."[61]

By the time a shaken Turner emerged from Alderson's Headquarters, British and Canadian troop movements had ceased for the night and the only action of any significance, albeit dying down, was at Locality C. Here, the steadily diminishing garrison had been under heavy pressure during the course of the day, repulsing one attack after another. The men relieved the dead and wounded of their ammunition to keep from exhausting their low supply. Of the original 300 defenders only 35 remained by 5:00 p.m.[62] Warden was himself badly wounded early in the afternoon, but remained until dusk, doing his best to assist and encourage those who were left. Before helped to the rear, he handed command over to Lieutenant Howard Scharschmidt, a 24-year-old native of British Columbia. Warden told his subordinate to hold on until he received help, was relieved, or ordered to retire. On the way back to a dressing station, Warden ran into a party of engineers and showed them the way to his old trench. Somewhat later, he approached a lieutenant-colonel and asked him to send out some men to help Scharschmidt. Warden could not recall the name of the lieutenant-colonel who claimed he was holding a trench in support of Turner's brigade, but he remembered his dismissive reply: "Cannot spare a single man."

Warden did manage to send a message to 2nd Brigade Headquarters, detailing the situation of his men and pleading for support. He was then taken to a dressing station where his wound was dressed and from there was transported by rail to a hospital in Boulogne. It was only later that he discovered what happened to his men. Around 4:00 a.m., Kemmis-

Betty ordered Scharschmidt to retire, by which time Locality C was completely surrounded. Under cover of a thick fog, Scharschmidt and 22 men managed to slip through the German cordon.[63]

At the end of the day's fighting, the Germans were dug in north of St. Julien and faced a British line that was very ragged and unguarded in places. A gap of two and three-quarter miles divided the 3rd Brigade from the 8th and 5th Battalions, which were still holding fast. In this opening there were only two detachments: one a mixed force of Suffolks, Northumberland Fusiliers, Cheshires, and Monmouthshires occupying about 800 yards near Boetleer Farm; the other, a battalion of 12th London and two companies of Suffolks, manning an isolated 1200-yards-long section of the Gravenstafel road. The survivors of the 3rd Brigade and the various attached units were in the GHQ Line north of Wieltje, at which point Geddes's Detachment and the 13th Brigade prolonged the line towards the canal.

The carnage on Saturday had left the Canadians utterly exhausted and in desperate straits. They had faced poison gas without respirators, been pounded relentlessly by German artillery, suffered massive casualties, lost the apex of the salient, and Locality C and been driven back steadily. But things were not as bad as they seemed. In fact, the Germans had taken punishment that was out of all proportion to their gains. Although they had a huge numerical superiority with no fewer than 39 divisions in the vicinity of the Canadian Division, they not only failed to gain their objectives for the day, but had been driven out of St. Julien after expending many lives to capture it. An aggressive advance during the night between Locality C and Mouse Trap Farm, which contained only a few British battalions, would have brought them the victory they were seeking. That they did not do so is striking testimony to the reception their attacking waves had met all along the line throughout the 24th. Thus the day that began ominously for the Canadians, with the shadow of defeat, ended with the situation more or less in hand. But more hard fighting lay ahead. In fact the next day would be just as bloody and harrowing for the Canadians as on the 24th.

CHAPTER 10
25 April: Another Awful Day

At the Headquarters of Duke Albrecht, Saturday 24 April had started with great expectations, but by the end of the day, the general sentiment, while not recorded, must have been at least one of concern. The German armies had made modest progress in some places, but nowhere had they gained their secondary objectives for the day. In the process, they had suffered staggering casualties. The XXIII Reserve Corps' drive against the French and Belgians had stalled and was nowhere near Vlamertinghe, where it needed to be to cut off the British army's main line of retreat from the salient. The XXVI Corps, assisted by poison gas and artillery barrages, had launched repeated assaults against the heavily outnumbered Canadians and had not succeeded in sweeping them away.

The experience of the 23rd and 24th convinced Albrecht that he must stop fruitless offensives on the west side of the canal and instead concentrate his efforts on cutting off the defenders in the salient. The idea now was to place the main attack in the hands of the XXVI Corps, which was ordered to capture St. Julien (which was believed to be in the hands of the Canadians) and then press on some 2500 yards to secure the ridges north of Wieltje and Frezenberg. At the same time, the XXVII Reserve Corps' right wing would deliver converging attacks, one against the eastern side of the salient at Broodseinde and the other in the Canadian sector against the Gravenstafel Ridge.[1] But the main German drive was forestalled by Hull's attack.

Arriving in Wieltje, Hull set up temporary headquarters in the ruins of a cottage and subsequently moved to Mouse Trap Farm, where he remained during the battle. Conferring with his own battalion commanders, he found that his brigade could only file out from two narrow openings in the wire of the GHQ Line before forming up again for the assault. This drawback, together with the congestion of traffic on the road, induced Hull to delay the operation for yet another hour.[2] Even then, he found himself with only the five battalions of his own 10th Brigade instead of fifteen. Of the remaining 10 battalions, some were committed elsewhere or did not receive their orders, while others, although notified, were delayed on the road.

Hull's objective was to capture Kitchener's Wood and St. Julien, a task that would have presented a huge challenge in the best of circumstances. But the conditions were anything but favourable. To begin with, the nature of the operation had changed. It was considerably smaller than originally planned and would be taking place, not at night, but in full view of the enemy. The delay in zero hour, coupled with poor communications, created further difficulties. No one had alerted the gunners that the time of the attack had been pushed back. Consequently, Canadian and British batteries opened fire at precisely 3:30 a.m., signalling an impending attack. To make matters worse, owing to a mistaken report that perhaps as many as 200 Canadians were still in St. Julien, a warning had been issued to avoid shelling the village. Several of the British batteries assigned to assist did not receive the message — with predictable consequences. The Germans were under the impression that St. Julien had been occupied by the Canadians after the German withdrawal on the previous evening. The bombardment of the village told them that it was not held by British troops. After the shelling was over, elements of the 51st German Reserve Division moved into the village, scattered snipers, and set up machine guns in the outlying houses, covering the flat terrain over which the 10th Brigade was about to advance.

Hull placed his four regular battalions in the front line with the 1st Royal Irish Fusiliers and 2nd Royal Dublin Fusiliers on the right, facing St. Julien and the 2nd Seaforth Highlanders and 1st Royal Warwickshire Regiment on the left, overlooking Kitchener's Wood. A Territorial battalion, the 7th Argyll and Sutherland Highlanders, was in support behind the left. The 10th Brigade, one of the best available to Alderson, was fresh, at war strength, and its regular battalions were experienced with a long tradition of service. This magnificent brigade was about to be sent to its doom.

The rain had stopped and a thick morning mist shielded the five British battalions when they passed through the GHQ Line. Before they could form up, they encountered fire from snipers hidden in the grass and crops of the farms. Discipline held and the brigade fanned out and, in faultless order, advanced against Kitchener's Wood and St. Julien, about a mile away. As the Britons moved forward, they also ran into a rising swell of bullets being fired from enemy machine guns, which began to take a toll. These were located not only in St Julien, but also in two places about 400 yards south of Kitchener's Wood, Juliet Farm, which had fallen to the Germans on the previous day, and Oblong Farm — all three positions in enemy hands were the direct result of Turner's obsession with manning the GHQ Line. Lieutenant Bruce Bairnsfather (1st Royal Wicks), described the early action from his perspective: "Ahead in semi-darkness I could just see the forms of men running out into the open fields on either side ... and beyond them a continuous crackling of rifle-fire showed me the main direction of the attack. A few men had gone down already, and no wonder — the air was thick with bullets."[3] Approaching their objectives by rushes, the men of the 10th Brigade ran into such a frightful tempest of fire that they were cut down like wheat before a scythe. From Mouse Trap Farm, Hull experienced a sick feeling as he held up his field glasses and watched the leading waves fall and remain prone in long regular lines. "Why do they stop?" asked a young officer. "They are dead," was the terse reply.[4]

Trapped in an open field and with the chances of survival slight, it required extraordinary discipline and courage for the men involved not to break and run for cover. A company of the Royal Dublin Fusiliers, which had suffered badly and found itself without officers, was on the verge of doing so, but rallied in time: An officer who took part in the attack wrote:

> One unforgettable scene remains in the writer's memory;
> one company, which had lost all its officers and which

had been ordered to retire, was doing so in disorder, when the small untidy figure of Colonel Loveband, clad in an ancient "British warm" and carrying a blackthorn stick, approached quietly across the open, making as he walked the lie down-signal with the stick. The effect was instantaneous and for hundreds of yards along the front the men dropped and used their entrenching tools.[5]

A handful of men in the leading waves struggled to find cover, but most never returned. The following lines were pinned to the ground and each time they rose to advance they encountered the same storm of fire. The Argyle and Sutherland Highlanders, sent in to reinforce the Royal Warwicks and Seaforth Highlanders, met the same fate. At no point did the attackers reach their objectives and come to grip with the Germans. The Royal Irish Fusiliers, who halted some 200 yards from St. Julien, came closest. With the view of lending additional weight to the attack on the right, Hull ordered the 4th and 7th Northumberland Fusiliers, two newly arrived battalions of the 149th Brigade, into action. These units lost their direction and veered to the right, lengthening the line instead of thickening it. By 7:00 a.m., the British attack had broken up and the survivors were surging back in search of cover. It was clear to Hull that the enemy's line could not be carried. He proceeded to consolidate the ground gained and his recommendation that the attack not be renewed was endorsed by the High Command. A new line was formed, running from west of Mouse Trap Farm to south of Fortuin, where it linked up with the entrenchments of the two York and Durham battalions. The operation had virtually annihilated the 10th Brigade, which lost 73 officers and 2346 other ranks in less than two hours.[6]

As horrible as the cost had been, it would have been even worse had it not been for the seven batteries of the Canadian field artillery that covered the attack. The Canadian guns had joined the batteries of the 27th and 28th Divisions in the preliminary bombardment at 3:30 a.m., but, on learning of the rescheduled assault in time, repeated the action two hours later. "The artillery fire was good," Hull wrote in his report, "but there was not enough of it to seriously damage the enemy who were entrenched in a very strong position." What Hull did not realize was that the men of the 51st German Division (XXVI Corps) were assembling behind Kitchener's Wood to sweep southward. The Canadian shells caught the Germans bunched up in a forming-up area and inflicted such huge losses on the 51st Division, its ranks already thinned by three days of hard fighting, that its attack was cancelled.[7] An additional benefit flowed from Hull's ill-fated assault. The survivors had closed the gap in the vicinity of St. Julien.

The right of the XXVII German Reserve Corps went ahead, as scheduled, with its two-pronged attack. The Germans heralded their first assault at Broodseinde on 25 April with an intense bombardment that began around 5:00 a.m., and rained shells on the trenches of the 85th British Brigade (28th Division) for the next eight hours. The Germans supplemented shrapnel and high explosives with gas shells, which seriously affected the defenders, rendering some unconscious. Then, at 1:00 p.m., a regiment of the 53rd Reserve Division charged across the 70 yards of no man's land and fell upon the trenches occupied by the 2nd East Surreys. There was hand-to-hand fighting and the Germans broke in at several places in this 1000-yard sector. On the right, the East Surreys drove off the Germans, capturing 29 and killing the others who had entered the trench. In the centre, the East Surreys retained possession of the trench with the help of a support company of the 8th Middlesex. It was a different matter on the left where the defence had been weakened by the loss of all the officers. The Germans gained the upper hand and remained in possession of 60 yards of breastwork, despite two subsequent attempts to dislodge them. In the sector of the 3rd Royal Fusiliers, on the left of the East Surreys, the Germans had to cross 200 yards of no man's land before reaching their trenches. The Germans never came close to doing so. Lieutenant Hallandain, who handled one of the machine guns, deserves much of the credit for breaking up the German attack. The War Diary of the 28th Division accorded him his proper due: "During the fighting the enemy collecting for the attack were caught in close formation by a Machine Gun ... under Lieutenant Hallandain, who seeing the situation, rapidly changed the position of his gun and catching the Germans in enfilade caused them to retire with very heavy casualties."[8]

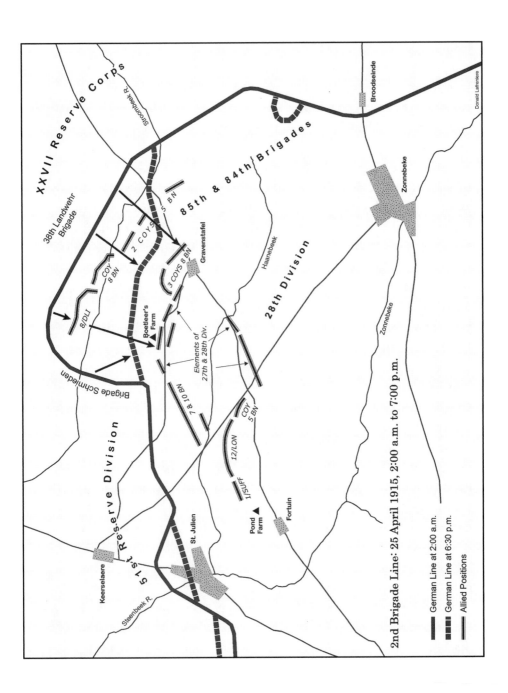

2nd Brigade Line: 25 April 1915, 2:00 a.m. to 7:00 p.m.

— German Line at 2:00 a.m.

▪▪▪ German Line at 6:30 p.m.

— Allied Positions

Farther west in the neighbouring Canadian sector, the Germans were relatively quiet until after dawn. In the meantime, the 8th Durham Light Infantry (151st Brigade) under Lieutenant-Colonel John Turnbull, arrived at at Boetleer Farm, Lipsett's headquarters, around 3:00 a.m. This fresh and inexperienced Territorial battalion had been sent by General Snow from the corps reserve at Potijze to assist the 85th Brigade. Along the way, Turbull's orders were changed and instead he was directed by his commanding officer, Brigadier-General Archibald Chapman, to fill the gap north of the Rangers facing Locality C. Lipsett explained that his battalion had been badly cut up from 48 hours of incessant fighting and bombardment and pleaded with Turnbull to relieve his three companies. Although Turnbull considered himself responsible only to General Chapman, he recognized Lipsett's desperate situation and agreed to replace his men in the trenches.

As a group, the Canadians had mixed feelings about turning over their line to the Durham Light Infantry. After being in the thick of things for a long time, they had endured more than could normally be expected of humans, were much reduced in number, and weak from want of food, so they were grateful for the respite. However, they thought it was unfair to plunge the raw recruits, who were very tired after two long marches and unfamiliar with the mental and bodily torment of trench warfare, into the horrors of the salient in their baptism of fire. "It was certainly a forlorn hope to expect them to take over and hold such an exposed flank under the circumstances," Major Harold Mathews wrote.[9] Although the Canadians had been overseas for two months and had seen little fighting before 22nd April, they considered themselves to be seasoned troops compared to the Durhams. Lester Stevens's reaction was typical of that of his comrades:

> I remember the Durham Light Infantry coming up and taking over from us. And they were all kids and I spoke to some of the kids, see. I said, "where are you from?"
>
> He says, "We've just come out from England."
>
> I said, "Haven't you been in any trenches before?"
>
> "Never been in any trenches before," he says. "We don't know nothing."

"Goodnight," I said, "I'm sorry for you." In fact I said
to one or two of our chaps, I said, "It's a damn shame
… for them to come in here and take over from us. We
should stay here and carry on." But … we got our orders
to get out and the Durham Light Infantry took over. [10]

The coming of daylight prevented the removal of the remaining dead
and wounded from the trenches and the relief of the Lipsett's right company
(No. 4), which stayed in the line. Two companies of Durhams (Nos.1 and
4) occupied the left of Lipsett's front while the other two were deployed
in support along the hedges near Boetleer Farm. Besides the Durhams
and one company of the 8th and the 5th Battalions, the area was defended
by mixed British units, which included a company of Northumberland
Fusiliers, two companies of Suffolks with two half companies of 8th
Middlesex, and a company of 1st Monmouthsires in support.

Behind the lines, Currie wasted no time in attending to the
instructions that he had received from Lieutenant-Colonel Gordon-
Hall, Alderson's emissary. He had been awakened from a dead sleep to
attend the conference and was exhausted. In view of his obvious fatigue,
Currie's single-mindedness struck Gordon-Hall, who observed that he
"collected his staff, walked out into the night to get in touch with Lipsett
and fill in, as far as he could, the gap between Lipsett's left and the
General Headquarters Line."[11] Concentrated near Currie's headquarters
were survivors of the 7th and 10th Battalions, whose combined strength
numbered roughly 360 all ranks. The 10th had lost its commanding officer,
Lieutenant-Colonel Boyle, its second-in-command, Major MacLaren, as
well as its adjutant, Major Ormond, while participating in the deadly
attack in Kitchener's Wood on 22 April and in assisting in the defence
of Locality C on Gravenstafel Ridge. The 7th was without its original
commander, Hart-McHarg, who had been mortally wounded, and it
had been practically destroyed in the action near Keerselaere. Currie
personally led the two battalions to the front lines where he merged them
into a composite unit. Dawn was breaking when he proceeded to placed
them in a southwesterly direction from the left of the Suffolks (end of
the 8th Battalion's line) to the Haanebeek. As the morning mist began to

dissipate, the Germans opened up with small-arms fire. Currie carried on with his work and paid no attention to the bullets whizzing around him to the disbelief of his men. It was clear to them that his size — six-foot-four and 250 pounds — and distinctive headdress made him an inviting target. Sidney Cox said in hindsight: "We thought he was crazy, standing up there with his red hat on, while we were taking all the cover we could till we dug in."[12]

Placing Major Odlum in charge of the composite unit, Currie hurried over to Boetleer Farm to confer with Lipsett. Satified with Lipsett's defensive arrangements, he left the farm and walked toward the headquarters of the 5th Battalion, located near Gravenstafel Crossroads. On the way, he suddenly came under machine-gun fire and jumped into a sap that ran into the 5th Battalion's line. He was furious, as he picked himself off the ground, for he assumed that he had been fired on by some of Tuxford's men. On reaching the battalion's headquarters, he exclaimed, "Tuxford, who the hell was that shooting at me?"[13] Tuxford explained that the shots had been fired by Germans, who occupied a house behind the battalion's front line. Currie was skeptical and thought Tuxford must be mistaken. Thereupon Tuxford led Currie outside and posted him behind a brick wall. "I directed him where to look and to withdraw at once," Tuxford wrote. "He did so and immediately after withdrawing, came a flight of machine-gun bullets against the brick wall." Currie was convinced. "Then those are the beggars who shot at me this morning," he said. Currie's earlier brush with death was driven home when, at breakfast, he reached down to draw something out of his pockets and found a bullet in the fold of his riding pants.[14]

Currie set up his command post at Tuxford's headquarters, hardly an ideal place. The telephone lines with Division Headquarters were soon severed and messages by runners, sent from either end, were slow to arrive if they did at all. Moreover, there was the issue of Currie's safety. Tuxford noted:

> The enemy bombardment intensified, and my H. Qrs were badly shelled. I tried to persuade General Currie to go back to Brigade H. Qrs, but he only said "I shall stay

with my men." We felt that the crisis was approaching. Enemy aeroplanes were very active in directing their artillery fire, flying low down. The brick buildings were rapidly disintegrating under the shell fire.[15]

The enemy had confined its activities during the early morning hours to rifle fire and occasional shelling, but after dawn, artillery of all calibres pounded the salient mercilessly, reaching as far as Potijze, some two miles behind the Canadian front line. The shelling gradually increased in volume and reached a crescendo at 9:00 a.m. and lasting until noon, when between 45 and 68 shells were falling every minute. What stood out for Lieutenant Edison Lynn was the cascade of shells and machine-gun fire sweeping the area: "Gunfire was not concentrated on any one area continuously. It would be heavy for a time at one point and then would shift, apparently being directed by observation planes or balloons against advancing troops. The gun fire came from several directions and at all angles."[16] Then, after noon, the shelling subsided slightly, but increased again before 2:00 p.m. Private Samuel Archer (7th Battalion), who was caught in the maelstrom of fire, and, like his mates, could do nothing but endure, received two wounds early in the afternoon, a bullet in the arm, and shrapnel in his thigh. While recovering from his wounds, he wrote to his parents in Ireland:

> It was an awful battle and one I shall never forget … After I got wounded I crawled half a mile to get my wounds dressed. I did not even know whether I would get to my destination. But thought I would have a try. The shells were bursting all around me, and bullets coming in all directions over my head, while the dead were lying everywhere. No matter where you went you could see nothing but dead bodies.[17]

For some, especially among the newcomers, the relentless shelling was more than they could bear. In the second line a group of Durham troops broke and fled in disarray. Tuxford later wrote:

About 1 p.m. a number of the Durhams came back from the left in disorder, and I gathered them in and placed them in the trenches with instructions to pick up and use the rifles that were lying around … Raw troops as they were, rushed into the midst of a veritable inferno, they had more than bravely borne themselves throughout that long morning's bombardment until the strain became more than human men could stand.[18]

On the morning of the 25th, the only enemy attack on the 2nd Brigade's front line, such as it was, occurred southwest of Locality C on the far left, manned by the composite 7th/10th Battalion. As Odlum's men were digging in, two soldiers were seen running from behind the cover of a ruined building and coming toward them. Without waiting for orders, some of the Canadians opened fire and the figures fell. Someone shouted that they were British, and so two Canadian soldiers went out to investigate. Fired on in turn, the two were hit, but managed to hobble back to their trench. Slightly ahead on the left, where Odlum assumed the Suffolks lay, a small group appeared and began exchanging shots with the Canadians. The distance between the two lines was only about 200 yards, but in the half light of dawn with a morning mist covering the field, Odlum was unable to determine whether those ahead were British or Germans. He ordered his men to cease firing. A young straggler from the 2nd Battalion, who spoke German, volunteered to find out who they were. He held up his hands and advanced, shouting out in German. He had gone about 50 yards when he was shot down. There was no longer any doubt that those on the other side were Germans. By now their numbers had increased considerably, and, although they tried to advance, they were cut down by rifle fire and the survivors were driven to the ground.[19] As it turned out, it was the prelude to the fight for the Gravenstafel Ridge.

At 11:00 a.m., large bodies of German infantry were seen advancing in close order southward from the direction of Poelcappelle and Locality C, and it was evident that another attempt to pinch off the northeastern salient was but a few hours away. The latest German threat came when Alderson's position in some ways had improved. The 10th Brigade and attached battalions had filled the wide gap south of St. Julien. Although most of the Canadian units were terribly reduced and weary, he had a considerable number of British units at his disposal with others on the way. Furthermore he had been advised that at 1:00 p.m. the French would launch an attack east of the canal toward Pilckem.

Still, there was an absence of a unified command structure made necessary by the intervention of British units. On top of this, some of the old problems remained. Far to the rear in the Château des Trois Tours and without adequate communications to control his forces, Alderson was compelled to base his decisions on reports that were often erroneous or out of date. Before 1:00 p.m., Alderson was handed information that suggested that the trenches running from the northern outskirts of St. Julien to Locality C were occupied by British forces. "This is undoubtedly the left of our 1st [Canadian] Bde. which was sent last night to connect with the 3rd Canadian Brigade," he notified General Hull. "Try to connect with them."[20] In fact, Mercer's men were dug in one mile south of St. Julien and the trenches in question were occupied by the Germans, not by the British. Before this was known, Alderson's hopeful thoughts were disrupted by alarming messages from the 28th and 5th Divisions. The former claimed that the enemy was advancing from the north in long columns between Locality C and Boetleer Farm, which meant that Currie's front line had been smashed and his units were being encircled; while the latter indicated that Fortuin had apparently fallen and that the German line now ran along the Haanebeek some 700 yards south of Boetleer Farm and the Gravenstafel Ridge.[21] Both reports were wrong. Fortuin was in British hands and the British line was 500 to 1500 yards north of the stream. But Alderson concluded from the announcements that the Ridge had fallen and with it the forces manning the 2nd Brigade's front. Consequently, he contacted General Snow at 1:45 p.m. and requested that the three remaining battalions of the 151st Brigade (Durham Light Infantry) move up, not to reinforce Currie's men, but to occupy a new line along the Fortuin-Gravenstafel road, between 500 to 1000 yards in rear of the Ridge, in order to halt the supposed enemy's advance.[22] Simultaneously, Alderson arranged to inform 2nd Brigade Headquarters at Wieltje of the change of plans so that the news could be transmitted to Currie. Over three hours would pass before the message reached Currie, who was at 5th Battalion headquarters.

Throughout the day, Currie directed and encouraged his commanders while trying to cope with developments on his front. The situation was not reassuring. The 2nd Brigade's line was exposed and tactically unsound. Currie hoped that the promised counterattack would clear the enemy off the toe of Gravenstafel Ridge and secure his left. But around 1:00 p.m., he learned that Hull's attack had been unsuccessful.[23] To compound his despair, what was left of the Canadian 1st Brigade and Bush's 151st Brigade had not moved into position on his left as Gordon-Hall had ordered the previous night. By way of encouragement, Alderson assured Currie at 11:50 a.m. that "strong reinforcements" were coming up to help.[24] But unless these arrived in time, Currie feared that his thin line, which was unsupported by artillery and reserves, would be swept away by a determined enemy assault.

At noon, Currie received a call for assistance from Odlum, whose men had been in action since the night attack on Kitchener's Wood. The Germans had been massing in strength on the high ground in the area of Locality C and a torrent of shells from front and flank were blasting his men out of the trenches. Odlum had pleaded with Turnbull to organize a counterstroke to clear his front, only to be turned down. He reported the following:

> In justice to the O.C. 5th [should be 8th] D.L.I. I should state that there seemed to be some doubt in his mind as to the source to which he should look for his orders … He had no instructions that he had been placed under the G.O. C. 2nd Canadian Inf. Bde. for orders, and felt that he should await instructions from his own Brigade before moving.[25]

When Odlum could not persuade Turnbull to take action, he contacted Currie, hoping for better results. Currie was powerless to offer anything. "We must hang on at least to night fall," Currie replied. Odlum sent word to Currie that his men were almost done in, but thought that they could hang on until nightfall.[26]

The German assault on the 2nd Brigade's front was in full swing by mid afternoon. On the left, the composite 7th/10th Battalion was up against hordes of grey-clad figures without artillery support or the prospects of receiving reinforcements. As chaotic as conditions were, the Canadians maintained a steady fire, but the Germans kept advancing like a gigantic landslide. Before long they began to work around the flanks of the Canadians, who kept fighting and showed no signs of breaking down.

A few hundred yards to the east, the weight of the German attack forced the Durhams back bit by bit. Turnbull ordered one of his two support companies (No. 2) forward to bolster his front-line troops. That Territorial company was unable to reach the front. As it emerged from the covering hedges into a shallow valley, it was subjected to a terrible shelling and machine-gun fire, which decimated its ranks. A Canadian who witnessed the scene recalled: "I have never seen such slaughter in my life. They were straight from England. They had never heard a shot fired in anger. They were lined up — I can see it still — in a long line — straight up and the Hun opened up on them with machine-guns. They were just raked down. It was pathetic."[27] Stunned and terrified by the unexpected turn of events, the survivors reeled back towards Boetleer Farm, the German fire following them step-by-step. The Germans next penetrated behind the two left companies in the line, but the fire of the Durhams, supplemented by the machine guns of the 8th Canadians (No. 4 Company), kept them temporarily at bay.

The weight of the German attack was directed against Boetleer Farm. Here, the elite battalions of Brigade Schmieden (XXVII Reserve Corps), backed by massive artillery bombardment, pressed hard and around 3:00 a.m. acquired a foothold on the edges of the farm. Major Harold Mathews, who went up to report to Lipsett, described the grim conditions at his headquarters: "The cellar and any outbuildings that remained standing were full of wounded men. The place was getting a most unmerciful shelling and was a regular shambles."[28] German troops continued to gain more ground, and, at 3:30 p.m., captured the farm.

Lipsett countered by moving up his three companies, which were in reserve near a turnip field southwest of Gravenstafel Ridge. His objective was to halt the enemy's advance by occupying old trenches below the fallen Boetleer Farm. The movement was spotted by the Germans, whose artillery quickly found the range. One shell, Mathews wrote, "dropped right in the trench and blew twelve of my men out at once, all of them being killed or wounded." [29] Consequently Lipsett gave the order to fall back to a farm about a quarter of a mile to the rear.

Odlum's quick action helped patch up the breach at Boetleer's Farm. Scurrying around in the neighbouring sector, Odlum saw British and Canadian troops pouring over the crest and retreating down the reverse slope of Gravenstafel Ridge. He hurried over, and, with the assistance of Major W.A. Monro (8th Battalion), tried to stem the tide. "We succeeded in getting them turned back and returned to the trenches near the crest," he wrote in his report.[30]

On the east of Boetleer Farm, pressure intensified as the afternoon wore on. At 4:00 p.m., Currie was alerted that No.1 and No. 4 Companies of the Durhams had fallen back to the Gravenstafel Ridge. Currie reported the withdrawal to, among others, General Hull, from whom he requested troops for a counterattack. Half an hour later, Currie received a note from Captain G.A. Stevens of the 8th Durhams that contradicted the earlier intelligence. Stevens wrote that, although all the men in the left front trench had been killed or wounded and one reserve company driven back, the line from Boetleer Farm to the road east of it was still intact. He added that the enemy did not appear to be pressing the attack except by artillery fire.[31] No sooner were Currie's cautious hopes raised than they were dashed by the receipt of two messages from Division Headquarters (relayed by 2nd Brigade Headquarters at Wieltje) around 5:00 p.m.

The first suggested that the Durhams had fled from the front and that No. 4 Company of the 8th (Canadian) Battalion had been surrounded and destroyed. This piece of intelligence was inaccurate. The three companies were still holding out in their allotted places, though they were surrounded on three sides and out of touch with the Gravenstafel Ridge. The other was a telephone call announcing that the 151st Brigade, which Currie assumed were the expected reinforcements, had been ordered to dig in a valley about half a mile behind his position on the Gravenstafel Ridge. Currie interpreted the message to mean that his exposed position had been judged hopeless.

A little after 5:00 p.m., Currie paused to take stock. Hull's attack had been repulsed; Mercer's men had failed to move up to guard his left flank; his line was crumbling and he believed that the Durhams had taken to their heels and No. 4 Company of the 8th Battalion destroyed; the reinforcements he expected had been diverted elsewhere; his request for troops from the 10th Brigade to make a counterattack had gone unanswered; his men were weary and close to the breaking point; and the most compelling factor was receipt of the message from Divisional Headquarters implying that Gravenstafel was about to be abandoned. Weighing everything, Currie concluded at 5:15 p.m. that in order to save the rest of his men he must withdraw.[32]

Currie immediately walked up to Tuxford and said, "We are ordered to retire." Tuxford was astounded. Executing a withdrawal in the midst of close contact with the enemy is dangerous enough in the best of circumstances, but to do so in broad daylight up an open slope swept by enemy fire is to invite annihilation. "But sir, it is impossible to retire," Tuxford replied. Currie, however, was adamant, insisting that the movement had to be carried out at once.[33] "God help us all," Frederick Bagshaw, Tuxford's orderly room sergeant, commented in his diary. "It is madness to go before dark."[34] Lipsett and Odlum learned of the retirement order around 5:30 p.m. and Currie claimed that they approved of it.[35] In making this assertion, Currie went perhaps too far. Their reaction, while not recorded, was probably the same as that of Tuxford. That is, they objected not so much to the withdrawal, as to the time of day it was to be carried out.

As the phone lines were down, Odlum sent an orderly to deliver the order to the 7th/10th Battalion to fall back. Lipsett sent a similar message to his 8th Battalion. But soon after he began to worry lest the runner fail to reach his destination, in which case his companies might be cut off. To set his mind at ease, he decided to personally carry the order forward, "exposing himself to great danger."[36] Both Captain Hilliam, the adjutant, and Major Hugh Dyer, the second-in-command, were adamant about carrying the retirement order to the 5th Battalion's two front-line companies, a task that, in the words of Tuxford, "courted almost certain death." Under incredible strain, Currie was not amused to see the two old men arguing like children on a playground. To end the embarrassing dispute, Tuxford duplicated the message, giving one to Hilliam to deliver to the right company and the other to Dyer for the left company. Starting from the cover of the hedges, they came to an open area that extended about 100 yards. Hilliam had gone only a few steps when a bullet pierced one of his lungs, but somehow he managed to get through. Dyer was also struck by a bullet which lodged within an inch of his heart. "Pulling himself together this man of iron," Tuxford wrote, "half scrambled, half dragged himself until he dropped some few yards short of the trench into which he was immediately dragged."[37] Dyer was carried back on a stretcher. Several soldiers, looking to pick up Hilliam, found instead a board on which was scrawled in mud, "I have crawled home."[38]

Currie's order was for all troops to retire to a switch line,[39] at some distance behind the Gravenstafel Ridge, which was to have been dug during the night. The line, however, did not exist because Snow, expecting an attack on his front, had not sent the 151st Brigade forward as Alderson had requested. This was unknown to Currie when he departed for Brigade Headquarters at Wieltje, running the gauntlet of German fire coming from cottages in Tuxford's rear.

Currie was also unaware that the survivors of the two Durham companies and No. 4 Company of the 8th Battalion remained in their trenches, fighting gamely against overwhelming odds. Cut off from their battalions and under an artillery barrage that was increasing in fury, their condition had become desperate. At 5:00 p.m., the three front-line commanders — two from the Durhams and Captain George Northwood of No. 4 Company — met behind a broken wall in the centre of their line and agreed that they must pull back. A message was dispatched to ask if they could withdraw, bur no answer came. Nevertheless, the operation proceeded, the first to go were small groups of wounded and gassed men. These disabled soldiers had to make their way rearward over a long stretch of open country upon which a torrent of fire was being directed. All but a few were mowed down before they reached the crest of the ridge. To cover the withdrawal, a platoon of the left company of Durhams, led by a subaltern, was sent to occupy a small house a short distance to the west. As the men crawled through a field of beets, a party of Germans, preparing for an assault, lay hidden amid foliage on slightly higher ground. Suddenly they sprang up, surrounded the Durhams, and took them prisoner.

By now the Germans realized that something was in progress. Accordingly, they turned a concentrated fire on the Anglo-Canadian front line, shelling it heavily, and raking it with machine guns. While a handful of Durhams remained behind to draw the enemy's attention, the rest of the left company moved eastward along the trench and made its way back successfully. A much harsher fate awaited the right company. Assaulted from all sides it was annihilated practically to a man.

Northwood's dwindling No.4 Company was still in the trenches when it was rushed and surrounded. All the machine guns were out of commission except the one that Sergeant William Alldritt, a physical director from the YMCA in Winnipeg, operated effectively. He continued to fire, mowing down in droves grey-clad soldiers swarming from all sides, until he was killed. The rest of the men, save for a small party under Sergeant Knobet that had been ordered to the rear before the onslaught, remained at their post until the bitter end. The casualties of No. 4 Company included all the officers and 139 other ranks.[40]

While these events were taking place, Lipsett and Tuxford began to carry out the withdrawal of their respective battalions. "The din of bursting shells and the noise of battle were bewildering," Tuxford wrote. The two officers had agree earlier that retirement, should the need arise, was to be conducted in succession of companies, starting from Lipsett's left — so as to provide mutual support. On receiving the order, however, Lipsett's companies left their trenches en masse, and, consequently, all cohesion was lost. As it was still light, it was not easy for the Little Black Devils to extricate themselves. Sergeant Aubrey Fisher recalled his harrowing experience:

> We were at the apex so we got cut off. They cut through
> us at both sides. And we had been given orders to retire.

Well, we said, tell H.Q. to come up and look at the slope on that ground at the back of us. They would have slaughtered us going up the hill. "Well," I said, "look, there is only one way we can get away. We can't run up that slope, we got to get down in the ditches. And they can't hit us with a machine gun or any other gun down in the ditch."

So we got down in the ditch and we moved, and then there was a lull, and Arthur and Bob decided they'd take a short cut. They both got killed, and I stayed in the ditch. I crawled through this hawthorn hedge and then when I came out I saw some other fellows, you see, so I just hooked up with them.[41]

Across open ground swept by machine-gun and artillery fire, the men of the 8th Battalion fled, as fast as their physical condition would permit, toward the rear. Once they had escaped from the grasp of the slowly pursuing Germans, they barely limped along. Fighting days and nights on end and seriously affected by the gas attack on 24 April, they had exceeded their powers of endurance and were drunk with exhaustion. Witnessing the retreat, Tuxford wrote with empathy: "It was pitiful indeed to see these men who had come from the very jaws of hell staggering along, absolutely dazed, gassed, hungry and parched with thirst." [42]

It was more difficult for the 5th Battalion to extricate itself from the grasp of the enemy, owing to the collapse of the retirement plan. Unhampered, the Germans closed in on the two front-line companies and prevented them from falling back beyond the Gravenstafel Ridge, where they were to join their reserve companies and the remnant of the 8th. Tuxford had sent his staff ahead and was alone in a house that served as his headquarters a short distance in the rear. He realized that without covering fire, the chances that his companies could escape were practically non-existent. Grabbing a rifle from the ground — it was the third as the bolt from the other two rifles were jammed — he ran back and collected 40 or 50 men from various units and ordered them up the hill. Dragging their tired bodies, they silently fell in without uttering a word of complaint. Their moral courage could not help but draw unbounded admiration from Tuxford:

> Having escaped by a miracle and having retired to practical safety at the Zonnebeke Road to mount the hill again under heavy fire to line the trench, and upon the order being passed down the line to fix bayonets a Sergeant called to me as he snapped his bayonet home with a click. "Tell me what to do sir, and we'll do it.[43]

Tuxford and his men were climbing the half-mile slope of the Gravenstafel Ridge when a German machine gun opened up from a farm house 400 yards to the left and everyone scrambled for cover. Tuxford could not have been terribly surprised since it was the same machine gun which, for the past few days, had periodically fired bursts into his headquarters from the rear. Changing the belt took about a minute, during which the men got up and ran 50 or 60 yards before dropping to the ground. Halfway up the hill, there was a loud explosion and the firing stopped. Tuxford turned toward the house where the machine gun was hidden in time to see it disintegrate into a cloud of flying debris. A British battery unit, firing behind Tuxford's right, had scored a direct hit.

Trudging along, Tuxford ran into Lipsett and several members of his staff, and together they led the men back to the top of the ridge. Tuxford placed his men in a shallow line of reserve trenches, and, as it was getting dark, sent word for the two front-line companies to break off action. The roar of exploding shells was so deafening that he had to shout to be heard. At one point he lost sight of Lipsett. He had last seen Lipsett lying alongside his batman and feared that he was wounded. He circled around the ridge three times looking for him, but without success. As it happened, Lipsett was unhurt, though he had a close call when a bullet went through his cap. But his batman was wounded and he had assisted him down the hill to the dressing station — which explained his absence from the ridge.

Soon after Tuxford returned from the search, he spotted the leading waves of the two companies with No. 1 on the right and No. 2 on the

Close up of Gravenstafel Ridge.

left. The movement, Tuxford noted with satisfaction, proceeded in good order, even though the Germans were in hot pursuit, beating drums and shouting, "We have got you Canadians now." Tuxford posted Sergeant Bowie and six men to guard his left at a distance of 80 yards from the main body. Bowie had barely established himself when he saw a party, which he estimated to number 150, appear over a mound ahead. Since he could not determine whether they were friend or foe, he immediately issued a challenge. Back came a reply "Do not shoot, ve was French." Bowie shouted, "Fire" and the Germans, who were caught in the open, were cut to pieces. Bowie alone claimed to have shot down 14 of the enemy.[44]

A few minutes later, another group of Germans belonging to the Schmieden Brigade approached Tuxford's main position. By now a number of stragglers, separated from their units, had joined the 5th Battalion. Among the newcomers was Sergeant Aubrey Fisher (8th Battalion), who heard the officer in charge say, "Now stay where you are and don't fire." Fisher continued with his account:

And we stayed there, and by then there must have been
two hundred of us collected from the 5th battalion and
a few other battalions. And then after that Fritzie got
more confident of his position and he just came forward
and then we had the order to let go. And we let go, and
they must have thought the whole Canadian Army was
at the back of it. It was an absolute surprise to them.[45]

The accurate and rapid fire of the Canadians broke up one rush after
the other. Although Tuxford had the situation well in hand, he realized
that if he stayed there much longer he would be outflanked and cut off.
Under cover of darkness, the delicate process of disengagement was
successfully completed. As Tuxford led his men to the rear, he searched
in vain for the switch line, which, as already mentioned, had not been
constructed. He was, however, elated to find that Lipsett had escaped
without a scratch.

On the way down the slope, the Canadians had passed by the
trenches of the 3rd Royal Fusiliers, the left battalion of the adjacent 85th
Brigade. Tuxford discovered that the Fusiliers were not conforming to
the retirement for they had received no orders to do so. It was apparent
that a general retirement had not been ordered. Both Tuxford and Lipsett
realized that by falling back they had uncovered the Fusilier's flank and
given the Germans an opportunity to roll up the 28th Division from
its left. Without reference to Currie, the two Canadian officers acted
quickly. They turned their men around, and, over the same fire-swept
ground, hastened up to the top of the ridge, where they reoccupied the
trenches. They remained there even after the Fusiliers, like the other
British units in the line, received orders to withdraw. "The Regulars fell
back to our right very steadily as if carrying out a tactical exercise under
peace conditions," observed Major Mathews. The Canadians were left in
comparative peace, although at one point it appeared as if they might
be attacked. "The Germans came up under cover of the slope and some
woods and buildings on our front to within perhaps 400 or 500 yards
of us," Mathews wrote, "blowing a trumpet that sounded like a small
hunting horn. We quite expected and hoped that they would attack and

charge our position, but evidently they had no idea of doing anything rash."[46] At 3:00 a.m. on 26 April, the Canadians received instructions to withdraw, which was carried out in a somewhat disorderly fashion, but silently and without the enemy realizing it.

When Tuxford raced back up the Gravenstafel Ridge, he was uncertain of what was happening on the other side of the line. Below Boetleer Farm, on what had been Lipsett's left, a collection of British forces — Suffolks, Monmouthshires, and Durhams under Lieutenant-Colonel Turnbull — continued to hold their ground. Turnbull had received Currie's order to withdraw, but doubtful that he was under Canadian jurisdiction remained in place until assured he could leave. Turnbull's left was covered by the mixed 7th/10th Battalion, which had not received the order to retire. In the absence of Odlum, the two senior officers in the line, Captain Stanley Gardner of the 7th and Major Percy Guthrie of the 10th, met and decided to stay where they were until the Suffolks had completed their retirement.

The withdrawal of the composite battalion was carried out over an extended period. The first runner sent to the 10th Battalion trenches apparently was killed, and, by the time the second one arrived at the 7th, the composite unit had reverted to separate commands. Odlum, although unaware of the breakup of the unit, was to remain in charge of the 7th Battalion while the 10th was placed under 30-year-old Major Gutherie, a former politician in New Brunswick. As the orders of the 7th Battalion no longer applied to the 10th, Guthrie was reluctant to retire without the direct authorization of Brigade Headquarters, even though units around him were leaving their trenches. While he set out for Currie's new advanced headquarters in Gravenstafel village, the 7th Battalion made its break to the rear. Sergeant Raymond MacIlree described how he and survivors of his platoon made their way to comparative safety:

> We were prepared to hold on forever when the order came to retire, as our flanks were turned. I took half my Platoon out along a hedge to cover the retreat of the Company, so I never saw them again. The Germans were coming in thousands, so we worked our way down

the trenches to the left. In this way, we kept up a running battle ... leaving one trench, and running across the open to another one in the rear. Our artillery ... gave us no help, while we were being mowed down by shrapnel, machine-guns, and rifles. It was sure a merry hell ... people kept getting killed, in such messy ways, that it became a nightmare. It is funny how calm you get. A man falls besides you, and you just heave him out of the way, like a sack of flour. Finally we reached the last trench, which was simply jammed with men from all our regiments.[47]

Guthrie, for his part, never reached Currie's headquarters. On the way, he came face to face with a German party and barely managed to escape capture. Hotly pursued by the enemy, he did not return to the 10th Battalion until after midnight. Lieutenant Walter Critchley had better luck when he tried to get through. The fleet-footed 23-year-old was able to elude the Germans in the darkness, and, before dawn on 26 April, returned from Currie's headquarters with a written order for retirement. "Without this order," Guthrie wrote to Currie a week later, "I would have maintained my position and been annihilated."[48] Thanks to the early morning mist, the 10th Battalion's withdrawal was unnoticed by the enemy.

During the fighting, several of Guthrie's men found themselves isolated and ended up with other units. A case in point was Sid Cox, a tough-minded survivor of Kitchener's Wood and Locality C who joined up with a small group of British soldiers — possibly belonging to the 2nd East Yorks — in a remote trench. For some reason, they did not receive the order to withdraw, and, to their horror, discovered they were cut off when they heard German voices in the darkness around them. There was a ditch that ran behind their trench and Cox was prepared to take his chances rather than surrender. Several of his comrades appeared to be wavering, which prompted an angry Cox to exclaim, "You can surrender if you damn well please. I'm going down the ditch." All but one of the British soldiers followed him in the ditch that fortunately led to the 11th Brigade's line.[49]

In his report, Odlum acknowledged that the 7th and 10th Battalions, "knowing that both their flanks were up in the air," had fought with dogged determination, "which undoubtedly held back and seriously delayed the German advance towards Fortuin."[50] Still, the idea of giving up ground rankled Guthrie: "I felt rotten about having to give way … There was nothing else to be done, as our right was left open and our men were worn out. If two new regiments had marched up to our help we need not have given way an inch."[51]

Odlum had become separated from his unit in the afternoon when he rushed over to rally the routed defenders of Boetleer Farm. He subsequently went over to Currie's advanced headquarters in Gravenstafel village to discuss the situation, and left a few hours later. By dusk, the 7th and 10th Battalions had not reported in and he began to worry over their fate. He had no idea where they were, and, in trying to locate them, made his way to the old 8th Battalion headquarters, which he discovered was in the hands of the Germans. A little after 8:00 p.m., he walked over to a place called Bombard Crossroads and found the remnants of the 7th Battalion, which he led back to Wieltje.[52]

None of the units under Turner's command were heavily engaged on the 25th, although they had a trying time, pounded as they were by nonstop shelling. Late in the afternoon, Turner and some of his officers had a narrow brush with death. Turner was studying a large map in rear of his headquarters at Mouse Trap Farm, when an airplane circled twice overhead. The plane must have been German, even though it bore Allied markings, for within a few minutes, incendiary shells came crashing in rapid succession on the farmhouse and the outbuildings that served as a dressing station. The farmhouse caught fire, as did the straw on which the wounded were lying. Eventually, the fire reached a dump of 200,000 rounds of rifle ammunition and the cartridges began to explode. The shelling continued and the whole place was filled with flames, Lyddite fumes, and flying bullets. Through this inferno, Captain Francis Scrimger, assisted by a small band of devoted stretcher-bearers, calmly brought the wounded into the open.

The farm was surrounded by a moat, which was crossed by only one road. But the entrance across the moat was on the exposed side, so that when Turner ordered the place evacuated, all the able-bodied men jumped into the water. Crawling out of the moat, they eventually reached a small house, some 300 yards to the south, which became their new headquarters. In the words of Villiers, the experience had left them "not much the worse, except that we were all soaked through, and a bit shaken."

Scrimger had supervised the removal of the wounded and personally looked after Captain Harold McDonald, a staff officer of the 3rd Brigade, whose wounds were so serious that no one expected him to live. Scrimger carried him out of the blazing house and laid him down in a shallow ditch near the moat. He remained beside McDonald, coiling his body around the wounded officer's head and shoulder, while shells exploded around them. Five shells fell within fifteen feet of the lying men, dazing and half-smothering them with flying mud. At length, help arrived. Two of Turner's staff officers swam the moat again, and, after waiting for a lull in the shelling, got the wounded man across the road onto a stretcher. McDonald lost an arm, but recovered from his injuries. For exceptional valour and devotion to duty, Scrimger was awarded the Victoria Cross.[53]

For the past three days, Alderson had been responsible for a front exceeding five miles, whereas the usual divisional sector by any of the belligerents on either side averaged two miles, rarely more than three. On top of this, the recent action in the salient by Canadian and British troops had left a fragile line held by intermingled and tired units, sometimes out of touch with groups on their flanks, and without a unified command. Thus, at 2:30 p.m. on the 25th, Plumer began the process of reapportioning divisional responsibilities, improving the command structure and separating the units. His order, effective at 7:00 p.m., placed Alderson in charge of the 1st and 3rd Canadian Brigades, the 10th, 13th, 149th Brigades, and Geddes's Detachment, as well as reducing his sector to the two miles between Turco Farm (the junction with the French) and Fortuin; and Major-General E.S. Bulfin, to whom was given the 2nd Canadian Brigade, the 150th (York and Durham) Brigade, the 8th Durham Light Infantry (151st Brigade), and the newly arrived 11th Brigade, was allocated the front from east of Fortuin to his own 28th Division. By dividing the sector and the troops therein between Bulfin and Alderson, an important step was taken in the direction of a unified command. It was further stated that as soon as circumstances permitted, all detached units were to be withdrawn and returned to their proper brigades. Finally, any units that could be spared were to be sent to General Snow, who remained in command of Corps Reserve in Potijze.[54]

The Germans, as usual, made no attacks during the night, permitting the movement and disentanglement of British units to commence. As hard as the British leadership tried to organize the defence in the areas where the bitterest fighting had taken place, there were still three substantial gaps in the line as dawn approached on the 26th.[55] Incredibly, the Germans had not discovered any of the openings, presumably because of careless or non-existent reconnaissance. Had the Germans exploited their chances, Albrecht would have had more reason to feel confident when contemplating his next move. Rejecting his general's proposal that he broaden the scope of his operation, he wrote: "The Corps must be satisfied with what it has gained ... The aim of the Army Operation was for the present to lop off the pocket east of Ypres by the advance of the XXVI Reserve Corps."[56]

During the evening on the 25th, Alderson took the opportunity to relieve some of his units, starting with those which had been sadly depleted. The 1st Canadian Brigade was sent to defend the bridges across the canal, replacing Wanless O'Gowan's 13th Brigade, which occupied the front vacated by Geddes's Detachment. The 10th Brigade marched to the GHQ Line and took over from Turner's 3rd Brigade, which was ordered to bivouac near La Brique (west of St. Julien).[57]

The fighting around Ypres had taught British generals on the spot that hasty, isolated attacks by the infantry alone could not stop the Germans from slicing off pieces of the front, much less expel them from the territory they had gained. Another offensive directed at the enemy was pointless unless carefully prepared, backed by sufficient artillery, and in conjunction with a resolute and powerful effort by the French. Contrary to Foch's assurances, the reinforcements, except for the leading regiment of the 153rd Division, had not arrived, so that the French contribution on the 25th had been limited to an abortive attack by a single battalion of Zouaves at midday on the east side of the canal. Putz had decided to postpone the counterattack until the following day when he would have more troops at his disposal.

At a high-level Anglo-French conference on the afternoon of 25 April, presided over by Smith-Dorrien, an agreement was reached on a plan for combined action the following day. The British, with two brigades of the newly arrived Lahore Division, were to push northward on Langemarck in support of the French attack. At the same time General Putz would launch a three-pronged attack: adjoining the British troops, General Joppé with his own fresh 152rd Division, plus the remainder of Mordacq's brigade of Zouaves (45th Division), would assault from the east side of the canal toward Pilckem. As soon as Joppé's advance permitted, General Quiquandon, commanding the rest of the 45th Division, along with the 87th Division, would cross at Boesinghe and join the northward drive. And on the left, General Curé, with the 153rd and 18th Divisions, assisted by the Belgians, would aim to dislodge the Germans on the west bank at Lizerne, Steenstraat, and Het Sas and then proceed in the direction of Bixschoote.[58]

That evening, Smith-Dorrien drove to Hazebrouck, where he was given Sir John's instructions. Smith-Dorrien had already concluded that the resources to expel the Germans from ground they had been fortifying for several days were unavailable. The French were organizing a vigorous offensive in Artois and their contribution to the ongoing battle at Ypres, half-hearted at best, was not likely to change. Sir John was committed to assist the French and he was in no mood to divide his resources between Ypres and his impending operation farther south. Yet to persist in a policy of fragmentary attacks was both futile and costly. And to remain in the salient, which was narrowing and overcrowded, was to put the troops at greater risk. The only sensible solution, as Smith-Dorrien saw it, was to withdraw to a shorter and more defensible line that was closer to Ypres.

Sir John, however, had already made up his mind. He indicated that he did not want to abandon any ground, but that he might have to unless the French regained what they had lost, or at least a good portion of it. He felt certain that the enemy's continuing attacks around Ypres were calculated to disrupt the projected Anglo-French offensive in the Artois region, scheduled to start at the end of April. Determined to see that these plans were carried out, he wanted the situation "cleared up and the area quieted as soon as possible," even if it meant a further withdrawal.

Sir John added irately that, "as the French had got the Second Army into the difficulty, they ought to get it out."[59]

Foch evidently did not see eye to eye with French. He considered the loss of territory around Ypres to be no more than a local setback. In his view, it was a problem that chiefly affected the British, since the French did not have much of a stake in defending the salient. In fact, Foch had made plans to relieve French troops from the Ypres area weeks before and only the diversion of the British 29th Division to the Dardanelles prevented him from following through.[60]

Smith-Dorrien had been led to believe that General Putz, supposedly reinforced by three divisions, would employ sufficient troops to drive home his attack. At 10:00 p.m., when a copy of Putz's orders arrived at Second Army Headquarters, it showed that he proposed to commit only one new division (less a brigade), together with those troops already in the line — a mere total of 17 battalions. This news was followed by another French message saying that zero hour was to be moved up from 5:00 p.m. to 2:00 p.m. Smith-Dorrien reeled under the double blow. He telephoned General Headquarters and was told that Sir John had retired for the night. At his insistence, the little field marshal was awakened and brought to the telephone. Smith-Dorrien protested first, that the French attack would not carry enough weight to have any effect, and second, that advancing it three hours would curtail the already limited period available for preparations and for the rest needed by the Lahore Division, which had marched all night. Smith-Dorrien expected a much more sympathetic hearing than he received. After all, Sir William Robertson, Sir John's chief of staff, had warned him earlier in the day to attack simultaneously with, but not before, the French.[61] Evidently Robertson was unwilling to accept Foch's assurances at face value. But Sir John was eager to please French leaders, even though, as the British Official Historian wrote, "at heart he was most anxious to withdraw from the impossible position in the Salient" so as to spare the unseasoned New Army divisions from engaging "in a losing battle as their first experience of war."[62] He disregarded Smith-Dorrien's objections and cut short the conversation by giving him a direct order to proceed as arranged.

CHAPTER 11
Lambs Led to the Slaughter

Ordered out of the front line on 25 April, the three Canadian brigades made their way to their assigned areas. All three had suffered heavily and were in awful shape. Evading corpses and shell holes littering the field, the men staggered along, and, as they were unshaven and grubby, and their uniforms were ragged, torn, and caked with mud, they appeared as bad as they felt. All looked forward to a bath, rest, and a hot meal upon arriving at their destination. But leisurely time for the 2nd and 3rd Brigades would have to wait.

Placed at the disposal of General Bulfin, Currie's Brigade had been ordered to take a position southeast of Fortuin to support the left of the 11th Brigade (4th Division) under Brigadier General John Hasler. Shortly after dawn on the 26th, Currie and Hasler were on their way to Fortuin to see Bulfin when a runner approached them with a message that the Germans had pierced the right of the 11th Brigade's line.[1] The information, as it turned out, was incorrect, arising from the 28th Division's overreaction to an inconsequential incident. Under cover of a heavy mist in the early morning, a large party of Germans had advanced through a gap, and, by pretending to be Royal Fusiliers, had wiped out an unsuspecting patrol belonging to the 1st Hampshires. The Hampshires had been sent up to seal the breach and were in the process of digging in when the Germans approached No. 3 Company. When challenged, they replied, "We are the Royal Fusiliers." Detecting a foreign accent, Captain Bennett ordered his men to open fire.[2] The Germans hastily took to their heels and that was the end of the threat, such as it was.

On hearing the news, Currie volunteered his brigade to help patch up the supposed break in the line. Hasler gave his blessing and Currie's men were roused from their brief slumber. By Currie's count he could only muster between 1200 and 1400 men out of a force that a few days earlier had numbered 4000 — there were, of course, stragglers who had temporarily fallen in with other units during the night and would eventually turn up. With its left resting on Fortuin, the brigade was ordered to advance three-quarters of a mile to a ridge. At 8:00 a. m., the brigade was on the march again with the 10th Battalion on the left and the 8th on the right, followed by the 5th and 7th in reserve. The fog had lifted and the sun shone brightly. All went well in the beginning. As the Canadians were in the midst of crossing a ploughed field, they were spotted by a German airplane and soon came under heavy shrapnel fire. They sustained few casualties, however, until they crossed a small stream and reached a line of farmhouses. Major Mathews explained what subsequently occurred: "Pushing on towards the ridge we came under an oblique fire from machine guns at our left front, but soon the rising ground protected us. We found the field exposed to a cross, as well as a frontal, fire of shrapnel and high explosive, and I [?] gave orders to dig in behind the crest."

While the ridge offered the Canadians protection from shrapnel fire, it also obstructed their view. Mathews crawled forward to reconnoiter the other side of the ridge when a shrapnel shell burst in front of him, sending fragments into his left leg, just below the knee. Mathews crawled back to the line and one of his men dressed his wound. In the evening, he was taken to a dressing station and from there passed through Ypres on his way to England.[3] Before the Canadian battalions withdrew from the area on the 27th artillery fire, described by Currie "as the heaviest yet experienced," accounted for a considerable number of casualties, though the exact number was not recorded.[4] What had to be the most frustrating part was that the suffering endured by the Canadians had been for nothing.

Turner's brigade assembled at La Brique (west of Ypres), as ordered, but, finding no staff to give it further directions, marched across the canal and spent the night of 25–26 April south of Brielen. Just after dawn, Turner and a few members of his staff went over to see Lieutenant-Colonel John Currie to congratulate him "on sticking it out at the hot corner." The brigadier had not slept since Thursday morning. "He was completely worn out," Currie wrote, "so I gave him and his officers a place under a piece of tarpaulin after they had had something to eat." Currie himself laid down for a nap, but was awakened half an hour later by a dispatch rider looking for Turner. Currie refused to wake him unless the matter was urgent. Assured that it was, Currie roused Turner, who was handed a message ordering his brigade to march to La Brique to support the Lahore Division.[5]

More than one soldier cursed when woken from a dead sleep and told that his battalion was returning to the battle zone. Half asleep, the men dragged themselves to the concentration area where they were issued rations and ammunition. The 3rd Brigade was as depleted as Currie's Brigade when it got underway at 8:00 a.m. The Canadians were spotted after crossing the canal on the way to La Brique and shelled heavily, though it thankfully resulted in few casualties. The men dug in when they reached their assigned place, but there was no let-up from the artillery blasts, some of which came from British shells falling short of their target. For a few of the battle-fatigued men, the strain was more than they could bear. According to the historian of the 16th Battalion, several of them suffered mental breakdowns.[6] Lieutenant F. Hawkins, a member of the nearby 9th Battalion, London Regiment (Queen Victoria Rifles), witnessed one such scene: "A Canadian Scotchman went mad this morning. He jumped out of the trench and commenced firing his rifle wildly in the direction of friend and foe alike. To have shot him down would have been the only way of protecting ourselves against him; but we were saved from this act as Fritz turned a machine gun on him and riddled him with bullets."[7]

Men and officers of the 3rd Brigade fully expected to enter the fray at any moment to assist the Lahore Division's assault. Lieutenant-Colonel Currie wrote: "We all thought we would be at it again in a few minutes, and the men began tightening up their puttees and looking to their rifles and ammunition." He went on to say, "Some began eating their rations, for as one poor fellow said they might as well enjoy them because they might not need any more after a few minutes."[8] But to their relief, the Canadians were not called on to fight. As they moved to take up a new position along the St. Jean Ridge that afternoon, they were unaware of the disaster that befell the Lahore Division.

The objective of the Lahore Division was identical to that of Geddes's Detachment on 23 April, namely the German line between Kitchener's Wood and the Langemarck road. In some respects, Major-General H. D'U. Keary, who commanded the Indian troops, was better off than Geddes had been. He had a complete staff, as did each CO of his two assaulting brigades, Ferozepore and Jullundur. He arrived at midday on the 25th, and, having discussed matters with Smith-Dorrien, sent out his officers to arrange for artillery support and to observe the roads, places of assembly, and the ground over which the men were to advance. Thus he had time to gain useful information about his mission, make preparations, and ensure that his orders reached all his units.

The Indian Division remained directly under the control of Smith-Dorrien whose operation orders for the 26th called on the V Corps to launch an attack on its immediate right.[9] In accordance with his instructions, Alderson directed the 149th Brigade to attack St. Julien astride the Wieltje road, and, at the same time, ordered the 10th Brigade to assign one battalion to advance between the two diverging forces. Geddes's three reserve battalions at St. Jean would move into the GHQ Line to support the attack. Canadian contribution to the operation was to be limited to a number of field batteries and the 3rd Brigade, which would serve as the divisional reserve.[10]

The attacking troops were more numerous, but everything else favoured the enemy. The length of the British artillery barrage, fixed by the amount of ammunition available, was wholly insufficient to cut wire and flatten strong entrenchments. Additionally, there was no time to lay lines to the observation officers and many of the batteries were too far from the front to zero in on their targets or else they were placed out in the open and clearly visible to German counter-battery fire. The Germans, on the other hand, had enjoyed three days in which to improve their defences. They had a limitless amount of ammunition for their field batteries, the majority of which had been moved forward into the captured territory. Aided by excellent observation on both ground and in air, German guns commanded every square inch of territory over which the Indian brigades had to advance.

On the way, the long column of marching British and Indian soldiers had been spotted by enemy observation planes and came under artillery fire. While there were some casualties, most of the shells detonated harmlessly amongst the rubble and torn fields. Around 12:30 p.m., the two assaulting brigades of the Lahore Division, each consisting of a British battalion and three Indian battalions, formed up side by side west of Wieltje. The Ferozepore Brigade deployed three battalions in the front line with, from left to right, the Connaught Rangers, the 57th Wilde's Rifles, and 129th Baluchis; while the 47th Sikhs on the left, the 40th Panthans in the centre, and 1st Manchesters on the right, made up the Jullundur Brigade's three front-line battalions.[11] Straight ahead lay the ground, much of it devoid of cover, where bitter fighting had taken place on 23 April. It was littered with bloated bodies of Canadian and British dead, a sight that could not have inspired confidence among the attacking troops. Like Geddes's Detachment, the Lahore Division had to ascend Hill Top Ridge and pass through a shallow valley, then sweep up the long, gentle slope toward the German trenches on the summit of Mauser Ridge.

At 1:20 p.m., the bombardment commenced and lasted 40 minutes, much longer than the barrage that had preceded the Canadian assault on Mauser Ridge three days earlier. Still, it proved rather ineffective, for the gunners had no knowledge of the precise location of the German trenches. At 2:00 p.m., before the bombardment ceased, the Indian division advanced with the Ferozepore Brigade on the left and the Jullundur Brigade on the right. The general direction of the attack was due north, but the exact location of the enemy's position was not known. "The idea had got about that the German trenches were two hundred yards away," recalled Major F.A. Robertson, in charge of a bombing party of his regiment, the 59th Scinde Rifles, which formed part of the second line of the Jullundur Brigade. "When our front line went over the top they found that there was anything from twelve to fifteen hundred yards to go."[12]

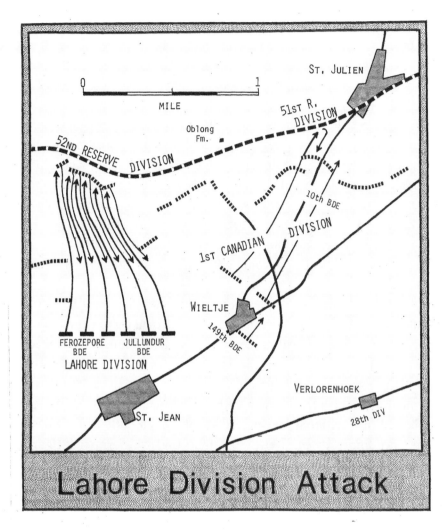

Lahore Division Attack

It was not long after the advance started that the Jullundur Brigade veered slightly northwest, crowding the neighbouring brigade and driving it across the line that separated the French troops from the Lahore Division.[13] German artillery followed the attack from the very beginning, and, as the leading waves of infantry raced down the reverse slope of Hill Top Ridge, German machine guns joined in the action. Men fell in heaps from the tornado of bullets. No less devastating were the exploding shells, particularly from 5.9-inch heavy field howitzers, which landed with pinpoint accuracy, tearing huge gaps into the advancing ranks. Since the troops instinctively bunched behind what little scrap of cover was available, there were instances when whole platoons were wiped out by a single shell. When the first of the attackers reached the bottom of the valley, the ground behind them was covered with bodies of the fallen.

Thus, in following the efforts of the individual assaulting units, the story is fairly repetitive. On the left of the Ferozeopore Brigade, the Connaught Rangers were slowed down by thick hedges through which passage was accessible only in a few places. Crowded as they were, they met the full blast of the enemy's fire when their supporting artillery bombardment ceased. Living up to their nickname of "The Devil's Own," they lost 15 officers, including their CO Lieutenant-Colonel S.J. Murray, and 361 other ranks before coming to a halt about 120 yards from the German trenches.

The 57th Wilde's Rifles advanced steadily until they crested Hill Top Ridge, when they ran into an inferno of fire and their casualties mounted rapidly. They closed to within 80 yards of the enemy, and, in the process, lost 17 officers and 258 men. There were here, as in other regiments on this day, acts of extreme heroism. Among the wounded officers was Captain P. d'A. Banks, whose orderly, a Sikh named Bhan Singh, had followed him faithfully. Seeing Banks fall, Singh, although seriously wounded himself, went over to help him. Under a storm of shell and machine-gun fire, Singh staggered along with Banks on his back, but, weak from his own wound, collapsed from exhaustion.[14] Disregarding his own safety, he remained with Banks for the rest of the afternoon, and, in the evening, pulled him out to safety. By the time Banks reached the British lines, he was dead. For his act of devotion and bravery, Singh was awarded the DSM.

The right battalion, the 129th Baluchis, was hampered in its forward movement by the Jullundur Brigade, which angled too much to the left. In turn, the 129th forced the other two battalions, the 57th Rifles and Connaught Rangers, to veer to the left. As with the other units, the 129th endured a hammering running down the ridge, but pushed on through the dark smoke until it approached the so-called Canadian Farm on its right, about 300 yards from the German line. Fire from an enemy machine gun located in the farm drove the 129th farther to the left and it seemed to lose direction.

The Jullundur Brigade was mauled as severely as its sister brigade. In fact, the 47th Sikhs sustained more casualties than any other regiment, losing all but one of its British officers. Left in command, Lieutenant A.E. Drysdale, a subaltern with only five years' service, rallied the men after they were moving away from their objective, and, under murderous fire, brought them to within 70 yards of the enemy. Still, at the end of the day's fighting, the 47th Sikhs had been reduced to a shadow of its former self. Of the nearly 450 men, the battalion could muster no more than 96 men and officers.

From the northwest frontier of India, the 40th Panthans, in their first battle since arriving in Belgium in April, fought like hardened veterans. They advanced rapidly to take advantage of the supporting bombardment, but, on crossing the ridge, encountered heavy fire and took appalling casualties. Merewether and Smith wrote: "At one moment they were moving forward as if nothing could stop them; the next second they had simply collapsed."[15] The machine-gun officer, Lieutenant F.L.R. Munn, with his crew, followed the regiment to provide support. On crossing a small brook, all those carrying the guns were shot down. Seapoy Muktiara successfully retrieved one of the guns by dashing 250 yards each way over bullet-swept ground. The gun was then set up, but alas proved to be useless. It jammed repeatedly, presumably damaged as a result of soaking in the muddy stream when its original carriers were hit.

In the meantime, the Panthans pressed forward by short rushes and came remarkably close to the enemy. Their bombing officer, Lieutenant R.J. Thornton, came nearer than anyone, reaching a point about 40 yards from the enemy's wire when he was wounded. Unable to move, he remained where he was throughout the daylight hours with no cover except a pile of manure. The losses for the Panthans were serious enough: five officers and 23 other ranks killed with 19 missing; while 15 officers and 258 others were wounded. The commanding officer, Lieutenant-Colonel F. Rennick, was mortally wounded and carried to a ditch until dusk, when he was taken away on a stretcher. He died while in an ambulance, one of five commanding officers to fall during the engagement. The command devolved upon Lieutenant-Colonel F.B. Hill, who cheated death on two occasions that afternoon: a bullet sheared his revolver case off his belt; and another went through a notebook in his breast pocket, and, travelling from left to right, left him without so much as a scratch.

In another sickening scene, the 1st Manchesters felt the inferno of fire while crossing the ridge with men and officers falling everywhere. Practically all the officers were killed or wounded, leaving sergeants and corporals in charge of the depleted companies and platoons. The stubborn Manchesters were ultimately stopped 60 yards from the German trenches. They had suffered 289 casualties, including their commanding officer, Lieutenant-Colonel H.W.E. Hutchins, who was killed by a stray bullet. In the course of the action, Corporal. Izzy Smith (born Ishroulch Shmeilowitz) went to the assistance of his immediate superior, Sergeant Rooke, who was seriously wounded and unable to move. Placing the sergeant on his back, he carried him 250 yards to safety, while all the time he was exposed to rifle and machine-gun fire. Rooke later described what happened: "During the attack I was shot through the liver and was quite helpless. Smith at once ran out to my rescue, put me on his back, and carried me through a terrific hail of shrapnel, rifle and machine-gun fire … I was lying only 200 yards from the German trenches and the fact that Smith escaped being hit was a sheer miracle." Smith's good luck held out on that day. He risked his life again and again by bringing in a number of other wounded men. He was awarded the Victoria Cross for exceptional gallantry under fire.[16]

Major Robertson was understandably horrified by what he witnessed. It may be of interest to quote part of his account:

> Our artillery preparation had not at all shaken the nerves of the Germans, and the two British and four Indian regiments who led the way were absolutely mowed down by rifles, machine guns, and artillery of every calibre. The slaughter was cruel … My bombers never even got to grips! It was a miracle that any men did manage to cross that wide shallow valley exposed

to a torrent of fire from the German line on the rising ground beyond… Heavy German howitzers … had the range and whole platoons were being knocked out by a single massive shell. All across the shallow valley the dead and the dying were tossed into the air and dropped in mangled heaps. But survivors of the leading waves pressed on until they were little more than a stone's throw from the German wire a hundred yards beyond.[17]

In the span of 20 minutes, the men of the Lahore Division had gone through hell, but unfortunately that was not the end of their anguish. To the west of the Ferozepore Brigade, General Joppé's attack had been launched punctually at 2:00 p.m., and some progress was made at the outset. Then, at 2:20 p.m., the Germans played their trump card, releasing chlorine gas opposite the 4th Moroccan Brigade on the right of the 153rd (French) Division. It appears that the Germans had installed cylinders in the area with the object of discharging gas, not for defensive purposes, but to assist an attack they were planning. However, the sight of a new wave of attackers, coming at a time when the German infantry's confidence had been shaken by the ordeal of the past few days, convinced local commanders to release some of the gas.

The steady approach of a six-foot wall of deadly fumes terrified the Moroccans, understandable enough, given what happened to their comrades on the front line on 22 April. Some tried to protect themselves by covering their mouth and nose with wet handkerchiefs, others could only think of pressing their faces into the earth, but most turned and ran, stumbling and gasping toward the rear. In a few minutes, the gas had engulfed the leading waves of Moroccans, leaving scores of men writhing on the ground, dying of slow suffocation as their faces turned a ghastly blue. The French official history makes no mention of a panic retreat in its one-sentence description of the event, merely stating that the "advance was unexpectedly stopped by a discharge of gas and the troops driven back in some places to the south of the jumping off places."[18]

Mixing with British and Indian troops on their right, the Moroccans carried many with them while they streamed back in hopeless confusion.[19]

Sergeant F.G. Udall, a member of a Territorial battalion (4th Londons) in the second line, was waiting for the order to go forward when he saw groups of Connaughts running back in acute distress. According to his account: "They were in no sort of order, and there was greenish colour about their clothing and they were coughing and staggering and some of them were dropping down on the way. I remember hearing an NCO shouting at them, 'Don't let the Territorials beat you!' And many of the Connaught Rangers actually turned round and went back again to their line."[20]

A mixed party of mostly Connaughts and Manchesters under Major H.R.G. Deacon, numbering around 120, refused to give up the ground they had gained during their advance. They stopped and dug themselves in. The Germans stormed their position and fierce fighting ensued, much of it hand-to-hand. Against overwhelming odds, Deacon's men were forced back 80 yards when the Germans broke off action and returned to their trenches. Deacon and his little band remained where they were, beating back several attempts by the enemy to dislodge them until relieved at 2:30 a.m. the next morning.[21]

The wind, blowing from west to east, carried much of the gas fumes across the front of the Lahore division. The Indian troops had never been exposed to poison gas, and, although they were warned about it, only had a vague idea of how to defend against it.[22] A handful of the men reacted by holding cloths wetted with urine or water against their nose and mouth. Most of the others, either taken by surprise or without means of protection, pressed their face against the scanty parapet. This was an exercise in futility. Shrieks of fear and uncontrollable coughing filled the air with soldiers clutching their throats or collapsing to the ground in agony. The survivors staggered to the rear to escape the gas cloud. During the confusion, with all the officers dead or incapacitated, Jemadar Mir Dast of the 57th collected as many men as he could find, some of whom were wounded or slightly gassed. By cajoling and bullying, he managed to hold his position until ordered to retire after dusk. On the way back, hearing cries from wounded comrades from nearby trenches, he picked up a number of officers and men, some of whom would probably have died without his help. What made his rescue efforts more remarkable was that he was wounded himself.[23] For his gallant conduct, he was awarded the Victoria Cross, the second soldier from the Lahore Division to receive that unique distinction for the action on the 26th.

The Germans took advantage of the hideous effects of the gas by pouring on more firepower, wrecking havoc on the troops trying to dig in or advance.[24] In the final analysis, the combined effects of the gas and massive shelling proved too much and the Lahore Division's assault, which was faltering, came to a dead stop. Beaten to a bloody pulp, it had been a dark day for the division, which had suffered 1829 casualties to all rank, including the deaths of two battalion commanders, for no purpose whatsoever. At nightfall, the division gave up what ground it had gained so that the line was more or less where it had been at the start of the day.

As awful as the Lahore Division's experience had been, it was, if anything, even worse for the 149th (Northumberland Fusiliers) Brigade on its right. Although the brigade was in reserve nearby at Wieltje, its commander, Brigadier-General J.F. Riddell, did not receive his orders to advance until 1:30 p.m., 30 minutes before the chosen hour of the attack. The delay in issuing the order was due not so much to a breakdown in staff work as it was to the lack of time to bring together all elements of the attack by 2:00 p.m. Smith-Dorrien had warned French of the inherent dangers of moving up the starting time by three hours, but to no avail. Had the attack proceeded at 5:00 p.m., as originally scheduled, Riddell would have been able to conduct a brief reconnaissance of the ground and gained some idea of the location of the enemy's trenches, rather than have them pointed out on a map. Then, too, he would have had time to usher his three Northumberland battalions — the 4th on the right, the 6th on the left, and the 7th behind the 4th — through the few narrow gap protecting the GHQ Line, deploy them, and, during the assault, take advantage of what little artillery support there was.[25] To further complicate matters, Hull's 10th Brigade, instructed to connect the Fusiliers with the attack of the Lahore Division, had not moved into position. Hull's telephone lines had been cut by German bombardment and he received his orders too late to participate in the action.

Riddell acted immediately on receiving his orders, for he realized that any failure on the part of his brigade to attack might compromise the operation.[26] Under heavy shelling, the Fusiliers, the first Territorial

Vanheule Farm near St. Julien.

brigade to go into action, assembled in attack formation and advanced on either side of the Wieltje–St. Jean road. By 2:45 p.m., they crossed over the 10th Brigade's shallow trenches and converged toward St. Julien, their objective. They were about to receive a harrowing introduction to trench warfare.

Deprived of artillery support, the Fusiliers forged ahead over practically level ground and in plain view of the enemy. Consequently, they were mowed down in droves by exploding shells and machine-gun fire, particularly from buildings in St. Jean. The Fusiliers showed remarkable gallantry, but they were able to advance only about 100 yards beyond the British front-line trenches. Pinned in no man's land, the men found shelter where they could and remained there with no thought of retiring.

At 3:15 p.m., Riddell, who had established his headquarters in the support trench, reported erroneously that his men had captured St. Julien.[27] At 3:30, he left his headquarters and headed towards Vanheule Farm to be closer to his battalion commanders.[28] As he approached the farm he was shot through the head and died instantly. "I did all I could to stop him going into what I knew was almost certain death," Riddell's brigade-major sadly related, "but it was of no avail, as he was too brave a man to think of self under the circumstances."[29] Temporary command of the brigade fell to Lieutenant-Colonel A.J. Foster, who ordered the men to dig in and stay where they were.[30] The abortive attack on St. Julien had cost the 149th Brigade a total of 42 officers and 1912 other ranks in killed, wounded, and missing — over two-thirds of its strength. Of all the senseless and bloody counterattacks during Second Ypres, this one ranks at, or close to, the top.

Elsewhere, we had left Joppé's Morrocans when they fell back in disorder upon the appearance of the gas cloud. But, as it blew diagonally, they rallied and pushed forward once more to regain the terrain they had lost. Enemy resistance stiffened when they came abreast of the Lahore Division and they went no farther. Joppé's failure to gain the commanding ground on the east side of the canal prevented General Quiquandon from developing his attack against Boesinghe. French efforts on the west bank met with only limited success. Desperate fighting raged throughout the night, ending with the capture of most of Lizerne. For a change, the French had shown a greater level of commitment, but nowhere had they achieved their objectives for the day.[31]

And so the fighting on the 26th came to a close. The incredible courage shown by the Lahore Division and the 149th Brigade had only resulted in their being smashed to a bloody pulp. They had not gained any ground that they were able to hold, and the worst part was that they had inflicted practically no losses on the enemy. Improvised counterattacks to stop an enemy from inflicting greater damage, even one claiming heavy casualties, can be justified. What was inexcusable, as on the 26th, was the horrendous loss of life in fruitless and ill-prepared attacks in broad daylight against an enemy well entrenched and possessing vastly superior firepower. Sir John French seemed oblivious to what was happening. He persisted in clinging to the notion that the French had to be given every opportunity to regain the territory they had lost. But how long did it take for him to realize that they had no intentions of taking charge of the operations. Time and time again the French had failed miserably to live up to their grand promises. The reason they did so should have been obvious.

From practically the outset, Foch considered the re-establishment of the line in the salient a British responsibility, and he proposed to limit, as much as possible, French involvement in the fighting.

The French planned to renew the assault the next day and it was again arranged that the British left would co-operate. When Smith-Dorrien received a copy of Putz's orders, he was horrified that the weight of the French attack, upon which the whole operation depended, would be no greater than on the previous day. He at once dispatched a note to Putz, pointing out that the British troops were too insufficient in numbers to achieve anything without substantial and effective French assistance. Putz responded to Smith-Dorrien's complaint by ordering Joppé, on the immediate left of the British, to employ his entire force, including the reserve regiment. When alterations were made, the net result added only two more battalions to the French attack.

Smith-Dorrien could no longer suffer in silence with the feeble French efforts that had cost him some of his best-trained and most experienced men. In the early morning hours of 27 April, he forwarded a long letter addressed to Sir William Robertson, but actually intended for French, along with a copy of Putz's note. He began by outlining the French plan and stressed that the number of troops they proposed to assign to its execution was wholly inadequate. In accordance with his instructions, he had ordered the Lahore Division to co-operate with the French attack at 1:15 p.m. on the 27th, but was "pretty sure that our line to-night will not be advanced of where it is at the present moment." He feared that the Lahore Division had suffered very heavy casualties, and, from all reports, so had the 149th Brigade. He continued on to say, "I am doubtful if it is worth losing any more men to regain the French ground unless the French do something really big." If a determined French push was not forthcoming (as seemed likely to him), it seemed best for the safety of his troops to effect a tactical withdrawal to a line that could be more easily defended. Smith-Dorrien warned that should the Germans break through the French lines and advance west of the canal, the British would have no alternative but to abandon the salient and Ypres itself.[32] Smith-Dorrien's comments reflected a reasoned and professional assessment of the hard facts.

While Smith-Dorrien waited for a reply from General Headquarters, the planned offensive went ahead on schedule. In the French sector, Putz had ordered a preliminary bombardment to begin at 12:30 p.m., followed by the advance of Joppé's mixed force — 4th Morrocan Brigade on the right, a brigade from the 18th Division in the centre, and Mordacq's Zouaves on the left — at 1:30 p.m. East of the Ypres-Langemarck road, the dividing line between the two forces, the Lahore Division was to support the French, but it was not to advance until its left flank was secure. It was clear that Smith-Dorrien had done his best to avoid throwing away additional troops based on empty French promises. But even if the French showed a more combative spirit, he must have known that the Allied attack, taking place over the same ground as on the previous day, and with ill-defined objectives, was doomed to fail. It must have pained him immensely to sacrifice the Lahore Division simply because his spineless chief wanted to keep the French happy.

The one change from the previous day was the replacement of the Jullundur Brigade by the Sirhind Brigade, commanded by Brigadier-General W.G. Walker. The freshest brigade of the Lahore Division, it was situated ahead of the French right. The Ferozepore Brigade, now much reduced in strength, was to extend the line to the east. It was arranged that this brigade, which was well to the rear, would leave its shelter trenches at 12:30 p.m., so as to arrive in line with the Sirhind Brigade by 1:15 p.m. Thereafter, the two Indian brigades, with the French right, would move forward simultaneously.

At 12:30 p.m., Walker, without seeing any signs of French activity or waiting for the Ferozepore to come up in line, ordered his battalions to advance to take advantage of artillery cover.[33] Walker's action was against the express wishes of Smith-Dorrien, not to mention that by outdistancing the Allied attack line, the enemy's entire firepower would be fixed on his brigade in the early stages. Over ground strewn with Canadian, British, and Indian dead, the Sirhind Brigade moved forward on a two battalion front, with the 1/4th Gurkhas on the right and the 1/1st Gurkhas on the left. From the mountainous region in Nepal, the Gurkhas were small in stature, extremely courageous, and carried the *kukri*, a broad, curved knife, with them into battle. They were devoted to King George V, loyal to their officers, and very popular with British and Canadian soldiers. Lieutenant Stan Lovelace, a member of the 9th CFA, watched the start of the Gurkhas attack from his observation post: "I witnessed a very exciting charge by the Gurkha troops. They started from somewhere near my observation station and moved quickly in groups of about a dozen to rush forward and then drop. Then a rush to the right or the left and on about 500 yards over a slight ridge. What wonderful little men."[34]

As soon as the Gurkhas passed across Hill Top Ridge, they fell in heaps under the enemy's shattering fire, which broke up the attack. Through the inferno, three British officers and some 30 Gurkhas persevered and managed to reach Canadian Farm at the bottom of Mauser Ridge. No reinforcements could reach the small party until 4:00 a.m. when it was joined by other members of the unit. That help arrived at all was due to the spirited dash of the 4th King's Liverpool, which, in the face of murderous fire, came to within 200 yards of the enemy's line. Here, the 4th Kings discovered that the wire protecting the German trench was uncut, which made it futile to push on any farther.

A little behind on the right, the Ferozepore Brigade, led by the 4th London Regiment and the 9th Bhopal Infantry, was similarly swept away by enemy fire. The Bophals did all that could be humanly expected, but their attack withered away after they gained touch with the Sirhind Brigade. Their losses totalled 122 men. The Londoners pushed on slowly and painfully until their movement ceased in the face of overwhelming fire. One of its leading companies had been reduced to a mere 30 men. The machine-gun detachment was cut up so badly that most of the men and all but one gun were put out of action.[35]

Although it probably would not have affected the outcome of the Lahore Division's attack, the French located west of the Ypres-Langemarck road did not even attempt to leave their assembly area. The French Official History offers us no explanation for their inaction, but its British counterpart does.[36] According to Edmonds, Joppé's men did not move because they were pinned down by a heavy enemy barrage.[37] It was no more intense than what the Indian Brigades had endured and yet they went ahead with their end of the operation. Instead of acting in support of the French, they ended up carrying the whole weight of the assault.

The French showed more determination west of the canal where General Curé completed the capture of Lizerne and regained Het Sas and the line of the canal up to Steenstraat.

The French were sufficiently encouraged to undertake another assault with the British to begin at 6:30 p.m., following an artillery barrage. The British planned to attack with their depleted Indian Division, supported by a composite brigade led by Lieutenant-Colonel H.D. Tuson of the Duke of Cornwall Light Infantry (D.C.L.I.). Tuson's detachment had recently been created out of the V Corps reserve — 2nd D.C.L.I., 1st York, and Lancasters, 5th King's Own, and 2nd Duke of Wellington — and totalled 1290 men, barely more than a battalion. This scratch force was about to be thrown against Mauser Ridge, where an entrenched enemy with unlimited firepower had destroyed practically an entire division in the span of a few hours on two successive afternoons.

The British attack got under way as scheduled and the moment the two Indian Brigades and Tuson's detachment came into view, enemy shells rained down with incredible fury. "In moving up under heavy fire from shell," the War Diary of the 5th King's Own noted, "one shell killed 12 men and wounded 5 others."[38] Men were falling fast, but the leading waves pressed on and there was hope that they would be able to reach the wire and possibly come to grips with the enemy. Much would depend on the progress of the French left.

Launched under cover of a heavy bombardment, Joppé's colonial troops got off to a good start, but as they crossed open ground, they were met with a tremendous burst of fire of all kinds, which tore great gaps in their ranks. As they struggled to move forward, they were deluged with gas shells. The cry of "Gas!" went up and the panic-stricken Turcos turned and ran all the way back through their own lines and across the canal bridges. What followed is unclear. There were unconfirmed rumours, perhaps unfair, that the Africans went on a rampage in the rear sector, looting, raping nurses in the dressing stations and shooting officers who tried to restrain them. All we know for sure was that General Putz appealed to the British V Corps for a brigade of cavalry to assist in restoring order — though their help was not needed, as two battalions of *Chasseurs*, who had been held in reserve, were able to bring matters under control.[39]

British troops nearby caught sight of the spectacle of Turco troops with their colourful uniforms, fleeing back in disarray, and heard them wailing and shouting "Gas." Word spread rapidly along the British line that the Turcos were running away. This dispirited news seemed to break the momentum of the attack, which was soon brought to a halt. The day's fighting, in which nothing had been accomplished, cost the Lahore Division 1,205 casualties, decimated the already understrength Tuson detachment, and left the British in a critical position. It is fortunate that the Germans did not launch a counterattack, for no support troops had moved up to man the trenches vacated by the Sirhind Brigade, which, in the assault, had been cut to ribbons and would have been incapable of prolong resistance.[40]

During the Lahore's Division's attack early in the afternoon, Smith-Dorrien received a telephone call from Robertson, who passed on Sir John's reaction to his letter. Sir John did not view the situation as unfavourably as he did and insisted that he had more than enough troops and reserves to co-operate effectively with the French in driving back the Germans. The field marshal also indicated that the French had the situation well in hand on the west side of the canal, which "seems to remove anxiety as to your left flank."[41] Sir John's observation of the battle was inconsistent with reality. First, the objective could not be met without the French committing themselves to an all-out effort, which they were unwilling to do as shown by their feeble response over and over again. Second, there may have been plenty of units in the British sector, but many of them were so greatly reduced by earlier fighting that, like the Canadians, they were unfit for further action. Third, not withstanding the modest progress around Lizerne, it was certainly not out of the question that a breakthrough could occur in the French sector, in which case the British troops in the salient would be trapped.[42]

Toward the end of the afternoon, Smith-Dorrien received a telegram from General Headquarters, directing him to hand over command of all the troops engaged around Ypres to Plumer.[43] Sir John, under the pretext that Smith-Dorrien had violated instructions, had chosen this time to settle old accounts.[44] The wire from General Headquarters was uncoded so that its contents would leak out, an act undoubtedly calculated to further humiliate Smith-Dorrien. Sir John's discourtesy aside, his decision to remove one of the best generals in the British Army at this critical juncture of the battle simply because he disliked him was another example of his unfitness to command. As might be expected, Smith-Dorrien was deeply wounded by his brutal treatment. Left without responsibilities, he suggested to General Headquarters on 6 May that he be transferred to a different command. That evening, Robertson paid him a visit and informed him that he was being sent home. It turned out to be the end of his military career, for he never held a field command again.

Plumer had a reputation for adopting tactics designed to keep casualties among his men to a minimum. He was a first-rate field general, calm, above-board, cautious, and attentive to details. On 28 April, General Headquarters notified him in writing that it would "in all probability be necessary to-night to commence measures for the withdrawal from the Salient to a more westerly line," and he was instructed to "take such preliminary for commencing retirement to-night, if in the C-in-C's opinion it proves necessary." Plumer was to inform General Headquarters as soon as possible the line that he proposed to occupy.[45] In short, Plumer was requested to prepare for the very withdrawal that Smith-Dorrien had suggested.

Plumer was stunned and indignant at the way French had treated Smith-Dorrien, an old comrade. He knew that Smith-Dorrien had done nothing to warrant dismissal. In a letter to his wife two days later, he wrote:

> Things have not been made better by Sir John French slighting Sir Horace, and taking practically all my force away from him and leaving me independent of him. It is the last thing I wanted. It is not fair because Smith-Dorrien and I were in absolute agreement as to what should be done, and I am only doing now what I should have been doing if I had remained under Smith-Dorrien.[46]

After issuing instructions to Plumer, Sir John visited Foch at Cassel around noon on the 28th to tell him of his intention to withdraw from his current position in the salient. He justified his decision on the grounds that his troops were extremely tired, the task of supplying them was becoming increasingly difficult, and he doubted he could continue to hold on to a tactically indefensible position. He added that he did not wish to compromise the coming offensive at Arras by frittering away his reserves in secondary operations. But Foch rejected any notion of withdrawal. He pointed out the tactical disadvantage of moving from the crest to lower ground and claimed that retirement would damage the morale of the Allied forces. He maintained, furthermore, that it be a confession of weakness and encourage the Germans to make fresh efforts to push the Allies further back and possibly capture Ypres. He maintained that a vigorous offensive to regain the Langemarck region was vital not only to secure the British supply line but to hold on to Ypres and its environs. Foch no longer promised reinforcements, simply insisting that there were enough troops on the spot to retrieve the lost ground. Although Sir John understood that clinging to the awkward salient was perilous and costly, he could not bring himself to cede any ground, which would be looked upon as a defeat for the British army and likely lead to the loss of Ypres. The upshot was that he agreed to postpone his retirement, pending the results of another major counterattack, which was to be launched toward Langemarck on the 29th, with the help of heavy artillery.[47] During the afternoon, Foch submitted a memorandum listing his arguments in favour of the attack and confirming the agreement reached with Sir John. In reporting the interview, Foch told Joffre: "I painted the picture of the consequences of withdrawal darker than they appeared to me."[48]

Crisis had the effect of generating in Foch a kind of excitable euphoria. His prescription never varied, imbued as he was with the French pre-war doctrine of the offensive on all occasions. His buoyant assurances or flattering entreaties invariably overwhelmed Sir John, who was nervous, indecisive, and subject to pressure. The scenes that followed behind the front could be likened to those of a comic opera if the consequences had not been so tragic. Day after day, Sir John would learn of the absence of the much-heralded French offensive and of the continued suffering of his men. Each time he would pass from optimism to pessimism, deriding the French and concluding that he must pull back his troops. And yet, when confronted by the self-assured and smooth-talking Foch, he would swing the other way, agreeing not only to wait a little longer before withdrawing his men, but also to co-operate in one more counterattack.

The arrangements reached at the conference on the 28th make it clear that neither Foch nor Sir John expected the French attack in the afternoon to achieve anything meaningful. It would have been difficult to arrive at any other conclusion, considering the resources Putz proposed to employ. The account of the operation can be summarized easily. The Curé group's objective was to expel the Germans from the west side of the canal, but it was stopped in front of Steenstraat. West of the Ypres-Langemarck road, Joppé's men, other than laying down a heavy barrage on the enemy lines, did not advance. The Sirhind Brigade, which had been told to move forward simultaneously with the French, remained stationary. A staff officer's report to Joffre, summarizing the day's events, ended by saying: "General Foch is very calm and very confident. But he does not want to call up other troops for he estimates that for the moment he has enough for his front. He is going to try to convince Field Marshal French of the necessity of the English making a violent effort to re-establish the situation."[49]

Foch postponed the planned assault on the 29th to allow the newly arrived artillery time to register. Sir John agreed to keep his troops in their forward position another day, even though they were being hammered on three sides by German artillery without much opportunity to reply.

Sir John's anxiety was not relieved when he received the General Staff's reply to Foch's memo of the previous day. The General Staff refuted practically all of the French general's points, stressing that they were based on his opinion, not facts. In particular, it pointed that there was no reason to suppose that falling back to the new line would be followed by still further retirements, or that the position in the rear would be less strong. It denied that readjustment of the line would adversely impact the morale of British troops, just because of the failure of the French on their left. The General Staff then dwelled on the obvious: that the reduced salient was overcrowded with troops and the risk to their safety increased; that the salient was a notoriously weak section in the line and only retained for political reasons; that straightening the line farther back and hinting preferably behind Ypres would be safer and reduce the number of troops required to man it. The memo ended by saying that the nature of operations proposed by Foch had little chance of success "now that the Germans are dug in."[50]

Sir John, however, had already committed himself and he could only hope for the best. On the 30th, Putz ordered an attack and slight progress was made, but the battalions of the Sirhind Brigade remained in their trenches because the French troops next to them did not budge. In the evening, Foch motored to General Headquarters at Hazebrouck, and, at his urgent representations, Sir John consented to delay the British withdrawal for yet another 24 hours. But clearly he was uneasy and asked Robertson to draw up a letter, which he intended to forward to Foch. He then paid a visit to Haig, and, during their discussion, a staff officer brought the letter for his signature. Haig recorded the following in his diary on 30 April: "Sir J. read me the letter. It was in the nature of an ultimatum, and stated that the withdrawal of the British from the salient would commence tonight, unless the French had succeeded in advancing their line." When French asked Haig for his opinion on the matter, he replied, "I considered that it was the Commander-in-Chief's duty to remove his men from what was really a 'death trap.'"[51] Still, Sir John could not bring himself to send the note. Ironically, the decision to write off the defence of the salient came from an unexpected quarter.

Putz, under pressure from Foch, ordered the attack renewed on 1 May, but when the hour came, his men refused to move. Later in the day, Foch visited Sir John, but this time he was not seeking a further delay. He had in his possession a telegram from Joffre ordering him to act on the defensive about Ypres so that troops from there could be sent to reinforce his projected offensive farther south. Sir John welcomed the news and it was agreed, or more precisely Foch decided, to adopt a defensive stance around Ypres, rather than all the way back to the canal as good sense dictated. It was with a good deal of relief that Sir John issued orders to Plummer to commence the planned withdrawal that same night with troops not required for the defence. The initial movement was carried out without a hitch during the night of 1–2 May.

On the afternoon of 2 May, before the next stage of the retirement could take place, a shift in the wind enabled the Germans to launch a gas attack on a three-mile front between Fortuin and Turco Farm. The area was defended by three brigades of the 4th Division — the newly arrived 12th Brigade and the remains of the 10th and 11th — all under the command of General Alderson. Fortunately for the British, their trenches here were far apart — between 300 and 500 yards — and the fitful wind distributed the gas unevenly. As a result, the poisonous fumes lacked the density to overwhelm the defenders, although every man was affected, some more than others. In some places, the troops in the trenches drew to one side to avoid the gas; in others they waited for the oncoming cloud of vapour and charged swiftly through it, falling with the bayonet on the Germans behind it. At the end of the day's fighting, the Germans had only gained two lengths of trench west of Mouse Trap Farm. On the first alarm, the Canadian brigades were alerted, but, as it turned out, were not required.

The Germans renewed the assault next day, concentrating near the junction of the 11th and 85th Brigades at Berlin Wood. The British had to rely mainly on rifle fire since all but three field batteries had been withdrawn from the area. Several units were badly mauled, but reinforcements were rushed up through the shelled zone in time to stop the enemy's advance. When the fighting died down, the 85th and 11th Brigades were in such close contact with the enemy that in places they were separated by only a few yards. Nevertheless, it was decided to proceed with the planned withdrawal of the 27th and 28th Divisions and the right of the Canadian Division.[52]

On the night of 3–4 May, the movement was carried out, in perfect order, and without the loss of a man. The enemy was unaware of the retirement until daylight. The new line formed a semicircle in front of Ypres and ran from Turco Farm, to Frezenberg, and to Sanctuary Wood, before joining the 2nd Corps trenches near Hill 60.[53] This line was about three miles shorter than the old one and so, with fewer troops needed to hold it, some of the brigades, which had been most sorely tired, were given a chance to rest.

The phase of the fighting between 24 April and 4 May, officially known as the Battle of St. Julien, had come to an end. At 10:00 a.m. on 4 May,

Alderson handed over his front to Major-General H.F.M. Wilson, GOC 4th Division. The Canadian Divisional Artillery remained in position attached to the 4th Division, covering the front between Mouse Trap and Turco Farm. The remaining units of the First Canadian Division, after as trying an initiation in battle as any troops ever received, retired to the Bailleul area for a well-deserved rest.

CHAPTER 12
The Patricias at Frezenberg

The Second Battle of Ypres lasted an additional three weeks, during which there were two bloody engagements, the Battle of Frezenberg Ridge (8–13 May) and the Battle of Bellewaarde Ridge (24–25 May). Some British units suffered appalling losses, more heavily than even the Canadians. It seemed as if the Germans, suddenly realizing how close they had come to achieving their goal, were making frantic efforts to recover their lost opportunity.

The only Canadian infantry battalion to participate in the ensuing action (Frezenberg Ridge) was Princess Patricia's Canadian Light Infantry, which consisted of an elite volunteer group of veterans. Because it was well-trained and capable of taking the field, it had been detached from the Canadian contingent shortly after its arrival in England and crossed over to France in late December 1914 as part of the 80th Brigade, 27th British Division. From 7 January to 23 March, the Patricias served in the St. Eloi sector, learning from trial and error and adjusting to life in the wet, rat- and lice-infested trenches. Whenever it rained, the trenches would fill with water and prolonged immersion produced the condition known as trench foot. Lieutenant Hugh Niven, the adjutant from Edmonton, describes how men tried to cope with the painful ailment: "Men would sit opposite each other, you'd take off his boots and his socks and the other man would rub them [feet] with a towel, dry them, put on another pair of socks and hurry on with the boots. It had to be done in thirty seconds or you never got your boots on again while you were alive."[1]

Compounding the misery of the Patricias was the constant bombardment and enemy snipers. Any man who happened to raise his head above the trench parapet was certain to attract an enemy bullet that proved fatal more often than not. The trenches were shallow and the parapets could not be built up, owing to the dearth of sandbags, so that the men could only move about in a crouched position. Nothing could be done about the shelling, but a special unit, made up of skilled marksmen, was formed to deal with enemy snipers. The group became exceptionally adept at locating and eliminating enemy snipers and, in a two-day period, accounted for 17 kills. Much of the unit's success was due to Corporal Jim Christie, a crack shot and durable hunter from the Yukon. Christie was interesting character. He had once tangled with a grizzly bear, resulting in his head nearly being torn off, but he had managed to finish his tormenter with a knife. In his maimed condition, he had walked five days before reaching civilization and seeking medical treatment. He was over 40 years old when he volunteered for service.[2]

On the night of 27–28 February, the Patricias engaged in their first operation, a minor foray against the enemy's opposing trenches. A party of 100 Patricias, under the leadership of Major Hamilton Gault, the founder of the regiment and second-in-command, made a successful raid, destroying 30 to 40 yards of enemy trench and inflicting an unknown number of casualties.[3] It was the beginning of a new type of warfare at which the Canadians excelled and carried out regularly, even when they occupied a stretch of the British line where the unwritten code of live and let live had existed.

The Patricias garrisoned the line, provided work parties, and in mid-March they participated in a local attack. Near St. Eloi, the Germans had captured a small hill covering half an acre, about 30 feet high, known as the "the Mound." Snow wrote in his narrative of the 27th Division: "As the country was flat it made a good observation post and so became a bone of contention."[4] The Patricias, together with elements of the 80th Brigade, were ordered to recover the lost ground, but alas, the operation failed. On the last days of the regiment's stay at St. Eloi, a sniper's bullet killed its commander, Lieutenant-Colonel Francis Farquhar. In the absence of Major Gault, who was recovering from a wound to his forearm, the command devolved upon the senior officer in the field, Captain H.C. Buller, who was given the temporary rank of lieutenant-colonel. On 23 March, the regiment left the St. Eloi front and moved into the Ypres salient a fortnight later, occupying a position in Polygon Wood some three miles behind the right of the 2nd Canadian Brigade. In two and a half months of trench warfare, the regiment had paid a heavy price for its aggressiveness, suffering 238 battle casualties.

The area was relatively quiet for the first two weeks or so, but during the bitter fighting on the northern salient the regiment was under constant bombardment and took 80 casualties. To avoid being outflanked when the withdrawal occurred on the night of 3–4 May, the Patricias moved back to Bellewaarde Ridge, half a mile east of Hooge. The Germans quickly located their new position, pushing machine guns to within 200 yards and unleashing an intensive bombardment. In their unfinished, shallow trenches, the regiment suffered 122 casualties on 4 May before the enemy's fire subsided that evening. The next morning, a shell fragment struck Buller in the eye and he was invalidated to England. Major Hamilton Gault, who had just returned to duty, assumed command of the battalion.[5]

Several days later, the Patricias confronted their first serious test. Encouraged by the British withdrawal from the apex, Duke Albrecht made another determined effort to reduce the salient. His plan was to send three corps of his Fourth Army — XXVI Reserve Corps, XXVII Reserve Corps, and XV Corps — to strike from the north against the sector between Mouse Trap Farm and Zillebeck. As a preliminary move, he ordered the capture of Hill 60 at the southern end of the salient. A favourable wind allowed the enemy to release gas at 8:45 a.m. on 5 May, which drifted along, rather than across, the British trenches. In case of a gas attack, the men had been ordered to hurry over to either flank to avoid it, but the direction in which the fumes wafted made the plan inoperative. In some places the fumes hung about the trenches and were so thick that that the makeshift respirators were of little help. Some of the men fell back to the reserve line, but those who stood firm were overpowered by German troops (elements of the XV Corps) following behind the gas cloud. Once the Germans gained control of the top of the hill, they withstood repeated attempts by the British to recover it.[6]

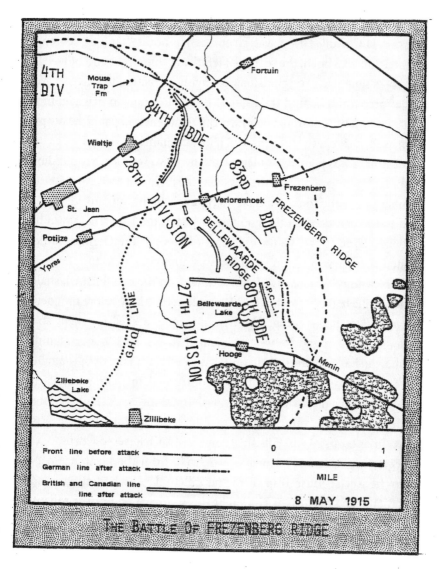

Front line before attack
German line after attack
British and Canadian line
line after attack

0   1

MILE

8 MAY 1915

THE BATTLE OF FREZENBERG RIDGE

The silence in the early hours of on the 8th was shattered an hour or so after dawn by the start of an enemy bombardment that grew in volume and intensity. By 7:00 a.m. the bombardment had reached a frightful crescendo, transcending anything the British had experienced before.[7] Along the front of the 27th and 28th Divisions, huge projectiles fell with remarkable precision, obliterating whole stretches of trenches and killing or burying alive its occupants. Losses were greater because the trenches had been hastily constructed and were narrow, shallow because of the water table and often without traverses. It was assumed that the tremendous volume of shells fired presaged a major enemy assault.

Deployed on Bellewaarde Ridge, the Patricias formed the extreme left flank of the 80th Brigade with the 4th King's Royal Rifle Corps, under Major John Harington, on their right. On their left lay units of the 83rd Brigade. The Patricias had two companys in the front line and two in the support trench. A little after dawn, a small party of Germans, no more than several hundred, came down a hill on the double in front of the Patricias' trenches. Their attack was broken up by heavy concentrated rifle fire and the survivors were sent scurrying back over the crest of the ridge into safety.

As the morning wore on, the Patricias were subjected to the same artillery blitz as the rest of the British units. According to George Pearson it defied description:

> Each burst of high explosive shells, each terrible
> pulsation of the atmosphere, if it missed the body,
> seemed to render the very brain or else stupefied it ...
> All spoken language is totally inadequate to describe
> the shocks and horrors of an intense bombardment.
> It is not that man himself lacks the imaginative gift of
> words but that he has not the work tools with which to
> work. They do not exist.[8]

Quite apart from the shattering effect on the Patricias' psyche, the fierce barrage that poured down smashed their flimsy front-line trenches, put out of action two of their four machine guns, cut and blew away the belts of wire in front, and severed communications with Brigade Headquarters. To add to their misery, they were in an exposed position and had no protection from the enfilading fire of machine guns situated on high ground to their right. Casualties were so heavy that Gault ordered signallers, pioneers, batmen, and orderlies into the support line. A little after 8:00 a.m., he sent a runner to 80th Brigade Headquarters with the following message:

Bellewaarde Ridge today. A telescopic view of the devastated area superimposed in the center of the ridge is a hint of the ferociousness of the battle ninety-five years earlier.

Have been heavily shelled since 7 a.m. Sections of front trenches made untenable by enemy's artillery, but have still 160 rifles in front line. German infantry has not yet appeared … Will advise O.C. Rifle Brigade should I require support. In lulls of gun fire there is heavy fire from rifles and machine guns. Please send me two m.g.'s if possible. I have only two left in front line. None in support.[9]

When the German guns lifted at 9:00 a.m., grey-clad infantrymen clambered out of their trenches and poured down in a mass, running and shouting as they came. The main German thrust was directed at the 83rd Brigade holding Frezenberg Ridge. Driven back twice, the Germans broke through on the third attempt, capturing the ridge and penetrating as far as Verlorenhoek, nearly a mile away. They advanced no farther because of stiffening British resistance. Thus turning to widen the breach, as was their practice in such circumstances, they began to roll up the flanks of the two British Brigades (84th and 80th) on either side.

Shortly after 9:00 a.m., the Germans struck in force against the sector defended by the Patricias. An observer on the scene wrote: "There seemed to be an astonishing silence with just an occasional rifle shot, and then we realized that the German infantry were upon us."[10] The fighting lasted throughout the daylight hours and was as fierce as anywhere in the British line. With their machine guns repeatedly buried and inoperable while they were being dug out, cleaned, and remounted, the Patricias fought mainly with rifles against overwhelming odds. "We were good shots; we were veterans [and] we had really been trained in the fifteen rounds rapid fire," observed Lieutenant Niven. "We were getting off the fifteen rounds a minute and the Germans thought they were machine guns, and they were rifles."[11] Equipped with the British Lee-Enfield, the men did not have to worry about their rifles jamming under steady fire. Interviewed in later life, H.C. Hetherington recalled: "I fired rifle after fire until they were actually too hot to hold. There was no difficulty picking out a cool rifle because they were lying all around one. They were coming in masses because I was aiming at Germans for hours that morning. There was always a target to aim at."[12]

Though the ranks of the Patricias had been thinned by the bombardment, every man, even the wounded capable of raising a rifle, brought a deadly fire to bear on the enemy's initial major rush. As the ground in front was open, No. 2 Company inflicted huge losses on the Germans and drove them back. The Germans had more success against No. 1 Company, whose trenches had been obliterated in places and abandoned. Trampling over the cut wire, the Germans began to penetrate through the right side of the trench, and, perhaps because of the heavy price they had paid, showed no mercy. A soldier who survived the onslaught recalled: "They reached our trench and the dogs bayoneted our wounded."[13] Since it was clear to Captain H.S. Dennison, the commanding officer, that his position was no longer tenable, he sent back the remnant of his company to the support line while he stayed behind with a handful of men to cover the withdrawal. The rear guard was all but wiped out. Only Sergeant Jordan and another soldier remained and they refused to budge, accounting for many enemy dead. Jordan, although wounded, survived the day and later received a DMC for his courage and devotion to duty.

The men of No. 2 Company continued to cling to what remained of their trenches. Under orders from the brigade to hold the ridge at all costs, they kept up a hot and steady fire on the enemy trying to close in. Finally, with their ammunition nearly expended and the knowledge that their right flank was in danger of being turned, they carried out a daring and successful retirement from the front line. By 10:00 a.m., No. 2 Company, or what was left of it, occupied the support line on the crest. Here, the Patricias endured a blistering bombardment that was relentless and punctuated only when the enemy's infantry sought to advance from the captured trenches, which they had quickly rebuilt and fortified. The Patricias were disgusted to see the Germans use the bodies of their dead comrades as material to strengthen their new line. George Pearson wrote:

> The Germans had already, with usual industry, gotten the trench into some sort of shape again, with the parapet shifted over to the other side and facing Bellewaarde Wood. And everywhere along its length I noticed the bodies of our dead built into it to replace sandbags while others lay on the parados at the rear. It was not nice. The faces of men we had known and called comrade looked at us now in ghastly disarray from odd sections of both walls. And they were taking on a brick like shape from the weight of the filled bags on top of them.[14]

Pearson and his mates paid the ultimate tribute to their fallen comrades by hurling back every German attempt to advance from the trenches. "Our most wonderful man on this day was Cpl J. Christie of the Scout section," Lieutenant Niven noted. "Christie … lay full length in front of our trenches and killed Germans. He was no 15-round a minute soldier as he only needed one shot and he never wasted a shot in his life."[15] At one point Sergeant-Major A.G. Fraser, half crazed from a serious head wound, jumped up on the parapet, waving the regimental colours and shouting abuse at the Germans. That he was not brought down by an enemy bullet was miracle (though he would die later in the day). "The Colours were riddled with bullets and even the staff was pierced by them," Niven remarked with incredulity. "I had to jump out and chase him and drag him into the trench."[16]

The leadership of Major Gault did much to strengthen the will and determination of the men. Lieutenant Niven remarked in hindsight: "With Hamilton Gault there, nobody could think of retiring ... Nobody knows why, but it gave everyone a tremendous lot of courage that nobody else in the world could give to the other regiments."[17] Unknown to but a few, Gault was put out of action not long after the battle began. He was wounded in the morning, but carried on until a second and more serious injury compelled him to hand over the command to Captain Agar Adamson, a 48-year-old Boer veteran who was blind in one eye.

As stretcher-bearers could not hope to pass through the curtain of deadly fire, neither Gault nor any of the seriously wounded could be evacuated during the daylight hours. Some lay at the bottom of the crumbling trenches, bleeding, sometimes buried by shell fire, and attended only by a medical corporal who did what he could to allay their suffering. Those who could walk or crawl took refuge in the nearby dugout. Many, like Fraser, died before they could be carried to the rear. Privtate James Vaughan described what happened to him after he was struck in the leg by a shell fragment:

> I was hit with a shell splinter and ... I lay there for six hours. That's as fast as they got me out ... When the first-aid men got to me a couple of fellows said, "Now, Jimmy, there's an artillery dug-out just fifty yards ahead. Now, you got to crawl over there, crawl to that dug-out and get down in there." And do you know how they did it? One took hold of my shoulders, the other took hold of my legs — and one leg was wounded, remember! — and they threw me over the back of the trench. That's the only way they could get me out. When I got my breath back and got myself together, I crawled along and

crawled along, and it felt like fifty miles not fifty yards. Well, I made it to the dug-out and when I did get in it was full of wounded men … and the moans and groans all over were something terrible. I squeezed in and lay down where I could and waited there for the dark, for the stretcher-bearers to come up.[18]

At noon a company of the 4th King's Royal Rifle Corps — which had been subjected to severe bombardment — gallantly pushed forward through the raging inferno with boxes of ammunition and two machine guns. Their arrival was a godsend and a boost to the morale of the bone-weary and beleaguered defenders. At the first anniversary of the regiment's stand at Bellewaarde Ridge, an NCO commented that "we saw the Angels and they wore the letters 'R.B.' on their shoulders; and the biggest of the Angels were those who bore the machine-guns on their shoulders too."[19] The newcomers were posted on the extreme right of the firing line, using the trees and hedges for cover.

As communications with the rear had been severed, Adamson could not determine the fate of the 83rd Brigade for certain. Throughout the morning he had seen movement in the trenches to the north and had established contact with the 3rd Monmouthshires, the right-handed battalion of the 83rd Brigade. When forced back to the support line, however, he lost touch with the Monmouths. Through artillery bursts and clouds of swirling smoke, he saw men on his left falling back to the rear and he assumed that the 83rd Division had entirely disappeared —which, if true, meant that his flank was in the air. As it happened, Adamson had been wrong about the 83rd Brigade. Cut off when the enemy broke through the centre, the Monmouths and the unit next to them, the 1st King's Own Yorkshire Light Infantry, continued to fight on the forward slope of the ridge, isolated and without support.

Upon learning of the break-in, General Snow arranged to extend the line to the northwest with reserve units of the 80th and 81st Brigades. Moving into the line, these formations eventually gained touch with counterattacking elements of the 85th Brigade (27th Division) and a tenuous line was established across the gap.

The Patricias were unaware of the movements on their left, occupied as they were on their own front. By now Adamson was wounded in the shoulder but he remained on his feet doing what he could to help out. "I recalled seeing Captain Adamson with an arm hanging down," W.J. Popey later remembered, "getting ammunition from the dead or dying and handing it to us."[20] In the afternoon, Major Harington took advantage of a brief pause in the shelling to come up to survey the scene. His report ran as follows: "P.P. have suffered 75 per cent casualties and the position is critical. Reinforcements badly wanted at once. All my battalion is up."[21]

When Adamson was unable to continue, command of the regiment passed to Lieutenant Niven, who received the order to withdraw shortly after. He refused to carry it out. Years later, in old age, he explained why:

> I had been told to retire, that the 27th Division couldn't help me, that they couldn't get up to me ... and it was just madness to stay there, and I wrote back and said that I had too many wounded. We had no stretcher bearers to take out the wounded and I wouldn't go and leave them. So then they sent for me and I had to go back about, oh about a mile, to talk to the Divisional Commander and tell him that I wouldn't go back. I wouldn't retire. I was only a lieutenant but no General in the British Army could make me go back without what was left. So we stuck it out.[22]

A little before 3:00 p.m., a platoon of Shopshires brought up a load of ammunition and were deployed on the left flank. They came at a propitious moment. Around 4:00 p.m., the Germans made their third and final major sally. The fighting lasted until it was nearly dark. "Our gun barrels were blistering hot from firing hours on hours," said T. Richardson, who manned the remaining machine gun. "Then they sent over another wave. We gave them all we had. It was nearly enough to stop them but not quite. A few of them entered our trench." Richardson was crouched and in the process of putting a fresh belt of ammunition into his machine gun when he saw a German soldier standing above the trench.

We looked into each other's eyes. He laughed hysterically and sprang down at me with his bayonet lunging at my stomach. The butt of his rifle was in his shoulder as he literally dived at me, bayonet first, trying to pin me through the body. I gathered my hands and feet under me faster than I can tell it, and tried to throw myself sideways and backwards. I was too weak to get quite clear. He pinned me to the ground through the side of my left thigh. He was laughing hysterically still. I never carried a rifle that day.... But I always carried a .45 Colt automatic pistol. Now as I lay there on my back with that German bayonet through my leg, and that German face laughing down at me, I pulled that pistol and shoved it up into his face. A more surprised man there never was. His expression changed as if a hand had wiped that hysterical laugh off his face. The laugh changed to a scream. His first word was "Kamerade." But I laughed now. And I pulled the trigger.[23]

The last attack, like the others, encountered such a deadly fire that the advance hesitated, faltered, and petered out as the survivors drew back, leaving their dead and wounded behind. Thereafter, the pressure slackened because the Germans became preoccupied with British counterattacks in other parts of the line. It would take several hours before the Patricias realized that the crisis had passed.

Around 11.30 p.m., the 3rd King's Royal Rifle Corps came forward to relieve what remained of the shattered Patricias. The defence of Bellewaarde Ridge had destroyed the core of the "Originals" of the regiment. Niven marched out of the line with three officers and 150 other ranks. With much on his mind, he had neglected to retrieve the colours, now smudged and torn in several places. "Our good old Colours had been forgotten and had been buried in a dugout," commented a member of the battalion. "Lieutenant Niven, in charge, was marching away when someone thought of it. I, with several others ... was sent back to get them and then rejoined the party."[24] As the Patricias marched toward the rear, reserve troops of their own 80th Brigade stood up and cheered as they passed. General Snow, not known to be a champion of Empire troops, paid them the ultimate compliment when he wrote in his report to the V Corps: "No regt. could have fought with greater determination or endurance, many would have failed where they succeeded."[25] The Patricias deserved all the accolades they received after the battle. Outgunned, outnumbered, outflanked, their numbers reduced and worn out, they had refused to let the enemy pass. In so doing they may have saved Ypres from falling.

The Patricias were not called upon to enter the front line again during the remainder of the fighting around Ypres, which died down out of pure exhaustion in the last week in May. The Germans made a last-ditch effort to reach Ypres on the 24th. They released a heavy concentration of chlorine on a front of over four miles, followed by an infantry assault. However, the British troops had been issued crude cotton masks, which shielded their lungs from the poisonous fumes. When the Germans advanced they met unexpected resistance and in many places were driven back to their trenches by the blazing fire. The Germans captured Mouse Trap Farm and Bellewaarde Ridge, but that was the extent of their gains.[26] The opposing lines in front of Ypres would remain practically unchanged until the summer of 1917.

Epilogue

The Second Battle of Ypres introduced two distinctive features in the fighting on the Western Front. The first, of course, was poison gas, against which the Allies had no defence whatsoever. Gradually a whole protective system was devised — alarms, respirators, gas-proof dugouts — so that gas, "while retaining its startling and insidious qualities, became far less lethiferous than high explosive shells and high velocity bullets."[1] The second matched materials against men. Since the Germans lacked the necessary reserves to swell the ranks of their infantry, or even replace all of its losses, they changed their tactics to take advantage of the formidable strength of their artillery to sweep away the Allied line. The object was to pulverize the defenders, release gas whenever possible, and then send in their troops to mop up the few survivors. The infantry, limited in numbers, and not of the highest quality, was seen as secondary to success. On the other hand, British troops were frequently compelled to rely almost solely on their rifles in their efforts to stop the enemy's steady encroachment. If the British leaders learned one lesson from Second Ypres it was that they needed many more heavy guns to match or counter the enemy's fire. Never again during the war were British infantrymen called upon to maintain so protracted and unequal a struggle.

Despite these novel elements, Second Ypres was remarkably similar to other battles in the war: the grim life in the trenches, the utter futility of massed infantry attacks with the terrible toll in killed and maimed, inept and callous leadership, the hardships and heroism of the troops, and, in the end, nothing achieved.

For its size, Second Ypres was one of the deadliest clashes of the First World War. Aggregate British losses amounted to 60,000 men, or nearly twice the official German total of 35,000. The disparity, however, is not as great as it seems, for the Germans did not include among their casualties soldiers who were lightly wounded and returned to duty. Even so, it is probable that the defenders suffered heavier losses than did the attackers.

Had the Allied generals paid closer attention to repeated warnings that the Germans intended to use gas, it is possible that the fighting at Ypres would not have developed into a major battle. The evidence, coming as it did from different sources, was strong enough to require that the army adopt preventative measures like thinning the front line and equipping troops with crude respirators patterned after those taken from the German deserters. But, even if little could have been done in the time available except warn the men to apply wet handkerchiefs to their nose and mouth, forewarning them would have reduced the psychological terror of the unknown and, perhaps, prevented the panic and rout that ensued among the French troops.

One may well ask what the Allies were doing in the salient in the first place? The primary reason given for its retention was emotional, not strategic. Both GQG and General Headquarters were under the impression that the occupation of additional Belgian territory by the rampaging German armies would impair the morale of their troops. But this is specious reasoning. Normally, strategic retreats do not have an adverse effect on trained soldiers, as was shown in 1917, when the Germans fought, if anything, better after the great withdrawal to the Hindenburg Line. Another argument frequently heard was that the salient was an admirable springboard for an Allied offensive to roll up the German left flank. In fact, it was so used in the second half of 1917 at the Third Battle of Ypres (popularly called Passchendaele), but the less said about the disastrous results of that battle the better. Finally, it was claimed that the salient stood directly at the crossroads to the Channel ports of Dunkirk, Calais, and Boulogne, and that the loss of Ypres would make it difficult for Britain to send supplies and reinforcements to the Western front. However, any German advance in the direction of the

Channel ports could have been blunted more easily several miles farther back where the defenders could have held a shorter and stronger line.

If the Allies, in defiance of military logic, were determined to hold on to the salient, they should at least have prepared a new line in the rear to which they could fall back in the event of a serious attack. At any rate, after the two French divisions had fled, the British should have exerted every effort during one of the periodic lulls to withdraw to a better defensive position on the other side of Ypres — which had been reduced to rubble shortly after the start of the battle and surely had lost much of its symbolic value. The effort to retain a small segment of Belgian territory, more vulnerable to enemy artillery than before, was certainly not worth the price paid.

The manner in which the British High Command managed the battle exacerbated the difficulties for the men in the field. Beginning with the first gas attack, Plumer can be criticized for making no change of divisional boundaries and leaving Alderson to cope with a five-mile gap in the line. The 28th Division enjoyed relative quiet and an extension of that unit's front to include part of the Canadian sector would have divided the responsibility and resulted in improving command and supply. Furthermore, it would have reduced confusion by negating the need to place the Corps reserve in the hands of General Snow, a soldier who was unfamiliar with the disposition of the troops there, the sector under attack, and the brigade commanders fighting in the line.

There were two viable options to counter siege warfare tactics as practised by the Germans at Ypres. The first was a quick sortie, to strike before the enemy had time to fortify its new position. The other was a deliberately prepared attack, requiring proper reconnaissance, adequate numbers and carefully arranged artillery co-operation. In the operations at Ypres, Sir John allowed the choice to be taken out of his hands when he bound himself to French plans and wishes.

It has been alleged by John Dixon that French was following Kitchener's instructions to act in a subordinate role to the French commanders.[2] How he arrived at such a conclusion is difficult to fathom. Kitchener was adamant that Sir John's command was to be independent and that he was to act in concert with, but not subordinate to, the

French military authorities. Kitchener told the field marshal, "I wish you distinctly to understand that your command is an entirely independent one, and that you will in no case come in any sense under the orders of any Allied General." While French was to act "most sympathetically with the plans and wishes of our Ally," he was to avoid embarking on reckless adventures and to keep in mind "that the greatest care must be exercised towards a minimum of loss and wastage."[3] The plain truth was that Sir John was intimidated by Foch, so much so that he never questioned his commitment or logic. Sadly he was more interested in pleasing Foch than in looking out for the well-being of his troops.

Foch led Sir John to believe that British action would merely entail assisting the French in recapturing the ground they had lost. The little Frenchman acted in bad faith for he really never tried to uphold his end of the bargain. Admittedly, he issued orders for counterattacks but General Putz did not have anywhere near the required strength, in either infantry or artillery, to execute them, and rarely budged. Foch quickly realized that restoration of the line by French local reserves was tactically impossible. As he had no intentions of compromising the projected Arras offensive by calling up large reinforcements, he cajoled and deceived Sir John into carrying out hasty and ill-prepared attacks. The result was that the initial stated roles of the two armies were reversed, with the British shouldering the main burden of retaking the lost ground, assisted (poorly at that) by the French. By egging on the gullible Sir John with false promises of co-operation, Foch placed British troops in the extreme danger of encirclement and annihilation. Discussing Foch's reprehensible conduct, Gordon-Hall wrote with some acerbity:

> He gained his point by deceiving Sir J. French at little loss of his own troops, but at a cost of confidence comparable to the early days of the war when the British Army felt that the French did not play the game, but were ready to sacrifice the British whenever pressed. This lost confidence was never restored, but rather increased and the war prolonged. History will not exonerate Foch.[4]

Again and again French pledges to engage the enemy vigorously failed to materialize and British counterattacks continued virtually alone, in a vain cause. All these counterattacks, save for the Canadian night assault on Kitchener's Wood, were operationally unsound. None could be considered as true deliberate counterattacks. Reconnaissance was inadequate, objectives were unrealistic, the routes chosen were dangerous, frequently suicidal, there was poor coordination between units, and, worst of all, there was nowhere near the amount of artillery support deemed necessary. Commanders have the right to demand the maximum from their men, but not the impossible. At Second Ypres, the impossible was demanded over and over again with predictably grievous losses.

The generalship at the very top of the Canadian Division may not have been exceptional, but it was no worse than that shown by commanders on either side. With communications to his Division Headquarters cut repeatedly, Alderson should have moved his command centre closer to the front. As it was, he was located too far back to keep abreast of what was going on in the front line. Plagued by uncertainty, he was slow in reacting to enemy moves and his instructions to subordinates were at times vague and confusing. But, in his defence, he was also handicapped by usual battle conditions and being responsible for forces that were too big for his staff to manage — at one point 33 Canadian and British battalions. In the final analysis, he was in no position to influence the course of events and generally could not do much more than pass on Corps instructions for counterattacks to be made and distribute what reinforcements were available, leaving the commanders on the spot to deal with the situation as it developed.

At the brigade level and below, nearly all the Canadian officers were amateur soldiers. This proved to be a benefit in some instances, a handicap in others. Overall the Canadians were guilty of few grave errors. Turner committed the most serious blunders. He may have been personally fearless but otherwise showed little understanding of how to control his forces or deal with uncertain battlefield conditions. Poorly served by his staff, especially Lieutenant-Colonel Hughes, his tactical moves on the 24th were seriously flawed. He was never certain of the position of his front line, and, throughout the day, sent conflicting reports of its location to Division Headquarters. Less excusable was his panic withdrawal to the GHQ Line, which caused not only additional suffering to his own men, but the near destruction of the 2nd Brigade. Only his hero status in Canada prevented him from being sacked. Several months later, Alderson tried in vain to block Turner's appointment as commander of the newly formed 2nd Canadian Division. He wrote to a friend: "I am sorry to say that I do not consider Turner really fit to command a Division and his name was not put forward for it by Sir John French, but Canadian politics, have been too strong for all of us and so he has got it."[5] The reprieve was only temporary. Turner was transferred to an administrative post in London after he bungled the 2nd Division's first battle at St. Eloi early in 1916.

Balancing Turner's mistakes was Currie's firm response to the enemy's break-in at the apex. He quickly formed an accurate picture of what was happening, and, considering the gravity of the situation, exercised remarkable control over his brigade. He possessed sound tactical judgment and did not hesitate when committing his reserves, an action that enabled the 2nd Brigade to maintain its position longer than anyone had the right to expect. Some, and I include myself, believe that Currie ought not to have left his command post during the midst of a battle — to acquire much-needed reinforcements when other means had failed — but at least he did so for the right cause. A natural leader, Currie won high praise from those who had witnessed his conduct during the battle. Lieutenant-Colonel C.H. Mitchell, 3rd Brigade, CFA, remarked that Currie "was the one outstanding figure in the Second Battle of Ypres." According to Captain T.C. Irving, an engineer, "if there is one man above another who should be given credit for holding back the Germans at Ypres, it is Currie." Colonel Cecil Romer, an Englishman serving on Alderson's staff, was no less effusive: "I was struck at once, both during my telephone conversations and visits to the general, by his calmness in a crisis; and what pleased me most of all was that he never lost a certain dry humour, which was typical of him."[6]

An excellent tactician, skillful in the use of artillery, cool under fire, and meticulous in his planning, Currie rose to command the Canadian Corps, never failing to gain his assigned objectives and doing so rapidly and with lower casualties than expected. Knighted in 1917 by King George, he received an array of other honours and at the end of the war retuned to Canada a national hero, greeted enthusiastically wherever he went by large crowds, officials, and press. In 1919, he was promoted to full general, the first Canadian to attain that rank. That same year, he was named inspector-general of the Military Forces of Canada, a position he held until 1920 when he resigned to become principal and vice-chancellor of McGill University.

Judgment on the performance of the remaining brigade commander, Brigadier-General Mercer, must be withheld, for he was only marginally involved in the battle. In fact, Mercer never really had a chance to prove himself in the war. In his first big action as commander of the 3rd Division, he was in the front lines at Mount Sorrel in the Ypres salient on 2 June 1916, when he was caught in a violent artillery barrage and fatally wounded.

Of the battalion commanders, three were killed and one, Lieutenant-Colonel J.A. Currie, was sent home. The others ranged from adequate to excellent. Tuxford, Leckie, Rennie, Meighen, Ormond, and Odlum attained the rank of brigadier-general, while Watson, Loomis, and Lipsett rose to command divisions as major-generals. The most able of the group was Lipsett, who deserves much of the credit for the heroic and critical stand of the 8th Battalion on the 24th and 25th. J. Upritchard (8th Battalion) was not exaggerating when he made the following comments about his former commander: "From what I gather, and things I heard afterwards ... I think that if they had a man of less caliber than Lipsett, we would probably been all taken because he stood firm. He was a wonderful soldier and wonderful man."[7] In June 1916, Lipsett was placed at the head of the 3rd Canadian Division following the death of Mercer. Transferred back to the British Army in September 1918 and given command of the 4th Division, he was killed the following month by a machine-gun blast while on reconnaissance — the 59th and last British general to die in the war.

It has often been said that the Germans committed the most serious blunder of the war through their premature and local use of poison gas. Properly exploited, the new weapon might have permitted the Germans to break the deadlock of trench warfare and win the war in the west. They missed an opportunity that would not come again, except in March 1918. In the long run, the introduction of poison gas did the Germans more harm than good. It laid them open to heavy reprisals because the prevailing winds, as a rule, were westerly. No less important was the damage that it did to Germany's reputation in the neutralist countries, particularly in the United States, where indignation was to be further fuelled by the sinking of the *Lusitania* on 7 May 1915.

German unwillingness to appreciate the potentiality of the new weapon led to a series of miscalculations at the outset of the battle: no follow-up plan had been prepared; there were insufficient reserves to exploit the initial success; the objectives were too limited; and the attack on the 22nd, even if pressed with enough determination, which it was not, was launched too late in the day to permit sweeping gains before last light. Still, the Germans quickly recognized their errors, and, taking corrective measures when possible, fought reasonably well during the remainder of Second Ypres. If their attack on the 22nd had been as carefully planned and executed as the one made two days later, it is almost certain that the salient would have fallen into their hands.

Yet, when everything has been said and done, it remains true that the principal reason for the German failure had been the presence of three Canadian brigades composed of men accustomed to civilian life — lawyers, college professors, graduates, lumberjacks, labourers, farmers, and clerks — and who, in thousands of cases, had never handled a gun before rallying to their country's call. During the crucial first three days of battle, these ill-equipped and untried amateur soldiers had held the vital left flank of the Second British Army against superior artillery and many times their numbers, and had not broken even under the horrible surprise of poison gas. By 25 April, enough British reinforcements had arrived to end the danger of a German breakthrough.

Duguid has claimed that the Canadians were too new at the game to know the seriousness of their predicament, otherwise they might not have responded so gallantry in the face of death to hold the line or literally to the order that ground "once lost must be retaken" and counterattacked with such reckless determination.[8] That may have been true in the beginning, but there were other factors that led Canadians to perform beyond expectations. The majority of Canadian soldiers came from farms and small towns and were accustomed to working outdoors in extreme cold weather, which inured them to the harsh conditions they faced in Flanders. Then, too, as an army without an identity, and small in comparison to the other European belligerents, they felt that in order to achieve recognition they had to prove that they were the best. Finally, their force was made up entirely of volunteers, and, by learning together, the gap between officers and the rank and file was much narrower than in European armies. The bonding among the men and their officers kept morale and the fighting spirit of the division at a high level. Sergeant-Major William Jones wrote that the loyalties that developed in the small groups found in all the Canadian battalions was a key factor in promoting cohesion in the face of the new and terrifying weapon:

> We met as strangers but were friends and true comrades from the first. The spirit born at Valcartier camp held good on foreign soil. We were really brothers now, and this feeling of unity had much to do with the courage and faith displayed by the men in holding the Huns back from Calais and at the second battle of Ypres in April, 1915.[9]

Unkown to Jones at the time, the Germans had no intentions of pushing on to the Channel ports, but, without the tenacious stand of the Canadians, they might have cut off and destroyed the 50,000 Allied troops in the salient. An additional benefit flowed from the accomplishment of the Canadians. By withstanding "the paralyzing surprise" of poison gas with only improvised and not altogether effective means, they had minimized its psychological impact and henceforth it would be downgraded as only another weapon of war.

Beginning in the latter part of April, the Canadian Division was deluged with ringing words of praise from every quarter. Prime Minister Robert Borden conveyed his warmest congratulations to

Alderson: "Report of splendid gallantry and efficiency of Division under your command has thrilled all Canada with pride."[10] As might be expected, newspapers across Canada echoed similar sentiments. "Canada saved the Day," maintained the Montreal *Daily Star*. "Our Canadian boys, unused to war and summoned to arms only at the close of last summer … bore the brunt of a savage German attempt to break the Allied line." The Toronto *Star* declared: "The last has been heard, we hope, from those poor sports among us who declared that our men were unequal to valors and sacrifices of war because they lacked … a requisite of discipline in army." The Winnipeg *Telegram* also trumpeted the glorious achievement of the Canadian troops: "They have worthily fulfilled the highest expectations of a nation that never for a moment has doubted their courage and their ability to hold their own with the best troops on the continent."[11]

The Allies were equally unsparing in paying tribute to the Canadians. Joffre, in a note to Sir John, expressed his deep appreciation for the prompt response of the Canadians during which they displayed "a valour and spirit … justly appreciated by all, and I should be glad if you would let them know how much the French forces admire their fine conduct."[12] Kitchener sent a communiqué to the press, reading: "The Canadians had many casualties, but their gallantry and determination undoubtedly saved the situation. Their conduct has been magnificent throughout."[13] The bearing and conduct of the Canadian troops, Sir John French reported in his dispatch, "had averted a disaster, which might have been attended with the most serious consequences."[14] Plumer was equally generous. He alluded to the vital part played by the Canadians during the heavy fighting and indicated "how proud I am to have had them under my command."[15]

No one was more delighted than Alderson. He could barely contain his emotion when he addressed his men:

> I would, first of all, tell you that I have never been so proud of anything in my life as I am of this armlet with "Canada" on it … I thank you, and congratulate you from the bottom of my heart, for the part each one of

you have taken in giving me this feeling of pride. I think it is possible that you do not, all of you, quite realize that, if we had retired on the evening of 22 April when our Allies fell back before the gas and left our left flank quite open — the whole of the 27th and 28th Divisions would probably have been cut off ... My lads, if ever men had a right to be proud in this world, you have.

I know my military history pretty well, and I cannot think of an instance, especially when the cleverness and determination of the enemy is taken into account, in which troops were placed in such a difficult position; nor can I think of an instance in which so much depended on the standing fast of one Division.

You will remember that the last time I spoke to you, just before you went into the trenches ... now over two months ago, I told you about my old regiment — the Royal West Kents — having gained a reputation for not budging from their trenches, no matter how they were attacked. I said then I was quite sure that, in a short time, the Army out here would be saying the same of you. I little thought — none of us thought — how soon those words would come true. But now, today, not only the Army out here, but all Canada, all England and all the Empire are saying it of you.[16]

Interesting enough, the Canadians even drew grudging admiration from the Germans, whose leaders had earlier dismissed them as inconsequential colonial rabble — upon learning of their arrival in England, the kaiser was reported to have said that he would send them "back in thirty rowboats."[17] The German Official History, published after the war, attributed the failure of Albrecht's forces to gain their objectives on the 24th mainly to the "obstinate resistance" and "tenacious determination" of the Canadians.[18] The men and officers of the 1st Canadian Division may have appreciated being the object of widespread adulation, but there were some who were exceptionally modest and questioned whether they deserved it. One survivor said "All I can remember … was that I was in the blooming old funk for about three days and three nights and now I am told I am a hero."[19] Odlum also took the matter in stride: "We mustn't boast too much because it wasn't heroism that made us stay there and fight through that battle. We just didn't know how to get out. We were out at the end of the Salient. Everything was happening and we couldn't get information. The only thing to do as far as we could see was just stay where we were.[20]

Measured by their accomplishment in their first serious engagement, the Canadians knew that they could hold up in comparison with any other troops, allied or enemy. When the French fled, had they not stood firm and faced poison gas with no protection? Had they not, under very trying circumstances and against heavy odds, proven themselves as more than a match for the enemy? The Second Battle of Ypres, tragic though it was, transformed the untested colonials, hitherto deemed fit only to hold the line and do useful spade work, into battle-hardened soldiers and gave them an indomitable confidence that carried them forward through the Somme, Vimy Ridge, Passchendaele, and ultimately, as Britain's shock troops, chosen to lead the drive that finally ended the war.

For the Canadian public, which had exuded enormous pride in the heroic stand of its division, the announcement of the number of casualties far exceeded the 1000 or so predicted by some newspapers and clearly drove home the horrors of war. A native of Pembroke, Ontario, Grace Morris had just received a letter from her boyfriend, Alfred Bastedo, who had been in the front line at Ypres, when the casualty lists were announced. There is a poignant piece in her memoirs worth quoting:

> The news of their heroic stand was received with great pride, and Canadians realized that their country … had decisively stepped on the world stage. Then came the casualty list. Beneath a banner headline, "Canada Forever and Forever," were the names of the gallant men who had fallen in battle. In Pembroke the long list was posted in the window of the telegraph office on Main

Street. People stood in the street to read it. There was the silence and deep sorrow. At the top of the list was the name "Captain Alfred Bastedo — killed in action."[21]

The figures from 22 April to 3 May were shocking, even when judged by the standards of the Great War. Out of a front-line infantry strength of some 10,000, the number of killed, wounded and missing amounted to 5506. The losses were almost equally distributed among the three brigades with 1839 for the 1st, 1829 for the 2nd, and 1838 for the 3rd. The total number of casualties for the period between 15 April and 17 May was 6,341. As part of the 27th Division, the Patricias sustained 658 casualties in their action between 10 April and 1 June.[22]

Canada, in grateful remembrance of her sons' suffering and sacrifice at the Second Battle of Ypres, erected a memorial that was formally unveiled by the Duke of Connaught on 8 July 1923. The moving and impressive ceremony was attended by such illuminaries as the Belgian Crown Prince, Marshal Foch, and Sir John French. The monument was designed by Frederick Clemesha of Regina and consists of a single giant shaft of flagstone court, on which is mounted the head and shoulders of a brooding Canadian soldier. His hands are folded, resting on a reversed rifle, and, under a steel helmet, his head is bowed in perpetual tribute to those who fell. On the front

Courtesy of In Flanders Fields Museum.

The Brooding Canadian soldier. The Canadian memorial at St. Julien.

The inauguration of the Menin Gate Memorial in Ypres on 1 July 1928. Every evening since 11 November 1929, except during the German occupation of Ypres, the Last Post has been sounded as a tribute to those who had died to preserve Belgian freedom and independence.

of the plinth is inscribed the word "Canada" and on each side — one in English and the other in French — is the bare statement:

> This column marks the battlefield where 18,000
> Canadians on the British left withstood the First
> German Gas Attack the 22–24 April 1915. 2000 fell and
> lie buried here.

Actually, the Canadians who perished at Ypres are not buried in the memorial plot, but may be found in the many British cemeteries in the area. Inscribed on the walls of the Menin Gate Memorial in the city of Ypres are the names of more than 55,000 British and Commonwealth soldiers whose bodies were never recovered. Of these, 6983 were Canadians who were declared missing after Ypres and subsequent battles in Belgium.[23] Many soldiers who could not be identified — identification

Courtesy of Bruce Liebowiz.

The illustration shows the daily memorial ceremony held beneath the arches of Menin Gate on 2 May 2008. The names of the missing from the Commonwealth countries are etched behind the crowd of onlookers.

tags came later — lie in British cemeteries. On their headstone is the insignia of a maple leaf, or regimental crest if known, with the inscription "Known Unto God."

There is another Canadian memorial commemorating the soldiers at Ypres for whom the Last Post had sounded — one that may outlast even the monument of stone. During the battle, John McCrae, a medical officer with the 1st Canadian Field Artillery Brigade, wrote what was to become perhaps the best known poem of the First World War.

Born in Guelph, Ontario, in 1872, McCrae studied medicine at the University of Toronto, earning a BM in 1898. Drawn to the military from the time he was a young boy, he interrupted his medical career in 1900 and volunteered for the South African War as an artillery subaltern. In 1901, he returned to Canada whereupon he entered McGill University, spending four years in the study of pathology. He went on to open his own practice, as well as teach and work at several hospitals. The years between 1905 and 1914 were extremely busy. He became a physician

Courtesy of Library and Archives Canada.

Lieutenant-Colonel John McCrae. Canadian medical officer and author of the most-recited poem of the First World War.

of some note and authored a number of scientific articles and two medical texts. In his idle moments he wrote poetry and occasionally contributed verses to the *University Magazine* and other periodicals. When the country rallied to arms in August 1914, McCrae, although a gunner at heart, joined the medical corps, where he felt he could best contribute.

At the time that the Germans launched their gas attack, McCrae was in charge of a dressing station at Essex Farm, a mile or so north of Ypres, dug into the bank of the Yser Canal. As a veteran of the Boer War, he had seen suffering before, but nothing that compared to the carnage that occurred during the battle. For more than a fortnight, he and the medical staff worked practically around the clock, feverishly tending to the hundreds of wounded and agonizing over those that were maimed or could not be saved. He became resentful and disillusioned. In a letter to his mother he wrote:

> The general impression in my mind is of a nightmare. We have been in the most bitter of fights. For seventeen days and nights none of us have had our clothes off, nor our boots even except occasionally. In all that time that I was awake, gunfire and rifle fire never ceased for 60 seconds— and behind it all was the constant sights of the dead and wounded, the maimed and the terrible anxiety lest the line should give way.[24]

One death, in particular, caused McCrae immense grief. On 2 May his closest friend and former student, Lieutenant Alexis Helmer of Ottawa, was blown to bits by an 8-inch shell. Helmer's remains were gathered and

Courtesy of Bruce Liebowitz.

The dressing station at Essex Farm.

buried next day in a small cemetery outside McCrae's dressing station. In the absence of the chaplain, McCrae performed the funeral service as best as he could. Deep in thought, words came easily to McCrae when he scribbled down 15 lines of verse during a lull in bombardment that same day. There are conflicting accounts as to where he was when he wrote his poem. A young medical NCO, Sergeant-Major Cyril Allinson, claimed that he was bringing mail to McCrae when he saw him writing on a pad while sitting on the back step of an ambulance. Allison waited until he had finished before approaching him and "as I handed him his mail, he handed me his pad." Allison was much moved by what he read, which he observed was almost "an exact description of the scene in front of us both."[25] Wild poppies were beginning to bloom between the crosses marking the graves in the nearby cemetery, and some of them were being blown by a gentle east wind.

Another source attributes a fellow officer, Lieutenant-Colonel E.W.B. Morrison, CO of the 1st Brigade, Canadian Field Artillery, with bringing the poem to light. As the story goes, Morrison dropped by the dressing station, and, seeing McCrae put his thoughts to paper, asked him to read what he had written. McCrae did so diffidently. Believing the poem to be worthless, he crushed the paper up in a ball and threw it into the wastebasket. Morrison, who in private life was the editor of the *Ottawa Citizen*, recognized the artistic merits of the poem and immediately retrieved it. He later sent it to the *Spectator* in London, which rejected it. Finally, it appeared in *Punch* magazine on 8 December 8 1915. It became an instant hit, particularly with the soldiers in Flanders, and was translated into many languages.[26]

Unfortunately, McCrae did not survive the war. His health progressively declined — owing to his medical workload, the damp climate, and asthma attacks which were further exacerbated by the effects of the chlorine gas he had inhaled at Second Ypres. Strickened by pneumonia, he developed meningitis and fell into a coma. He died on 28 January 1918, at the age of 45. He was honoured by one of the largest military funerals, at which several generals were among the hundreds in attendance, and buried in Wimereux communal cemetery, just north of Boulogne.

McCrae lives on through his memorable poem, which still touches a nerve today. It is a tribute to the fallen soldiers and a call to the living to carry on their unfinished task. Because of its great popularity, the poppy was adopted as a symbol of remembrance for the war dead in Canada, Britain, and the other Commonwealth countries, as well as in the United States and France. "In Flanders Fields" is a lasting legacy of the tragic Second Battle of Ypres and a fitting note on which to close this story:

> In Flanders fields the poppies blow
> Between the crosses, row on row,
> That mark our place; and in the sky
> The larks, still bravely singing, fly
> Scarce heard amid the guns below.
>
> We are the Dead. Short days ago
> We lived, felt dawn, saw sunset glow,
> Loved, and were loved, and now we lie
> In Flanders fields.

Take up our quarrel with the foe:
To you from failing hands we throw
The torch; be yours to hold it high.
If ye break faith with us who die
We shall not sleep, though poppies grow
In Flanders fields.

Appendix

Order of Battle, First Canadian Division

Commander: Lieutenant-General. E.A.H. Alderson
1st Brigade: Brigadier-General M.S. Mercer
    1st (Western Ontario) Battalion: Lieutenant-Colonel F.W. Hill
    2nd (Eastern Ontario) Battalion: Lieutenant-Colonel D. Watson
    3rd (Toronto) Battalion: Lieutenant-Colonel R. Rennie
    4th (Central Ontario) Battalion: Lieutenant-Colonel A.P. Birchall
2nd Brigade: Brigadier-General A.W. Currie
    5th (Western Ontario) Battalion: Lieutenant-Colonel G.S. Tuxford
    7th (Western Ontario) Battalion: Lieutenant-Colonel W.R.F. Hart-McHarg
    8th (Winnipeg) Battalion: Lieutenant-Colonel L.J. Lipsett
    10th (Calgary-Winnipeg) Battalion: Lieutenant-Colonel R.L. Boyle
3rd Brigade: Brigadier-General R.E.W. Turner
    13th (Royal Highlanders of Canada) Battalion: Lieutenant-Colonel F.O.W. Loomis
    14th (Royal Montreal Regiment) Battalion: Lieutenant-Colonel F.S. Meighen
    15th (48th Highlanders of Canada) Battalion: Lieutenant-Colonel J.A. Currie
    16th (Canadian Scottish) Battalion: Lieutenant-Colonel R.G.E. Leckie
Divisional Artillery: Brigadier-General H.E. Burstall
    1st Brigade, CFA: Lieutenant-Colonel E.W.B. Morrison
    2nd Brigade, CFA: Lieutenant-Colonel J.J. Creelman
    3rd Brigade, CFA: Lieutenant-Colonel J.H. Mitchell

NOTES

Chapter 1 — Creating an Army

1. Henry Borden, ed., *Robert Laird Borden: His Memoirs*, Vol. 1 (Toronto: Macmillan, 1938), 452.
2. The British reply can be found in Appendix 42 in the companion volume of documents to Colonel A. Fortescue Duguid, *Official History of the Canadian Forces in the Great War, 1914–1919* (Ottawa: King's Printer, 1938). Henceforth, it will be cited as *Official History Documents*. During the 1920s, Colonel Duguid, director of the Historical Section, was instructed to compile an eight-volume official history of the Canadian Army in the First World War. The first one was published in 1938, together with the aforementioned volume of appendices and maps. However, the outbreak of the Second World War and the retirement of Duguid led Ottawa to cancel the project.
3. Sir Charles Lucas, *The Empire At War*, Vol. 2 (London: Oxford University Press, 1923), 82.
4. G.F.C. Stanley, *Canada's Soldiers, 1604–1954* (Toronto: Macmillan, 1954), 310; Duguid, *Official History*, 97–98.
5. Colonel G.W.L. Nicholson, *Official History of the Canadian Army in the First World War 1914–1919* (Ottawa: Queen's Printer, 1962), 14. In 1956 the Canadian government, in response to requests from individuals and veterans' organizations, authorized Colonel Nicholson, then deputy director of the Historical Section, to write a single-volume study of the Canadian forces during the Great

War. On the whole, Nicholson produced an admirable and detailed account, except for the first year of the conflict, which is essentially a condensation of Duguid's volume. He does not appear to have dug deeply into the enormous collection of official records and letters from survivors of the Second Battle of Ypres that Duguid and his staff had assembled.

6. *Official History Documents*, Appendix 11.

7. Ronald G. Haycock, *Sam Hughes* (Waterloo: Wilfrid Laurier University Press, 1986), 180–81.

8. *Official History Documents*, Appendix 44.

9. Duguid, *Official History*, 26–28.

10. Canadian House of Commons, *Debates*, 26 January 1916, Vol. 1, 292.

11. *Official History Documents*, Appendix 52.

12. Oscar Douglas Skelton, *Life and Letters of Sir Wilfrid Laurier*, Vol. 2 (New York, 1922), 432–33.

13. Cited in H.M. Urquhart, *The History of the 16th Battalion in the Great War, 1914–1919* (Toronto: Macmillan, 1932), 369.

14. Cited in Urquhart, *16th Battalion*, 369.

15. Don Gillmour, *Canada: A People's History* (Toronto: McClelland & Stewart, 2001), 91.

16. Elizabeth H. Armstrong, *The Crisis of Quebec* (New York: AMS Press, 1967), 55ff.

17. "Flanders Fields: Canada Answers the Call," 2/5 (Program no. and page no. of transcript). The CBC aired a 17-part radio series in 1964 on the 50th anniversary of the outbreak of the Great War. The transcripts for the programs are accessible at the National Archives of Canada in Ottawa, and, for the ones I used, are in RG41, Vol. 6. Hundreds of interviews of survivors of Second Ypres and other battles were conducted by CBC for its radio series and these can be found in alphabetical order under the following call numbers: RG 41, Vol. 7 contains the transcripts for the men in the first four battalions: RG 41, Vol. 8 for the men in battalions 5, 6, 7, and 10; and RG 41, Vol. 9 for the men in battalions 13, 15, and 16. Those used in this study, but not included in the radio programs are simply referred to as "CBC interview."

18. John Swettenham, *To Seize the Victory* (Toronto: Ryerson Press, 1965), 31–32.

19. "Flanders Fields," 2/6.

20. "Flanders Fields, "2/9

21. "Flanders Fields," 2/6.

22. Colonel George G. Nasmith, *Canada's Sons and Great Britain in the World War* (Toronto: Winston, 1919), 80–81.

23. Bill Freeman and Richard Nielson, *Far From Home: Canadians in the First World War* (Toronto: McGraw-Hill Ryerson, 1999), 13–14.

24. J.L. Granatstein, *Canada's Army* (Toronto: University of Toronto Press, 2002), 57.

25. Both excerpts in the paragraph are from "Flanders Fields," 2/7–8.

26. William D. Mathieson, *My Grandfather's War* (Toronto: Macmillan, 1981), 12.

27. Both excerpts are from "Flanders Fields," 2/5–6.

28. "Flanders Fields," 2/10.

29. Mathieson, *Grandfather's War*, 13.

30. "Flanders Fields," 2/10.

31. Urquhart, *16th Battalion*, 9.

32. Urquhart, *16th Battalion*, 11.

33. "Flanders Fields," 2/9.

34. "Flanders Fields," 2/12.

35. Harold R. Peat, *Private Peat* (Indianapolis: Bobbs-Merrill, 1917), 4.

36. Mathieson, *My Grandfather's War*, 15.

37. Gordon Reid, ed., *Poor Bloody Murder* (Oakville, ON: Mosaic Press, 1980), 14.

38. Reid, *Bloody Murder*, 12.

39. "Flanders Fields," 2/9.

40. Desmond Morton and J.L. Granatstein, *Marching to Armageddon* (Toronto: Lester and Orpen Dennys, 1989), 10; Haycock, *Sam Hughes*, 182–83.

41. Hughes, deeming that being a general was more suitable for a man of his position, badgered the prime minister until he reluctantly yielded. Hughes was promoted to the rank of major-general in October 1914, an appointment that was made retroactive to 1912.

42. Canon Frederick George Scott, *The Great War as I Saw it* (Vancouver: Clark and Stuart, 1934), 17.

43. Stanley, *Canada's Soldiers*, 311.

44. Robert F. Zubowski, *As Long as Faith and Freedom Last* (Calgary: Bunker to Bunker Books, 2005), 2.

45. Jeffrey Williams, *Princess Patricia's Canadian Light Infantry* (London: Leo Cooper, 1972), 1–5.

46. "Flanders Fields, 2/27.

47. Borden, *Memoirs*, Vol. 1, 464–66.

48. Freeman and Nelson, *Far From Home, 18.*

49. "Flanders Fields: The Great Expedition," 3/2.

50. "Flanders Fields," 3/2.

51. Nicholson, *Canadian Expeditionary Force*, 22.

52. Desmond Morton, *When Your Number's Up: The Canadian Soldier in the First World War* (Toronto: Random House, 1993), 15.

53. Swettenham, *To Seize*, 30–31.

54. Granatstein, *Canada's Army*, 59.

55. Borden to Perley, 14 August 1914; Perley papers, MG27 II DI2, Vol. 1, CNA.

56. Kitchener to Perley, 16 August 1914, Perley papers.

57. Borden to Perley, 29, August 1914, Perley papers; Desmond Morton, "Exerting Control: The Development of Canadian Authority Over the Canadian Expeditionary Force, 1914–1919," in Timothy Travers and Christon Archer, eds., *Men At War* (Chicago: Precedent, 1982), 12.

58. Kitchener to Perley, 5 September 1914, Perley papers, Vol. 1.

59. On 25 August, Hughes asked Kitchener "whether force will be maintained as a division or broken up into brigades." The War Office replied the following day: "With reference to your telegram … the Canadians will most probably be used as organized and be sent in a complete division." See *Official History Documents*, Appendices, 118 and 119.

60. Nicholson, *Canadian Expeditionary Force*, 34.

61. Duguid, *Official History*, 126–27.

62. Brigadier-General Charles F. Winter, *Lieutenant-General the Hon. Sir Sam Hughes* (Toronto: Macmillan, 1931), 53.

63. CBC interview.

64. Both excerpts are from "Flanders Fields," 3/11.

65. "Flanders Fields," 3/11.

66. "Flanders Fields," 3/11.

67. Duguid, *Official History*, 88.

68. CBC interview.

69. The other excerpts in the paragraph are from "Flanders Fields," 3/5.

70. "Flanders Fields," 3/8.

71. Sergeant-Major William R. Jones, *Fighting the Hun from Saddle and Trench* (Albany, NY: Aiken, 1918), 14–15. The episode is also related, but in less colourful terms, in the unpublished account of W.S. Lighthall's experience in the First World War, 4; 81/9/1, IWM. A member of the Royal Canadian Dragoons at the start of the war, Lighthall would soon turn in his horse for an airplane, eventually attaining the rank of Wing Commander.

72. Granatstein, *Canada's Army*, 54–55, 59; Haycock, *Sam Hughes*, 185; Lucas, *Empire*, Vol. 1, 83–84.

73. CBC interview.

74. Jones, *Fighting the Hun*, 22.

75. *Official History Documents*, Appendix, 130.

76. Haycock, *Sam Hughes*, 186.

77. Colonel G.W.L. Nicholson, *The Gunners of Canada* (Toronto: McClelland & Stewart, 1967), 201.

78. Nicholson, *Canadian Expeditionary Force*, 31.

79. Lighthall account, 6–7.

80. "Flanders Fields," 3/15.

81. All newspaper citations are taken from Nasmith, *Canada's Sons*, 110–11.

82. R.C. Fetherstonhaugh, *The Royal Montreal Regiment 14th Battalion, C.E.F. 1914–1925* (Montreal: Gazette, 1927), 15; Urquhart, *16th Battalion*, 27–28; John Macfie, *Letters Home* (Meaford, ON: Oliver Graphics, 1990), 8–9.

83. Kirkpatrick diary, 15 October 1914, MG30 E3I8, Vol. 23, file 179, CNA.

84. Both excerpts are from "Flanders Fields," 3/17.

85. Fetherstonhaugh, *14th Battalion*, 16.

86. Tim Cook., *At the Sharp End*, Vol. 1 (Toronto: Viking, 2007), 74–75; Duguid, *Official History*, 119; Desmond Morton, "Edwin Alfred Hervey Alderson," in *Dictionary of Canadian Biography*, Vol. 12.

87. Nicholson, *Canadian Expeditionary Force*, 35

88. Kirkpatrick diary.

89. Swettenham, *To Seize*, 52.

90. Cited in Freeman and Nielsen, *Far From Home*, 32.

91. "Flanders Fields," 3/19.

92. "Flanders Fields," 3/20.

93. Kirkpatrick diary, 12 November 1914.

94. Nicholson, *Canadian Expeditionary Force*, 36–37.

95. Cited in Frederick C. Curry, *From the St. Lawrence to the Yser* (London: Smith, Elder and Co., 1916), 34.

96. Urquhart, *16th Battalion*, 30–31.

97. Duguid, *Official History*, 152.

98. Swettenham, *To Seize*, 52.

99. Both excerpts are from "Flanders Fields," 3/28.

100. Scott, *The Great War*, 31.

101. Kirkpatrick diary, 30 November 1914.

102. CBC interview.

103. *Official History Documents*, Appendix, 205.

104. *Official History Documents*, Appendix, 227.

105. Nicholson, *Canadian Expeditionary Force*, 26.

106. *Official History Documents*, Appendix, 227.

107. Haycock, *Sam Hughes*, 119–23, 246–52; Swettenham, *To Seize*, 58–59.

108. CBC interview.

109. *Official History Documents*, Appendix, 111.

110. Urquhart, *16th Battalion*, 32.

111. Sir Andrew Macphail, *Official History of the Canadian Forces in the Great War: The Medical Services* (Ottawa: King's Printer, 1925), 257–58.

112. Nasmith, *Canada's Sons*, 123.

113. Peat, *Private*, 21–22. Peat does not identify the speaker. He merely states that it was a brigadier-general who was subsequently killed in battle, but he must have been mistaken about the officer's rank. There were only three brigadiers at the time and none had the given

name of Bill or William.

114. Crerar diary, 5 December 1914, MG30 E157, Vol. 15, CNA.

115. Cited in Nicholson, *Canadian Expeditionary Force*, 38.

116. Creelman diary, 19 December 1914.

117. Colonel A. Currie, *The Red Watch: With the First Canadian Division in Flanders* (Toronto: McClelland, Goodchild and Stewart, 1916), 84–85.

118. Ralph Hodder Williams, *Princess Patricias' Canadian Light Infantry, 1914–1919 Vol. 1* (London: Hodder and Stoughton, 1923), 14–17.

119. Nicholson, *Canadian Expeditionary Force*, 39–40.

120. Currie, *Red Watch*, 98–99.

121. Colonel George C. Nasmith, *On the Fringe of the Great Fight* (New York: Doran, 1917), 29.

122. Duguid, *Official History*, 151.

123. Nicholson, *Canadian Expeditionary Force*, 40.

Chapter 2 — Off to the Front

1. The excerpts in the paragraph are from "Flanders Fields: Baptism of Fire," 4/6–7.

2. Nicholson, *Canadian Expeditionary Force*, 39.

3. Duguid, *Official History*, 172–73.

4. Cited in Duguid, *Official History*, 173.

5. Nicholson, *Canadian Expeditionary Force*, 39.

6. CBC interview.

7. Peat, *Private*, 37.

8. Villiers diary, Villiers papers, MG30 E236, Vol. 4, CNA.

9. Peat, *Private*, 33–34.

10. A.C. McLennan (16th Battalion) interview with CBC.

11. Fetherstonhaugh, *14th Battalion*, 26–27.

12. Lucas, *Empire at War*, Vol. 2, 86.

13. Sir John French, *The Dispatches of Lord French* (London: Chapman and Hall, 1917), 249. French expressed himself similarly in his diary (20 February 1915), which forms part of his collection housed in the

Imperial War Museum.

14. Nicholson, *Canadian Expeditionary Force*, 45–46; Brigadier-General J.E. Edmonds and Captain G.C. Wynne, *Military Operations: France and Belgium, 1915*, Vol. 1 (London: Macmillan, 1927), 22–23.

15 Smith-Dorrien diary, February 17 1915, Smith Dorrien papers, 87/47/10, IWM.

16. A.B. Tucker, *The Battle Glory of Canada* (London: Cassell, 1915), 46.

17. Nicholson, *Canadian Expeditionary Force*, 49.

18. Cited in Daniel D. Dancocks, *Welcome to Flanders Fields* (Toronto: McClelland & Stewart, 1988), 86.

19. Nicholson, *Canadian Expeditionary Force*, 49.

20. *Official History Documents*, Appendix, 267.

21. CBC interview.

22. Both excerpts in the paragraph are from "Flanders Fields," 4/15.

23. Duguid, *Official History*, 157, 180.

24. Morton and Granatstein, *Armageddon*, 57.

25. Cited in Freeman and Nielsen, *Far From Home*, 44.

26. Desmond Morton, "Malcom Smith Mercer," in *Dictionary of Canadian Biography*, Vol. 12; Gordon MacKinnon, "Major-General Malcolm Smith Mercer," *www.cavalryhighlanders.com/history/2ndbrigade.htm*.

27. Press clipping of a newspaper article entitled "I Remember Currie," MG30 E78, Vol. 3, CNA.

28. A.M.J. Hyatt, *General Sir Arthur Currie: A Military Biography* (Toronto: University of Toronto Press, 1987) and Daniel G. Dancocks, *Sir Arthur Currie: A Biography* (Toronto, Methuen, 1985) are two good recent studies of Currie.

29. Duguid, *Official History*, 64; "Richard Ernest William Turner," *http// en.wikipedia.org/wiki/Richard_Ernest_William_Turner*; Thomas P. Leppard, "'The Dashing Subaltern:' Sir Richard Turner in Retrospect," *Canadian Military History* 6, No. 2 (1997): 21–24.

30. The background information of the battalion commanders, or most of it, can be found online.

31. Duguid, *Official History*, 52–53.

32. CBC interview.

33. *Official History Documents*, Appendix, 270.

34. CBC interview.

35. Peat, *Private*, 140.

36. CBC interview.

37. Louis Keene, *"Crumps:" The Plain Story of a Canadian Who Went* (Boston: Houghton and Mifflin, 1917), 109–10.

38. Crerar diary, MG30 E157, Vol. 15, CNA.

39. "Flanders Fields," 4/12.

40. "Flanders Fields," 4/13

41. "Flanders Fields,"4/18.

42. Cited in Freeman and Nielsen, *Far From Home*, 44.

43. Keene, *"Crumps,"* 113.

44. "Flanders Fields,"4/19.

45. Keene, *"Crumps,"* 113.

46. Whitehouse, "Recollections of service in the army, from 1913 to 1919," 52–53; 4/37/1, IWM.

47. CBC interview.

48. "Flanders Fields,"4/18.

49. "Flanders Fields,"4/18.

50. "Flanders Fields," 4/17.

51. Cited in Morton and Granatstein, *Marching, 55–56.*

52. "Flanders Fields," 4/10.

53. Freeman and Nielsen, *Far From Home*, 46.

54. "Flanders Fields: A World of Stealth," 6/25.

55. CBC TV Production "The Killing Ground."

56. Bruce Tascona and Eric Wells, *Little Black Devils* (Winnipeg: Royal Winnipeg Rifles, 1983), 75; Fred Gaffen, *Forgotten Soldiers* (Penticton: Theytus, 1985), 20–28.

57. Edmonds and Wynne, *France and Belgium, 1915*, Vol. 1, 66–69.

58. George H. Cassar, *The Tragedy of Sir John French* (Newark, DE: University of Delaware Press, 1985), 205–10.

59. Nicholson, *Canadian Expeditionary Force*, 51.

60. The battle is described in detail in Edmonds and Wynne, *France and Belgium, 1915,* Vol. 1, chs. 6–7. A good, brief version can be found in John Keegan, *The First World War* (New York: Knopf, 1999), 192–97.

61. Nicholson, *Gunners*, 212.

62. Currie diary, 10 March 1915, Currie papers, MG30 E100, CNA.

63. Both excerpts are from "Flanders Fields," 4/26.

64. Currie diary, 24 March 1915.

65. Canadian Field Comforts Commission, *With the First Canadian Contingent* (Toronto: Hodder and Stoughton/Musson, 1915), 55.

66. *Official History Documents*, Appendix, 306.

67. Cassar, *Sir John French*, 216–20.

68. Geoffrey Powell, *Plumer* (London: Leo Cooper, 1990), 106–07.

69. *Official History Documents*, Appendix, 306a.

70. He was then in command of the 19th Brigade, which included the 2nd Battalion, Royal Canadian Regiment.

71. Hugh Urquhart, *Arthur Currie* (Toronto: Dent, 1950), 58–59.

Chapter 3 — Unheeded Warning

1. Nicholson, *Canadian Expeditionary Force*, 55.

2. Hugh B.C. Pollard, *The Story of Ypres* (New York: McBride, 1917), 65.

3. John Giles, *The Ypres Salient (London: Leo Cooper*, 1970), 31; Tonie and Valmai Holt, *Ypres Salient* (London: Leo Cooper, 1999)13–14.

4. Pollard, *Ypres*, 14–15.

5. Pollard, *Ypres*, 51–55.

6. Nicholson, *Canadian Expeditionary Force*, 55–56.

7. Edmonds and Wynne, *France and Belgium, 1915*, Vol. 1, 271.

8. Duguid, *Official History*, 205.

9. *Official History Documents*, Appendix, 330a.

10. *Official History Documents*, Appendix, 334

11. CBC interview.

12. Alldritt diary, 20 April 1915, MG30 E1, CNA.

13. "Flanders Fields," 4/27.

14. Fred Bagnall, *Not Mentioned in Despatches* (Ottawa: CEF Books, 2005), 57.

15. Edmonds and Wynne, *France and Belgium, 1915*, Vol. 1, 161.

16. Historical Section, Historical Staff, *Canadian War Records: Narrative*

on the Formation and Operation of the First Canadian Division to the Second Battle of Ypres, Vol. 1 (Ottawa: Mulvey, 1920), 130–33. The narrative itself is unreliable and should not be used as a work of reference. But it has value because it contains war diaries and other official records, some of which cannot be found in the archives. A copy of the publication, which had a very limited circulation, can be found in the Canadian National Archives in Ottawa.

17. Edmonds and Wynne, *France and Belgium, 1915,* Vol. 1, 160–61n3.
18. Edmonds and Wynne, *France and Belgium, 1915,* Vol. 1, 161–62.
19. *Official History Documents,* Appendix, 330a.
20. Charles, L. Foster, ed., *Letters from the Front, 1914–1919,* Vol. 1 (Toronto: Bank of Commerce, 1920), 13.
21. Foster, ed., *Letters,* Vol. 1, 13.
22. Edmonds and Wynne, *France and Belgium, 1915,* Vol. 1, 162.
23. General Erich von Falkenhayn, *The German General Staff and its Decisions,* 1914–1916 (New York, 1920), 94.
24. G.L. Lewin, *Die Gifte in der Weltgeschichte* (Berlin: Springer, 1920); J.R. Partington, *A History of Greek Fire and Gunpowder* (Cambridge: Heffer, 1960); Adrienne Mayor, *Greek Fire, Poison Arrows and Scorpion Bombs in the Ancient World* (Woodstock: Overlook Duckworth, 2003); J.R. Wood, "Chemical Warfare — A Chemical and Toxicological Review," *American Journal of Public Health* 34 (1946): 455–460.
25. For details of the proceedings see J.B. Scott, ed., *The Reports of the Hague Conferences of 1899 and 1907* (Oxford: Clarendon Press, 1917).
26. Major-General C.H. Foulkes, *Gas!* (Edinburgh: Blackwood and Sons, 1934), 23
27. Ulrich Trumpener, "The Road to Ypres: The Beginnings of Gas Warfare in World War I," *Journal of Modern History* 47 (1975): 463.
28. William Moore, *Gas Attack!* (London: Leo Cooper, 1987), 16–17; Winston S. Churchill, *The World Crisis,* Vol. 2 (New York: Scribner's Sons, 1951), 72–75.
29. Trumpener, "The Road to Ypres," 464–70.
30. Trumpener, "The Road to Ypres," 469.
31. Daniel Charles, *Between Genius and Genocide* (London: Cape, 2005), 155–56.

32. Augustin M. Prentiss, *Chemicals in War* (New York: McGraw-Hill, 1937), 150.

33. General Max Schwarte, *Die Technik im Weltkriege* (Berlin: Mittler, 1920), 280–81.

34. Ludwig F. Faber, *The Poisonous Cloud: Chemical Warfare in the First World War* (Oxford: Clarendon Press, 1986), 28.

35. Moore, *Gas Attack!*, 16–17.

36. Faber, *Poisonous Cloud*, 29.

37. Morris Goran, *The Story of Fritz Haber* (Norman: University of Oklahoma Press, 1967), 68–69.

38. Holger H. Herwig, *The First World War: Germany and Austria-Hungary 1914–1918* (London: Arnold: 1997), 169.

39. *Der Weltkrieg*, Band 8, 37.

40. Faber, *Poisonous Cloud*, 30–32.

41. General Jacques Mordac, *Le Drame de l'Yser* (Paris: Editions des Portiques, 1933), 219–20.

42. General Edmond Ferry, "Ce qui s'est passé sur l'Yser," *La review des vivants* (July 1930): 898–899.

43. Ferry, "Ce qui s'est passé sur l'Yser," 899.

44. Ferry, "Ce qui s'est passé sur l'Yser, 900.

45. Ferry, "Ce qui s'est passé sur l'Yser," 900.

46. Kim Beattie, "Unheeded Warning," *Maclean's*, 1 May 1936, 69–70.

47. Ministère de la guerre, Etat Major de l'armée. Service Historique. *Les armées françaises dans la grande guerre*, Tome II, Vol. 2, Annexe 1392.

48. The *Times*, 13, 14, and 17 April 1915.

49. *Official History Documents*, Appendix, 320.

50. Edmonds and Wynne, *France and Belgium, 1915*, Vol. 1, 164.

51. Smith-Dorrien diary, 15 April 1915, Smith-Dorrien papers, 87/47/10, IWM.

52. *Official History Documents*, Appendix, 331.

53. Bulfin to Edmonds, 10 March 1925, CAB 45/140, BNA.

54. Edmonds and Wynne, *France and Belgium, 1915*, Vol. 1, 166.

55. "An Account of German Gas Cloud Attacks on British Front in France," WO 32/5483.

56. Alderson to Edmonds, 28 March 1925, CAB 45/140.

57. Currie diary, 15 April 1915, MG30 E100, Vol. 43, file 194, CNA.

58. "Flanders Fields," 4/28; See also a speech Odlum gave before a group of army veterans in 1923; Odlum papers, MG30 E300, Vol. 24, CNA.

59. CBC interview.

60. Bagnall, *Not Mentioned in Despatches*, 57.

61. Cited in Rudolph Hanslian, *The Gas Attack at Ypres* (Edgewood Arsenal, MD: Chemical Warfare School, 1940), 14.

62. William Rae to Duguid, 29 June 1926, RG24, Vol. 2680, file 2/HQC4950, CNA.

63. Odlum speech, Odlum papers.

64. Nigel Cave, *Hill 60* (Barnsley: Leo Cooper, 1998); Edmonds and Wynne, *France and Belgium, 1915*, Vol. 1, 166–70; John Dixon, *Magnificent But Not War: The Battle For Ypres, 1915* (Barnsley: Leo Cooper, 2003), Chs. 2 and 3.

65. Pollard, *Story of Ypres*, 69–76.

66. Scott, *Great War As I Saw It*, 57.

67. Duguid, *Official History*, 219.

68. *Der Weltkrieg*, Band. 8, 38–39; Duguid, *Official History*, 224.

69. *Der Weltkrieg*, Band 8, 39.

70. Edmonds and Wynne, *France and Belgium, 1915*, Vol. 1, 190, n2.

Chapter 4 — A Higher Form of Killing

1. Maxwell-Scott's account of his experience in the Ypres salient, 97/38/1, IWM.

2. Herbert Rae, *Maple Leaves in Flanders Fields* (London: Smith, Elder and Co., 1917), 139–40.

3. Divisional Headquarters replied: "There are one hundred mouth organs ... for you. Please call for them. No cards available just now but will send you some out of next consignment." See *Official History Documents*, Appendix, 339.

4. German field batteries were silent from 5 p.m. to 5.10 p.m. to avoid disturbing the gas clouds.

5. Beatrix Brice, *The Battle Book of Ypres* (London: John Murray,

1927), 18.

6. "Flanders Fields: The Second Battle of Ypres," 5/3.

7. The French Official History, which frequently places nationalism ahead of accurate reporting, is regrettably circumspect on the details following the gas attack in this sector. To reconstruct what occurred, one must rely on the few memoirs of the French officers involved, as well as Canadian and British sources.

8. "Flanders Fields," 5/ 3.

9. Edmonds and Wynne, *France and Belgium, 1915*, Vol. 1, 177–78.

10. Nicholson, *Canadian Expeditionary Force*, 62.

11. Recording of James Pratt, tape 000495/06 R03, IWM.

12. Swettenham, *McNaughton*, Vol. 1, 44–45.

13. Cited in Dancocks, *Flanders Fields*, 115.

14. Capt. W.D. Ellis, Secretary of the Canadian Corps Battalion Association, to author in 1982; Odlum, speech given in 1923, Odlum papers, MG30 E300; and interview for CBC; F.C. Arnold (7th Battalion) in "Flanders Fields," 5/3; Andrew McNaughton in CBC interview.

15. Peat, *Private*, 144.

16. "Memo Regarding Poison Gas," RG24, Vol. 1810, file GAQ 1–10, CNA.

17. Colonel George C. Nasmith, *Canada's Sons and Great Britain in the World War* (Toronto: Winston, 1919), 178–79.

18. "Memo Regarding Poison Gas."

19. "Flanders Fields," 5/4.

20. Major F. Davy, "Ypres, 1915–1916," in *Canada in Khaki*, Canadian War Records Office, ed. (London: Pictorial Newspaper, 1917), 66.

21. "Flanders Fields," 5/3.

22. Morrison account, RG24 C5, Vol. 1832, file GAQ 8–15, CNA.

23. Hawkins diary, 22 April 1915, 75/113/ 1 and DS MISC/25, IWM.

24. Colonel Jacques Mordacq, *Le drame sur l'Yser* (Paris: Editions des Portiques, 1933), 63.

25. Mordacq, *Le drame*, 64.

26. CBC interview.

27. Odlum in a speech given in 1923, Odlum papers, MG30 E300, Vol. 24, CNA.

28. CBC interview.

29. CBC interview.

30. Nicholson, Canadian *Expeditionary Force*, 64.

31. Nicholson, *Canadian Expeditionary Force*, 62.

32. McCuaig, Report of Operations from 22 to 24 April, 1915, in *First Canadian Division, 268–69.*

33. "Flanders Fields," 5/4.

34. "Flanders Fields," 5/4.

35. Ian Sinclair to his mother, 28 April 1915, MG30 E432, Vol. 1, CNA.

36. Cited in Norm Christie, *For King and Empire* (Ottawa: CEF Books, 2005), 26.

37. McCuaig, Report of Operations, 272.

38. Dancocks, *Flanders Fields*, 24.

39. J.A. Currie, *Red Watch*, 226.

40. Norm Christie, *Gas Attack: The Canadians at Ypres* (Ottawa: CEF Books, 1998), 28.

41. King to Duguid, 19 May 1926, RG24, Vol. 2680, file 2/HQC4950, CNA.

42. "Flanders Fields," 5/5.

43. Peter Batchelor and Chris Matson, *VCs of the First World War*, 62–63; A.T. Hunter, "The Second Battle of Ypres," in *Canada in the Great World War*, Vol. 3 (Toronto: United Publishers, 1919), 110.

44. Alderson to Edmonds, 28 March 1925, CAB 45/140, BNA.

45. Alderson report, RG9 III 3, Vol. 4011, fol. 15, file 1, CNA.

46. *Official History Documents*, Appendix, 341.

47. *Official History Documents*, Appendix, 342.

48. Villiers diary, 22 April 1915, Villiers papers, MG30 E236, Vol.4, CNA.

49. *Official History Documents*, Appendices, 347, 351, 357.

50. Andrew Iarocci, *Shoestring Soldiers: The 1st Canadian Division at War, 1914–1915* (Toronto: University of Toronto Press, 2008), 106.

51. *Official History Documents*, Appendix, 370.

52. See especially *Official History Documents*, Appendices, 355, 358.

53. *Official History Documents*, Appendices, 353, 354, 355, 358.

54. "Flanders Fields," 5/7.

55. Peat, *Private*, 149.

56. "Flanders Fields," 5/8.

57. "Flanders Fields," 5/5–6.

58. Arthur Currie to General MacBrien (then Canadian Chief of Staff), 24 April 1926, RG24, Vol. 2680, file 2/HQC4950, CNA.

59. Edmonds and Wynne, *France and Belgium, 1915*, Vol. 1, 180.

60. Edmonds and Wynne, *France and Belgium, 1915*, Vol. 1, 180–81.

61. *Official History Documents*, Appendix, 370. The message, dispatched at 8:25 p.m., did not reach Divisional Headquarters until after 9:00 p.m.

62. "Flanders Fields," 5/8. Others interviewed expressed themselves in similar terms.

Chapter 5 — The Deadly Counterattacks

1. Shand was mistaken when he referred to the medical aid post as a clearing station. For one thing, he was too close to the front. For another, the dying were not conveyed to the clearing station.

2. Reid, *Poor Bloody Murder*, 82.

3. Colonel J.G. Adami, *The War Story of the Canadian Army Medical Corps, 1914–1915*, Vol. 1 (London: Canadian War Records Office, 1918), 118.

4. Cited in Dancocks, *Flanders Fields*, 137.

5. Morton, *When Your Number's Up*, 181–82.

6. As usual in such circumstances, we receive no enlightenment from the French Official History.

7. *Official History Documents*, Appendix, 375.

8. Leckie to Duguid, 28 April 1926, RG24, Vol. 2680, file 2, CNA.

9. "Flanders Fields," 5/9.

10. Duguid, *Official History*, 253.

11. Dancocks, *Gallant Canadians*, 29.

12. Urquhart, *16th Battalion*, 58.

13. Foster, ed., *Letters*, Vol. 1, 10.

14. CBC interview with A.M. McLennan (16th Battalion).

15. "Flanders Fields," 5/9; Ormond, "War Diary of 10th Battalion, 1st Canadian Division, 1–30 April 1915," in *First Canadian Division, 242*.

16. Leckie to Duguid, 28 April 1928, RG24, Vol. 2680, file 2, CNA.

17. "Flanders Fields," 5/10.

18. Ormond, War Diary, 249.

19. Impressions of a Platoon Commander, "The Canadian Scottish at the Second Battle of Ypres, April 1915," *Canadian Defence Quarterly*, Vol. 2 (1924–25).

20. Private Percy Allen, bound volume of extracts from letters sent, 98/24/1, IWM. Hereafter cited as Allen Letters.

21. Tucker, *Battle Glory*, 92.

22. Cited in *The Times History of the War*, Vol. 5 (London: *The Times*, 1915), 61.

23. Ormond, War Diary, 249.

24. Foster, ed., *Letters*, Vol. 1, 10.

25. Tucker, *Battle Glory*, 93

26. Tucker, *Battle Glory*, 95.

27. Leckie, "Official Report," 29 April 1915 in *First Canadian Division*, 292.

28. Foster, ed., *Letters*, Vol. 1, 15.

29. Cited in the *Times History*, Vol. 5, 61–3.

30. Cited in Urquhart, *16th Battalion*, 59

31. "Flanders Fields," 5/10.

32. Leckie, "Account of the Charge of the Canadian Scottish," n.d., MG30 E 236, Vol. 4, CNA.

33. Allen Letters.

34. Leckie, "Account of the Charge of the Canadian Scottish."

35. Urquhart, *16th Battalion*, 59.

36. Ormond, War Diary, 249.

37. Nicholson, *Canadian Expeditionary Force*, 66

38. Sir Max Aitken (later Lord Beaverbrook), *Canada in Flanders*, Vol. 1 (London: Hodder and Stoughton, 1916), 54–55.

39. "Flanders Fields," 5/10.

40. *Official History Documents*, Appendix, 394.

41. Duguid, *Official History*, 256–57.

42. Watson diary, 23 April 1915, MG30 E69, CNA.

43. CBC interview.

44. Urquhart, *16th Battalion*, 62.

45. Ormond, War Diary, 244.

46. Leckie, "Official Report," 293

47. Cited in Dancocks, *Flanders Fields*, 134.

48. Allen Letters.

49. Dancocks, *Flanders Fields*, 134.

50. BBC interview with William Rae (16th Battalion), 4201/1, IWM

51. Cited in Urquhart, *16th Battalion*, 72.

52. Allen Letters.

53. Peat, *Private*, 156–61.

54. *Officia History Documents*, Appendix 412.

55. Currie, "2nd Canadian Infantry Brigade – Narrative of Events 22nd to 27th April, 1915," in *First Canadian Division*, 207.

56. McCuaig, Report of Operations, 269–70.

57. Tomlinson, "Narrative of Events, April 22 and 23," WO 95/2278, BNA.

58. *Official History Documents,* Appendix 404.

59. Duguid, *Official History*, 265–66.

60. "Narrative of Operations of Col. Geddes' Detachment, 22–28 April 1915", WO 95/2267, IWM.

61. *Official History Documents*, Appendix 425.

62. "Flanders Fields," 5/12.

63. Andrew Iarocci, "1st Canadian Infantry Brigade in the Second Battle of Ypres: The Case of the 1st and 4th Infantry Battalions, 23 April 1915 , *Canadian Military History*, Vol 12, No. 4 (2003): 13.

64. Duguid, *Official History*, 269.

65. Iarocci, "1st Canadian Infantry Brigade in the Second Battle of Ypres," 13

66. Duguid, *Official History*, 269–70.

67. Iarocci, "1st Canadian Infantry Brigade in the Second Battle of Ypres," 9.

68. Cited in Dancocks, *Flanders Fields*, 142.

69. Mathieson, *Grandfather's War*, 105.

70. "Flanders Fields," 5/13.

71. Duguid, *Official History*, 270.

72. A.T. Hunter, "The Second Battle of Ypres," in *Canada in the Great World War* (Toronto: United Publishers, 1919), 105.

73. *Official History Documents*, Appendix, 442.

74. "Flanders Fields," 5/13.

75. *Official History Documents*, Appendix, 481.

76. Edmonds and Wynne, *France and Belgium*, Vol. 1, 198.

Chapter 6 — Securing the New Flank

1. Mathieson, *My Grandfather's War*, 106.
2. Ormond, War Diary, 249.
3. Foster, ed., *Letters*, vol. 1, 15.
4. McCuaig, Report of Operations, 270.
5. Ian Sinclair to his mother, 28 April 1915, MG30 E432, Vol. 1, CNA.
6. McLaren, Report of No. 3 Company, 15th Battalion, in First Canadian Division, 286.
7. War Diary of 5th Battalion in First Canadian Division, 220.
8. *Official History Documents*, Appendix, 453.
9. *Official History Documents*, Appendix, 462.
10. *Official History Documents*, Appendix, 472.
11. *Official History Documents*, Appendix, 474.
12. Edmonds and Wynne, *France and Belgium, 1915*, Vol. 1, 200.
13. Odlum in a speech given in 1923, Odlum papers. MG30 E300, vol. 16, CNA.
14. Odlum to Mrs. McHarg (Hart-McHarg's mother), 26 April 1915, Odlum papers.
15. War Diary of 7th Battalion in First Canadian Division, 225.
16. Odlum to T.G. Roberts, 10 July 1915, Odlum papers, MG30 E300, Vol. 16, CNA.
17. Odlum's account of Hart-McHarg's death, as told to Major Mathews, September 1928, Odlum papers, MG30 E300, Vol. 16, CNA.
18. Odlum in a speech given in 1923, Odlum papers.
19. Odlum to Currie, n.d., Odlum papers, MG30 E300, vol. 16, CNA.
20. Odlum's account of Hart-McHarg's death, as told to Major Mathews, September 1928.
21. "A Brave Soldier and a Gallant Gentleman," March 1929, MG30 E100, Vol. 1, CNA.
22. Odlum's account of Hart-McHarg's death, as told to Major Mathews, September 1928.
23. Odlum, 7th Battalion — Narrative of Events, 22–27 April 1915, in First Canadian Division, 225.
24. Odlum to Mrs. McHarg, 26 April 1915.

25. George H. Cassar, *The Tragedy of Sir John French* (Newark, DE: University of Delaware Press, 1985), passim.

26. On the subject of Foch, see especially Captain B.H. Liddell Hart, *Foch: The Man of Orleans* (Boston: Little, Brown and Co., 1932) and General Sir James Marshall-Cornwall, *Foch as Military Commander* (London: Batsford, 1972).

27. Les armées françaises dans fa grande guerre, Tome II, 701.

28. Official History Documents, Appendix, 705.

29. Edmonds and Wynne, *France and Belgium, 1915*, Vol. 1, 201

30. Der Weltkrieg, Band 8, 41–42

31. Der Weltkrieg, Band 8, 42–43.

32. Edmonds and Wynne, *France and Belgium, 1915*, vol. 1, 199–200.

33. Official History Documents, Appendix, 485.

34. Official History Documents, Appendix, 486.

35. Official History Documents, Appendices, 489, 493.

36. Dancocks, *Flanders Fields*, 151.

37. Official History Documents, Appendix, 484.

38. Edmonds and Wynne, *France and Belgium, 1915*, Vol. 1, 203–03.

39. Wanless, O'Gowan, Report of Operations of the 13th Infantry Brigade on 23 April 1915, WO 95/1548, BNA.

40. War Diary of the 1st Royal West Kents for 23 April, WO 95/1553, BNA.

41. "Flanders Fields," 5/13.

42. Report of the 2nd Yorkshires Regiment on Action of 23 April 1915, WO 95/2267, BNA.

43. Peat, *Private*, 164–65.

44. The letter is reproduced in F. Douglas Reveille, History of the County of Brant, Vol. 2 (Branford: Hurley, 1920), 457.

45. "Flanders Fields," 5/14.

46. Romer to Duguid, 26 April 1926, CAB 45/156, BNA.

47. Brown to Duguid, 7 May 1926, RG24, Vol. 2680 HQC-5046 CNA.

48. Duguid to Edmonds, 25 July 1925, CAB 45/155, BNA.

49. Edmonds and Wynne, *France and Belgium, 1915*, Vol. 1, 207.

50. John Dixon, *Magnificent*, 76.

51. Gordon-Hall to Duguid, 27 April 1926; RG24, Vol. 2680, file 2/HQC4950, CNA.

52. Loomis, Report on Action in Front of Ypres, in First Canadian Division, 263.

53. Tomlinson, "Narrative of Events, April 22 and 23," WO 95/2278, BNA

54. McCuaig, Report of Operations, 270–71.

55. Loomis, Report of Action, 264.

56. Edmonds and Wynne, *France and Belgium, 1915*, Vol. 1, 213.

57. H.H. Mathews, "An Account of the Second Battle of Ypres, April 1915," 10, Mathews papers, MG30 E60, Vol. 4, file 17, CNA. The story was written for friends in June 1915, about a month after the fighting ended.

58. McLaren, Report of No. 3 Company, 286.

59. Currie, *Red Watch*, 235.

60. Anon., "The Canadian Scottish at the Second Battle of Ypres, April 1915," *Canadian Defence Quarterly* (January 1925): 140.

61. Duguid, *Official History*, 287.

62. Odlum, Narrative of Events, 225.

63. Official History Documents, Appendix, 522.

64. Mathews, "An Account of the Second Battle of Ypres," 10.

65. *Les armées françaises dans fa grande guerre*, Tome II, 704.

66. Edmonds, *France and Belgium, 1915*, Vol. 1, Appendix, 22.

Chapter 7 — 24 April: The Onset of the Battle of St. Julien (4:00 a.m. to 1:00 p.m.)

1. Edmonds and Wynne, *France and Belgium, 1915*, Vol. 1, 214.

2. *Der Weltkrieg*, Band 8, 44; Nicholson, *Canadian Expeditionary Force*, 71.

3. Mathews, "An Account of the Second Battle of Ypres," 10, Mathews papers, MG30 E60, Vol. 4, file 17, CNA.

4. Mathews, "An Account of the Second Battle of Ypres," 10.

5. Odlum Report, in *First Canadian Division*, 226.

6. "Flanders Field," 5/16.

7. Sergeant Harold Baldwin, *Holding the Line* (Chicago: McClurg, 1918), 162.

8. Creelman to Duguid, 22 September 1936, RG24, Vol. 1503, CNA; Duguid, *Official History Documents*, Appendix, 526.
9. "Flanders Fields," 5/15.
10. Cited in Dancocks, *Flanders Fields*, 160.
11. McLaren, Report of No. 3 Company, 15th Battalion, *in First Canadian Division*, 286.
12. Lipsett, "Narrative of Events, 22nd to 26th April 1915," in *First Canadian Division*, 235.
13. Even after crude respirators were issued to the British and Canadian troops in May, a report on their reliability in the wake of a recent gas attack concluded that, "Where gas was at its greatest concentration, no respirators or helmets appear to have been absolutely effective." Report by Captain R. Dwyer and Lieutenant Jones, S.L. Cummins collection, LHCMA.
14. "Account of Lieutenant Herbert Maxwell-Scott's experience in the Ypres Salient," 97/38/1, IWM.
15. Mathews, "An Account of the Second Battle of Ypres," 11.
16. Lipsett, "Narrative of Events," 235ff; McLaren, Report of No. 3 Company, 15th Battalion, 286; Kim Beattie, *The 48th Highlanders of Canada, 1891–1928* (Toronto: 48th Highlanders of Canada, 1932), 70–71.
17. Lipsett, "Narrative of Events," 235.
18. Mathews "Account of the Second Battle of Ypres," 11.
19. Mathews, "Account of the Second Battle of Ypres," 11.
20. Tuxford, "The Second Battle of Ypres — The 5th Battalion and the 2nd Brigade," 1, RG24, Vol. 1829, file GAQ 7–35, CNA.
21. J. Upritchard (8th Battalion) interview from "Flanders Fields," 5/15.
22. Tuxford, "The Second Battle of Ypres," 1.
23. CBC interview.
24. Tucker, *Battle Glory*, 128–29.
25. Cited in Dancocks, *Flanders Fields*, 161.
26. Mathews, "Account of the Second Battle of Ypres," 11.
27. Cited in Dancocks, *Flanders Fields*, 161.
28. Duguid to Edmonds, 8 January 1925, CAB 45/155, BNA.
29. McLaren.Report, 286.

30. Cited in McWilliams and Steele, *Gas!*, 106.

31. Morley, "A detail account of the part of No. 3 Company, 90th Rifles (8th Battalion), played in the Battle of Langemarck-St.-Julien-Ypres," n.d., RG24 C5, Vol. 1831, GAQ 7–45, CNA.

32. Duguid, *Official History Documents*, Appendix 529

33. Duguid, *Official History Documents*, Appendix 528

34. "Flanders Fields,"5/16.

35. "Flanders Fields," 5/17.

36. "Flanders Fields," 5/ 17.

37. Lipsett, "Narrative of Events," 237.

38. Both excerpts are from "Flanders Fields," 5/17.

39. Warden, "Report of Narrative of Events, Ypres, April 22nd/26th 1915"in *First Canadian Division*, 232.

40. "Flanders Fields," 5/17.

41. CBC interview.

42. *Thirty Canadian V. Cs*, 7–9; Batchelor and Matson, *VCs of the First World War*, 66–67.

43. Odlum Report, 226

44. Reid, *Bloody Murder*, 81–82.

45. "Flanders Field," 5/16.

46. Duguid, *Official History Documents*, 298.

47. Greenfield, *Baptism of Fire*, 212–13.

48. McCuaig Report, *in First Canadian Division*, 271.

49. Osborne, "Report on Operations," in *First Canadian Division,* 280–81.

50. Odlum to Currie, 24 April 1915, Odlum papers, MG30 E300, Vol. 16, CNA.

51. L.C. Scott interview from "Flanders Fields," 5/18.

52. McWilliams and Steele, *Gas!*, 118.

53. McWilliams and Steele, *Gas!*, 119.

54. T.B. Scudamore, *A Short History of the 7th Battalion CEF* (Vancouver: Anderson and Odlum, 1930). There is no pagination in this brief book.

55. L.C. Scott interview from "Flanders Fields," 5/18.

56. Cited in Greenfield, *Baptism of Fire*, 228.

57. Cited in Greenfield, *Baptism of Fire*, 227.

58. Odlum Report, 224–25.

59. Odlum to Turner, 24 April 1915, Odlum papers, MG30 E300, Vol. 16, CNA.
60. Duguid, *Official History Documents*, Appendix, 532.
61. 2nd Canadian Brigade, Narrative of Events, 210.
62. Duguid, *Official History Documents*, Appendix, 539.
63. Burland had assumed command of the battalion when the CO, Lieutenant-Colonel F.S. Meighen, was placed in charge of the GHQ Line.
64. Duguid, *Official History Documents*, Appendix, 540.
65. Duguid, *Official History Documents*, Appendix, 541.
66. Duguid, *Official History Documents*, Appendix, 543.
67. Beattie, *48th Highlanders*, 79.
68. Duguid, *Official History Documents*, Appendices, 542, 545.
69. Duguid, *Official History Documents*, Appendix, 544.
70. Duguid, *Official History Documents*, Appendix, 544a.
71. Duguid, *Official History Documents*, Appendix, 549.
72. Duguid, *Official History Documents*, Appendix, 557.
73. Edmonds and Wynne, *France and Belgium, 1915*, Vol. 1, 220.
74. Odlum to Duguid, 26 September 1934, RG24, Vol. 1503, file 1, CNA.
75. Currie's case is a sad one. In the afternoon he came across a 2nd Brigade outpost where he erupted and had to be restrained by a staff officer. Later he went back to Ypres looking for stragglers to move forward, so he says in his account (258–59), but no one was crazy enough to to seek refuge in the city, which continued to attract almost uninterrupted shelling. After the battle, he disappeared and resurfaced in Boulogne, a port on the French coast, where Turner ordered him to return at once or face arrest. Sent back home soon after, he would spend the rest of his life defending himself against accusations of cowardice. Notes by Duguid, MG30 E8, CNA.
76. "Flanders Fields," 5/18.
77. Duguid, *Official History Documents*, Appendix, 560.
78. Odlum Report, 227.
79. Ormond Report, 250.
80. "Flanders Fields," 5/18.
81. Brotherhood Report in *First Canadian Division*, 265.

82. Beattie, *48th Highlanders*, 76.

83. Duguid, *Official History*, 309.

84. Duguid, *Official History Documents*, Appendix 564

85. "Flanders Fields," 5/18.

86. McWilliams and Steel, *Gas!*, 121.

87. Dancocks, *Flanders Fields*, 178.

88. McWilliams and Steel, *Gas!*, 122.

89. Greenfield, *Baptism of Fire*, 240.

Chapter 8 — 24 April: The Crisis Deepens (1:40 p.m. to 7:00 p.m.)

1. W.W. Murray, *The History of the 2nd Canadian Battalion in the Great War, 1914–1919* (Ottawa: Mortimer, 1947), 51–52.

2. Streight, "Report of Operations," 30 March 1918, in *First Canadian Division*, 204.

3. Duguid, *Official History*, 310.

4. *Official History Documents*, Appendix, 566.

5. *Official History Documents*, Appendix, 580.

6. "Flanders Fields," 5/19.

7. Report of No. 2 Company, 2nd Battalion, MG30 E318, Vol. 23, file 178B, CNA.

8. Watson, "Detailed Report on Operations of the 2nd Canadian Battalion, From 22nd April to 26th April, 1915," in *First Canadian Division*, 198. .

9. Watson to Turner, 27 April 1915, RG24 C5, Vol. 1822, GAQ 5–29, CNA.

10. Murray, *2nd Canadian Battalion*, 52.

11. Report of No. 2 Company, 2nd Battalion.

12. Foster, ed., *Letters from the Front*, 36.

13. "Flanders Fields," program 5/19.

14. Cited in Dancocks, *Flanders Fields*, 184.

15. Report of No 2 Company, 2nd battalion.

16. Cited in McWilliams and Steel, *Gas!*, 139–40.

17. Murray, *2nd Canadian Battalion*, 53.
18. Murray, *2nd Canadian Battalion*, 55.
19. Report of No. 2 Company, 2nd Battalion.
20. Foster, ed., *Letters from the Front*, 37.
21. "Flanders Fields," 5/20.
22. Kirkpatrick Report on circumstances leading up to his capture on 24 April 1915, in *First Canadian Division*, 202. The report was written on 3 December 1917, after Kirkpatrick was repatriated from Switzerland.
23. "Flanders Fields," 5/20.
24. Kirkpatrick Diary, 24 April 1915, MG30 E318, Vol. 23, file 179, CNA.
25. Both excerpts cited in Dancocks, *Flanders Fields*, 186.
26. Reid, *Poor Bloody Murder*, 83.
27. Goodspeed, *Battle Royal*, 110.
28. *Official History Documents*, Appendix, 601.
29. Sutherland-Brown to J.A. MacBrien (Canadian Chief of Staff), 25 November 1925, RG24, Vol. 2680, file 1/HQC4950, CNA.
30. *Official History Documents*, Appendix, 612.
31. *Official History Documents*, Appendix, 330a.
32. Edmonds and Wynne, *France and Belgium, 1915*, Vol. 1, 224.
33. *Official History Documents*, Appendix, 535.
34. Edmonds and Wynne, *France and Belgium, 1915*, Vol. 1, 224–27.
35. *Official History Documents*, Appendix, 600.
36. Cited in Dancocks, *Flanders Fields*, 198.
37. Duguid, *Official History*, 324–25.
38. Bulfin told Edmonds that not long afterward, he had engaged in a row with Snow, who he felt had no right to touch his divisional reserve without his permission. He added: "I had meant to use them to regain Gravenstafel the loss of which I had heard at Alderson's Headquarters where I was when Snow snaffled them in his panic." Bulfin to Edmonds, October 28, 1925, CAB 45/140, BNA.
39. *Official History Documents*, Appendix, 630.
40. Dancocks, *Flanders Fields*, 199.
41. Gordon-Hall to Duguid, 16 January 1935, RG24 Vol. 1503, file 1/HQ683-1-30-5, CNA.
42. Duguid, *Offical History*, 311.

43. Duguid to Canadian Chief of Staff, 23 June 1936, RN24, Vol. 2680, file 2/HQC4950, CNA

Chapter 9 — 24 April: The 2nd Brigade Stands Fast

1. Urquhart, *Currie*, 76.
2. *Official History Documents*, Appendix, 545b.
3. Tuxford, "The Second Battle of Ypres — The 5th Battalion," RG24, Vol. 1829, file GAQ 7–35, 2, CNA.
4. Urquhart, *Currie*, 82–83.
5. Urquhart, *Currie*, 84.
6. *Official History Documents*, Appendix, 559.
7. Currie, "Narrative of Events", 211.
8. *Official History Documents*, Appendix, 565.
9. Currie, "Narrative of Events", 211–12.
10. *Official History Documents*, Appendix 570.
11. Urquhart, *Currie*, 87–88.
12. *Official History Documents*, Appendix, 574.
13. Currie to Duguid, 7 May 1926, Urquhart papers, MG 30 E75, Vol. 2, file 3, CNA. Currie is commenting on Edmonds's second draft of his Official History of the battle.
14. Tuxford to Duguid, 15 April 1926, RG24, Vol. 1755, file 1, CNA.
15. Currie to Duguid, 7 May 1926, Urquhart papers.
16. Lipsett, "Narrative of Events, 237.
17. Tuxford to Duguid, 19 July 1926, RG24, Vol. 2680, file 2. Tuxford penned the following note to Duguid on 14 April 1926: "Lipsett always claimed that he and I were the only two men who knew the inner history of the fight of the 2nd C.I.B. and Lipsett was killed later." RG24, Vol. 1755, file 1, CNA.
18. Tuxford, "The Second Battle of Ypres," 2.
19. Duguid, *Official History*, 321–22, and Appendices, 577, 579, 582, 587, 587a, 615, 626.
20. Cited in Lieutenant-Colonel Wilfred Bovey, "Sir Arthur Currie: The Corps Commander," *The Legionary* (July 1934): 6.

21. Currie to Duguid, 7 May 1926, Urquhart papers.

22. Currie, Narrative of Events, 211–12.

23 . Currie to Duguid, 7 May 1926, Urquhart papers.

24. Lynn to Urquhart, 22 June 1936, Urquhart papers, MG30 E75, Vol. 2, file 3, CNA. Lynn kept meticulous records of everything that concerned or interested him from the day he enlisted with the 2nd Battalion, R.G.R.I. on 21 October 1899, when he was only 17. This lengthy and graphic account of the Snow/Currie interview, from which I obtained most of my information, was based on his diary. See also Villiers to Duguid, 31 December 1935, MG30 E246, Vol. 4, file 7, CNA.

25. Lynn to Urquhart, 22 June 1936, Urquhart papers.

26. Lynn to Urquhart, 22 June 1936, Urquhart papers.

27. Currie to Duguid, 7 May 1926, Urquhart papers.

28. Lynn to Urquhart, 22 June, 1936, Urquhart papers.

29. Lynn to Urquhart, 22 June, 1936, Urquhart papers.

30. Lynn to Urquhart, 22 June, 1936, Urquhart papers.

31. Currie to Duguid, 7 May 1926, Urquhart papers.

32. Snow, "Narrative of the 27th Division from the Date of Formation to the End of its Tour on the Western Front," WO 95/2254, 39, BNA.

33. Edmonds to Duguid, RG24, Vol. 1503, file 3, CNA.

34. The full text is available in *Official History Documents*, Appendix, 607.

35. Edmonds to Duguid, 12 November 1936, RG24, Vol. 1503, file 3, CNA.

36. Edmonds to Duguid, 12 November 1936, RG24, Vol. 1503, file 3, CNA. See also Edmonds to Duguid, 23 September 1936 RG24, Vol. 1503, file 3 and Edmonds to Duguid, 5 February 1934, RG24, Vol. 1503, file 1, CNA.

37. Duguid, *Official History*, 321.

38. Currie to Duguid, 7 May 1926, Urquhart papers, MG 30 E75, Vol. 2, file 3, CNA.

39. Lynn to Urquhart, 22 June 1936, Urquhart papers.

40. Watson diary, 1 March 1919, MG30 E69, Reel M-10. Watson's discussion with Kirkcaldy can be found in the back of his diary under the heading "Of Interest to Turner." See also, Kirkcaldy to Duguid, 23 November 1934, RG24, Vol. 1503, file 1, CNA.

41. Tuxford, "Second Battle of Ypres," 2.

42. Lipsett, Narrative of Events, 237.

43. *Official History Documents*, Appendix, 587, 590.

44. Tuxford, "Second Battle of Ypres," 2.

45. Cited in Swettenham, *McNaughton*, Vol. 1, 45–46.

46. Tuxford, "Second Battle of Ypres," 2–3.

47. Edmonds, *France and Belgium, 1915*, Vol.1, Appendix, 23.

48. Edmonds, *France and Belgium, 1915*, Vol.1, 233n.

49. Edmonds, *France and Belgium, 1915*, Vol.1, 234.

50. *Official History Documents*, Appendix, 619.

51. Currie to Duguid, 7 May 1926, Urquhart papers, MG 30 E75, Vol. 2, file 3, CNA.

52. Nicholson, *Canadian Expeditionary Force*, 80.

53. Tuxford, "Second Battle of Ypres," 3–4.

54. Tuxford, "Second Battle of Ypres," 3–4. Tuxford wrote another unpublished account of the battle on 10 March 1916, entitled "Narrative of Brig.-Gen. G.S. Tuxford," RG24, Vol. 1825, file GAQ 5–61, CNA.

55. Tuxford, "Second Battle of Ypres," 4.

56. *Official History Documents*, Appendix, 630.

57. *Official History Documents*, Appendices, 618, 631.

58. *Official History Documents*, Appendix, 634.

59. Duguid, *Official History*, 339.

60. Several months later, Alderson attempted in vain to prevent Turner's appointment as commander of the newly formed 2nd Canadian Division. He wrote the following to a close friend: "I am sorry to say that I do not consider Turner really fit to command a Division and his name was not put forward for it by Sir John French, but Canadian politics have been too strong for all of us and so he has got it." Alderson to Major-General E.T.H. Hutton, 21 August 1915, Hutton papers Add 50096, 310, British Library. I am indebted to Professor Desmond Morton for sending me a copy of the letter.

61. Sutherland-Brown to J.A. MacBrien (Canadian Chief of Staff), 25 November 1925, RG24, Vol. 2680, file 1/HQC4950, CNA.

62. According to Warden, he had his own company of 234 men, plus 50 Turcos, and 2 officers and 12 other ranks belonging to the 16th Battalion.

63. Warden, "Narrative of Events," in *First Canadian Division*, 233–34.

Chapter 10 — 25 April: Another Awful Day

1. *Der Weltkrieg*, Band 8, 44.
2. Hull, "Report on Operations," WO 95/1478, BNA.
3. Bruce Bairnsfather, *Bullets and Billets: Fragments from France* (London: Great Richards, 1916), 274.
4. Duguid, *Offical History*, 347.
5. Colonel H.C. Wylly, *Crown and Company: The Historical Record of the 2nd Battalion Royal Dublin Fusiliers, 1911–1922*, Vol. 2 (Aldershot: Gale and Polden, 1923), 41.
6. Edmonds and Wynne, *France and Belgium, 1915*, Vol. 1, 240–43.
7. Duguid, *Official History*, 350.
8. Report of Operations undertaken by the 28th Division from 20th April to 4th May, 1915, WO95/2267, BNA.
9. Mathews, "Account of Second Battle of Ypres," 15, Mathews papers, MG30 E60, Vol. 4, file 17, CNA.
10. "Flanders Fields," 5/21.
11. Cited in Urquhart, *Arthur Currie*, 97.
12. CBC interview.
13. CBC interview with F.B. Bagshaw.
14. Tuxford, "The Second Battle of Ypres," 5, RG24, Vol. 1829, CNA.
15. Tuxford, "The Second Battle of Ypres," 5.
16. Lynn to Urquhart, 22 June 1935, Urquhart papers, MG30 E75, Vol. 2, file 3, CNA.
17. Tucker, *Battle Glory*, 130–31.
18. Tuxford, "The Second Battle of Ypres," 5.
19. Odlum, 7th Battalion — Narrative of Events, 228; "Flanders Fields," 5/21.
20. *Official History Documents*, Appendix 664.
21. *Official History Documents*, Appendices 665, 666.
22. *Official History Documents*, Appendix 667.
23. Currie, 2nd Brigade — Narrative of Events, 214.
24. *Official History Documents*, Appendix 659.
25. Odlum, *7th Battalion — Narrative of Events*, 228–29.
26. Currie to Odlum, 12:45 p.m. and Odlum to Currie, 2:00 p.m., 25

April 1915, MG30 E300, Vol. 16, CNA.

27. "Flanders Fields," 5/22.

28. Mathews, "Account of the Second Battle of Ypres," 16,

29. Mathews, "Account of the Second Battle of Ypres," 16.

30. Odlum, 7th Battalion — Narrative of Events, 229.

31. Currie, 2nd Brigade — Narrative of Events, 215–16.

32. Currie, "2nd Brigade — Narrative of Events," 216.

33. Tuxford, "The Second Battle of Ypres," 5.

34. "Flanders Fields," 5/23.

35. Dancocks, *Flanders Fields*, 216–17.

36. Odlum, 7th Battalion — Narrative of Events, 229.

37. Tuxford, "The Second Battle of Ypres," 6.

38. Cited in McWilliams and Steel, *Gas!* 174.

39. A trench dug at an oblique angle from the front to where troops could fall back if driven from the main line.

40. Lipsett, 8th Battalion — Narrative of Events, 239.

41. "Flanders Fields," 5/23.

42. Tuxford, "The Second Battle of Ypres," 6.

43. Tuxford, "The Second Battle of Ypres," 7.

44. "Narrative of Brigadier-General G.S. Tuxford," 16 March 1916, Vol. 1825, GAQ 5–51, 6-f, CNA.

45. Tuxford, "The Second Battle of Ypres," 7.

46. Mathews, "Account of the Second Battle of Ypres," 17.

47. Cited in Dancocks, *Flanders Fields*, 214.

48. Cited in Dancocks, *Gallant Canadians*, 41.

49. CBC interview.

50. Odlum, 7th Battalion — Narrative of Events, 229.

51. Cited in Dancocks, *Gallant Canadians*, 42.

52. Odlum, 7th Battalion — Narrative of Events, 229.

53. Villiers diary, 25 April 1915, MG30 E236, Vol. 4, CNA: *Thirty Canadian V.C.s.,* 9–10; Adami, *Canadian Army Medical Corps,* 146–47; *London Gazette,* 22 June 1915.

55. Edmonds and Wynne, *France and Belgium, 1915,* Vol. 1, 248 and n2.

55. Edmonds qand Wynne, *France and Belgium, 1915,* Vol. 1, 250.

56. *Der Weltkrieg,* Band. 8, 45.

57. *Official History Documents*, Appendix, 675.

58. *Les armées françaises dans la grande guerre,* Tome II, 708.

59. Edmonds and Wynne, *France and Belgium, 1915*, Vol. 1, 254; French Diary, 25 April 1915, French papers, IWM.

60. Edmonds and Wynne, *France and Belgium, 1915*, Vol. 1, 271n.

61. A. J. Smithers, *The Man Who Disobeyed* (London: Leo Cooper, 1970) 289n.

62. Edmonds and Wynne, *France and Belgium, 1915*, Vol. 1, 271–72.

Chapter 11 — Lambs Led to the Slaughter

1. Dancocks, *Flanders Fields*, 223.

2. C.T. Atkinson, *Regimental History: The Royal Hampshire Regiment, 1914-1918,* Vol. 2 (Glasgow: Robert Maclehose, University Press, 1952), 58; Edmonds and Wynne, *France and Belgium, 1915*, Vol. 1, 263.

3. Mathews, "Account of the Second Battle of Ypres," 19–21.

4. Currie, 2nd Infantry Brigade —Narrative of Events, 217.

5. J.A. Currie, *Red Watch*, 264.

6. Urquhart, *16th Battalion*, 67.

7. Hawkins Diary, 26 April 1915, 75/113/1 and DS Misc/25, IWM.

8. J.A. Currie, *Red Watch*, 265.

9. Edmonds and Wynne, *France and Belgium, 1915*, Vol. 1, Appendix, 26.

10. *Official History Documents*, Appendix, 684.

11. Lieutenant J.W.B. Merewether and Sir Frederick Smith, *The Indian Corps in France* (London: John Murray, 1918), 290.

12. Cited in Macdonald, *1915*, 251.

13. Brigadier-General E.P. Strickland, "Report on Action taken by Jullundur Brigade NE of Ypres," 26 April 1915, WO 95/3926, BNA.

14. Merewether and Smith, *Indian Corps*, 300.

15. Merewether and Smith, *Indian Corps*, 294–95.

16. Peter Batchelor and Chris Matson, *VCs of the First World War* (Stroud, Gloucestershire: Sutton, 1997), 81–83.

17. Cited in Macdonald, *1915*, 251–52.

18. *Les armées françaises dans la grande guerre*, tome 2, 710.

19. Brigadier-General R.G. Egerton, "Report on Operations Carried out by Ferozepore Brigade," WO 95/3922, BNA.

20. Cited in Macdonald, *1915*, 252.

21. Egerton, Report of Ferozepore Brigade.

22. Gordon Corrigan, *Sepoys in the Trenches* (Staplehur, UK: Spellmount, 1999), 190.

23. Batchelor and Matson, *VCs of the First World War*, 76–77.

24. Edmonds and Wynne, *France and Belgium: 1915*, Vol. 1, 260.

25. "Report of the 149th Brigade's Sction at St. Julien on 26 April 1915," WO 95/2826, BNA.

26. Report of 149th Brigade.

27. Duguid, *Official History*, 374.

28. Report of 149th Brigade.

29. Anon., *Bond of Sacrifice: A Biographical Record of All British Officers Who Fell in the Great War*, Vol. 2 (London: Anglo-African Publishing Contractors, 1916), 394.

30. Brigadier-General G.P.T. Feilding succeeded Riddell in command of the brigade.

31. *Les armées françaises dans la grande guerre*, Tome II, 709–710.

32. Smithers, *Man Who Disobeyed*, 252–55.

33. Merewether and Smith, *Indian Corps*, 314–15.

34. Cited in McWilliams and Steele, *Gas!*, 201.

35. Merewether and Smith, *Indian Corps*, 316–20.

36. The French Official History discusses only very briefly — about seven lines — the fighting on 27 April. See *Les armées françaises dans la grande guerre*, Tome II, 711.

37. Edmonds and Wynne, *France and Belgium, 1915*, Vol. 1, 273.

38. Cited in Dixon, *Magnificient*, 152.

39. Edmonds and Wynne, *France and Belgium, 1915*, Vol. 1, 274.

40. Merewether and Smith, *Indian Corps*, 321–23.

41. Edmonds and Wynne, *France and Belgium, 1915*, Vol. 1, Appendix, 30.

42. Dixon, *Magnificient*, 151.

43. Edmonds and Wynne, *France and Belgium, 1915*, Vol. 1, Appendix, 31.

44. For the details of the long-standing antipathy between Sir John and Smith-Dorrien, see Smithers, *Man Who Disobeyed*, Ch. 21; Cassar,

Sir John French, 223–25; and Brigadier-General C.R. Ballard, *Smith Dorrien* (New York: Dodd, Meade and Co., 1930), ch.18.

45 Edmonds and Wynne, *France and Belgium, 1915*, Vol. 1, 278.

46. Cited in Powell, *Plumer*, 121.

47. Edmonds and Wynne, *France and Belgium, 1915*, Vol. 1, Appendix 33; *Les armées françaises dans la grande guerre*, Tome II, Vol. 2, annexe 1465.

48. *Les armées françaises dans la grande guerre*, Tome II, Vol. 2, annexe 1466.

49. *Les armées françaises dans la grande guerre*, Tome II, Vol. 2, annexe 1468.

50. General Staff Memorandum, 29 April, 1915, WO 158/17.

51. Haig Diary, 30 April 1915, Haig papers.

52. Edmonds and Wynne, *France and Belgium: 1915*, Vol. 1, 289–92.

53. Edmonds and Wynne, *France and Belgium, 1915*, Vol. 1, 293–94.

Chapter 12 — *The Patricias at Frezenberg*

1. Cited in Bercuson, *The Patricias*, 43.

2. J. Williams, *Princess Patricia's*, 8.

3. Ralph H. Williams, *Princess Patricia's Canadian Light Infantry 1914–1919*, Vol. 1 (Toronto: Hodder and Stoughton, 1923), 30–34.

4. Snow, "Narrative of the 27th Division," 10, WO95/2254, BNA.

5. J. Williams, *Princess Patricia's*, 13.

6. Dixon, *Magnificent*, 206–12

7. J. Williams, *Princess Patricia's*, 13.

8. George Pearson, *The Escape of a Princess Pat* (New York: Doran, 1918), 35.

9. R. Williams, *Princess Patricia's*, 61.

10. R. Williams, *Princess Patricia's*, 62.

11. "Flanders Fields," 5/25–26.

12. "Flanders Fields," 5/26.

13. Cited in Bercuson, *The Patricias*, 63.

14. S.K. Newman, *With the Patricias in Flanders 1914–198* (Sannichton, B.C.: Bellewaerde, 2000), 57.

15. Cited in Newman, *With the Patricias*, 55.

16. Cited in Newman, *With the Patricias*, 54.
17. Cited in Bercuson, *The Patricias,* 64.
18. Cited in Lyn Macdonald, *1915*, 287 and 292.
19. Cited in R. Williams, *Princess Patricia's*, 65.
20. Cited in Newman, *With the Patricias*, 54.
21. Cited in R. Williams, *Princess Patricia's*, 65.
22. "Flanders Fields," 5/26.
23. Zubowski, *As Long as Faith*, 88–89.
24. Cited in Newman, *With the Patricias*, 58.
25. "Report by Major-General Thomas D'Oyly Snow," in *First Canadian Division*, 139.
26. Dixon, *Magnificent*, Ch. 18.

Epilogue

1. Duguid, *Official History*, 407–08.
2. Dixon, *Magnificent*, 63, 147.
3. French of Ypres, *1914* (London: Constable, 1919), 14–15.
4. Gordon-Hall to Duguid, 16 January 1935, RG24, Vol. 1503, file 1, HQ683-1-30-5, CNA.
5. I am indebted to Professor Desmond Morton for sending me a copy of the letter, together with the call number, which can be found in the Hutton collection, British Library. Alderson to Hutton, 21 August 1915, Add MS 50096, 310.
6. All three citations can be found in Dancocks, *Arthur Currie*, 54–55.
7. CBC interview.
8. Duguid, *Official History*, 422.
9. Jones, *Fighting the Hun*, 11.
10. *Official History Documents*, Appendix, 699a.
11. All the newspapers citations were drawn from Dancocks, *Flanders Fields*, 241.
12. *Official History Documents*, Appendix, 704.
13. *Official History Documents*, Appendix, 701a.
14. *Official History Documents*, Appendix, 705.

15. *Official History Documents*, Appendix, 699a.

16. "Alderson's speech to the 1st Canadian Division," 4 May 1915, MG30 E92, CNA.

17. Urquhart, *16th Battalion*, 35.

18. *Der Weltkrieg*, Band 8, 40ff.

19. Scott, *Great War*, 72.

20. CBC interview.

21. Grace Morris Craig, *But This is Our War* (Toronto: University of Toronto Press, 1981), 28.

22. Duguid, *Official History*, 421.

23. Norm Christie, *For King and Empire* (Ottawa: CEF Books, 2005), 67.

24. John F. Prescott, *In Flanders Fields: The Story of John McCrae* (Erin, ON: Boston Mills, 1985), 98.

25. Mathieson, *My Grandfather's War*, 264.

26. Andrew McNaughton, origins of "In Flanders Fields," McNaughton papers, MG30 E133, Vol. 4, CNA.

BIBLIOGRAPHY

Archival Collections

Imperial War Museum, London
>   Percy Allen
>   Sir John French
>   F. Hawkins
>   W.S. Lighthall
>   Herbert Maxwell-Scott
>   James Pratt (recording)
>   William Rae
>   Horace Smith-Dorrien
>   Percy Whitehouse

Liddle Hart Centre for Military Archives
>   S.L. Cummins

National Archives of Canada, Ottawa
>   William Alldritt
>   CBC transcript of radio series "In Flanders Field," Programs 2–6, and interviews with survivors. Also CBC TV Production "The Killing Ground."
>   J.J. Creelman
>   Harry Crerar
>   Arthur Currie
>   Edward Hilliam

Arthur Kirkpatrick

Henry Lamb

John Leckie — Served as major in the 16th Battalion along with his older brother Robert who was the CO of the regiment.

Robert G. Edwards Leckie

Harold Mathews

Andrew McNaughton

Victor Odlum

Official records — These include the massive Duguid correspondence and notes, as well as operational orders, papers of various units, and War Diaries — those of the division, brigades, and battalions were published and also are available online.

George Perley

Richard Turner

Hugh Urqurhart — Currie's biographer served in the 16th Battalion and later became its historian.

Paul Villiers

David Watson

National British Archives (formerly Public Record Office), London

Account of German Gas Cloud Attacks on British Fronts in France

Edmonds correspondence

Snow — Original diary along with his papers are housed at the Imperial War Museum.

War Diaries — Geddes's Detachment, 149th and 150th Brigades (50th Division), Lahore Division and its Brigades, 27th and 28th British Divisions, and their Brigades and Regiments.

Official Histories and Publications

Canada, House of Commons. *Debates.*

Canadian War Records Office. *Thirty Canadians VCs.* London: Skeffington, 1918.

Duguid, Colonel A. Fortescue. *Official History of the Canadian Forces in the Great War, 1914–1919.* Vol. 1 and Appendices. Ottawa: King's Printer, 1938.

Edmonds, Brigadier-General Sir James E. and Captain G.C. Wynne. *Official History of the Great War: Military Operations: France and Belgium, 1915.* Vol. 1. London: Macmillan, 1927.

France. Ministère de la guerre, Etat Major de l'armée. Service Historique. *Les armées françaises das la grande guerre.* Tome 2 and accompanying volume of annexes. Paris: Imprimerie Nationale, 1930.

Historical Section. Historical Staff. *Narrative on the Formation and Operation of the First Canadian Division to the Second Battle of Ypres.* Ottawa: Mulvey, 1920.

Macphail, Sir Andrew. *Official History of the Canadian forces in the Great War, 1914–1919: The Medical Services.* Ottawa: King's Printer, 1925.

Nichlson, Colonel G.W.L. *Canadian Expeditionary Forces, 1914–1919.* Ottawa: Queen's Printer, 1952.

Reichsarchiv. *Der Weltkrieg 1914 bis 1918.* Band 8. Berlin: Mittler and Sohn, 1932.

Scott, J.B., ed. *The Reports of the Hague Conferences of 1899 and 1907.* Oxford: Clarendon Press, 1917.

Regimental Histories

Atkinson, C.T. *Regimental History: The Royal Hampshire Regiment, 1914–1918.* Vol. 2. Glasgow: Robert Maclehose, University Press, 1932.

Beattie, Kim. *48th Highlanders of Canada, 1891–1928.* Vol. 1. Toronto: 48th Highlanders of Canada, 1932.

Bercuson, David J. *The Patricias.* Toronto: Stoddart, 2001.

Dancocks, Daniel G. *Gallant Canadians: The Story of the Tenth Canadian Infantry Battalion.* Calgary: Calgary Highlanders Regimental Funds Foundation, 1990.

Fetherstonhaugh, R.C. *The 13th Battalion, Royal Highlanders of Canada, 1914–1919.* Montreal: 13th Battalion, Royal Highlanders of Canada, 1925.

_____. *The Royal Montreal Regiment, 14th Battalion, CEF 1914–1925.* Montreal: Royal Montreal Regiment, 1927.

Goodspeed, Major D.J. *Battle Royale: A History of the Royal Regiment of Canada, 1862–1962* [3rd Battalion]. Montreal: Royal Regiment of Canada Association, 1962.

Holland, J.A. *The Story of the Tenth Canadian Battalion*. London: Canadian War Records Office, 1918.

Murray, W.W. *The History of the 2nd Canadian Battalion in the Great War, 1914–1919*. Ottawa: 2nd Canadian Battalion, 1947.

Newman, Stephen K. *With the Patricias in Flanders, 1914–1918*. Sannichton, B.C: Bellewaerde, 2007.

Scudmore, T.V. *A Short History of the 7th Battalion, CEF*. Vancouver: Anderson and Odlum, 1930.

Urquhart, H.M. *The History of the 16th Battalion (The Canadian Scottish) Canadian Expeditionary Force in the Great War, 1914–1919*. Toronto: Macmillan, 1932.

Williams, Jeffrey. *Princess Patricia's Canadian Light Infantry*. Vol. 1. London: Leo Cooper, 1972.

Williams, Ralph Hodder. *Princess Patricia's Canadian Light Infantry, 1914–1919*. Vol. 1. Toronto: Hodder and Stoughton, 1923.

Wylly, Colonel H.C. *Crown and Company: The Historical Record of the 2nd Battalion Royal Dublin Fusiliers, 1911–1922*. Vol. 2. Aldershot: Gale and Polden, 1923.

Wyrall, Everard. *The Duke of Cornwall's Light Infantry, 1914–1919*. London: Methuen, 1932.

——————. *The East Yorkshire Regiment in the Great War, 1914–1918*. London: Harrison and Sons, 1928.

——————. *The History of the 50th Division, 1914–1919*. London: Percy Lund, Humphries and Co., 1939.

Memoirs, Diaries, and Letters

Anon. *With the First Canadian Contingent*. Toronto: Hodder and Stoughton, 1915.

Bairnsfather, Captain Bruce. *Bullets and Billets: Fragments from France*. New York: G.P. Putnam's Sons, 1917.

Baldwin, Sergeant Harold. *Holding the Line*. Chicago: McClurg, 1918.

Borden, Henry, ed. *Robert Laird Borden: His Memoirs*. Vol. 1. Toronto: Macmillan, 1938.

Canadian Field Comforts Commion, *With the First Canadian Contingent*. Toronto: Hodder and Stoughton, 1915.

Christie, Norm, ed. *Not Mentioned in Despatches: The Memoirs of Fred Bagnall, 14th Battalion, CEF 1914–1917*. Ottawa: CEF Books, 2005.

Keene, Louis. *"Crumps": The Plain Story of a Canadian Who Went*. Boston: Houghton Mifflin, 1917.

Currie, Colonel J.A. *The Red Watch: With the First Canadian Division in Flanders*. Toronto: McClelland, Goodchild and Stewart, 1916.

Curry, Frederick C. *From the St. Lawrence to the Yser*. London: Smith, Elder and Co., 1916.

French, Lord. *1914*. London: Constable, 1919.

Foster, Charles L., ed. *Letters From the Front, 1914–1919*. Vol. 1. Toronto: Bank of Commerce, 1920.

Jones, Sergeant-Major Wlliam R. *Fighting the Hun from the Saddle and Trench*. Albany, NY: Aitken, 1918.

Macfie, John. *Letters Home*. Meaford, ON: Oliver Graphics, 1990.

Mathieson, William D. *My Granfather's War*. Toronto: Macmillan, 1981.

Mordacq, General Jacques. *La Drame de l'Yser*. Paris: Editions des Portquies, 1933.

Pearson, George. *The Escape of a Princess Pat*. London: Doran, 1918.

Peat, Harold R. *Private Peat*. Indianapolis: Bobbs-Merrill, 1917.

Rae, Herbert. *Maple Leaves in Flanders Fields*. London: Smith, Elder and Co., 1917.

Reid, Gordon. *Poor Bloody Murder*. Oakville, ON: Mosaic, 1980.

Scott, Canon Frederick G. *The War as I Saw It*. Vancouver: Clark and Stuart, 1934.

Tascona, Bruce, and Eric Wells. *Little Black Devils*. Winnipeg: Royal Winnipeg Rifles, 1983.

Taylor, Charles L, ed. *Letters from the Front*. Vols. 1 and 2. Toronto: Canadian Bank of Commerce, 1920.

Tucker, A.B. *The Battle Glory of Canada*. London: Cassell, 1915.

Von Falkenhayn, General Erich. *The German General Staff and its Decisions, 1914–1916*. New York: Dodd, Mead and Co., 1920.

Other Relevant Books

Adami, Colonel J.G. *War Story of the Canadian Army Medical Corps*. Vol. 1. London: Canadian War Records Office, 1918.

Aitken, Sir Max (later Lord Beaverbrook). *Canada in Flanders.* Vol. 1. Toronto: Hodder and Stoughton, 1916.

Anon. *Unknown Soldiers by One of Them.* New York: Vantage, 1959.

Armstrong, Elizabeth H. *The Crisis of Quebec.* New York: AMS Press, 1967.

Brice, Beatrice. *The Battle Book of Ypres.* London: John Murray, 1927.

Cassar, George H. *The Tragedy of Sir John French.* Newark, DE: University of Delaware Press, 1985.

Charles, Daniel. *Between Genius and Genoicide.* London: Jonathan Cape, 2005.

Christie, Norm M. *The Canadians in the Second Battle of Ypres, April 22 to 26 April, 1915.* Ottawa: Bunker to Bunker Books, 1996.

_____. *For King and Empire.* Ottawa: CEF Books, 2005.

_____. *Gas Attack!: The Canadians at Ypres, April–May,1915.* Ottawa: CEF Books, 1998.

Churchill, Winston S. *The World Crisis.* Vol. 2. New York: Charles Scribner's Sons, 1951.

Cook, Tim. *At the Sharp End: Canadians Fighting the Great War, 1914–1916.* Vol. 1. Toronto: Penguin Group, 2007.

_____. *No Place to Run.* Vancouver: UBC Press, 1999.

Dancocks, Daniel G. *Sir Arthur Currie.* Toronto: Methuen, 1985.

_____. *Welcome to Flanders Field.* Toronto: McClelland & Stewart, 1998.

Dixon, John. *Magnificent But Not War: The Battle For Ypres, 1915.* London: Leo Cooper, 2003.

Faber, Ludwig F. *The Poisionous Cloud: Chemical Warfare in the First World War.* Oxford: Clarendon Press, 1986.

Freeman, Bill, and Richard Nelson. *Far From Home: Canadians in the First World War.* Toronto: McGraw-Hill, 1999.

French, Lord. *The Complete Despatches of Lord French, 1914–1916.* London: Chapman and Hall, 1917.

_____. *1914.* London: Constable, 1919.

Foulkes, Major-General C.H. *Gas!* Edinburgh: William B. Blackwood and Sons, 1934.

Gaffen, Fred. *Forgotten Soldiers.* Penticton, B.C: Theytus Books, 1985.

Giles, John. *The Ypres Salient.* London: Leo Cooper, 1970.

Gilmour, Don. *Canada: A People's History*. Toronto: McClelland & Stewart, 2001.

Goran, Morris. *The Story of Fritz Haber*. Norman: University of Oklahoma Press, 1967.

Granatstein, Jack. L. *Canada's Army*. Toronto: University of Toronto Press, 2002.

Greenfield, Nathan M. *Baptism of Fire: The Second Battle of Ypres*. Toronto: HarperCollins, 2007.

Hanslian, Rudolph. *The Gas Attack at Ypres*. Edgewood Arsenal, MD: Chemical Warfare School, 1940.

Herwig, Holger H. *The First World War: Germany and Austria-Hungry 1914–1918*. London: Edward Arnold, 1997.

Hyatt, A.M.J. *General Sir Arthur Currie: A Military Biography*. Toronto and Ottawa: University of Toronto Press and Canadian War Museum, 1987.

Haycock, Ronald G. *Sam Hughes*. Waterloo, ON: Wilfred Laurier University Press, 1986.

Iarocci, Andrew. *Shoestring Soldiers: The 1st Canadian Division at War, 1914–1915*. Toronto: University of Toronto Press, 2008.

Keech, Graham. *St. Julien*. London: Leo Cooper, 2001.

Keegan, John. *The First World War*. New York: Knopf, 1999.

Lewin, G.L. *Die Gifte in der Weltgeschichte*. Berlin: Springer, 1920.

Lucas, Sir Charles. *The Empire at War*. Vol. 2. London: Milford and Oxford University Press, 1923.

Macdonald, Lyn. *1915: The Death of Innocence*. London: Headline Book, 1993.

Macfie, John. *Letters Home*. Meaford, ON: Oliver Graphics, 1990.

McWilliams, James L. and R. James Steel. *Gas! The Battle for Ypres, 1915*. St. Catherine, ON: Vanwell, 1985.

Mayor, Adrienne. *Greek Fire, Poison Arrows and Scorpion Bombs in the Ancient World*. Woodstock: Overlook Duckworth, 2003.

Merewether, Lieutenant J.W.B. and Sir Frederick Smith. *The Indian Corps in France*. London: John Murray, 1918.

Moore, William. *Gas Attack!* London: Leo Cooper, 1987.

Morrison, J. Clinton. *Hell upon Earth*. Summerside, PEI: Morrison, 2005.

Morton, Desmond. *When Your Number's Up: The Canadian Soldier in the First World War.* Toronto: Random House, 1993.

Morton, Desmond and Jack L. Granatstein. *Marching to Armageddon.* Toronto: Lester and Orphen Dennys, 1989.

Nasmith, Colonel George C. *Canada's Sons and Great Britain in the World War.* Toronto: Winston, 1919.

_____. *On the Fringe of the Great Fight.* New York: Doran, 1917.

Nicholson, Colonel G.W.L. *The Gunners of Canada.* Toronto: McClelland & Stewart, 1967.

Partington, J.R. *A History of Greek Fire.* Cambridge: Heffer, 1960.

Pollard, Hugh B.C. *The Story of Ypres.* New York: McBride, 1917.

Powell, Geoffrey. *Plumer.* London: Leo Cooper, 1990.

Prescott, John F. *In Flanders Fields: The Story of John McCrae.* Erin,ON: Boston Mills Press, 1985.

Prentiss, Augustin M. *Chemical in War.* New York: McGraw-Hill, 1937.

Reveille, F. Douglas. *History of the County of Brant.* Vol 2. Brantford, ON: Hurley, 1920.

Schwarte, General Max. *Die Technik im Weltkriege.* Berlin: E.S.Mittler and Son, 1920.

Skelton, Oscar Douglas. *Life and Letters of Sir Wilfred Laurier.* Vol. 2. London: Milford and Oxford University Press, 1922.

Swettenham, John. *McNaughton.* Vol. 1. Toronto: Ryerson Press, 1968.

_____. *To Seize the Victory: The Canadian Corps in World War I.* Toronto: Ryerson Press, 1965.

Swinton, Lieutenant-Colonel E.D. and Earl Percy. *A Year Ago.* London: Edward Arnold, 1916.

The Times History of the War. Vol. 5. London: The *Times*, 1915.

Urquhart, Hugh M. *Arthur Currie.* Toronto: J.M. Dent and Sons, 1950.

Winter, Brigadier-General Charles F. *Lieutenant-General the Hon. Sir Sam Hughes.* Toronto: Macmillan, 1931.

Zubowski, Robert F. *As Long as Faith and Wisdom Last.* Calgary: Bunker to Bunker Books, 2005).

Articles

Beattie, Kim. "Unheeded Warning." *Maclean's Magazine* (1 May 1936).

Bovey, Lieutenant-Colonel Wilfred. "Sir Arthur Currie: The Corps Commander." *The Legionary* (July 1934).

Godefroy, Andrew B. "Portrait of a Battalion Commander: Lieutenant-Colonel George Stuart Tuxford at the Second Battle of Ypres." *Canadian Military Journal* (Summer 2004).

Ferry, General Edmond. "Ce qui s'est passé sur l'Yser." *La revue des vivants* (July 1930).

Iarocci, Andrew. "1st Canadian Infantry Brigade in the Second Battle of Ypres: The Case of the 1st and 4th Infantry Battalions, 23 April 1915." *Canadian Military History* 12, No. 4 (2003).

Impressions of a Platoon Commander. "The Canadian Scottish at the Second Battle of Ypres, April 1915." *Canadian Defence Quarterly* 2 (1924–25).

Leppard, Thomas P. "'The Dashing Subaltern.' Sir Richard Turner in Retrospect." *Canadian Military History* 6, No. 2 (1997).

Travers, Tim. "Currie and 1st Canadian Division at Second Ypres, April 1915: Controversy, Criticism and Official History." *Canadian Military History* 5, No. 2 (Autumn 1996).

_____. "Allies in Conflict: The British and Canadian Official Historians and the Real Story of Second Ypres." *Journal of Contemporary History* 24, No. 2 (April 1989).

Trumpener, Ulrich. "The Road to Ypres: The Beginnings of Gas Warfare in World War I." *Journal of Modern History* 47 (1975).

Wood, J.R. "Chemical Warfare — A Chemical and Toxicological Review." *American Journal of Public Health* 34 (1946).

INDEX

OF RELATED INTEREST

Dancing in the Sky
The Royal Flying Corps in Canada
by C.W. Hunt
978-1-55002-864-5
$28.99

Dancing in the Sky is the first complete telling of the First World War fighter pilot–training initiative established by the British in response to the terrible losses occurring in the skies over Europe in 1916. This program, up and running in under six months despite enormous obstacles, launched Canada into the age of flight ahead of the United States. This is the story of the talented and courageous men and women who made the training program a success, complete with the romance, tragedy, humour, and pathos that accompany an account of such heroic proportions.

Amazing Airmen

Canadian Flyers in the Second World War
by Ian Darling
978-1-55488-424-7
$24.99

Canadian and British airmen engaged in fierce and deadly battles in the skies over Europe during the Second World War. Those who survived often had to overcome incredible obstacles to do so — dodging bullets and German troops, escaping from burning planes, and enduring forced marches if they became prisoners. These painstakingly researched stories will enable you to feel what now-aging veterans endured when they were young men in the air war against Nazi Germany.

Hell & High Water

Canada and the Italian Campaign
by Lance Goddard
978-1-550027-280
$29.99

Although it has been overshadowed by other events of the Second World War, Canada's part in the Italian Campaign, from 1943 to 1945, was significant. Canadian forces played a major role in this campaign, whose goal was to open a second front in order to ease the pressure on Russian forces in the east. Canada fought under British command alongside British and American units, but our soldiers saw some of the fiercest fighting and achieved glory many times, including at the Battle of Ortona, one of Canada's greatest military accomplishments. The pictorial history examines the Italian Campaign from the view of the soldiers serving there.